Toward Excellence with Equity

Toward Excellence with Equity

An Emerging Vision for Closing the Achievement Gap

by Ronald F. Ferguson

HARVARD EDUCATION PRESS

Cambridge, Massachusetts

Second Printing, 2008

Library of Congress Control Number 2007932119

Paperback ISBN 978-1-891792-78-6
Library Edition ISBN 978-1-891792-79-3

Published by Harvard Education Press,
an imprint of the Harvard Education Publishing Group

Harvard Education Press
8 Story Street
Cambridge, MA 02138

Cover Design: Alyssa Morris

The typefaces used in this book are ITC Stone Serif for text and
ITC Stone Sans for display.

To my children
Daniel, Darren, and Marcus

Contents

Introduction

> The history of the United States includes slavery, genocide, racial discrimination, war—in other words, it's a country like all others. What is exceptional is that this country has created a vision of a new world and a new human being. Through its rhetoric, its poetry and prose, it has succeeded in investing the word "America" with enormous symbolic power. . . . Rhetoric can also shape reality.
>
> —*Sacvan Bercovitch, September 2007*[1]

American rhetoric has changed the reality of race in the United States only very gradually over the past few hundred years, and only under the pressure of sustained struggle. Some among us are still treated as less "American" than others, and thus the struggle continues, albeit with more allies and less resistance. In the face of current conditions, we have a collective responsibility to carry on the work of previous generations to ensure that all are treated as being equally American—irrespective of race, ethnicity, gender, or national origin—in both rhetoric and reality. We also have a responsibility to strive for excellence as a way of investing in continuing, long-term national vitality. Working to raise achievement levels for all segments of the population is a key to keeping America strong and vital. Striving to remove group identities as predictors of achievement—in other words, to close achievement gaps between groups—will help make the fruits of America's vitality more equally available. These are the goals toward which this book is directed and that reflect the meaning of the title, *Toward Excellence with Equity*.

This book chronicles an intellectual journey that I began nearly two decades ago that initially focused on black-white inequality in earnings. At that time, I was among the many economists who were intrigued by a large and unexplained increase in earnings disparities from the middle 1970s

1

through the late 1980s. Earnings disparity had grown between racial groups, between workers of the same race with different amounts of schooling, and even between workers who had an equal number of years of schooling. Since 1990, rising earnings at the very top of the income distribution has been the most prominent form of growing inequality. However, from the mid-1970s to the early 1990s, inequality grew throughout the income distribution and, as of the late 1980s, the reasons for this were poorly understood.

A major advance came around 1990, when economists and other social scientists began using the National Longitudinal Survey of Youth (NLSY) to study the issue. The NLSY was a nationally representative, longitudinal data-collection project sponsored by the U.S. government. It surveyed participants annually, beginning in 1979 when they were teenagers. By the late 1980s, participants were young adults, and many had jobs. The NLSY data on employment, earnings, attitudes, and living conditions, combined with a great deal of information about family backgrounds and other variables collected from the same people in earlier years, shed light on one aspect of the inequality puzzle: the growing black-white gap in earnings.

The leading hypothesis was that growing inequality was due in part to technological changes that made workers who could use reading and math skills on the job more valuable to employers and, at the same time, made those who could not do so less valuable. What made the NLSY especially useful was that the data included reading and math test scores for survey participants. Most participants took the Armed Forces Qualifications Test (AFQT) in 1980. In previous research, AFQT scores from young black and white males tested between 1949 and 1953 had provided no explanation for the substantial black-white economic disparities that obtained during the early 1960s, when those men were adults with jobs in the regular workforce (Jencks & Phillips, 1998, p. 3, citing Cutright, 1972, 1974). Indeed, AFQT scores were not key predictors of earnings in the early 1960s. However, by the early 1990s, our analyses showed that AFQT scores were quite important predictors of hourly earnings for young adult males and females. Furthermore, scores raised by any given amount predicted about the same increase in earnings, irrespective of race. Analyses showed that black-white disparities in AFQT scores predicted at least 50 percent of the black-white hourly earnings gap among young adults in the NLSY data, even after controlling for years of schooling and key family background measures.

The pattern was clear, and I became hooked on the idea of raising test scores. Apparently, improving reading and math skills among black youths was a very promising strategy for reducing racial earnings inequality.

Chapter 1, "Shifting Challenges: Fifty Years of Economic Change toward Black-White Earnings Equality," was first presented as a paper at a Morehouse College conference that commemorated the fiftieth anniversary of Gunnar Myrdal's classic book, *An American Dilemma*. In this chapter I trace shifts in black-white earnings inequality from the 1940s to the 1990s and highlight the growing importance of reading and math skills as causes of earnings inequality. I suggest further that efforts to improve basic skills need to become central to our strategic understanding of how to achieve racial equality in the United States.

My research also led me to investigate why test scores stopped rising for black and Hispanic teens at the end of the 1980s. In chapter 2, "Test-Score Trends along Racial Lines, 1971 to 1996: Popular Culture and Community Academic Standards," I discuss ways that a shift in black and Hispanic youth culture might partially account for this plateau.[2] Youth culture profoundly affects what young people do with their time, how free they feel to be ambitious, and how inclined they are to do what they know is right without fear that their peers might disapprove. This chapter, which foreshadows my more recent work in the same area, focuses particularly on the role of rap music and the impact of peer expectations in shaping young black students' attitudes toward achievement. In the Afterword to chapter 2, I describe some more recent findings from subsequent analyses of test-score trends.

The fact that reducing black-white test-score disparities has the potential to reduce other forms of racial inequality inspired Christopher Jencks to conceive the *Black-White Test Score Gap*, a landmark volume Jencks coedited with Meredith Phillips in 1998. In the introduction, Jencks wrote:

> Reducing the test-score gap is probably both necessary and sufficient for substantially reducing racial inequality in educational attainment and earnings. Changes in education and earnings would in turn help reduce racial differences in crime, health, and family structure, although we do not know how large these effects would be. (p. 4)

This followed another passage from Jencks that has become a standard quotation in writings on the black-white test-score gap: "If racial equality is America's goal, reducing the black-white test-score gap would probably do more to promote this goal than any other strategy that commands broad public support" (p. 3).

Jencks and Phillips invited me to contribute a chapter to their book that reviewed the best available research concerning the potential of school-related strategies to help close the black-white test-score gap. Preschool, grouping and tracking, class size, matching teacher and student race, teacher quality, and a few other topics were to be included. I also wanted to explore whether teachers' expectations were biased downward for black students, as compared to white students. In the course of my investigations, I learned that there are three distinct conceptions of bias in the literature on teacher expectations, and that the verdict on whether a teacher's expectations are biased along racial lines depends on which definition of bias is implicit in making the judgment. My investigation of teacher expectations became a separate chapter. Both chapters appear in this book: chapter 3, "Can Schools Narrow the Black-White Test Score Gap?" and chapter 4, "Teachers' Perceptions and Expectations and the Black-White Test Score Gap." Together they tell a nuanced but hopeful story about the ways that schools, teachers, and teaching affect achievement levels and gaps. They hold out promise that high-quality schooling, beginning with preschool, can indeed help close these gaps.

While I was working on these chapters, my friend Reuben Harris asked me to meet with Mark Freeman, the school superintendent in Shaker Heights, Ohio, to discuss ways that achievement gaps in the district could be reduced. Harris had become a parent leader at Shaker Heights High School and served on a committee of parents and school officials that had compiled student data in a report on achievement gaps within the school. The student newspaper at the high school got hold of the report and published grade-point averages and average standardized test-scores. Black students were embarrassed and upset by the results and also by the fact that they were released. Freeman asked me to present some of my research findings to his principals and to the community, so I met with the principals and some three hundred citizens on a summer Sunday afternoon.

This relationship with Shaker Heights eventually led to chapter 5 of this volume, "A Diagnostic Analysis of Black-White GPA Disparities in Shaker Heights, Ohio," which is based on findings from the Ed Excel survey of student culture developed by John Bishop of Cornell University. Bishop created the survey as a tool for studying achievement cultures in high schools. He invited me to help him find districts in which to administer it. Shaker Heights became one of the first. The findings I describe in chapter 5 indicate that black-white gaps in student skill levels had been developed before middle school, and that one key area of black-white differences in middle and high school was the sometimes rowdy behavioral expectations that black students often have for one another. The survey also highlighted some powerful challenges to the standard inferences teachers and other adults make about student effort and commitment to academic success, based on group-level differences in homework completion rates and behavior patterns. Black students reported lower homework completion rates than white classmates but no less time devoted to homework. They self-reported worse behavior than whites but no less desire to do well academically. Teachers and school officials found both of the latter findings surprising, and it changed their understanding of black-white differences in homework completion rates and behavior.[3]

Shaker Heights joined the Minority Student Achievement Network (MSAN) around 1999. Psychologist Edmund W. Gordon helped MSAN founder Alan Alson, then superintendent of the high school district in Evanston, Illinois, to convene a research advisory council. I joined that advisory council and began working with the MSAN Practitioner Research Council (PRC). The PRC, aware of the findings in Shaker Heights, decided in the spring of 2000 that they wanted to administer the Ed Excel survey to middle and high school students in all fifteen member districts. So, in November 2000, we administered the survey to roughly 40,000 middle and high school students. Slightly updated from the version that Shaker Heights students had taken, the survey touched on many issues of student motivation, peer relations, effort, aspirations, music preferences, family background supports, and use of time.

The results of this second survey are discussed in chapter 6, "What Doesn't Meet the Eye: Understanding and Addressing Racial Disparities in High-Achieving Suburban Schools." Patterns in the data for all fifteen districts were strikingly similar to those for Shaker Heights. The findings in this chapter pertain to racial differences and similarities in student effort and motivation, and to variations in the achievement gap by family socioeconomic status.

Chapter 6 also introduces the Tripod Project for School Improvement, which I conceived in collaboration with educators in Shaker Heights, partly in response to the MSAN Ed Excel survey findings. (The three legs of the "tripod" are teachers' content knowledge, pedagogy, and teacher-student relationships.) The project surveys students and teachers in participating schools to document attitudes, perceptions, experiences, and practices. The resulting data are returned to each school in forms suitable to inform and influence deliberations about ways to improve the school, raise achievement, and narrow gaps. The Tripod Project spread from Shaker Heights to other MSAN districts and now operates in both suburban and inner-city schools in several states. A central focus of the project is to provide classroom-level data for whole schools, which allows school leaders to discern how different classrooms are from one another in the quality of instruction and of student engagement in learning. The data inform school-level strategic efforts to improve instruction and school climate, raise achievement levels, and close achievement gaps. In the Afterword to chapter 6, I discuss additional data derived from Tripod Project surveys concerning youth culture, academic achievement, and the "acting white" hypothesis.

An all-too-constant concern among Tripod Project leaders in schools has been the resistance that they experience when trying to involve teachers deeply in school-level change. While it has been relatively easy to engage small, enthusiastic groups of teachers in change efforts—let us call them "the choir"—engaging the vast "congregation" of teachers in any school requires stronger leadership than many schools have developed. The failure of many schools to fully engage their "congregation" in implementing professional development programs, including but not limited to our "teaching the hard stuff" and other Tripod Project programs, led me to develop a special section on the Tripod Project survey for teachers. A key finding from this section indicated that professional development programs had not worked *because teachers had not implemented them*. In chapter 7, "Five Challenges to Effective Teacher Professional Development," I describe these and other conclusions based on the survey. I highlight the importance of introducing professional development in ways specifically designed to inspire teacher buy-in, of having in place specific monitoring and accountability procedures, of providing sufficient follow-up training and support, and of making space and time for the new activities within the context of a coherent professional development strategy.

While I began this journey focused on schools and still believe that schools are extremely important, I have slowly come to view parenting as a very important strategic emphasis for raising achievement and closing gaps. Therefore, I made parenting the major focus of chapter 8, "Toward Excellence with Equity: The Role of Parenting and Transformative School Reform." In this chapter, I draw on evidence from many sources that parenting practices, beginning at infancy, are important determinants of school achievement and that racial, ethnic, and socioeconomic groups differ in the degree to which practices most correlated with high achievement are the norm. Some of these differences seem related to resources, some to parenting beliefs, and some to the simple transmission of parenting norms and practices from generation to generation. Inducing people to raise their children differently is not easy, but if we can successfully influence parents to do so within the context of a national movement for excellence with equity, I believe the impact on

← like the Manhattan Project.

improving achievement levels and closing achievement gaps could be quite significant.

In the concluding chapter of this volume I discuss where we go from here. In it I outline basic ideas for framing our thinking about a social and cultural movement for excellence with equity—a movement that goes beyond the boundaries of the schoolyard to include families, communities, out-of-school supports, youth culture, and civic engagement. The key conception of equity is that group-level identities should be worthless as predictors of achievement. While all groups should rise toward excellence, those farthest behind should rise most rapidly until our society has reached a state of "group-proportional equality." In chapter 8 and the conclusion, I call on all Americans to provide high-quality developmental supports and experiences to children from all racial, ethnic, and social-class origins until excellence is a normal outcome and membership in a particular group no longer predicts anything of consequence in our society. American rhetoric will then have become our American reality.

CHAPTER 1

Shifting Challenges

Fifty Years of Economic Change toward Black-White Earnings Equality

INTRODUCTION

When Gunnar Myrdal published *An American Dilemma* in 1944 three of every four Negroes in the United States lived in the South where the reigning ideology, mirrored to a substantial degree in the nation at large, was white supremacy. Decade after decade, the leading proponents of white supremacy decreed that Negroes had neither the right nor the human potential to participate on a par with whites in the economic and political life of the nation. White citizens broadly subscribed to this dictum, as did many blacks. Consequently, a full eight decades after the formal abolition of slavery, social, political, and economic opportunities for Black Americans remained severely circumscribed.

In some ways, the South's racial caste system was more restrictive than the institution of slavery. As Myrdal wrote:

> Before Emancipation it was in the interest of the slave owners to use Negro slaves wherever it was profitable in handicraft and manufacture. After Emancipation no such proprietary interest protected Negro laborers from the desire of white workers to squeeze them out of skilled employment. They were gradually driven out and pushed down into the "Negro jobs," a category which has been more and more narrowly defined.[1]

Consequently, in the early 1940s blacks trailed far behind whites on virtually every important social and economic indicator. They attended poorly equipped schools and for only half as many years as whites. The average black male earned less than half as much as his white coworker. He labored, more often than not, in the most menial and low-wage jobs, receiving less pay than white workers even when doing the same work. Such was the situation in 1944.

Fifty years later, in 1994, remnants of white supremacist ideology continue to color the thoughts and behaviors of whites and blacks alike, but the most pernicious customs are largely outdated and most are violations of federal law. Furthermore, beyond formal legal structures, the Civil Rights and Black Power movements have achieved for African Americans a presence in public affairs and elective offices that few would have thought possible at the time that Myrdal wrote.

Still, legacies from three centuries of enforced social and economic subordination abound: economic advantage and disadvantage still correlate with race much more than might happen by chance; social relations between the races remain clumsy, suspicious, and fragile. Moreover, tenets of conventional wisdom regarding the causes of economic inequality between blacks and whites are legacies of the past as well.

This essay reviews explanations for changes in earnings inequality between black and white males since the publication of *An American Dilemma*. In addition, it aims to inform conventional wisdom concerning sources and remedies for inequality between black and white labor force participants *in the 1990s and beyond*. This essay contends that the most strategically relevant fact for understanding and reducing remaining wage and employment differences between young black and white male adults is the following: the basic skills (e.g., basic reading and math skills) of young black male workers are not, on average, as well matched to shifting patterns in the market demand for labor as are the basic skills of young whites who have the same years of schooling and live in the same regions. For young males in their twenties and early thirties, research from the late 1980s and early 1990s suggests that economic disparities between blacks and whites due to differences in skills and behaviors outweigh those associated with other proximate causes.

Measurable racial disparities in skill and commitment to work are complex manifestations of deep-rooted historical and contemporary social forces that produce self-fulfilling prophesies of poor performance for many African American youths and adults alike. These forces include the demeaning and discouraging messages that society delivers to black males as a group and the long tradition of excluding black workers from many positions for which they have had the qualifications. Discouraging messages that communicate low expectations to black male youths, buttressed by inadequate schools and talk "on the street" that the economic game is "rigged," foster skeptical and often half-hearted engagement by many black youths, and some adults as well, in "mainstream" activities that purport to prepare them for expanded opportunity.[2]

Substantially reducing racial disparity among young adults in the labor market requires supporting *and* holding accountable the institutions that should inspire, educate, and nurture African American children.[3] In addition, it requires continued vigilance against racial bias in the workplace that validates young people's expectations that the game is rigged against them even when they do their part to prepare and perform. Given the complexity of the social forces that affect the acquisition of skill and success in labor markets, and given that social forces are malleable, this author rejects any assertion that the remaining differences in skill among blacks and whites that this paper explores are genetically predetermined (as some pundits are again suggesting) or that society should acquiesce and be content to tolerate them.

PROGRESS FROM 1940–1975[4]

The period from 1940–1975 was one of substantial economic progress for blacks relative to whites. Each successive cohort of blacks after 1940 entered adulthood on a more equal social and educational footing with whites than the one before.[5] The dark diagonal line up the center of Figure 1–1 represents the composite earnings ratio for sixteen to sixty-four year olds. The narrower and flatter lines portray the patterns for ten-year cohorts that entered the labor market during consecutive decades. The label on each line shows the decade that the cohort entered the adult labor force.

Figure 1–1 shows that improvement for blacks relative to whites came from progress both within and between cohorts. However, the pattern was uneven over time. The 1940s saw rapid relative progress because heavy demand for labor during World War II broke down barriers that in the past had excluded blacks from certain jobs. The 1950s were relatively flat within cohorts but the composite pattern was slightly positive because the young men who entered the market had higher relative earnings (i.e., relative to their white peers) than did the older men who retired. The 1960s produced progress for all cohorts, while the 1970s saw progress through mid-decade and then a decline. Hence, the decade ended with relative wage levels for

**FIGURE 1–1   Black Weekly Wage as a Percentage of White Weekly Wage
(Adult Males, 1940–1980)**

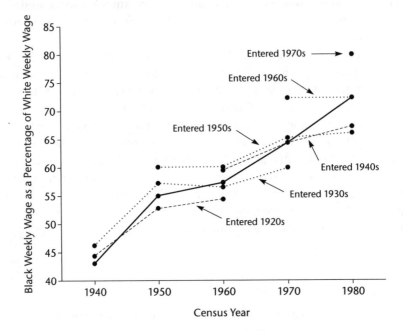

Source: James P. Smith and Finis R. Welch, "Black Economic Progress after Myrdal," *Journal of Economic Literature* XXVII (2) (June 1989), constructed from data in table 8.

individual cohorts roughly where they began in 1970. Nevertheless, successive cohorts continued to move ahead of those before them. The cohort that entered during the 1970s had wages that were higher relative to those of whites in 1980 than for any previous cohort—over 80 percent.[6]

why?   Three clusters of explanations seem to account for black economic progress relative to whites between 1940 and 1975: black migration away from Southern states and rural areas; improvements in the quality and quantity of schooling that blacks received; and the dismantling of discriminatory barriers in labor markets.

Migration

The fact that many blacks lived in the rural South—the poorest region in the nation—helps to explain why the black-white wage gap for the nation was greater than 50 percent in 1940. In 1940, 90.6 percent of blacks in the United

States had been born in the South and 74.8 percent still lived there.[7] Only 28 percent of the nation's whites were Southerners.

From 1940 through the mid-1960s, blacks abandoned the rural South in massive numbers. They found greater economic opportunity in the urban South and in the cities of other regions. The large difference between what blacks could earn in the South versus other regions was not, however, a permanent condition. Regional differences in the quality of opportunity narrowed substantially after the mid-1960s.

For example, analyses of annual data from the Current Population Survey (CPS) demonstrate that wage rates for black men in the South in 1965 were still 35 percent below those for whites of the same age and the same years of schooling. Outside of the South, the analogous gap was 17 percent.[8] By 1973, the gap for the South had shrunk to between 19 and 20 percent. The percentage difference for blacks in other regions had moved by less than 2 percentage points. Curiously, and suddenly, the data show a large positive spike in relative improvement for blacks outside the South between 1973 and 1975.[9] During these two years, the black-white wage gap outside the South was cut in half, from near 16 percent down to 8 percent. By 1980, however, the gap outside the South had returned to its 1973 level. Nearly all of the sustained wage gains for black men relative to white men in the fifteen years from 1965 through 1980 occurred in the South.[10] In addition, wage levels in the South for all racial groups, including whites, were slowly catching up with those in the rest of the nation.[11]

Hence, the economic incentive for blacks to leave the South decreased rather dramatically after 1965. The direction of migration reversed during the 1970s with a small net migration back to the South. Today, roughly half of all Black Americans live in the South and over 80 percent live in urban areas.

Younger cohorts of blacks in the South migrated away in larger numbers than did their elders. This helped to increase their wages more rapidly relative to whites. Overall, migrants out of the South comprised 14.6 percent of Southern blacks during the 1940s, 13.7 percent during the 1950s, and 11.9 percent during the 1960s.[12] These numbers are lower than those for twenty to twenty-four year olds. Net migration figures show that 26.3 percent of the South's twenty to twenty-four year old black males left the South in the 1940s, 24.5 percent left in the 1950s, and 19.3 percent left in the 1960s.[13]

James Smith and Finis Welch estimate that migration boosted the black-white wage ratio by 20 percent between 1940 and 1970 for young men with five or fewer years of work experience.[14] The gains were smaller for older cohorts who migrated in smaller numbers.

Schooling

There is little agreement concerning how to best measure school quality. It is clear, however, that the gross differences in resources available to black and white children in the South in the earlier part of the twentieth century could not possibly have provided them with equal opportunities to learn.

When Gunnar Myrdal wrote *An American Dilemma,* disparities in educational resources for black and white children in the South were diminishing, but they were still large. David Card and Alan Krueger have assembled data that show average pupil/teacher ratios, term length, and teacher pay for eighteen segregated states between 1915 and 1966. These disparities were not inadvertent. For example, Myrdal quotes from a report on teacher salaries:

> An additional argument in favor of the salary differential [between black and white teachers] is the general tradition of the South that negroes and whites are not to be paid equivalent salaries for equivalent work. . . . The custom is one . . . that the practical school administrator must not ignore.[15]

Figure 1–2 shows the patterns that Card and Krueger document.[16] In 1915, black students tolerated classes that were nearly twice as large as those that whites enjoyed. They attended school only two-thirds as many days as did whites. Furthermore, black teachers earned less than half of what white teachers earned. The fifty years between 1915 and 1965 saw hard-fought battles for educational equity. Those battles produced convergence in at least some measures of school quality. Figure 1–2 shows that by 1965 black schools in the South had achieved near parity on pupil/teacher ratios, term length, and teacher pay.

This convergence along several dimensions of school quality helps to explain why younger cohorts in the labor market did better both absolutely and relative to whites than did their elders.[17]

Card and Krueger present evidence of a link between the school resource variables in Figure 1–2—pupil/teacher ratios, term length, and teacher pay— and later earnings for men who attended the Southern schools that Figure 1–2 represents. Specifically, Card and Krueger estimate rates of return to additional years of schooling for men in nine Northern states in 1960, 1970, and 1980 who were born and educated in the South. They show that state-by-state differences between blacks and whites in the economic return to an additional year of schooling are correlated with black-white differences in schooling resources in the Southern states at the times that the men attended school.

FIGURE 1–2   Relative School Quality in Eighteen Segregated States, 1915–1966

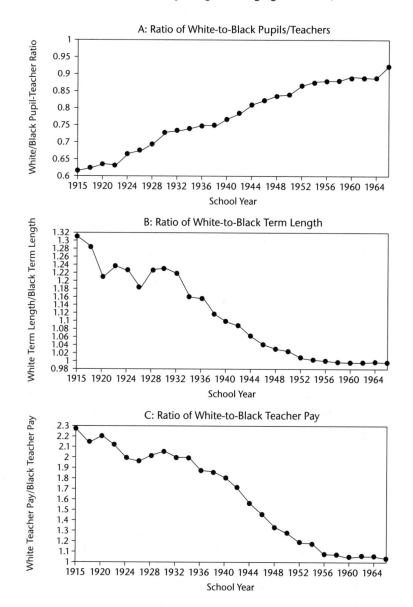

Source: David Card and Alan B. Krueger, "School Quality and Black-White Relative Earnings: A Direct Assessment," *The Quarterly Journal of Economics* CVII (1) (February 1992).

FIGURE 1–3   Difference in Rate of Return to Schooling Versus Difference in Pupil-Teacher Ratio (Men Born in 1910–1939 in the South)

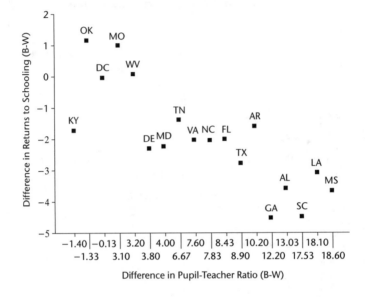

Source: David Card and Alan B. Krueger, "School Quality and Black-White Relative Earnings: A Direct Assessment," *The Quarterly Journal of Economics* CVII (1) (February 1992).

Figure 1–3 shows one of the patterns that their work reveals. The vertical axis shows the black-white difference in the percentage increase in income associated with an additional year of schooling. The horizontal axis shows the black-white difference in average pupil-teacher ratios. While the pattern in the diagram does not prove causation, the correlation is clearly negative: smaller class sizes appear to increase the value of an additional year of schooling.

During the period from 1960 to 1980, the relative rate of return to an extra year of schooling for black men educated in the South and working in the North was higher for younger cohorts than for older ones. The rate of return to schooling for the younger cohorts of Southern-born blacks was higher not only relative to whites but relative to Northern-born blacks as well. This increase as compared with Northern-born blacks who worked in the same Northern labor markets suggests that the gain for Southern blacks between 1960 and 1980 was not due simply to Civil Rights pressures on employers. These pressures would presumably have affected all blacks living in the

North in a similar way, regardless of the region of their birth. Instead, Card and Krueger argue, the higher rates of return to schooling for the younger cohorts reflect improvements in the relative quality of the schools that younger cohorts of Southern-born blacks attended. In addition, the increasing quality of the schools that black youths in the South attended probably helps to explain why younger cohorts chose to attend school longer.

Indeed, the gain in years of schooling for blacks in the United States after 1940 is truly impressive. Since the majority of blacks lived in the South, the national pattern reflects Southern progress disproportionately. In 1940, the average sixteen to sixty-four year old black male in the United States had only 4.70 years of schooling. The average for whites was 9.38. By 1980, average years of schooling had risen to 12.50 for whites and 11.00 for blacks. For the youngest adults, the difference by 1980 was less than one year.[18] Not only was the gap in average years of schooling closing, the gap in what an extra year of schooling contributed to earning power was closing as well. Some estimates show that blacks and whites with fewer than fifteen years of work experience had virtually the same rate of return to an additional year of schooling in 1980.[19]

Civil Rights

While some effects of the Civil Rights movement on relative earnings may have begun before 1960, most probably came afterward. The topics addressed above—migration, improvements in school quality, and more years in school—leave roughly one-third to one-half of the gain in relative earnings for blacks between 1960 and 1980 unexplained.[20] Research on the link between black economic progress and the Civil Rights movement has not produced a definitive estimate of how important affirmative action and Civil Rights enforcement were to black economic gains after 1960. We know, for example, that black employment increased in firms that were federal contractors and subject to federal affirmative action requirements. This improvement was concentrated in the South where black wage gains were greatest.[21] In addition, we know that relative improvements in black earnings between 1960 and 1980 were concentrated between the late 1960s and the early 1970s when formal and informal pressures to provide equal employment opportunity were especially strong. What we do not know with any precision is what percentage of observed improvements in employment outcomes for blacks were due to these and other Civil Rights pressures. Given that one-third to one-half of the gains after 1960 are not otherwise easily explained, the impact may have been substantial.

FIGURE 1–4   Black-White Percentage Earnings Gap by Level of Schooling (Young Men with Fewer than Ten Years of Experience)

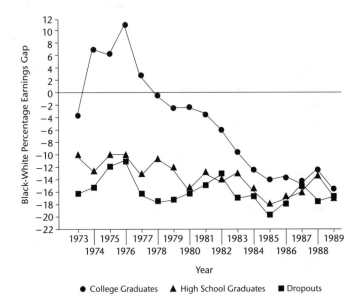

Source: John Bound and Richard B. Freeman, "What Went Wrong? The Erosion of Relative Earnings and Employment Among Young Black Men in the 1980s," *The Quarterly Journal of Economics* CVII (1) (February 1992).

However important federal pressure may have been, the period of advancement in labor market outcomes for black males ended, at least temporarily, in the mid-1970s.

THE LACK OF PROGRESS AFTER 1975

By 1975, black males had earnings that were within 8 percentage points of those for whites who shared the same patterns of working and had equal years of schooling.[22] Since the mid-1970s, however, the level of wage disparity between black and white males older than forty-five years of age has been roughly constant. Disparity among younger males has increased, with younger blacks falling further behind.[23] The possible reasons are complex and not fully understood.[24]

The CPS provides the data that researchers use most commonly to track annual changes in earnings and employment. Based upon analyses of CPS

FIGURE 1–5   Black-White Percentage Earnings Gap by Region (Young Men with High School or Less Education and Fewer than Ten Years of Experience)

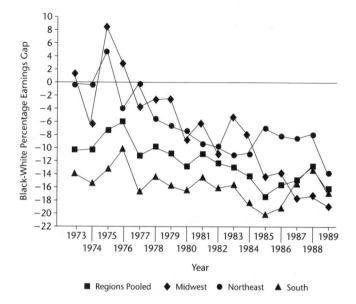

Source: John Bound and Richard B. Freeman, "What Went Wrong? The Erosion of Relative Earnings and Employment Among Young Black Men in the 1980s," *The Quarterly Journal of Economics* CVII (1) (February 1992).

data, several authors have reported the decline in relative earnings for young black males.[25] Figures 1–4 and 1–5 show the percentage gap since 1973 between blacks and whites (black minus white) in usual weekly earnings, holding constant years of schooling and potential experience.[26] Figure 1–6 shows employment-to-population ratios for men with fewer than twelve, exactly twelve, and exactly sixteen years of schooling. All of the numbers in Figures 1–4, 1–5, and 1–6 are for young men eighteen years old and older, with nine or fewer years of labor market experience.[27]

Figures 1–4 and 1–5 show that the pattern of change differed across regions and for men with different amounts of schooling. The greatest deterioration in relative earnings was for groups that experienced the most equality in the mid-1970s: college graduates, men in the Midwest, and, to a lesser extent, men in the Northeast.

Figure 1–6 shows that the employment-to-population ratio deteriorated at least slightly for all but white college graduates after the mid-1970s.[28] How-

FIGURE 1–6   Employment-to-Population Ratios by Levels of Schooling (Black and White Males with Fewer than Ten Years of Experience)

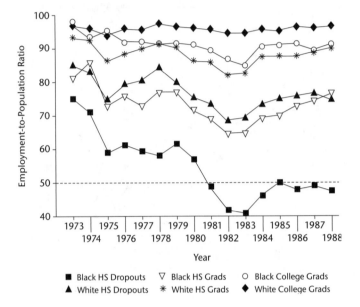

Source: Current Population Survey, tabulations by John Bound.

ever, the only group with large and perhaps permanent deterioration in its position—diverging sharply from employment levels of the mid-1970s—are black high school dropouts. Figure 1–6 shows no time after 1981 when more than 50 percent of black male dropouts in this age range were employed.

Increased Demand for Skill

A partial explanation for the increasing wage disparity between young blacks and whites after the mid-1970s is an increase in the demand for, and the price of, skill.[29] Even though it appears that the gap in skill has been closing,[30] the "price of skill" (defined below) may have been growing more rapidly during this period than the racial gap in skill has been closing.[31]

Consider a hypothetical example. Imagine that points on a particular test are a good measure of proficiency in basic reading and math skills. Employers buy (or, more accurately, rent) these skills by hiring employees to use their skills in the workplace. In effect, employers are bidding against one another for employees with good basic skills. The "price" of "ten points worth of skill" is the difference in wage rates that the employer pays for the skills associated with the ten points. If the "price of skill" were $0.10 per point in 1980 and rose to $0.25 per point by 1990, then two otherwise identical people whose test scores were ten points apart could expect the difference in their wages to rise from $1.00 per hour in 1980 to $2.50 per hour by 1990. If the test score gap closed from ten points in 1980 to become, say, seven points in 1990, then the gap in wages would not grow as much, but it would grow nevertheless. For the wage gap to remain constant at $1.00 in this example, the gap in test scores would have to fall from ten in 1980 to four in 1990.

Why do we believe that the market value of skill has risen? One piece of evidence is that the gap in earnings between high school and college graduates grew on the order of 1 percent per year during the 1980s.[32] Card and Krueger report that the percentage gap in earnings between blacks and whites with equal years of schooling tends to move up and down as the percentage gap in earnings between high school and college graduates rises and falls.[33] Another reason to believe that the market value of skill has risen is that differences in wages predicted by differences in test scores that measure basic reading and math skills have, by some estimates, grown. This evidence of the increasing importance of test scores as predictors of earnings, however, is based on data that are not completely appropriate.[34] Hence, while the story is quite plausible, the question remains open among researchers.

Skill-Biased Economic Change

Changes in the economy that have differential impacts on workers according to their proficiencies in relevant skills are examples of what I call "skill-biased economic changes." Employment in the United States has been falling in the public sector and in jobs protected by unions. Public-sector and union jobs tend to insulate workers from head-to-head competition based on proficiency. At the same time, competition from immigrants and foreign workers for the least skilled jobs that pay the lowest wages has been increasing. This increase in the supply of low-skilled labor suppresses the wage rate and thereby increases the cost to any given worker of not having better skills. Better skills could earn him or her a job in a segment of the labor market not affected so much by immigration. In addition, modernization in both manufacturing and service-sector technology is requiring new modes of workplace organization that entail more learning on the job, more responsibility among workers for managing technology, more reading of manuals, more writing of reports, and more working in groups.[35] These trends appear to be increasing the demand for both cognitive and social skills, thereby increasing wage differences between people at different skill levels.

John Bound and Richard Freeman attempt to measure the degree to which some of the factors listed above help to predict the trends shown in Figures 1–4 and 1–5.[36] The factors that they study include changes over time in location patterns, industrial and occupational employment shares, unionism, and the real value of the minimum wage. All may be causes or consequences of changes in the price of skill, as defined above, and associated increases in economic disparity. Table 1–1 summarizes their findings. The "Average Annual Change" at the top of each column represents the average annual change from 1973 through 1989 of average weekly earnings for blacks as a percentage of those for whites, holding constant years of schooling and potential experience. Rows 1 through 5 show how much of the "Average Annual Change" Bound and Freeman estimate may be associated with each respective category of explanatory variables.

The "Average Annual Change" is most negative for college graduates (–1.547 percent per year) and for men in the Midwest with twelve or fewer years of schooling (–1.424 percent per year). The most important factor in the Midwest is industry, which explains the disproportionate shift of young black men in the Midwest out of manufacturing jobs as manufacturing plants closed in the central cities where blacks were most concentrated. The biggest drop for college educated men is associated with occupation. Numbers not shown here demonstrate that 80 percent of the effect of occupation reflects greater shifts into lower-wage occupations for college educated blacks than for college educated whites, and 20 percent reflects reductions in the wages of occupations that blacks already tended to occupy more than whites in the early 1970s. However, even after all of the categories of variables are included, 59 percent of the trend for college graduates remains unexplained in the Bound and Freeman analysis.

The trend in earnings inequality for black dropouts in Table 1–1 is not as negative as that for high school and college graduates. Indeed, the fall in the real value of the minimum wage alone is sufficient to account for the trend. This, however, is not the most important story for black dropouts. First, white dropouts experienced a large amount of erosion in the inflation-adjusted value of their weekly earnings, so the fact that blacks did almost as well as whites is not grounds for solace. Second, recall the divergent employment trend for black high school dropouts in Figure 1–6. It appears that changes in the relative demand for black labor appeared more through changes in weekly earnings (Figure 1–4) for men with high school and college educations and through falling employment rates for high school dropouts (Figure 1–6).

TABLE 1–1   Annual Change in Black-White Earnings Gap as a Percentage of White Earnings (Males with Fewer than Ten Years of Experience, 1973–1989

	Level of Education				Region (High School Education or Less)		
	Total	College Grad.	High School Grad.	Dropout	Mid-west	North-east	South
Column:	1	2	3	4	5	6	7
Average Annual Change	−0.565	−1.547	−0.449	−0.208	−1.424	−0.797	−0.241
1. Due to Location	−0.062	−0.167	−0.041	0.109	−0.188	−0.311	−0.014
2. Due to Industry	−0.058	−0.108	−0.046	−0.106	−0.455	−0.140	0.062
3. Due to Occupation	−0.109	−0.296	−0.157	0.018	−0.162	−0.042	−0.106
4. Due to Unionism	−0.027	−0.024	−0.046	−0.047	−0.126	−0.108	−0.058
5. Due to Minimum Wage	−0.097	−0.042	−0.120	−0.203	−0.101	−0.034	−0.181
TOTAL OF LINES 1–5	−0.353	−0.637	−0.410	−0.229	−1.132	−0.624	−0.185

Source: Adapted from estimates presented in John Bound and Richard B. Freeman, "What Went Wrong? The Erosion of Relative Earnings and Employment Among Young Black Men in the 1980s," *The Quarterly Journal of Economics* CVII (1) (February 1992): table III, 213.

An important source of job competition for black dropouts is immigration. Immigration is a skill-biased economic phenomenon because it has different effects on workers at different skill levels. Immigrants have increased the supply of labor in low-wage low-skill segments of the labor market. One study estimates that legal and illegal immigrants together comprised a group equal to 17 percent of high school dropouts in 1975.[37] This number nearly doubled to 31 percent by 1985. The same study found that the number of high school dropouts apparently displaced by net imports to manufacturing grew from 1.5 percent to 12 percent over the same period. These numbers are large enough to be partly responsible for the deterioration in employment that less skilled young workers, especially black dropouts, experienced between 1975 and 1985.

The queuing theory of labor demand helps to explain what may be happening to young black males. This theory posits that employers hire from the front of an implicit labor queue. The applicants whom the employer expects will be most desirable as employees are at the front of the queue. The workers whom the employer expects will be less productive or otherwise less desirable are at the back of the queue. Employers will hire them last, if at all.

If employers hire from the front of the queue, and if blacks are disproportionately at the back—behind immigrants and native-born members of other racial groups—then blacks will suffer the greatest deterioration in employment when the number of immigrants grows. Precise estimates of the effect that immigration has on employment for black dropouts are not available. Nevertheless, growth in the size of the immigrant labor force probably helps to explain the trend in employment-to-population ratios for black high school dropouts shown in Figure 1–6.

A more disaggregated set of industrial and occupational categories in the study by Bound and Freeman would probably have explained an even larger percentage of the trends in earnings inequality. Nevertheless, even at the levels of aggregation that they used, Bound and Freeman identified an increasing propensity after 1973 for blacks to occupy less lucrative occupations and to work in industries that offered lower pay. For high school dropouts, some of this appears to be the consequence of increasing competition from immigrants. For high school graduates and college graduates, further analysis suggests that some of the shifting across occupations and industries may be the consequence of changing skill requirements and differences in how well blacks versus whites meet those requirements. In addition, a non-trivial share of this shifting is almost certainly the consequence of declining pressure for affirmative action.

Equal Opportunity and Affirmative Action

Declining pressures by the federal government and by other parts of society for equal employment opportunity and for affirmative action probably account for some of the industry and occupation effects in Table 1–1, as well as for some of the trends that remain unexplained. During the early 1970s, affirmative outreach for young minority workers, especially college graduates, was in style. The Civil Rights movement and the federal laws and regulations that resulted from that movement significantly reduced the possibility that past customs of racial exclusion could go unquestioned during the 1960s and early 1970s. Many employers in the late 1960s and early 1970s probably responded to the mood of the times and "voluntarily"—without court orders or contract compliance obligations—hired blacks into positions that they had reserved for whites in the past.

Title VII of the Civil Rights Act of 1964 and President Johnson's Executive Order 11246 provided official enforcement powers to the federal government. With these powers, the government put pressure on firms that discriminated against racial minorities and also on federal contractors who may in the past have had no concern for racial balance. Acting under the provisions of Title VII, federal courts awarded damages against firms convicted of racial bias. For example, the famous case of *Griggs* v. *Duke Power Company* put the business community on notice that even the appearance of a discriminatory motive—use of an exam that had a racially disproportionate impact and without sufficient job relatedness—could put them at risk for heavy fines and penalties.

Pressures for affirmative action by federal contractors waned during the 1980s. According to Jonathan Leonard, who has studied these issues extensively, ". . . affirmative action under the contract compliance program virtually ceased to exist in all but name after 1980."[38] As partial evidence, Leonard points out that the black share of employment in the early 1980s grew more rapidly in firms that were not federal contractors than in firms that were. He remarks, "It was as though contractors were returning to a growth path they had been forced off by previous affirmative action efforts."

It is no secret that economic opportunity for racial minorities was not a priority during Ronald Reagan's presidency. Neither, for that matter, were these issues as focal during the Carter administration of the late 1970s as they had been during the Johnson administration of the late 1960s. Hence, even in the absence of changes in the actual performance of federal enforcement agencies, it seems reasonable to expect that employers after the late 1970s may have, as Leonard suggests, largely returned to the patterns that they would have followed in the absence of federal pressure.

Changes from the 1970s to the 1980s in the relative occupational distributions of young blacks and whites are consistent with this interpretation. In the 1970s, young black college graduates were as likely as their white counterparts to be in managerial and professional occupations. By the late 1980s, they were 13 percent less likely than young whites to be in these occupations.[39] Black high school graduates lost ground as well. In the 1970s, young blacks had more than their share of jobs as operatives but fewer than their share of craftworker positions. By the late 1980s, the percentage of young black workers in operatives was the same as that for whites, and blacks had lost even further ground as craftworkers.[40]

THE IMPORTANCE OF SKILLS AND BEHAVIORS

Audit studies of hiring practices that send equally qualified blacks and whites to apply for the same job openings find that whites receive more job offers by small but nevertheless important margins of difference.[41] The need to comply with caste-based custom, however, is no longer a standard explanation as it may have been fifty years ago. Instead, both employers who discriminate and many researchers who seek to explain employers' behaviors usually point to what researchers call "statistical discrimination."[42]

By definition, statistical discrimination based on race is when employers use race as a signal of potential productivity and hire whites over blacks even when the two appear otherwise equal. In any particular example, an employer's assumption that race is a valid signal of skills and behaviors may be correct, or not. Still, if he expects on average to be correct, he will continue the practice. While this practice may be rational for employers, statistical discrimination is illegal and unfair to its victims who must prove that they are exceptions to the stereotype.

It is true that young black males *on average* rank lower than whites on dimensions that are unobservable to employers at the time of hiring but that help to predict later productivity on the job. These characteristics that are initially "invisible" may sometimes include basic reading and math skills as well as some employment behaviors, such as absenteeism and the propensity to quit.[43] Attempting to change employers' screening strategies without also changing the workers' skills and behaviors that produce and confirm those strategies is an expensive and potentially unworkable policy both for employers and for society at large. Conversely, permitting employers to practice a strategy of statistical discrimination is unfair to those it unjustly excludes from jobs. From a societal perspective, neither alternative is desirable.

Basic Skills and Wages

The National Longitudinal Survey of Youth (NLSY) provides the only nationally representative data that include measures of basic reading and math skills as well as the variables that researchers need in order to estimate standard wage and employment equations. The NLSY began in 1979 with a sample of twelve thousand fourteen to twenty-two year old respondents. Half were males. Interviewers have revisited the original sample each year since 1979. Ninety-five percent of the sample completed the Armed Services Vocational Aptitude Battery (ASVAB) in 1980. Here, I report results using a composite score called the Armed Forces Qualifications Test (AFQT). The AFQT is calculated by summing the scaled scores from tests of mathematic reasoning, word knowledge, reading comprehension, and half the score from a speed test of numerical operations. It is essentially a test of basic reading and math proficiencies.

Several authors have written recently concerning how well the AFQT score helps in predicting otherwise unexplained differences between blacks and whites in hourly wage rates.[44] In an analysis conducted for this paper, wage rates for 1988–1992[45] were based on the reported earnings for the "current or most recent job" for each of the five years[46] of 1,731 men (1,122 white and 609 black) aged twenty-three to thirty-five. For the present set of estimates, the wage from the most recent job at the time of the interview is averaged across the five years.[47]

The estimates that form the basis of this discussion include controls for years of schooling, census region, area of residence (i.e., urban, suburban, or rural), and years of potential experience.[48] This is the same type of procedure that Bound and Freeman used in estimating the numbers that Figures 1–4 and 1–5 report.[49]

Results.[50]   When our estimates do not include the AFQT score among the explanatory variables, the estimated wage differences between blacks and whites closely resemble those that Bound and Freeman found (see Figures 1–4 and 1–5) for the late 1980s in their analysis of data from the CPS. When test scores are not controlled, the unexplained racial difference in earnings for the late 1980s is between 13 and 20 percent in their analysis using the CPS as well as in my analysis using the NLSY. One-half to three-quarters of this difference disappears, however, once differences in basic skills, as measured by the AFQT, are taken into account.

Figure 1–7 shows three different methods of demonstrating the importance of reading and math skills (AFQT scores) in accounting for black-white differences in hourly earnings. Each panel of Figure 1–7 shows two bars. The longer bar in each panel is from estimates that exclude the AFQT score and the shorter bar is from estimates that include it.[51]

Regression coefficients estimated from the data for a given racial group reflect the "rules" in the market that determine wage rates for members of that group. We can use the rules estimated for one group to simulate what the average wage rate would be for the other group, if the second group were subject to the same treatment in the market as the first. Panels A and B of Figure 1–7 rely on this technique.

For example, "treating blacks as whites," for purposes of prediction, means taking the rules estimated on the data for whites and applying those rules to the raw data for blacks. This simulates what the average wage would be for

FIGURE 1–7 Difference in Wage (in percentage) If Treated as Black Versus If Treated as White (Males Aged 23–35, 1988–1992)

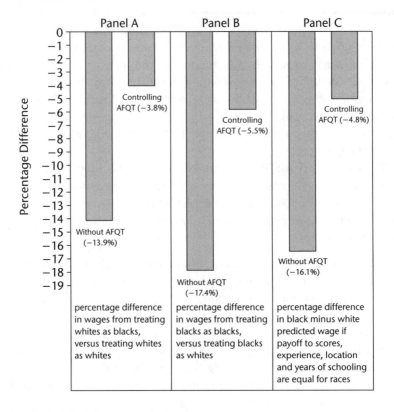

Note: Length of each bar is shown in parenthesis.

Source: National Longitudinal Survey of Youth, calculations by Ronald F. Ferguson.

blacks if the market treated them as whites. An analogous statement applies for treating whites as blacks.

Panels A and B of Figure 1–7 show that the apparent differential in the consequences of being treated as black versus being treated as white diminishes when the AFQT is included in the analysis. Without the AFQT, whites who are treated as blacks have predicted wages that are 13.9 percent lower, and blacks who are treated as blacks have wages that are almost 17.4 percent lower than if they were treated as whites.[52] Including the AFQT brings these differences down to –3.8 for whites and to –5.5 for blacks.

Panel C of Figure 1–7 uses the same estimation procedure that Bound and Freeman used. It uses equations that pool blacks and whites together and

FIGURE 1–8   **Black-White Percent Difference in Wage Rate (Males Aged 23–35, 1988–1992)**

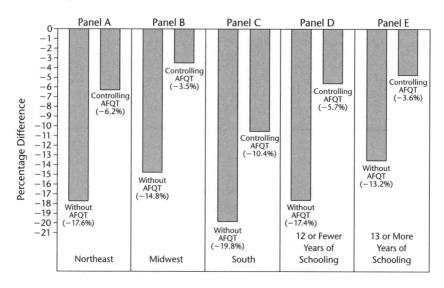

Note: The length of each bar is shown in parenthesis.

Source: National Longitudinal Survey of Youth, calculations by Ronald F. Ferguson.

includes a variable that captures the black-white difference in earnings that is otherwise not accounted for. The close similarity between Panel C and the other two panels of Figure 1–7 shows that regressions that pool the races together and use a variable to capture the unexplained racial difference, as in Panel C, produce essentially the same results as the more cumbersome procedure of estimating separate equations for the racial groups, as in Panels A and B.[53] Without including the AFQT, Panel C estimates that the unexplained gap between blacks and whites is 16.1 percent. With the AFQT, it becomes 4.8 percent.[54]

Figure 1–8 applies the method that Panel C uses in Figure 1–7, but for separate regions and education levels. Panels A, B, and C of Figure 1–8 use a separate equation for each region.[55] The AFQT score predicts roughly two-thirds of the remaining black-white wage gap in the Northeast, three-fourths of the remaining gap in the Midwest, and half of the remaining gap in the South. The South has the largest remaining gap: 10 percent after controlling for the AFQT in the analysis and 20 percent before.[56]

Panels D and E in Figure 1–8 show results separately for men with twelve or fewer years of schooling and for men with thirteen or more years. The estimated gap in earnings before the AFQT is in the analysis is –17.4 percent for men with twelve or fewer years of schooling. Introducing the AFQT reduces the gap to –5.7 percent—a reduction of two-thirds. For men with thirteen or more years of schooling, the gap of –13.2 percent before including the AFQT drops to –3.6 percent afterwards—a plunge of almost three-quarters.[57]

Figures 1–7 and 1–8 show that reading and math skills measured by the AFQT are important predictors of black-white wage differences. Figures 1–4 and 1–5 show that the greatest erosion in relative earnings after 1973 was outside the South, in the Midwest and Northeast, and for college graduates. The gaps that Figure 1–8 displays, after taking the AFQT into account, are too small to support the proposition that the erosion after the mid-1970s was mostly the result of increasing racial bias. Instead, the erosion probably results from some combination of the following: an increase in the market value of skill (e.g., the types of skills that the AFQT measures); or the deflation of an affirmative-action "bubble" that temporarily inflated wages for young blacks to be above those of whites with similar skills in the 1970s. These interpretations are not inconsistent with those in the Bound and Freeman analysis. With an average wage gap of roughly 5 percent in 1988–1992 (see Figure 1–7), an explanation of the trends in Figures 1–4 and 1–5 that rests on increased discrimination simply is not plausible.

Skills, Behaviors, Incarceration, and Work[58]

The typical African American male works fewer weeks per year than his white male counterpart (see Figure 1–6). The analysis below uses the NLSY to test several hypotheses concerning differences in employment between blacks and whites aged twenty-three to thirty-one who had thirteen or fewer years of schooling in 1986–1988. Together, these hypotheses account for virtually all of the disparity in weeks worked per year between the least skilled young black and white males in the NLSY sample. Using no explanatory variables other than location and schooling leaves an unexplained black-white difference of about three months per year, with blacks working less.[59] With a number of additional explanatory variables included, the remaining unexplained difference is on the order of one to three weeks per year for men in the least complex jobs. This difference is not statistically distinguishable from zero. The difference is larger for more complex blue-collar jobs. Before explaining this statement, the other explanatory variables in the analysis must be introduced.

Measures of both skill and behavior in this analysis help in predicting black-white differences in employment for young men with fewer than thirteen years of schooling. Clearly, these differences in skill and behavior are associated with differences in schools, family backgrounds, youth peer cultures, and other pre-labor-market institutions. The lack of equal opportunity for employment success may begin even before black youths enter the labor market, causing them to enter the market less well prepared than their white counterparts.

Skills. Skill-related measures in the analysis of weeks worked per year include not only the AFQT score, but also the NLSY interviewer's rating of the respondent's comprehension during the interview, and a complexity rating for the respondent's occupation in the year before the analysis.[60] All three— the test score, the interviewer's rating, and the occupational complexity rating—come from an earlier year. Each is a statistically significant predictor of weeks worked and helps to explain racial disparity in employment for young males. Black-white differences in the AFQT score predict roughly three weeks less employment per year for blacks, and the interviewer's rating predicts an additional one week less, for a total of one month from these two sources.

Behaviors. Research in sociology and anthropology shows that socialization processes differ within and across communities. Even in the poorest urban neighborhoods many children receive the nurturance and protection that they need to mature and prosper. However, many schools, families, and community institutions lack the social and material resources to cope successfully with all of the youth development challenges that they face. Negative influences that tend to distract youths from wholesome development and from investing in their own futures can overwhelm the defenses that parents and their allies are able to muster. Mischief and crime are often the consequences.

Results from my research with the NLSY show that two indices related to crime are instrumental in predicting the number of weeks worked. The first measures whether the respondent was ever incarcerated in the years prior to the analysis. The second is an "incarceration-likelihood index" that uses prior behaviors and other background factors to estimate the likelihood that the respondent has ever been incarcerated. This pair of variables is important in explaining black-white differences in employment. Young black males are more likely than young white males to experience incarceration. Moreover, actual prior incarceration has twice the negative effect on weeks worked for blacks as for whites.

Prior incarceration for a young white male predicts that, other things being equal, he will work an average of two months less per year than a young white male who has no history of incarceration. For young black males, the average difference between those with and without prior incarceration is four months per year. This measured effect of actual prior incarceration on weeks worked probably reflects both labor supply behavior (including reincarceration) and, on the demand side, employment discrimination that penalizes blacks who have criminal records more than it penalizes similar whites. Even for men with a history of incarceration who were *not* reincarcerated during the 1986–1988 study period, the effect of prior incarceration is more than twice as negative for blacks as for whites: roughly one month per year less work for whites and more than two months per year for blacks.

The strongest predictors of incarceration are locational and behavioral. Behaviors that help in predicting incarceration are: expulsion from school, unwed fatherhood, age of first intercourse (younger is worse), income from crime during adolescence, drug use, and dropping out before completing high school. Race, test scores, attitudes, family background, and local unemployment rates help in predicting these behaviors, but they do not help in predicting incarceration once the listed behaviors are controlled. Aside from indices associated with individuals, the incarceration rate in the geographic area where a young man lives is an important predictor of incarceration, explaining 30 percent of the black-white difference in incarceration rates. This signals the importance of local differences in law enforcement practices, youth cultures, and other features of local environments.

Among the indices of adolescent behavior that predict incarceration, only income from crime shows a statistically significant relationship to local unemployment (for the year during adolescence when the income from crime was earned). However, self-reported income from crime during adolescence does not differ much by race. In contrast, for example, the average age of first intercourse is more than one year earlier for blacks, bears no relationship to the state of the local economy, and is an important predictor of later incarceration.[61] The same is true for unwed fatherhood. These empirical results suggest that both economic and noneconomic forces predict differences in behavior that lead to mediocre labor market outcomes. Black-white differences in actual and predicted incarceration in this analysis account for an average difference between *all* blacks and whites in the sample (not simply those who have been incarcerated) of roughly one month per year in time employed.

Together with the one month which is estimated to be due to skill differences, this adds to a total difference in time employed of two months per year between black and white males aged twenty-three to thirty-one with thirteen or fewer years of schooling.

Quit Rates. Among the unanticipated findings from this work is that the black-white difference in job-resignation rates for noncollege-educated males in their twenties increases with occupational complexity—the quit rate for blacks rises with occupational complexity while that for whites falls.[62] In a multivariate statistical analysis that includes a number of controls, the difference between blacks and whites in the effect on employment of raising occupational complexity (as measured in the job held in 1985) predicts an average difference in employment of between four and five weeks per year for young blacks and whites during the period from 1986 to 1988. Again, this pattern is measured with years of schooling, test scores, and other background variables being held constant.

Table 1–2 shows the pattern in the raw data. It divides the jobs that men with thirteen or fewer years of schooling occupy into two categories—"low skill" and "high skill." This splits the sample rather evenly. The table covers three years, from 1986 to 1988. The NLSY interviewed respondents three times during this period, and the table tabulates the reason each respondent gave for leaving the last job. The answer comes from the first of the three interviews at which time the respondent reported that he was not currently employed. The bottom line of the table shows the percentages of blacks and whites who had jobs at all three interview dates, and who therefore never gave a reason for leaving a job. The percentage of blacks employed at all three dates is virtually the same for the "high skill" occupations (63.87 percent) as for the "low skill" occupations (62.66 percent). For whites, the percentage employed at all three dates rises from 75.08 percent in the "low skill" category to 85.60 percent in the "high skill" jobs.

The fact that increasing job complexity has different effects on employment longevity for blacks and whites reinforces the general proposition that skill differences are central in explaining racial differences in employment for young males, but, especially here, the mechanisms are not transparent.

As previously stated, after taking account of explanatory variables, the remaining unexplained difference in weeks worked for the least skilled blacks and whites is roughly one to three weeks. This difference applies to men in the least skilled jobs. For a job of average complexity, we need to add the four to five weeks per year (higher unemployment for blacks than whites) associated with the occupational complexity of the average job that blacks without college educations occupy. Whether one counts the four to five weeks asso-

TABLE 1–2   Reason for Leaving Most Recent Job (Males Aged 23–31 with Fewer than Thirteen Years of Schooling, 1986–1988)

| | "Low Skill" Occupations | | | "High Skill" Occupations | | |
	Black	White	Black-White Difference	Black	White	Black-White Difference
Column:	1	2	3	4	5	6
Percent Laid Off	10.95	10.91	0.04	6.32	5.12	1.20
Percent Job Ended	3.38	3.20	0.18	6.54	1.46	5.08
Percent Quit	14.01	7.13	6.88	19.05	5.15	13.90
Percent Fired	6.81	2.37	4.44	3.04	1.69	1.35
Percent Other	2.19	1.31	0.88	1.18	0.98	0.20
Percent Employed at All Three Survey Dates	62.66	75.08	12.42	63.87	85.60	21.73

Source: National Longitudinal Survey of Youth, compiled by Ronald F. Ferguson.

ciated with occupational complexity as "explained," because it is associated with a particular meaningful variable (occupational complexity), or "unexplained," because we do not understand why the black-white difference in this relationship exists, depends upon one's purpose.

Certainly, this effect is "unexplained" if one's purpose is to shape an intervention. A speculative explanation is that blacks and whites in the workplace are sometimes caught in a cycle of negative and self-fulfilling expectations: blacks expect that whites will expect less of them and will be less supportive to them than to whites; whites expect that blacks will have chips on their shoulders and will be less cooperative; each lives down to the other's expectations and the expectations are confirmed. If blacks respond by quitting, as Table 1–2 suggests that they often may, then they accumulate less experience and, over time, the deficit in their experience may further harm their employment prospects and performance. Human relations across racial lines in the workplace, especially in blue-collar workplaces, present issues that deserve much more attention than they currently receive. Current ethnographic work by other researchers may help to explain the workplace dynamics associated with these interesting and important patterns.[63]

SUMMARY

World War II created new employment opportunities for African Americans. It brought growth in earnings that did not disappear when the war ended. While the causes shifted, the positive momentum of progress continued from the 1940s through the 1960s as younger blacks lead a mass migration away from the rural South. Some settled in Southern cities. Others migrated further to the cities of the North where, until the mid-1970s, economic opportunities were far superior.

Thanks to the Civil Rights movement, economic progress for blacks accelerated in the South after the mid-1960s. For the first time, more blacks returned to the South than left it during the 1970s. In addition to its many other achievements, the Civil Rights movement was a major force behind decisions by the Congress and the President of the United States to enact Title VII of the Civil Rights Act of 1964 and Executive Order 11246. Both of these measures apparently helped to sustain income growth for blacks relative to whites well into the mid-1970s. These Civil Rights measures helped to insure, for example, that blacks would receive the growth in earnings that they deserved, commensurate with the gains that they were achieving in academic attainment. Blacks improved relative to whites in educational attainment and in various measures of school quality through the entire period after 1940. Researchers agree that this probably accounts for between one-quarter and one-half of the progress that blacks achieved in closing the gap in earnings, even without explicitly accounting for Civil Rights pressures.

After the mid-1970s, progress toward closing the gap in earnings stopped. In fact, for younger blacks, the trend reversed. Disparity grew.

A number of economic shifts, including racially disparate shifts in industry and occupational employment patterns, contributed to growth in racial disparity among young workers after 1975. Several may have common roots in the growing value of skill and in reduced federal pressure for affirmative action. Changing technology, the falling minimum wage, declining unionism, and increased immigration help to account for why the value of skill has grown both within and across racial groups.

The National Assessment of Educational Progress shows that basic skills for black high school students have been rising relative to those for whites since at least the early 1970s. The increase from –6 percent (in 1975) to –16 percent (in 1989) in the disparity in wage rates between young blacks and whites (measured without controlling for test scores) occurred not because blacks' skills have deteriorated. Instead, either the value of skill rose faster after 1975 than the black-white gap in skill closed—thus inflating the financial significance of remaining skill differences—or blacks in 1975 were earning more than whites who had similar qualifications, and the apparent erosion of earnings after 1975 was simply bringing them back in line. Both explanations may have some merit.

Based on the evidence, these explanations for what happened after 1975 seem more plausible than one that relies on an increase in discrimination. If an increase in discrimination were the major explanation for the increase in black-white earnings disparity, then one should expect an unexplained gap in earnings that is larger than 4.8 percent for 1988–1992. (Recall that 4.8 percent is the black-white gap in earnings that this essay estimates for 1988–1992 after accounting for differences in basic skills; before accounting for basic skills, the gap is 16.1 percent.)

Therefore, while this essay notes the continuing importance of discrimination and endorses the vigorous enforcement of Civil Rights laws, there are other explanations for the increase in disparity after 1975. Similarly, black-white differences in employment levels for men with thirteen or fewer years of schooling reflect various skill and behavioral differences, including a greater propensity to resign from occupations that require more skill. The latter pattern may be a response to racial bias in the social relations of work for more complex occupations. It warrants further investigation.

CONCLUSION

The most important disparities in opportunity may occur before young people even enter the labor market: in the provision of schooling and other resources that influence skill-building and the socialization of youths. These include not only current disparities in the quality of schooling and recreation and discouraging messages from society at large, but also racial inequities in past generations of institutions that prepared parents and grandparents for their roles as teachers and care givers. Certainly, efforts to fight unfair racial bias in hiring and promotion must continue. However, interventions to strengthen schools, families, and other institutions that prepare children for adulthood must be the highest priority in responding to the economic disparities that remain among young adults in the 1990s.

These are different times from the 1940s, 1950s, and 1960s. The task now is to utilize more effectively the legal and institutional resources that the Civil Rights and Black Power movements helped to put in place. The dream that inspired these movements was that African Americans might lead more healthy, happy, and productive lives, free from the hardships and degradations of social and economic subordination. The dream has not fully come true. Indeed, America may never cast off completely the ideology of white supremacy. Similarly, social class interests that align with wealth and privilege will remain challenges to many visions of social fairness and equity. Nevertheless, the evidence that this essay reviews demonstrates that progress for Black Americans over the past fifty years has been remarkable. In the face of resistance, discipline, courage, and perseverance have paid dividends. The same will be true in the future. Just as our African American parents and grandparents taught this lesson to us, so we must teach it to our children and insist that they put it to practice.

On the last page of *An American Dilemma,* Myrdal writes:

> The rationalism and moralism which is the driving force behind social study, whether we admit it or not, is the faith that institutions can be improved and strengthened and that people are good enough to live a happier life. . . . To find the practical formulas for this never-ending reconstruction of society is the supreme task of social science. The world catastrophe places tremendous difficulties in our way and may shake our confidence to the depths. Yet we have today in social science a greater trust in the improvability of man and society than we have ever had since the Enlightenment.[64]

This paper was written for the Morehouse Research Institute's Fiftieth Year Commemoration of the publication of Gunnar Myrdal's *An American Dilemma*. The author gratefully acknowledges support from the Rockefeller Foundation for some of the research upon which this paper reports and from the Russell Sage Foundation for sponsorship of the Morehouse conference.

Afterword to Chapter 1

In this chapter I focus to a substantial degree on rising wage disparity between young black and white males from the middle 1970s through the end of the 1980s. The most likely reason disparity grew is that the importance employers put on basic reading and math skills was rising more rapidly than the black-white gap in skills was closing. Indeed, the period from the mid-1970s through the end of the 1980s was a period of growing disparity not only between racial groups, but also between people of different income levels. The real purchasing power of hourly wages fell for young men with high school educations or less, and rose for workers who were college graduates.

The leading hypothesis for the increase in wage inequality from the mid-1970s through the end of the 1980s continues to be "skill-biased technological change." Specifically, rising skill requirements associated with technological changes caused employers to value workers with basic reading and math skills relatively more by the end of the 1980s than they had during the middle 1970s.

Since this chapter was written, the nature of growing inequality in the economy has changed. From the mid-1970s through the end of the 1980s, workers at the 10th percentile in the wage distribution fell further behind those at the 50th percentile, and workers at the 50th percentile fell further behind those at the 90th percentile. In contrast, from the early 1990s until recently (i.e., 2004), real wages have grown slightly more at the 10th percentile of the wage distribution than at the 50th. The story about inequality since the early 1990s is that workers at the top end of the distribution have seen their wages rise much more rapidly than people near the middle or the bottom.

The leading hypothesis is that demand for workers in the middle of the wage distribution has fallen in relative terms because more of their work has been automated using computer technology.[1] There are many relatively low-wage manual-labor jobs, such as making beds in hotels and waiting tables in restaurants, that computer-assisted machines cannot do. However, there are other jobs that used to be in the middle of the wage distribution, jobs like sorting checks in banks, which computer-assisted machines can do very well. It is these jobs that seem to have disappeared more recently.

The implication of these developments for black-white wage inequality has been that wage inequality between black and white young adults has slightly decreased since 1990.[2] Still, wage gaps remain, and skill gaps are contributing factors. Further, there remain major employment and incarceration rate differences by race and education level.[3] These latter gaps are also due, at least in part, to the education and skill disparities upon which this book is focused.

CHAPTER 2

Test-Score Trends along Racial Lines, 1971 to 1996

Popular Culture and Community Academic Standards

> Between me and the other world, there is ever an unasked question: unasked by some through feelings of delicacy; by others through the difficulty of rightly framing it. All, nevertheless, flutter round it. They approach me in a half-hesitant sort of way, eye me curiously or compassionately, and then, instead of saying directly, How does it feel to be a problem? they say, I know an excellent colored man in my town; or, I fought at Mechanicsville; or, Do not the Southern outrages make your blood boil? At these, I smile. . . . To the real question, How does it feel to be a problem? I answer seldom a word.

So ends the first paragraph of W. E. B. Du Bois's classic masterpiece, *The Souls of Black Folk* (1903:3). Today, more than 90 years later, black folk are still considered by some to be a problem. People approach furtively, with the same unasked question. A major reason is that blacks, Hispanics, American Indians, and some sub-groups among Asians have lower test scores than whites. This complicates efforts to achieve racial and ethnic balance in selective institutions. If test scores were equal, on average, among the races, there would be little need for current debates about affirmative action in college admissions. There would be no need for race norming on entry examinations for professions such as police and firefighters. Certification testing for new teachers would not so dramatically affect the racial composition of the nation's teacher work-force. The hourly earnings gap among racial groups would be only a fraction of what it is currently. Whether we like it or not, test scores, and the skills they measure, matter.

YES !

In an act of substantial wisdom, the U.S. Congress in the late 1960s directed the U.S. Department of Education to create a nationally representative data series with which to make academic proficiency comparisons across age, gender, race/ethnicity, and time. The result was the National Assessment of Educational Progress (NAEP), administered by the Educational Testing Service (ETS) under contract with the National Center for Education Statistics (NCES). Before NAEP, no nationally representative data existed for making test-score comparisons across time for school-aged children. Relying heavily on data from NAEP, this chapter summarizes and offers tentative explanations for trends in reading and math scores among black, Hispanic, and white children from the early 1970s through 1996. Neither American Indians and Alaska Natives nor Asians and Pacific Islanders was separately identified in NAEP during the period examined here and, therefore, neither of these groups is addressed.

Black-white and Hispanic-white achievement test-score gaps of 30 years ago were neither genetically preordained nor otherwise immutable. The headline is that progress has occurred. Average scores for all groups are higher. Racial disparity is lower. NAEP data show that the black-white reading-score gap for 17-year-olds narrowed 45 percent since 1971. The Hispanic-white gap narrowed 27 percent since 1975—the first year Hispanics were distinguished separately. The mean gap in math scores has fallen by 33 percent for blacks and 35 percent for Hispanics, compared with whites. These and other numbers show that black and Hispanic children have made important progress since the early 1970s, both absolutely and relative to whites.[1] For blacks especially, however, progress has been variable—at times rapid, but at other times halted or even reversed. The reasons for this variability are not clear. Changes in such areas as parenting, curriculum, teacher skill, and class size occur unevenly over time and might well be part of the story. Popular culture might be important as well.

The chapter begins with a review of test-score trends for blacks, Hispanics, and whites. The middle of the chapter tries to explain the pattern of stops and starts in progress for teenagers, especially black teenagers. The last third of the chapter reviews some ideas and evidence about how communities of students' peers, parents, and teachers affect education incentives and standards differently for Black youth.

WHAT ARE THE TRENDS?

To determine trends, the content of the NAEP trend assessments has remained virtually constant since they began for reading in 1971 and for math in 1973.

The other type of NAEP exam, called the "main assessment," changes to reflect current ideas and priorities. Each trend assessment was repeated every four years through 1990; then the schedule shifted to every two years, with smaller samples. NAEP scores range from 0 to 500. Scores for 9-, 13-, and 17-year-olds are all expressed on the same scale. Tables 2–1 and 2–2 show scores for reading and math. Both tables cover mean scores for blacks, Hispanics, and whites through 1996. In any given year, the standard deviation (SD) of scores within an age group is about 30 points for math and 40 points for reading. The standard errors (SE) of the mean scores are shown in parentheses on the tables.

Trends for Nine-Year-Olds

Reading scores for nine-year-olds rose mostly during the 1970s, but the increase in math scores occurred mostly in the mid-to-late 1980s. It seems almost certain that effective curricular and instructional changes focused more on reading in the 1970s and more on math in the 1980s. In support of this proposition—that instruction in different subjects was improved at different times—is the fact that reading scores declined slightly for black and Hispanic nine-year-olds in the late 1980s at the same time that math scores improved the most.

O'Day and Smith (1993) conjecture that the increased emphasis on basic skills between the late 1960s and the early 1980s contributed importantly to improvement in reading scores for all students, but especially for racial-minority students. Measures to strengthen math instruction helped all three groups of nine-year-olds to achieve roughly equal progress in the late 1980s.

Changes in disparity do not follow the same general timing as changes in overall performance. All of the catching up with whites that black nine-year-olds achieved was done by 1986 for math and 1988 for reading (Table 2–2). After that, blacks lost a little ground but regained it by 1996. For reading, Hispanic-white disparity follows a pattern similar to the black-white disparity, but there is a strangely unstable pattern for math. It seems likely that the composition of the Hispanic student sample was changing in ways that, for the broad group, make these comparisons over time less dependable. For blacks, however, it is noteworthy that reductions in black-white disparity follow a similar time pattern for both reading and math. This suggests that the factors helping blacks narrow the gap on one subject, also helped in the other.

I have shown elsewhere (Ferguson, 1998b) that black-white disparity in reading and math scores for nine-year-olds follows the same nonlinear trajec-

TABLE 2–1   NAEP Scores for Black, Hispanic, and White 9-, 13-, and 17-Year-Olds

A. Reading Scores, 1971 through 1996

	Age	1971	1975	1980	1984	1988	1990	1992	1994	1996
Black	17	238.7 (1.7)	240.6 (2.0)	243.1 (1.8)	264.3 (1.0)	274.4 (2.4)	267.3 (2.3)	260.6 (2.1)	266.2 (3.9)	265.4 (2.7)
	13	224.4 (1.2)	225.7 (1.3)	232.8 (1.5)	236.3 (1.2)	242.9 (2.4)	241.5 (2.2)	237.6 (2.3)	234.3 (2.4)	235.6 (2.6)
	9	170.1 (1.7)	181.2 (1.2)	189.3 (1.8)	185.7 (1.4)	188.5 (2.4)	181.8 (2.9)	184.5 (2.2)	185.4 (2.3)	190.0 (2.7)
Hispanic	17	n.a.	252.4 (3.6)	261.4 (2.7)	268.1 (4.3)	270.8 (4.3)	274.8 (3.6)	271.2 (3.7)	263.2 (4.9)	264.7 (4.1)
	13	n.a.	232.5 (3.0)	237.2 (2.0)	239.6 (2.0)	240.1 (3.5)	237.8 (2.3)	239.2 (3.5)	235.1 (1.9)	239.9 (2.9)
	9	n.a.	182.7 (2.2)	190.2 (2.3)	187.1 (3.1)	193.7 (3.5)	189.4 (2.3)	191.7 (3.1)	185.9 (3.9)	194.1 (3.5)
White	17	291.4 (1.0)	293.0 (0.6)	292.8 (0.9)	295.2 (0.7)	294.7 (1.2)	296.6 (1.2)	297.4 (1.4)	295.7 (1.5)	294.4 (1.2)
	13	260.9 (0.7)	262.1 (0.7)	264.4 (0.7)	262.5 (0.6)	261.3 (1.1)	262.3 (0.9)	266.4 (1.2)	265.1 (1.1)	267.0 (1.0)
	9	214.0 (0.9)	216.6 (0.7)	221.3 (0.8)	218.2 (0.9)	217.7 (1.4)	217.0 (1.3)	217.9 (1.0)	218.0 (1.3)	219.9 (1.2)

B. Math Scores, 1973 through 1996

	Age	1973	1978	1982	1986	1990	1992	1994	1996
Black	17	270.0 (1.3)	268.4 (1.3)	271.8 (1.2)	278.6 (2.1)	288.5 (2.8)	285.8 (2.2)	285.5 (1.8)	286.4 (1.7)
	13	228.0 (1.9)	229.6 (1.9)	240.4 (1.6)	249.2 (2.3)	249.1 (2.3)	250.2 (1.9)	251.5 (3.5)	252.1 (1.3)
	9	190.0 (1.8)	192.4 (1.1)	194.9 (1.6)	201.6 (1.6)	208.4 (2.2)	208.0 (2.0)	212.1 (1.6)	211.6 (1.4)
Hispanic	17	277.0 (2.2)	276.3 (2.3)	276.7 (1.8)	283.1 (2.9)	283.5 (2.9)	292.2 (2.6)	290.8 (3.7)	292.0 (2.1)
	13	239.0 (2.2)	238.0 (2.0)	252.4 (1.7)	254.3 (2.9)	254.6 (1.8)	259.3 (1.8)	256.0 (1.9)	255.7 (1.6)
	9	202.0 (2.4)	202.9 (2.2)	204.0 (1.3)	205.4 (2.1)	213.8 (2.1)	211.9 (2.3)	209.9 (2.3)	214.7 (1.7)
White	17	310.0 (1.1)	305.9 (0.9)	303.7 (0.9)	307.5 (1.0)	309.5 (1.0)	311.9 (0.8)	312.3 (1.1)	313.4 (1.4)
	13	274.0 (0.9)	271.6 (0.8)	272.4 (1.0)	273.6 (1.3)	276.3 (1.1)	278.9 (0.9)	280.8 (0.9)	281.2 (0.9)
	9	225.0 (1.0)	224.1 (0.9)	224.0 (1.1)	226.9 (1.1)	235.2 (0.8)	235.1 (0.8)	236.8 (1.0)	236.9 (1.0)

Note: Standard errors (SE) of mean scores are shown in parentheses. Source: National Assessment of Educational Progress (1996).

tory as national reductions in pupil-to-teacher ratios for elementary schools. Not only do inflection points match closely when class-size and black-white disparity are graphed, but multiple regression lines fit well even after including a separate control for a linear trend (see Ferguson, 1998b, Figure 9–4). One might expect this association between test-score disparity and class size if (1) reducing class size helps black students more than white students or (2) class sizes fell more in schools where blacks attend. It appears that both are true for the period since 1970.

First, the proposition that smaller classes help students learn was tested in the Tennessee Star Experiment conducted in the 1980s, the largest random-assignment study ever done to test that theory. Roughly 6,500 students in 80 schools were assigned randomly to either small (13 to 17 students) or large (22 to 25 students) classes. Estimated benefits of small classes were larger for black than for white students and larger in inner-city schools. Second, elementary pupil-to-teacher ratios fell nationally by roughly 25 percent between 1970 and 1990 (National Center for Education Statistics, 1996b). Moreover, class sizes appear to have been reduced more for blacks than for whites. When Coleman (1966) conducted the classic study *Equality of Educational Opportunity,* class sizes were still somewhat larger for blacks than for Whites. By 1990, national data show no overall differences in pupil-to-teacher ratios by race (black/white) or by socioeconomic status, as measured by the percentage of students eligible for free-and-reduced lunch subsidies.[2] Certainly, more than class size was changing over this period in the schooling of nine-year-olds. Civil rights gains and positive changes in family educational background might be important as well (Grissmer et al., 1998). Nonetheless, it appears quite likely that class-size reductions that affected blacks (and perhaps Hispanics) more than whites are part of the explanation for reductions in black-white test-score disparity from 1970 through the late 1980s.

Despite this evidence, there is an active debate among researchers about whether class size matters at all. My reading of the evidence (Ferguson, 1998b) is that it does, at least for elementary schools. However, Hanushek (1998), Krueger (1997), and Greenwald et al. (1996) argue on various sides of the debate.

Trends in Learning after Age Nine

The fact that black and Hispanic children reach the age of nine with fewer math and reading skills on average than whites is mostly because black and Hispanic children begin school with fewer skills. Once enrolled in school there is the chance that black and Hispanic children could learn more than

TABLE 2–2   NAEP Score Gaps and Percentage of Gap Remaining

A. Gaps in Reading Scores

	White-Black Gap			White-Hispanic Gap		
	17-year-olds	13-year-olds	9-year-olds	17-year-olds	13-year-olds	9-year-olds
1971	52.7	36.5	43.9	n.a.	n.a.	n.a.
1975	52.4	36.4	35.4	40.6	29.6	33.9
1980	49.7	31.6	32.0	31.4	27.2	31.1
1984	30.9	26.2	32.5	27.1	22.9	31.1
1988	20.3	18.4	29.2	23.9	21.2	24.0
1990	29.3	20.8	35.2	21.8	24.5	27.6
1992	36.8	28.8	33.4	26.2	27.2	26.2
1994	29.5	30.8	32.6	32.5	30.0	32.1
1996	29.0	31.4	29.9	29.7	27.1	25.8

	Percentage of the 1971 Gap Remaining			Percentage of the 1975 Gap Remaining		
1971	100.0	100.0	100.0	n.a.	n.a.	n.a.
1975	99.4	99.7	80.6	100.0	100.0	100.0
1980	94.3	86.6	72.9	77.3	91.9	91.7
1984	58.6	71.8	74.0	66.7	77.4	91.7
1988	38.5	50.4	66.5	58.9	71.6	70.8
1990	55.6	57.0	80.2	53.7	82.8	81.4
1992	69.8	78.9	76.1	64.5	91.9	77.3
1994	56.0	84.4	74.3	80.0	101.4	94.7
1996	55.0	86.0	68.1	73.2	91.6	76.1

B. Gaps in Math Scores

	White-Black Gap			White-Hispanic Gap		
	17-year-olds	13-year-olds	9-year-olds	17-year-olds	13-year-olds	9-year-olds
1973	40.0	46.0	35.0	33.0	35.0	23.0
1978	37.5	42.0	31.7	29.6	33.6	21.2
1982	31.9	32.0	29.1	27.0	20.0	20.0
1986	28.9	24.4	25.3	24.4	19.3	21.5
1990	21.0	27.2	26.8	26.0	21.7	21.4
1992	26.1	28.7	27.1	19.7	19.6	23.2
1994	26.8	29.3	24.7	21.5	24.8	26.9
1996	27.0	29.1	25.3	21.4	25.5	22.2

TABLE 2–2   NAEP Score Gaps and Percentage of Gap Remaining *(continued)*

	Percentage of the 1973 Gap Remaining			*Percentage of the 1973 Gap Remaining*		
1973	100.0	100.0	100.0	100.0	100.0	100.0
1978	93.8	91.3	90.6	89.7	96.0	92.2
1982	79.7	69.6	83.1	81.8	57.1	87.0
1986	72.2	53.0	72.3	73.9	55.1	93.5
1990	52.5	59.1	76.6	78.8	62.0	93.0
1992	65.2	62.4	77.4	59.7	56.0	100.9
1994	67.0	63.7	70.6	65.2	70.9	117.0
1996	67.5	63.3	72.3	64.8	72.9	96.5

Source: National Assessment of Educational Progress (1996).

whites but still have lower levels of skill because they start so far behind. We know that, on average, black and Hispanic four- and five-year-olds score lower on tests of school readiness than whites and lower on exams in early school years (Phillips et al., 1998a, 1998b). Phillips et al. (1998b) use a congressionally mandated, nationally representative, longitudinal data set called Prospects. Data collection began in 1991 for three birth cohorts—one in the first grade, one in the third grade, and one in the seventh grade. Phillips et al. conclude from their analysis of the Prospects data that blacks appear to have learned less than whites during the 1990s. Indeed, data from NAEP suggest the same; however, NAEP data for the 1970s and 1980s tell a different story. For the 1970s and 1980s, both black and Hispanic gains appear much of the time to be greater than those for whites. Hence, the answer to whether blacks or Hispanics learn more or less than whites during the school years may differ across time.

ETS selects a new NAEP sample each year, so children tested at one age from a particular birth cohort are not the same as those tested from the same birth cohort four years later. Nonetheless, data showing differences between 9- (or 13-) year-olds' scores one year and 13- (or 17-) year-olds' scores four years later provide the best nationally representative approximations available for measuring learning gains from ages 9 to 13 and 13 to 17, and measuring changes over time (see Figure 2–1).

Of course, using NAEP in this way only makes sense if we assume that children tested at, for example, age 13, had roughly the same distribution of scores at age 9 as the members of their cohort that NAEP actually tested at age 9. This seems likely, since NAEP samples are constructed to be nationally representative. Still, using NAEP for this type of approximation is necessarily imperfect for three reasons: (1) the 17-year-old sample does not cover dropouts; (2) the 13- and 17-year-old samples include recent immigrants who, of course, were not tested four years earlier; and (3) NAEP does not test children labeled as having learning disorders. The first two of these three reasons are probably greater problems for data for Hispanic students than for blacks or whites because the Hispanic dropout rate is higher, as is the Hispanic immigration rate. (The interval properties I assume below for comparing test score gains are probably only appropriate for comparing intervals where the average scores are very similar. I do not assume, for example, that a gain of say 20 points, from 170 to 190 for 9-year-olds, represents the same amount of learning or degree of difficulty as a 20-point gain, from say 250 to 270, for 17-year-olds. No such comparisons across disparate ranges are necessary for the way that I use the scores.)

Tables 2–1 and 2–2, along with Figure 2–1, represent a fairly complete summary of trends for reading and math scores over the past few decades. There is too much here to discuss it all in detail. However, there is one pattern that deserves special attention. Specifically, the test-score pattern for black students who were age 9 in 1984 is a fascinating anomaly. As 13-year-olds in 1988, this cohort had scores that were closer to white children's than for any other cohort of 13-year-old blacks. Indeed, the difference between black and white 13-year-olds in 1988 was less than half the difference that existed for the same age group in 1971. After 1988, however, by the time that they were 17 years old, the gap between blacks and whites in the cohort more than doubled. This represents a marked deceleration in academic progress both absolutely and relative to whites and Hispanics. It is typical in statistical time series for rapid advancements to be followed by "corrective" periods of slower growth (i.e., regression to the mean). I cannot rule out that this accounts for some of the pattern; however, I suspect something more fundamental was happening.

To investigate further, I examined unpublished NAEP data that give breakouts by region, type of community, type of school, and parents' education. For this cohort of black children, the pattern of rapid progress from ages 9 to 13, followed by very slow progress from ages 13 to 17, shows up for all four census regions, all four types of communities, public and nonpublic schools, and all three levels of parents' education! The fact that it shows up for both public and nonpublic schools suggests that the explanation is not some fundamental change in public school policies or practices. Further, this period shows the biggest ever gain for whites from ages 13 to 17, which also suggests

FIGURE 2–1   Standardized NAEP (A) Reading and (B) Math Scores for Black 9-, 13-, and 17-Year-Olds (Metric = S.D.'s below 17-year-old whites' 1996 mean). Labels on lines give the year that the tests were taken.

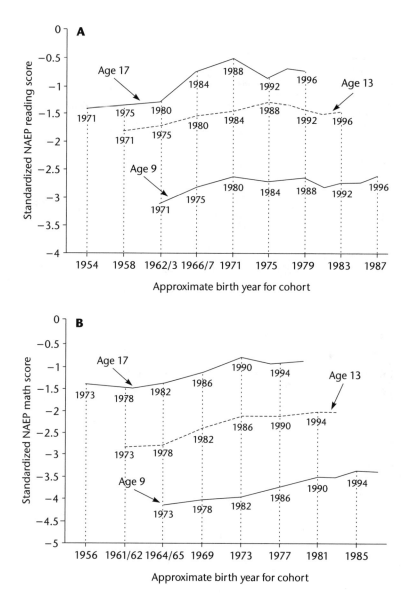

FIGURE 2–1   Standardized NAEP (C) Reading and (D) Math Scores for Hispanic 9-, 13-, and 17-Year-Olds (Metric = S.D.'s below 17-year-old whites' 1996 mean). Labels on lines give the year that the tests were taken. *(continued)*

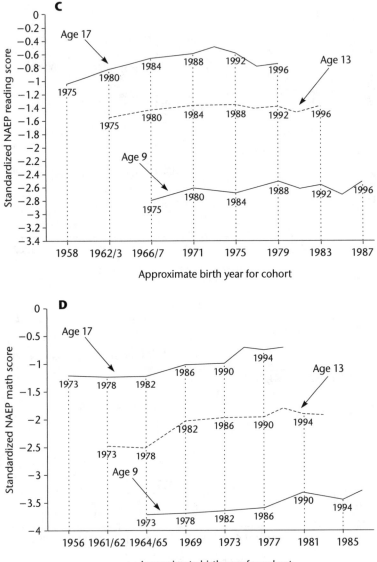

FIGURE 2–1   Standardized NAEP (E) Reading and (F) Math Scores for White 9-, 13-, and 17-Year-Olds (Metric = S.D.'s below 17-year-old whites' 1996 mean). Labels on lines give the year that the tests were taken. *(continued)*

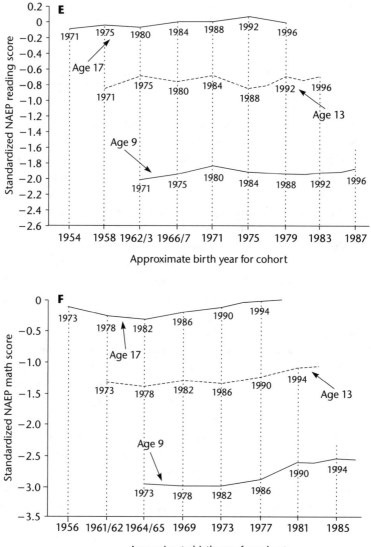

that something other than school policy is at work. Again, there is a possibility that the pattern is an artifact of the way the data were collected and processed. This possibility deserves investigation. For the time being, however, it seems reasonable to assume that the pattern is not an artifact.

This pattern of poor performance in high school is not unprecedented. The paltry 0.44 SD (16.2 points) that the 1975 birth cohort of black youth gained as 13- and 17-year-olds, in 1988 and 1992, is essentially the same as the 0.45 SD (17.7 points) that another cohort achieved in 1971 and 1975. In addition, it is highly suggestive to compare 13-year-olds in 1975 with 17-year-olds in 1980. The mean score for black 13-year-olds in 1975 is only 0.44 SD below the mean for 17-year-olds in 1980. Hence, it appears that black teenagers were not developing their reading skills in the 1970s. For 13- to 17-year-olds, both blacks and whites (NAEP did not distinguish Hispanics in 1971), similarities between 1971–1975 and 1988–1992 are striking. In both periods, the score at the 5th percentile for black 17-year-olds was actually lower than the score at the 5th percentile for 13-year-olds in the same cohort four years earlier (Table 2–3). With this negative change in scores, it is not surprising that disparity in scores—even among blacks—became much greater by age 17 than it was at age 13. However, gains near the top of the distribution were comparatively low as well: growth in scores in the top 10 percent of these cohorts that were 13 in 1971 and 1988 was only two-thirds as great as for the cohort that was 13 in 1984. The latter cohort appears to have been more academically engaged after age 13. The 13-year-old cohort of blacks in 1988 scored higher at every point in the distribution than blacks who were 13 in 1984; yet, by age 17, the rank ordering of the two cohorts had reversed, with the younger cohort doing worse at every point in the distribution. This is not true for whites. The younger cohort of 17-year-old whites outscored its older siblings at every point in the distribution except the very bottom.

Progress over the next few decades similar to the rates that 17-year-olds attained from 1980 to 1988 could produce a dramatic narrowing of black-white gaps in reading and math, and Hispanic-white gaps in reading. On the other hand, if the lack of relative progress achieved after 1988 continues, disparities will remain or widen. Whether one chooses to be hopeful or pessimistic depends on what one believes about the underlying causes for the leveling off that occurred after the late 1980s. [See the Appendix for a discussion of Scholastic Aptitude Test (SAT) score trends. Similar to NAEP, for both reading and math, racial gaps narrowed rapidly during the 1980s, but this stopped by 1990.]

TABLE 2–3 Percentiles of NAEP Reading Scores for 13- and 17-Year-Olds by Race, for Four Cohorts

	Whites			Blacks			
	Score Age 13	Score Age 17	Diff. Col. 2 Minus 1	Score Age 13	Score Age 17	Diff. Col. 5 Minus 4	Diff. Col. 3 Minus 6
Column	1	2	3	4	5	6	7
	1984 Cohort						
Year Percentile	1988	1992	1992– 1988	1988	1992	1992– 1988	
5	204.0	228.1	24.1	190.6	187.9	–2.7	26.8
10	217.1	244.9	27.8	202.2	206.2	4.0	23.8
25	238.3	272.3	34.0	222.0	235.1	13.1	20.9
50	262.2	300.1	37.9	242.4	262.5	20.1	17.8
75	285.1	324.5	39.4	263.6	288.3	24.7	14.7
90	304.2	346.6	42.4	283.6	312.0	28.4	14.0
95	315.8	359.0	43.2	298.9	327.0	28.1	15.1
95th minus 5th	111.8	130.9	19.1	108.3	139.1	30.8	–11.7
90th minus 10th	87.1	101.7	14.6	81.4	105.8	24.4	–9.8
	1980 Cohort						
Year Percentile	1984	1988	1988– 1984	1984	1988	1988– 1984	
5	204.9	232.6	27.7	180.1	214.4	34.3	–6.6
10	218.3	247.3	29.0	192.4	227.8	35.4	–6.4
25	240.6	271.4	30.8	213.3	250.5	37.2	–6.4
50	263.4	295.4	32.0	236.4	274.3	37.9	–5.9
75	285.6	319.9	34.3	259.3	299.6	40.3	–6.0
90	305.0	339.7	34.7	280.3	321.0	40.7	–6.0
95	316.8	351.6	34.8	292.7	333.1	40.4	–5.6
95th minus 5th	111.9	119.0	7.1	112.6	118.7	6.1	1.0
90th minus 10th	86.7	92.4	5.7	87.9	93.2	5.3	0.4

TABLE 2–3   Percentiles of NAEP Reading Scores for 13- and 17-Year-Olds by Race, for Four Cohorts   *(continued)*

	Whites			Blacks			
	Score Age 13	Score Age 17	Diff. Col. 2 Minus 1	Score Age 13	Score Age 17	Diff. Col. 5 Minus 4	Diff. Col. 3 Minus 6
Column	1	2	3	4	5	6	7
	1976 Cohort						
Year Percentile	1980	1984	1984–1980	1980	1984	1984–1980	
5	209.0	228.5	19.5	178.6	201.9	23.3	−3.8
10	221.8	243.5	21.7	190.6	216.0	25.4	−3.7
25	242.8	267.7	24.9	210.9	239.0	28.1	−3.2
50	265.1	293.6	28.5	232.6	264.0	31.4	−2.9
75	286.9	318.8	31.9	254.8	288.3	33.5	−1.6
90	305.7	340.6	34.9	275.0	310.5	35.5	−0.6
95	316.9	353.5	36.6	286.2	323.6	37.4	−0.8
95th minus 5th	107.9	125.0	17.1	107.6	121.7	14.1	3.0
90th minus 10th	83.9	97.1	13.2	84.4	94.5	10.1	3.1
	1967 Cohort						
Year Percentile	1971	1975	1975–1971	1971	1975	1975–1971	
5	204.6	225.9	21.3	166.3	164.7	−1.6	22.9
10	217.9	241.7	23.8	178.0	182.1	4.1	19.7
25	239.4	267.0	27.6	199.1	210.4	11.3	16.3
50	262.0	294.0	32.0	223.3	239.3	16.0	16.0
75	283.5	319.9	36.4	245.5	268.1	22.6	13.8
90	302.2	343.2	41.0	264.8	294.1	29.3	11.7
95	313.1	357.0	43.9	276.8	309.7	32.9	11.0
95th minus 5th	108.5	131.1	22.6	110.5	145.0	34.5	−11.9
90th minus 10th	84.3	101.5	17.2	86.8	112.0	25.2	−8.0

Source: Adapted from National Assessment of Educational Progress (1992: A-153 to A-156), and author's calculations.

WHAT DISTINGUISHED THE 1980S?

After teenagers gained so little in the 1970s, what explains such extraordinary progress during the 1980s, especially for blacks? Grissmer et al. (1998) tested a number of hypotheses and found that "Positive changes in family characteristics can explain nearly all the White gains but only a small part of the Black gains" (p. 221). The evidence they reviewed suggests that gains for black students who were in elementary school during the 1970s and in high school during the early-to-mid 1980s are at least partly explained by reduced class sizes, racial desegregation, and more-demanding coursework. I agree; more-demanding coursework was part of a broad-based movement for accountability in the 1980s.

Heightened Accountability

The 1980s were a period of heightened accountability for teachers and administrators in public education, and perhaps private education as well. Publication of *A Nation at Risk* (Gardner et al., 1983) was a major event, but only one among many events that symbolized a concern that failure to produce a well-educated citizenry would seriously threaten the nation's future stability and prosperity. Hence, the decade produced statements of concern about disparities in educational performance. The Commission on Minority Participation in Education and American Life (1988) wrote:

> If these disparities are allowed to continue, the United States inevitably will suffer a compromised quality of life and a lower standard of living. Social conflict will intensify. Our ability to compete in world markets will decline, our domestic economy will falter, our national security will be endangered. In brief, we will find ourselves unable to fulfill the promise of the American dream.

Whatever the degree of overstatement, this was not a plea for altruism. It was a declaration of national self-interest that many people believed then as they do now.

The appointment of this commission and others reflected forces that had been building since the late 1970s. Among the most visible changes in primary and secondary education during the 1980s was the proliferation of initial state-certification testing for new teachers: 3 states in 1980, 20 in 1984, 40 in 1988, and 42 in 1990 (National Center for Education Statistics, 1991, Table 148). Over time, certification testing has the greatest effect on schools where the teachers who fail the tests would otherwise have taught. In many cases, these are schools that serve disproportionate numbers of black children. Most studies that consider the question find that teachers' test scores are statistically significant predictors of their students' scores [see Greenwald et al. (1996) for a meta-analysis that includes teacher test scores; see also Ferguson (1998b) for discussion and evidence on teacher testing].

I am not suggesting that certification testing, per se, is a major reason that black students made such remarkable gains during the 1980s. It seems unlikely that new teachers would have such a sudden impact. The introduction of certification testing was part of a movement in American education to improve the quality of schools, especially the weakest. A clear possibility is that black students benefited disproportionately from that movement. The rise in math scores that virtually all groups achieved during the decade seems to be further evidence of the movement's impact.

Higher-Level, More Demanding Courses

Figure 2–2 shows annual changes in the number of students taking math (algebra and higher) and English courses among those students graduating from high school during the 1980s and the early 1990s. There was not much change in the number of students taking English, possibly because most students are automatically enrolled in an English course most semesters. The only way to increase the number would have been for students to take more than one English course per semester. For math, however, increases were substantial.

From 1982 through 1990, the average number of math courses that students took (algebra or higher) rose by almost a full course for blacks and Hispanics and by almost half a course for whites. From 1990 through 1994, however, the propensity to take more advanced courses in math slowed for blacks but accelerated for whites and Hispanics. This timing coincides with trends in NAEP math scores. From 1982 through 1990, NAEP math scores for 17-year-olds rose about 4 points for whites, about 9 points for Hispanics, and about 17 points for blacks. Conversely, from 1990 through 1994, NAEP math scores fell by 3 points for blacks, but rose by 3 points for whites and 7 points for Hispanics. Using the SE of the average NAEP scores (shown in parentheses in Table 2–1B), we see that the changes in average math scores during the early 1990s were of the same order of magnitude as their SEs. Hence, they are not statistically distinguishable from zero; nonetheless, their directions seem consistent with changes in course taking. This general similarity in timing does not prove causation, but it tends to support the conjecture that course taking is part of the explanation for the NAEP trends in math, especially for the 1980s.

FIGURE 2–2   Annual Growth in Average Number of Math (Algebra and Higher) and English Courses, for Students Graduating from High School, by Race/Ethnicity

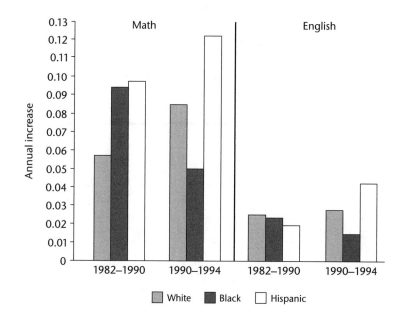

Source: Adapted from National Center for Education Statistics (1998:Table 136).

Blacks were taking higher-level courses as the 1990s approached. As shown in Figure 2–2, their scores were rising, compared to blacks who took the same courses (or at least courses with the same titles) in 1978 (Table 2–4). The same is true for whites and Hispanics, but to a lesser extent. In addition, Figure 2–1 (B, D, and F) indicates that math-score gains for 17-year-olds during the 1980s were building on the positive trends of the same cohorts at ages 9 to 13. Hence, improvements in the quality of math instruction at all levels—elementary, middle, and high school—probably helped to account for rising scores.

Trends in reading scores are not as similar among blacks, whites, and Hispanics, as are trends for math scores. Trends for black 17-year-olds in particular, present a real puzzle. Their mean reading score in 1988 was 274 with an SE of 2.4 points. By 1992, the mean score had fallen by almost 14 points—6 times the SE. Indeed, the mean reading score for black 17-year-olds was lower in 1992 than in 1984. Changes in such things as parenting, school resources, curriculum, instruction, and even school violence ". . . do not appear to be

TABLE 2–4 Mathematics Proficiency of 17-Year-Olds, by Highest Math Course Taken and Race/Ethnicity, 1978 and 1990

	All Areas	General Math or Pre-Algebra	Algebra I	Geometry	Algebra II	Calculus or Pre-Calculus
1978						
White	306	272	291	310	325	338
Black	269	247	264	281	292	297
Hispanic	277	256	273	294	303	306
1990						
White	310	277	292	304	323	347
Black	289	264	278	285	302	329
Hispanic	284	259	278	286	306	323
Change 1978–1990						
White	4	5	1	−6	−2	9
Black	20	17	14	4	10	31
Hispanic	7	3	5	−8	3	17

Source: National Center for Education Statistics (1996a, Table 121).

large enough to explain the drop in Black seventeen-year-olds' reading scores. This important question remains unresolved" (Grissmer et al., 1998:223).

The distributions of NAEP reading-score gains from ages 13 to 17 are remarkably similar for the 17-year-old black cohorts in 1975 and 1992. That both groups achieved small gains from ages 13 to 17 is also apparent in Figure 2–1.

WHAT ROLE MIGHT POPULAR CULTURE HAVE PLAYED?

Rhythm and blues artist James Brown is not known for enunciation, but his words were as clear as could be in 1969 when he shouted "I'm black and I'm proud!" on his hit record that remains an anthem for the period. In an act of collective self-determination, young black leaders in the late 1960s and early 1970s no longer accepted the labels "Negro" or "colored." Their political message rejected the hegemony of white society, asserted a need to mobilize "black power," and spurned integration as a legitimate goal for blacks in a racist society. The Civil Rights Movement of the 1950s and 1960s had pushed for integration and assimilation. It had raised hopes that equal opportunity was possible and could make the American dream real for blacks. But impatience grew. Riots rocked the cities and black leadership evolved.

In the early 1970s, court-ordered busing for school integration disrupted the lives of middle and high school students. Simultaneously, any focus on academic excellence was being blurred by oppositional messages decrying assimilation—muddying what, before, had been a clear consensus that it was okay to aspire to the white American dream. Allegations proliferated that schools were not teaching the whole truth about history; and with their legitimacy thus questioned, some schools, especially those serving blacks, tried to make their curriculums more multicultural. Students agitated for black history courses, not advanced algebra. Academic excellence was not categorically rejected by black youth culture, but neither was it effectively promoted as a worthy and legitimate pursuit by many adults. Gradually, tensions seemed to fade. In music, R&B lost its political edge and disco reigned supreme (George, 1998). Still, neither the early nor the late 1970s delivered a clear message to black teenagers that they should focus on schooling and learning. It seems entirely plausible to me that forced busing, mixed messages from black leaders, and a youth culture searching for ways to be authentically black are key parts of the explanation for why black 13- to 17-year-olds achieved such meager reading-score gains during the 1970s.

The unusually small gains black teenagers achieved in reading during the 1970s are matched only by what they achieved from 1988 to 1992. It appears that black (and perhaps also Hispanic) youth were relatively disengaged from activities that could otherwise have enhanced their reading skills. Clearly, their disengagement from academic endeavors was not total; gains in math scores seem less affected, and there were minimal gains in reading. Still, it seems that something important was different; popular culture is a prime suspect.

Less Leisure Reading

A natural place to look for changes in youth culture is in the ways that youth spend their time. Fortunately, ETS collects data on such things when it administers the NAEP reading exams. Table 2–5 includes data for leisure reading, telling friends about good books, and watching television; Table 2–6 addresses time spent doing homework. Table 2–5 shows that blacks spend more time watching television than whites and Hispanics, and Hispanics

TABLE 2–5   Trends in NAEP Reading Scores, Leisure Reading, Telling Friends about Good Books, and Watching Television among 17-Year-Olds

	1984	*1988*	*1990*	*1992*	*1994*	*1996*
NAEP reading scores						
Black	264.3 (1.0)	274.4 (2.4)	267.3 (2.3)	260.6 (2.1)	266.2 (3.9)	265.4 (2.7)
Hispanic	268.1 (2.2)	270.8 (4.3)	274.8 (3.6)	271.2 (3.7)	263.2 (4.9)	264.7 (4.1)
White	295.2 (0.7)	294.7 (1.2)	296.6 (1.2)	297.4 (1.4)	295.7 (1.5)	294.4 (1.2)
Percent who read almost daily for fun						
Black	30.5 (1.9)	35.3 (6.0)	20.0 (5.7)	14.7 (3.3)	16.4 (4.5)	21.0 (4.6)
Hispanic	26.1 (2.2)	n.a.	n.a.	n.a.	13.4 (3.7)	19.6 (7.5)
White	31.3 (0.9)	27.6 (2.3)	35.4 (2.2)	29.2 (1.8)	32.6 (3.3)	23.6 (2.5)
Percent who at least occasionally tell friends about good books						
Black	74.8 (1.9)	78.1 (3.8)	71.3 (5.0)	65.1 (5.4)	61.9 (5.0)	67.3 (8.0)
Hispanic	78.2 (2.4)	n.a.	n.a.	n.a.	72.2 (5.1)	66.5 (8.2)
White	77.1 (1.0)	73.7 (2.2)	69.0 (2.5)	70.6 (1.9)	70.8 (2.5)	69.6 (3.4)
Percent who spend more than 2 hours daily watching television						
Black	62.9 (1.0)	63.1 (2.0)	65.0 (1.9)	66.4 (1.5)	66.2 (2.5)	64.8 (2.3)
Hispanic	48.2 (1.5)	44.4 (3.0)	37.8 (5.2)	45.5 (2.8)	50.7 (2.2)	49.9 (3.0)
White	40.2 (0.9)	35.2 (1.1)	32.9 (0.9)	30.3 (0.9)	29.7 (1.4)	28.4 (1.2)

Note: Standard errors of mean scores are in parentheses.

watch more than whites. There is not, however, much of a trend in hours watched that might help explain why test scores peaked for minority youth at the end of the 1980s. Hence, if a change in television habits is part of the story for test scores, it has to be a change in what youth watched, not how long they sat in front of the television.

Table 2–6 shows that black 17-year-olds devoted somewhat more time to homework in 1988, when their reading scores peaked, than in 1992, when their scores were lowest. Generally, however, reports of time on homework are remarkably similar for the three racial groups, and there appear to be no major racial differences in trends. Lacking a much more elaborate multivari-

TABLE 2–6   Trends in Time Spent on Homework for Black, Hispanic, and White 17-Year-Olds, 1980 to 1996

	1980	1984	1988	1990	1992	1994	1996
Hispanics							
None	38.1	30.5	13.5	26.7	26.4	23.2	25.8
	(2.7)	(1.4)	(2.8)	(3.5)	(3.0)	(2.4)	(2.6)
Didn't do it	11.5	11.0	15.3	10.2	10.1	11.2	13.7
	(1.5)	(1.0)	(2.8)	(2.1)	(1.8)	(2.0)	(1.8)
Less than 1 hour	23.1	23.4	27.5	26.0	30.4	31.5	28.6
	(1.8)	(1.8)	(3.9)	(2.9)	(3.3)	(4.0)	(2.4)
1–2 hours	20.2	22.6	26.3	23.1	23.6	24.6	24.9
	(2.0)	(1.2)	(4.1)	(2.0)	(2.4)	(2.4)	(2.6)
More than 2 hours	7.0	12.5	17.4	14.0	9.6	9.5	7.1
	(0.7)	(0.8)	(2.5)	(2.1)	(1.3)	(1.8)	(1.3)
TOTAL 1 HOUR OR MORE	27.2	35.1	43.7	37.1	33.2	34.1	32.0
Blacks							
None	39.0	24.6	24.2	27.6	32.2	27.3	25.2
	(2.6)	(1.4)	(2.4)	(1.9)	(3.8)	(3.1)	(3.5)
Didn't do it	8.4	7.2	9.8	8.6	7.3	9.1	11.2
	(0.5)	(0.6)	(1.0)	(1.3)	(1.1)	(1.5)	(1.6)
Less than 1 hour	19.7	25.8	27.9	25.7	28.4	23.3	25.3
	(1.0)	(1.2)	(2.3)	(2.2)	(2.2)	(1.8)	(2.3)
1–2 hours	23.0	30.0	27.0	26.5	24.3	29.5	26.8
	(1.7)	(1.1)	(2.1)	(2.2)	(2.2)	(1.9)	(3.1)
More than 2 hours	9.9	12.4	11.1	11.5	7.8	10.9	11.5
	(0.9)	(0.6)	(2.0)	(1.5)	(1.3)	(1.8)	(2.0)
TOTAL 1 HOUR OR MORE	32.9	42.4	38.1	38.0	32.1	40.4	38.3

TABLE 2–6   Trends in Time Spent on Homework for Black, Hispanic, and White 17-Year-Olds, 1980 to 1996   *(continued)*

	1980	*1984*	*1988*	*1990*	*1992*	*1994*	*1996*
Whites							
None	30.3	21.7	21.1	21.8	20.5	22.7	22.6
	(1.3)	(0.9)	(1.6)	(1.1)	(1.0)	(1.6)	(1.6)
Didn't do it	13.1	12.2	14.1	13.4	13.1	11.8	14.0
	(0.5)	(0.5)	(0.8)	(0.7)	(0.6)	(0.7)	(0.7)
Less than 1 hour	24.3	26.6	28.0	28.6	29.2	27.8	28.6
	(0.6)	(0.5)	(1.1)	(1.0)	(1.0)	(1.0)	(1.1)
1–2 hours	22.6	26.6	25.8	24.5	25.7	25.2	23.6
	(0.6)	(0.6)	(1.6)	(0.8)	(0.9)	(1.3)	(1.1)
More than 2 hours	9.6	12.9	10.9	11.7	11.5	12.5	11.2
	(0.5)	(0.7)	(1.1)	(0.8)	(0.9)	(1.1)	(0.8)
TOTAL 1 HOUR OR MORE	32.2	39.5	36.7	36.2	37.2	37.7	34.8

Note: Standard errors of mean scores are in parentheses.

Source: Unpublished NAEP data provided to the author by the Educational Testing Service.

ate analysis, trends for time spent doing homework and watching television appear to have no clear implications for trends in reading scores.

Conversely, there appears to be a strong (one might even say striking) correlation between reading scores and leisure reading. Jencks and Phillips (1999) found that leisure reading is a statistically significant predictor of reading, but not math, scores for high school students. Reading scores for black youth follow both ups and downs in leisure reading from 1988 through 1996 (see Table 2–5 and Figure 2–3). For whites, leisure reading held steady from 1984 through 1994, then dipped in 1996. For blacks and Hispanics, the percentage of 17-year-olds reporting that they read almost daily for pleasure dropped by half from 1984 to 1994. The drop for black youth who were 13 years old in 1988 is especially dramatic. In 1988, 35.5 percent of 17-year-old blacks read almost daily for pleasure, but by 1992 the number for 17-year-old blacks was only 14.7 percent. This 14.7 percent represents a cohort of which 36.6 percent answered affirmatively that they read almost daily for

FIGURE 2–3   Trends in NAEP Reading Scores and Reading for Pleasure among Black 17-Year-Olds, 1984 to 1996

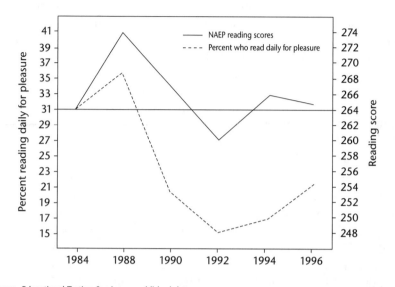

Source: Educational Testing Service, unpublished data.

pleasure as 13-year-olds in 1988. This essentially matches the 37.2 percent who answered affirmatively among whites.

Hip Hop's Explosive Growth

The year 1988 was the watershed year for "hip hop." After only 3 gold records before 1988, there were 17 in 1988 alone. It was the year that mainstream music video outlets forcefully embraced this movement in black and Hispanic youth culture that had been developing on urban streets since the mid-to-late 1970s. George's book *Hip Hop America* (1998) is regarded by many as the definitive text on hip hop's origins and evolution (also see Rose, 1994; Southern, 1997). Hip hop is a multifaceted blend of the new and the old in black and Hispanic culture. The nation first glimpsed it in the late 1970s when national media exposed wide audiences to the artistic graffiti on New York City subway trains and the acrobatic "break dancing" on New York City's streets. Elements of it spread quickly across the country. George (1998) describes hip hop as "a product of post-civil rights America" (p. viii).

For black and Hispanic youth, more than for whites, hip hop probably transcends the realm of entertainment to become an integral aspect of identity and a lens through which to understand the world. Many of the messages in hip hop mix social-class perspectives with racial commentary from an explicitly black and Hispanic point of view, especially in "gangsta" rap, which became popular rapidly during precisely the period under focus here; messages were oppositional and challenging to mainstream culture in an "in-your-face" confrontational style (see, for discussion, Rose, 1991; Dyson, 1996; Martinez, 1997; McLaurin, 1995).

Gangsta rap and associated forms of dress and personal expression began as legitimate cultural insignia among a minority of black youth. Indeed, it has been noted that "hip hop culture is one of the few cultural movements that has been shaped and, to a large extent, controlled by young Black males" (Nelson, 1991, cited in McLaurin, 1995). Drugs, gangs, and activities associated with the marketing and consumption of crack cocaine, admittedly relevant to a minority of black youth, are a factor in the effect of this popularized form of expression. The music that emanated from such lifestyles was highly original, entertaining, and marketable. Although the experiences that it reflected may have been authentic for only some youth, others embraced the expressions and began to mimic the styles and behaviors of gangsta rap and other hip-hop personalities. Did this affect learning and school engagement more for black and Hispanic youth than for whites? I think the answer is almost surely yes. The drop in leisure reading after 1988 may well have been the result of a shift toward listening to this popular new music.

Of course, rap is not unique in affecting identity. Various forms of music are integral to most human cultures and identities. For blacks, "Negro spirituals" emanated from the time of slavery, jazz and blues from early in the twentieth century, rhythm and blues from after World War II, and so on through funk and disco to rap. Rap is simply the latest addition, and it combines elements of all the others. Concerning the effect of rap in black identity, one pair of music historians go so far as to write "After a number of years of being lulled into complacency by popular music and disco, rap music has reintroduced Black identity and consciousness" (Berry and Looney, 1996:266).

Rap Music and Achievement-Related Judgments

Students derive their aspirations and standards for academic performance from parents, teachers, peers, carriers of popular culture, and their own sense of what is achievable and appropriate. Generally, an adolescent's sense of what is appropriate for him or her feels more autonomously determined than it actually is (Muuss, 1988). Different literatures have different emphases, but, generally, identity involves the internalized self (what youth think about themselves), the persona (how youth behave), and the reputation (what others think about the youth). Social forces and the demands they place on youth—for styles of dress, speech, time use, and behavior—affect all three aspects of identity. A few recent studies have sought to examine whether rap music can affect the identities and achievement orientations of Black youth (Johnson et al., 1995; Zillmann et al., 1995; Hanson, 1995; Orange, 1996).

Johnson et al. (1995) sought mainly to assess the effects of exposure to violent rap videos on attitudes toward the use of violence. However, their other purpose was to study the effect of exposure to rap music on perceptions of the usefulness of education. Their study involved 46 black males, ages 11 to 16, in Wilmington, North Carolina. All were enrolled in school (grades 6 through 10) and were participants at an inner-city boys club. They were randomly assigned to three groups. One group watched a series of eight rap music videos containing violent lyrics or imagery. The second group watched the same number of videos, but not containing any violence. The third group, the controls, watched no videos at all.

Following the videos, the boys were invited to participate in an exercise to assess their decision-making skills. The study found that those youth who had watched the violent videos were more likely, by a statistically significant margin, to condone the use of violence in the decisions they were asked to consider. More important for our purposes here, the study also found statistically significant effects on perceptions related to achievement. Specifically, the subjects were asked to read a passage "involving two young friends who chose different paths in life. Bobby chose to go to college and pursue a law degree and Keion chose not to go to college. Bobby came home for a break and Keion came to pick him up in his new BMW and he was wearing nice clothes and nice jewelry. When Bobby asked Keion how he could afford all those nice things without a job, Keion told Bobby to go for a ride with him and not worry about how he could afford the things. Keion picked up four girls and they all commented on how nice his clothes and car were. Bobby told Keion that he would have nice cars, and so on, when he finished school and Keion replied that he 'did not need college' to get nice things" (Johnson et al., 1995:33).

When asked whether they wanted to be like Bobby or Keion, youth in the control group, who had not watched either set of rap videos, wanted to be more like Bobby, the aspiring lawyer, by a statistically significant margin. There was no difference between the youth who had watched the violent and nonviolent videos, in who they wanted to emulate—Keion. When asked about the likelihood that Bobby would successfully complete law school, youth in the control group were more optimistic about Bobby's chances, again by a statistically significant margin.

If watching rap videos and listening to rap music promote cynicism about societal fairness, and about the prospects of people who work hard experiencing success, then it might also detract from academic engagement and performance. Mickelson (1990) found that those students earn lower grades who agree more with statements such as ". . . my parents tell me to get a good education to get a good job," but "[b]ased on their experiences, people like us are not always paid or promoted according to our education." Mickelson calls these "concrete beliefs," as opposed to "abstract beliefs"—i.e., that success requires education and effort. Mickelson also noted that black students agreed as much as, or more than, white students, that success requires effort; but the black students did not believe as much as white students that life is fair and that people always get what they deserve.

Hanson (1995) conducted a number of studies using "schema theory." Schema theory, in this context, suggests that popular music and music videos are structured around themes that are "schematically represented in memory" (p. 46). Subjects tend rather automatically to use these schema as the basis for interpretations, social judgments, and decisions soon after the video has been viewed, or soon after memories of the video are brought to mind. Hanson reports that violent hard-rock videos often affect attitudes about violence in a manner similar to what Johnson et al. (1995) found using violent rap videos; she concludes that both her and Johnson and colleagues' studies "clearly indicate the power of the themes contained in music videos to alter, at least temporarily, the kinds of social judgements people make" (Hanson, 1995:50). She goes on to suggest that, at least theoretically, cognitive priming of the type contained in rap videos "has the capacity to make frequently primed schemas become chronically highly accessible" (Hanson, 1995).

Hence, youth who devote a lot of time to listening to any type of music, including rap, may be more likely to interpret the world in ways consistent with the messages in that music. This might be especially so for those who come to use rap music consciously as a source of information about the world. One well-known performer, Chuck D of the group Public Enemy, has asserted that "Rap music is Black folks' CNN" (McLaurin, 1995:306).

The degree to which black youth use rap music as a source of information or insight is unclear. Similarly, my suggestion here that the rise of rap music may help account for the drop in leisure reading and reading scores for black and Hispanic students should be regarded as tentative until more evidence is found to support it.

Δ. Harris   NB

PEER PRESSURE TO NOT "ACT WHITE"

One often hears that fear of "acting white" prevents black and Hispanic students from striving to meet higher standards.[3] To illustrate the subtle influence of the acting-white challenge, provided below are three examples from an inner-ring suburb of a Midwestern city, from unpublished transcripts of interviews and focus groups conducted by anthropologist John Ogbu in May 1997. The racial composition in the district is roughly 50:50 black/white, but there is a wide difference in academic performance. The vast majority of the children in top academic sections are white and most of those in the lower sections are black. Many of the black and white parents are professionals; and most people agree that the black students underperform.

For each example, consider whether the fear of acting white might be an impediment to closing the black-white achievement gap, and whether it might be affected by elements of the hip-hop culture, as discussed above.

First Example: A Middle-School Principal Seeks Answers

[The principal is speaking.]

> We had a youngster working in our office during his study halls. He was very bright. And I go and evaluate classes all the time. He sat in front of me in one of our science classes. The teacher asked a question. He didn't put his hand up. I heard him mutter under his breath—the right answer. I poked him, and said, "Hey, what's going on here?" He said, "You don't have to ride home on the bus like I do." I said, "You're right; I don't." "You don't have to play in the neighborhood with all the other kids." I said, "You're right. I don't understand." He said, "I don't want 'em to know I'm smart. They'll make fun of me. I won't have any friends." I said, "So you'd rather sit there and pretend that you don't know than face kids who might say you're smart?" And he even said, "Worse than smart." I said, "Well, what's worse than that in your world?" He said, "Where I live, they're gonna say I'm White." I said, "Oh." I said, "Now I, I think I understand. I don't agree with you, but I hear what you're saying."

We lack good quantitative evidence of whether the pattern in this passage—i.e., holding back for fear of ostracism—happens more often for black students than for Whites, and how much it affects academic performance, but this is not an unusual report.

Second Example: Ambivalence of a Black Student Leader

The following speaker is a male student selected for interviewing from among a small group of black student leaders. First, he addresses the challenge of being smart without acting white and his own feeling that people who sound white are selling out:

> I just love to hear Michael Jordan because he sounds very intelligent without, you know, sounding white, like, what other people call, like, a [sic] "oreo sound." He sounds actually like a strong, black male who can actually talk to the people intelligently, which is actually hard to do. I mean, hard to sound like, "Oh, I'm not selling out," or things like that. . . . I've seen some people who, like (I wouldn't want to say, I don't know), but, you know, that's good for them if that's the path they chose to lead.

Second, he struggles with the trade-off between staying with other black students in college preparatory (CP) courses, versus getting a better education in the honors courses. He begins by saying that it is not important to take honors courses, but then explains that honors courses provide a better atmosphere for learning.

> I don't really find it very important to take honors. I've taken all kinds of, like, honors, CP, and everything. I just feel you that you should take whatever you can do well in. I mean, being in some CP classes it's, like it's a different atmosphere. It's, like, it's harder for the teacher to teach in some of those classes; she has to, like, deal with people causing problems and laughing and throwing people out of class. And I feel it hurts the people who want to learn. . . . And then honors classes, it's, like, everybody just sits there nice and soft and everybody listens in those classes. Everybody's more, everybody puts their education at the top of their priorities. Within the CP classes, everybody is just, like, chillin', laughin', jokin' at the teacher. And you see, like, everybody coming out of these Saturday schools. . . . I mean, not all of 'em are troublemakers, but I mean you hardly see White people wantin' a Saturday school.

Should he stay mostly in the honors classes, where he's one of only a few blacks, or should he take the CP courses where the majority of the students are black? Does his apparent ambivalence reflect a concern about being able to do well in the honors courses, a concern about acting white and selling out, or both? Do white students face such pressures equally? Would the black-white achievement gap be affected if black students received help in coping with such issues?

Third Example: Acting Ghetto

One way to not act white is to act ghetto. Here, the same black male student as above reflects on, and clearly rejects, the polar opposite of acting white:

It seems to me, almost, like black students act as ghetto as possible, like, as much of the time as they can. And I think that that's a lot of the problem. Because you'll be sitting in class, and people will just leave, or, like, we're in class, and the teacher handed a test to somebody, and they just, like, here you can have it back. That's just ridiculous.

Similarly, Ainsworth-Darnell and Downey (1998), found, using national data, that teachers rate black students as more frequently disruptive and as putting forth less effort. The black-white differences that they found were not very large, but remained statistically significant after accounting for family income, parental occupations, and parental education.

These issues need to be handled at the community level, in alliances among teachers, students, parents, and administrators. As I describe in Ferguson (1998a), evidence tends to support the conclusion that teachers' perceptions and expectations have an important effect on the performance of black students, more than whites (Casteel, 1997; Kleinfeld, 1972; Jussim et al., 1996). If we can equip teachers with the skills to encourage and motivate students, the fear of acting white and the peer norms that sometimes reward "acting ghetto" need not carry the day. Professional development opportunities that help teachers in this regard could be quite important next steps.

PARENTAL AND TEACHER STANDARDS

Teachers hold to higher standards those students they expect can perform at higher levels. One student who earns a grade of C may receive a reprimand for slacking off, while another with the same grade receives praise because it seems to reflect his best effort. The literature is clear on finding that teachers expect less, on average, from black students than whites (Ferguson, 1998a; Brophy, 1985; Good, 1987; Howard and Hammond, 1985; Jussim et al., 1996; Taylor, 1979). The few studies that take students' past grades and test scores into account find that teachers have the same expectations on average for black and white students who have performed equally in the past. Hence, by this notion of expectations conditional on past performance, teachers are not racially biased, even though they expect less of blacks, because blacks' past performance predicts their lower future performance. Using a notion of expectations based on students' latent potentials, teachers may or may not underestimate black or Hispanic students' latent potentials by more than they underestimate whites'. Because potential is not apparent until it shows itself, there is no way of proving or calibrating whether bias has a role here. Nonetheless, teachers who underestimate their students' potentials probably underinvest in the search for ways of unlocking it. Reverend Robert Schuller says, "Any fool can count the seeds in an apple, but only God can count the apples in a seed." If we believed more in children's potential, we might invest more effort in cultivation and aim for larger harvests.

These statements about expectations and standards apply as much to parents as to teachers. Figure 2–4 is based on a survey of students in nine high schools in Wisconsin and San Francisco during the 1980s.[4] It provides a striking illustration of the fact that parental standards can differ by race and parents' education. Students were asked, "What is the lowest grade you can get without your parents getting upset?" The mean answer was between C and C+, with a standard deviation of about one marking level (e.g., the difference between C+ and B–).

The most outstanding feature of Figure 2–4 is the performance Asian students perceive that their parents hold them accountable for; it is a higher level of performance than the other student groups perceive is expected of them. Asians whose parents are high school dropouts report higher grade-level thresholds for provoking parental anger than do white, black, or Hispanic students whose parents have four-year college degrees. Conversely, black students whose parents are college graduates report, on average, almost the same parental standards as whites whose parents are high school graduates and have not attended college at all. If teachers, parents, and peers hold black and sometimes Hispanic students to lower standards than Whites and Asians, part of the reason is that black and Hispanic students have historically performed at lower levels. But this can change. Especially when help is available, students tend to strive at least for the minimum standards that people around them set. National surveys show that students of all racial groups think the standards are too low.

WHAT STUDENTS THINK ABOUT THEIR SCHOOLS

Trends in NAEP indicate that achievement scores have risen over the past three decades. Presumably, minimum standards have risen as well. A nationally representative survey of high school students conducted in 1996, however, indicates that neither black, Hispanic, nor white students feel that standards are high enough (Public Agenda, 1997). The survey covered 1,000 randomly selected high school students, plus another 1,120 over-sample interviews for blacks, Hispanics, private high school students, middle school students, and students from two metropolitan areas. Tables 2–7 through 2–9 present selected items from the report. For the most part, I have selected

FIGURE 2–4   "What Is the Lowest Grade You Can Get without Your Parents Getting Upset?" Answers by student's race/ethnicity and mother's education. Y-axis is in standard deviations (1 letter grade per s.d.) around a mean of C+. Sample sizes for bars, from left to right on the diagram: 56, 15, 128, 31; 46, 47, 99, 115; 150, 126, 167, 866; 128, 137, 111, 882; 328, 138, 78, 1525.

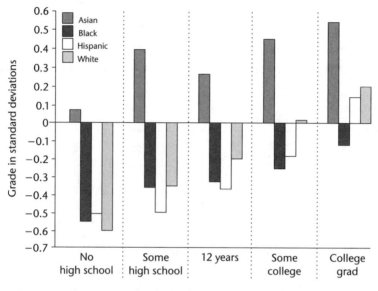

Source: Author's calculations, using data supplied by Laurence Steinberg for high schools in Wisconsin and San Francisco during the 1980s.

items that show racial differences or items that have direct bearing on the question of standards.

Fifty-six percent of black students, 45 percent of Hispanic students, and 36 percent of white students reported "Too many teachers are doing a bad job" is a "very serious" or "somewhat serious" problem in their school (Table 2–7). Items related to "doing a bad job" included not emphasizing basics such as reading, writing, and math; passing students to the next grade when they should be held back; and allowing students to get away with being late to class and not doing their work. More black than Hispanic students and more Hispanic than white students report these to be problems. It appears either that black students have higher standards for their schools (which seems unlikely) or that black students receive a lower standard of instruction. Stu-

TABLE 2–7   Percent Responding That the Problem Is "Very Serious" or "Somewhat Serious" in Their School

(Question: Here are some problems different schools could have. Please tell me how serious a problem this is in your school.)

	High School Students			
	Whites	Blacks	Hispanics	Private School
Too many teachers are doing a bad job	36	56	45	22
Not enough emphasis on the basics such as reading, writing, and math	30	49	41	16
Too many kids get passed to the next grade when they should be held back	41	58	49	16
Too many students get away with being late to class and not doing their work	49	58	50	35
Students pay too much attention to what they're wearing and what they look like	73	81	79	42
Classes are too crowded	42	52	45	14

Source: Public Agenda (1997, Table 4). Reprinted with permission from Public Agenda, New York.

dents in the private school sample, which is not differentiated by race, report far fewer of these problems than do students in public schools.

Sixty-two percent of blacks, 49 percent of Hispanics, and 48 percent of whites say they would learn "a lot more" if they knew that companies in the area were using high school transcripts to decide whom to hire (Table 2–8). Other measures that might get them to learn "a lot more" include having more good teachers, having work checked and then redoing it, removing chronic troublemakers from class, and receiving material incentives from parents. Answers on each of these questions indicate that children of all three racial groups believe they could learn a lot more than they currently do.

Table 2–9 lists 10 characteristics of effective teachers, and whether students believe that "most" of their current teachers have these characteristics. A majority of students respond that teachers with any of 9 characteristics (the exception is "knows how to handle disruptive students") could inspire them to learn "a lot more." For all characteristics, no public-school students reported that most of their teachers had the characteristics listed. On the other hand, for 5 of the 10 characteristics, a majority of private-school students say that most of their teachers fit the description. For most of the items

TABLE 2–8 Percent Responding That the Proposed Change Would Get Them to Learn "A Lot More"

(Question: Now I'm going to read a list of things that might get you to learn more and ask if you think they'll really work. Remember, I'm not asking if you like these ideas, only if you think they will actually get you to learn more.)

	High School Students			
	Whites	Blacks	Hispanics	Private School
Having more good teachers	60	75	69	74
Getting your class work checked and redoing it until it's right	58	74	69	61
Kicking constant troublemakers out of class so teachers can concentrate on the kids who want to learn	50	66	58	50
Knowing that more companies in your area are using high school transcripts to decide who to hire	48	62	49	46
Knowing you'll get something you want from your parents if you do well	27	43	44	27

Source: Public Agenda (1997, Table 5). Reprinted with permission from Public Agenda, New York.

in Table 2–9, black and Hispanic students rate their teachers higher on average than white students rate theirs. How do we reconcile this with Table 2–7, where larger percentages of black and Hispanic than white students report that too many teachers are doing a bad job? One possibility is that schools serving black and Hispanic students have a larger percentage of dedicated teachers *and* a larger percentage of teachers doing a bad job. Another possibility is that black and Hispanic students have lower threshold standards than whites do for judging teachers, so that blacks would rate any given teacher performance higher than whites would. If this latter interpretation is closer to correct, then it is even more a problem that a larger percentage of black and Hispanic than white students agree that "too many teachers are doing a bad job." The correct interpretation is impossible to glean from these data, but the issues are important, and the Public Agenda survey has at least begun to inform the discussion.

The Public Agenda survey results as well as the more extended discussion of standards-related issues above, suggest that children can do more than we are asking of them. Moreover, they know it. It appears that standards of effort and performance for black and Hispanic students, and perhaps for teachers

TABLE 2–9   Percent Responding That Certain Kinds of Teachers Would Lead Them to Learn "A Lot More"/Percent Responding "Most" of Their Teachers Are Like That Item Now

(Question: Now I'm going to talk about different kinds of teachers and ask you if you think they lead you to learn more or not.)

	High School Students			
	Whites	Blacks	Hispanics	Private School
A teacher who tries to make lessons fun and interesting	79/25	76/25	78/23	84/39
A teacher who is enthusiastic and excited about the subject they teach	71/29	71/28	72/32	71/32
A teacher who knows a lot about the subject they teach	70/47	74/49	72/47	77/63
A teacher who treats students with respect	68/42	75/37	68/50	73/63
A teacher who gives students a lot of individual help with their work	67/33	76/31	69/31	78/51
A teacher who uses hands-on projects and class discussion	68/23	67/31	68/19	70/33
A teacher who explains lessons very carefully	64/33	72/38	72/35	71/48
A teacher who challenges students to constantly do better and learn more	63/33	79/42	69/36	74/51
A teacher who personally cares about his students as people	62/30	68/31	66/31	71/58
A teacher who knows how to handle disruptive students	45/28	52/35	44/35	52/44

Source: Public Agenda (1997, Table 11). Reprinted with permission from Public Agenda, New York.

and parents as well, are lower than what will be required to avoid a future of continued racial disparity in academic achievement. We have underestimated children's potentials. We can and should produce a larger harvest.

CONCLUSION

Children's knowledge includes what they already know before arriving at school and what they learn once there. The average black or Hispanic child in the United States has fewer school-related skills than the average white child at the beginning of kindergarten. This is true even among households that appear equal in parental schooling and socioeconomic status [see Chapters 4 and 7 in Jencks and Phillips (1998)]. Once a child enters school already less proficient than his peers, catching up requires more than keeping up; equal progress merely maintains initial disparities.

Basic skill gaps among white, black, and Hispanic children, as measured by standardized test scores, have narrowed substantially over the past 30 years. Large gaps remain, but more progress is possible if we set high standards and do what it takes to achieve them. If we care about equality of results, then we must face the fact that catching up requires running faster than the competition: the only way for black and Hispanic students in a given birth cohort to narrow the gap with whites during the school years is for them to learn more than whites do. Although NAEP cannot measure changes in proficiency between school entry and age nine, data from NAEP suggest that black and Hispanic children often have learned more than whites after age nine, but not for all time periods, and not enough to come even close to closing the test-score gap. Accelerating progress on closing these gaps can be facilitated by a more supportive popular culture, by teachers and parents who set high standards, and by a society that provides the necessary resources and incentives to keep it all on track. Responsive teaching can weaken the link between past and future performance for an individual child. Similarly, a responsive and determined society can change prospects for large numbers of children—of all races and ethnicities—whose potential otherwise might be wasted.

This paper was initially prepared for the National Research Council Conference on Racial Trends in the United States, held October 15 and 16, 1998, at the National Academy of Sciences in Washington, D.C. Work on the paper has benefited from the financial support of the Annie E. Casey Foundation, the John D. and Catherine T. MacArthur Foundation, and the Rockefeller Foundation, through their support for the National Community Development Policy Analysis Network Project on Education and Youth in Community Development. Jordana Brown helped to collect the materials on which this paper is based and has provided helpful comments that improved the paper. William T. Dickens, Christopher Jencks, and Meredith Phillips also provided helpful comments.

Appendix:
Trends in Scholastic Aptitude Test Scores

Scholastic Aptitude Test (SAT) scores represent that segment of the high school population planning to apply to colleges where the SAT is required in the application. Hence, SAT scores and trends are not based on a random sample of all students. Further, characteristics of the sample, such as what percentage of students it represents, change over time. Still, SAT does provide a national time series of scores with which to compare the NAEP scores. Figure 2–A shows changes since 1976 in SAT scores for blacks, Mexicans, and whites. (Note that Mexicans' scores for the SAT are for a smaller segment of the Hispanic population than NAEP because NAEP includes additional Hispanic nationalities. Do not assume close comparability.) All three groups achieved higher scores in math during the 1980s. (College enrollment rates for new high school graduates during the mid-to-late 1980s were rising.) This is consistent with trends in the NAEP. The similarity of math trends for different racial groups and across both NAEP and SAT indicates that there was probably a narrow range of forces causing the changes across the board. These probably included changes in course-taking, curriculum, and instruction. For both NAEP and SAT, verbal scores are more variable than math, with less of a common pattern across groups. However, just as with NAEP, the most salient thing to notice about blacks in these two figures is that both verbal and math progress stops abruptly at the end of the 1980s, after a decade of rapid improvement.

FIGURE 2–A   Changes since 1976 in SAT (A) verbal and (B) math scores by racial/ethnic background (three-year moving averages).

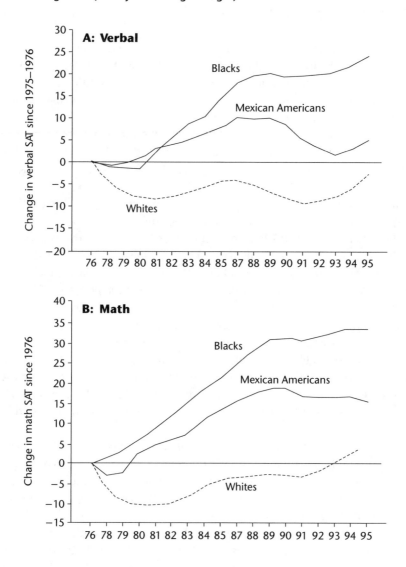

Source: National Center for Education Statistics (1996a, Table 128).

Afterword to Chapter 2

The primary data in this chapter on test-score trends come from the National Assessment of Educational Progress Long-Term Trend Assessment (NAEP-LTT). Since the initial publication of this chapter, NAEP-LTT has released additional data, for the years 1999 and 2004.[1] The good news is that reading and math scores for nine-year-olds have risen for whites, blacks, and Hispanics. Scores for all three groups in 2004 were the highest they have been since the NAEP-LTT was first administered in the early 1970s. Moreover, scores rose faster in recent years for blacks and Hispanics than for whites, so the achievement gap has narrowed.

Among 13-year-olds, math scores for all three groups were higher than ever in 2004. Racial gaps between blacks/Hispanics and whites were smaller in 2004 than during the 1990s, but still larger than during the late 1980s. Black and Hispanic 13-year-olds had higher reading scores in 2004 than in 1996, but the 2004 scores were about the same as an earlier cohort had scored in 1988, before reading scores for black and Hispanic teens slid backward. Reading scores for white 13-year-olds in 2004 were basically the same as throughout the 1990s. So the more recent story for 13-year-olds is mixed, but there is at least a moderate degree of recent progress.

The bad news is for 17-year-olds. None of the three groups—blacks, Hispanics, and whites—made progress in raising reading or math scores from the early 1990s through 2004. Racial gaps for 17-year-olds in 2004 were about the same as in the early 1990s, when they exceeded the gaps that existed in 1988.

The summary statement for math is this: Elementary schools have been preparing children better, but the gains appear to be squandered by the time students are 17 years old.[2] It may be that secondary schools have not upgraded their curricula to take advantage of the better-prepared students they have been receiving.

Finally, in this chapter I consider ways that school and youth cultures may have affected test-score disparities, especially the sudden halt in progress for black teenagers at the end of the 1980s. Recent work by Meredith Phillips finds that the drop in reading for leisure that I report here for the end of the 1980s is not replicated in another large data set.[3] However, she does find evidence of behavior changes for 17-year-olds that match the timing of the stalled progress. I am continuing to explore these issues.[4]

CHAPTER 3

Can Schools Narrow the Black-White Test Score Gap?

Proposals for improving the test performance of black children and closing the black-white test score gap are numerous and varied. This chapter evaluates the evidence for and against (six) of the most popular proposals that are related to schools: expanding enrollment in preschool programs; reducing ability grouping and curriculum tracking; supporting instructional interventions for youth at risk of failure (mainly in elementary school); matching students and teachers by race; selecting teachers with strong basic skills (as measured by teachers' own test scores); and maintaining smaller classes.[1] To judge the effectiveness of these proposals, I focus on studies of the highest methodological quality and pay special attention to whether and to what extent each measure would affect test scores.[2]

DOES PRESCHOOL PROVIDE A LASTING HEAD START?

Most policymakers and advocates for the poor believe that preschools can compensate for factors that place children from disadvantaged backgrounds behind their peers in academic terms before they even enter kindergarten. In reviewing the evidence, two questions are of concern. First, does attending compensatory preschool raise test scores in kindergarten? The best research on this question finds that the answer is yes. Second, do the effects of attending preschool persist into adulthood? The evidence on this question is, at best, mixed.

Experimental and Quasi-Experimental Studies

In the field of education, high-quality studies that use random assignment or good comparison groups, have large samples, and follow subjects over many years are rare. For an evaluation of compensatory preschool programs, Steven Barnett searched out such studies.[3] To qualify for his sample, studies had to cover programs serving children of low-income families and be based in a fixed location. They also had to include data on academic performance through at least the third grade. Eight of the studies that Barnett identified used random-assignment control groups or had comparison groups of similar children who did not attend the program. Almost all of the children in the studies were African American.

These eight studies find IQ gains ranging from 5 points to 13 points during preschool. Such gains are, respectively, equivalent to almost one-third and almost one full standard deviation on the standard scale for measuring IQ. All of the studies, including the Perry Preschool experiment which I discuss below, also show substantial declines in IQ relative to control or comparison groups by the third grade. Only one, the Philadelphia Project, reports statistically significant differences as late as fifth grade. These studies yield no firm evidence that preschool programs produce IQ gains that last past the early years of elementary school, but neither do they disprove the possibility.[4]

Five of the eight studies report achievement scores (distinct from IQ scores) for the third grade or higher. Of these five, only Perry Preschool shows a continuing and statistically significant advantage over the comparison group. The other four studies suffer from serious methodological problems. The Early Training Project uses only thirty-three experimentals and fifteen controls. The remaining three rely on achievement tests administered routinely by the schools; there are strong reasons to believe that doing so biases against detecting effects that might be present.[5] On balance, therefore, Perry Preschool is the strongest study.

Perry Preschool.   From 1962 to 1965, the Perry Preschool experiment randomly assigned five cohorts of children to be participants or members of the control group.[6] Children were eligible if their families had low ratings on a scale of socioeconomic status, their measured IQ was at least one standard deviation below the national mean, and they "showed no signs for organic causation for mental retardation or physical handicap." For the first wave, children enrolled at the age of four, but thereafter at age three. The treatment group attended preschool for 2.5 hours a day, Monday through Friday, from October to May. In addition, a teacher visited these children once a week to provide about 1.5 hours of instruction in a home setting.

An IQ difference of 12 points opened between experimentals and controls by the end of preschool. But this difference was not statistically significant

TABLE 3-1   Perry Preschool Project: Estimated Standardized Effects on Achievement Scores, Selected Ages[a]

Item	Age					
	Seven	Eight	Nine	Ten	Fourteen	Nineteen
Effect size	0.23	0.34	0.39	0.42	0.45	0.36
Probability[b]	0.219	0.079	0.042	0.040	0.003	0.059
Sample size						
Treatment group	53	49	54	49	49	52
Control group	60	56	55	46	46	57

Source: Author's calculations based on data from Barnett (1992, table 8).
a. Different examinations were used for different ages; details were unavailable.
b. Values given indicate probability of the estimated effect if the true effect is zero.

by the time the children were nine years old (see note 4). For achievement, the story is more encouraging. Table 3–1 shows approximate effect sizes for achievement tests.[7] Instead of diminishing over time, the size and statistical significance of the preschool effect on achievement test scores actually increased. The reasons remain unclear: they may be cognitive, motivational, or both.

Perry Preschool is not a typical program. It had more funding, was more intensive, and had better trained staff than most. Given, on the one hand, the small sample size in the Perry Preschool experiment and the fact that the intervention is atypical, and on the other, the weaker results from other experimental and quasi-experimental studies, a large random assignment longitudinal study for a program such as Head Start is overdue. In addition to measuring effects for standard programs, such a large-scale study might enrich a randomly selected sample of programs by strengthening their focus on reading and mathematics readiness, in order to compare the impacts of the basic and enriched interventions.

Child-Parent Center, Chicago.   In a study published after Barnett's review of the literature, Arthur Reynolds and colleagues examine the preschool program of the Child-Parent Center, which has operated since 1967 in low-income neighborhoods of Chicago.[8] The data cover 240 children who finished the preschool program in 1986 and follow them through sixth grade. A comparison group is composed of 120 nonparticipating children from families similar in characteristics to those of the participants and living in the same neighborhoods.

Because the Child-Parent Center study uses a comparison group rather than a randomly selected control group, and because the children were not tested at the time they entered preschool, it is impossible to be sure that the treatment and comparison groups were initially equivalent. Nevertheless, as of sixth grade, program participants scored about a third of a standard deviation higher than the comparison group in reading and mathematics on the Iowa Test of Basic Skills, after controlling for gender, age, parental education, eligibility for free lunch, and any additional years of Child-Parent Center participation after preschool. These results are comparable to those from the Perry Preschool program for similar age groups, and hence reinforce the proposition that benefits from preschool can be lasting.

Nonexperimental Evidence

The classic problem with using nonexperimental data to measure program effects of any type is that people are not selected (or do not select themselves) into programs randomly. Therefore statistical analyses that fail to correct for selection bias will tend to over- or underestimate program effects. A recent study of the federal Head Start program by Janet Currie and Duncan Thomas is notable for the way in which it tries to overcome this problem.[9]

Currie and Thomas use the National Longitudinal Survey of Youth's Child-Mother file to estimate effects of Head Start and other preschool programs on several outcomes, including one test score, the Peabody Picture Vocabulary Test (PPVT). Currie and Thomas estimate the difference in PPVT scores between siblings who attend Head Start and those who stay at home.[10] They measure whether the effects of Head Start are lasting by estimating differences between siblings through age ten.

Both African-American and white five-year-olds who attend Head Start score about 7 percentile points higher on the PPVT than their siblings who stay at home. These effects are highly statistically significant. However, while this benefit persists for whites, it decays rapidly for African Americans.[11] By age ten, the estimated effect of Head Start on the PPVT scores of black children has disappeared, but for white children it is roughly 5 percentile points. In addition, Head Start appears to reduce the probability of grade repetition for white children but not for blacks. The finding that effects die out for African Americans is consistent with results from many of the studies reviewed by Barnett that were less methodologically sound than the Perry Preschool study.

These results of Currie and Thomas are not definitive.[12] In order for their results to be unbiased, there must be no systematic difference between the child sent to Head Start and the sibling kept at home. Second, the parents' decision on whether to send the second child to Head Start should not depend on the quality of the first child's experience.[13] Third, the child who stays at home must not benefit from the fact that the sibling attended Head Start. Fourth, the children of families who send some but not all of their children to Head Start must derive the same average benefits as other children. There is some evidence to suggest that the second and third of these assumptions may not hold for African Americans. Specifically, Currie and Thomas report (but do not show) that the effect of Head Start for first-born children is "significantly negative" (that is, smaller) for African Americans.[14]

Further, the sample of sibling pairs fitting the study's requirements is small.[15] Both Currie and Thomas's study, which finds that achievement effects fade for black children, and the Perry Preschool study, which finds that these effects persist, are small and possibly unrepresentative samples from which to generalize about national impacts of preschool.[16]

Do Poor Schools Squander Gains from Head Start?   Seeking an explanation for why Head Start's benefits to black children might not persist, Currie and Thomas (1996a) use nationally representative data on eighth graders from the 1988 National Education Longitudinal Study (NELS:88).[17] They examine the proposition that the quality of the schools subsequently attended explains some of the difference in performance between students who attended Head Start and those who did not. Before controlling for school quality, eighth-graders who attended Head Start have lower scores on achievement tests than those who did not. But Currie and Thomas find that "among black children, the gap between Head Start children and other children is virtually eliminated if we include fixed effects for the school the child attends."[18] This suggests that black children who attend Head Start go on to weaker schools than black children who do not attend Head Start.

It would be too big a stretch, however, to conclude from this evidence that the Head Start effect fades as a result of weaker schools. Siblings who are close in age are very likely to attend the same schools. For school quality to explain why Head Start advantages fade for black children but not for whites, one would need to show that inferior schools reduce the difference between higher and lower achieving siblings by depressing high achievement disproportionately. This hypothesis is certainly plausible—even likely—but it awaits evidence other than what the NELS:88 can provide.

There is no disagreement that preschool programs, including Head Start, produce nontrivial gains in children's IQ and achievement scores by the time they enter kindergarten. However, given the nature of the evidence, no strong conclusions are warranted regarding whether these benefits persist. A large-scale random-assignment longitudinal study is needed to answer this question. In the meantime, preschools deserve continuing support.

DO ABILITY GROUPING AND TRACKING EXACERBATE THE BLACK-WHITE TEST SCORE GAP?

In this section, I examine the effects of ability grouping and curricular track-ing. Ability grouping usually refers to the practice of clustering elementary school children for instruction, based mostly on demonstrated or expected performance, but also on factors such as motivation, work habits, and behav-ior. Groups may be taught in the same or different classrooms, for a sin-gle subject or for the entire curriculum. Although the practice is not docu-mented by any national survey, it seems that the vast majority of elementary schools in the United States use in-class ability grouping for reading and whole class instruction for other subjects. Most U.S. high schools organize instruction around curricular tracks. Students in a particular track take a sequence of courses that distinguish their multisemester curriculum from that taught in other tracks. Students with greater academic interests and pro-ficiency tend toward academic, as opposed to general or vocational, tracks.[19] This in effect turns tracks into ability groups much of the time. There are also tracks within tracks: college prep, honors, and advanced placement are some standard labels for progressively more exclusive subdivisions.

Researchers and activists hotly debate the impact of ability grouping on achievement. Fashions in the research literature change with the political climate. James Kulik notes: "In an age of ability testing, reviewers concluded that ability grouping could benefit students. When progressive education was in style and ability testing fell from fashion, reviewers concluded that grouping was more likely to harm than help students. In an era that stressed excellence as an educational goal, reviewers concluded that there were great benefits in the special grouping of higher aptitude students. In an era of educational equity, they concluded that grouping was harmful for disadvan-taged and minority students. The times sensitized the reviewers to certain truths about grouping; they also blinded reviewers to other truths."[20]

I consider three questions. First, are blacks distributed among ability groups, curriculum tracks, and courses in equal proportion to their representation in schools? The answer is clearly no. Second, is there evidence that placements in ability groups or curriculum tracks are racially biased? While there are small racial differences in placement associated with socioeconomic status, most such differences are associated with measurable differences in proficiency (that is, past performance). But there are no consistent racial differences in placements after controlling for these two factors. Third, is it likely that ability grouping and curriculum tracking help to sustain or exacerbate black-white differences in achievement? The highest quality research suggests that ability grouping and tracking are not harmful—compared to the most likely alternatives.

Critics are not wrong in saying that instructional practices in lower groups and tracks are worse, that instruction in such tracks is not tailored to the needs of low-performing students, or that membership in lower tracks is stigmatizing. But that does not mean necessarily that heterogeneous classrooms are better. Most proposed alternatives to ability grouping and tracking involve changes in teaching, not simply the standard practices of today's heterogeneous classrooms. Without major changes in teacher training—and probably even with them—there seems little reason to expect that more heterogeneous grouping would be a panacea for any students, black or white. Children can succeed or fail under a variety of grouping arrangements.[21]

Racial Bias in Elementary School Group Placement

Elementary school teachers have virtually complete autonomy in choosing ability group placements for their students. It is therefore very plausible that group placements may be biased by children's race or socioeconomic status. Chapter 4 outlines three types of racial bias, each with a characteristic benchmark: unconditional race neutrality; race neutrality conditioned on past performance and other appropriate criteria; and race neutrality conditioned on future potential. Whether a pattern shows bias or not depends on the benchmark for neutrality that one has in mind.

Discourse on racial imbalance in grouping and tracking often takes any racial imbalance as prima facie evidence of bias. Jomills Braddock and Robert Slavin, for example, cite a study by Emil Haller as evidence of racial imbalance in elementary school and continue: "The U.S. Office of Civil Rights has estimated that more than half of U.S. elementary schools have at least one 'racially identifiable' classroom in its highest or lowest grade. A racially identifiable classroom is one in which the proportion of students of a given race in a class is substantially different from that in the school as a whole. This is considered an indication of discriminatory ability grouping."[22]

Haller asked teachers in the spring of 1982 to assign their current students to reading groups for the next school year.[23] Seventy-eight percent of the children recommended for the highest groups were white, and 63 percent of those recommended for the lowest groups were black. This imbalance is large. Nonetheless, Haller's findings are not an indication of discriminatory ability grouping.

Haller does not find any violation of racial neutrality, once test scores and other reasonable criteria are taken into account. Table 3–2 shows that the criteria teachers applied in judging blacks and whites are nearly identical. If their decisions were racially biased, it seems highly unlikely that teachers would use such similar criteria in discussing students.[24] Table 3–3 compares teachers' reading group recommendations with what placements would be if they were based on students' scores on the Comprehensive Test of Basic Skills, by race. Black-white differences in the percentage of students displaced upward or downward are small and well within the range of simple random variation.[25]

I have found only a few other studies that test for race neutrality conditioned on past performance in ability group placement.[26] None of these find racial bias after controlling for other factors, including test scores. Evidence for bias due to socioeconomic status is more mixed, and may account for a small percentage of the observed racial differences.[27] Still, by far the most important predictor of the black-white disparity in placements is proficiency, which produces large racial imbalances in group membership. The claim of racial discrimination in group placement by teachers is not supported by research.

Effects of Ability Grouping

Since black and white students are not equally distributed across groups, ability grouping will contribute to the black-white achievement gap if group placements affect how much students learn. Studies leave no doubt that lower ability groups cover less material than higher groups. This finding says nothing, however, about whether students learn different amounts in ability groups than under heterogeneous arrangements. Indeed, it is conceivable that students in lower ability groups might learn less if placed in heterogeneous groups where material is covered more rapidly.

The best way to estimate the impact of ability grouping is to compare grouped students with similar students who are not grouped. The most extensive meta-analytic reviews of such studies are those of James and Chen-Lin Kulik.[28] Drawing upon their work, Tables 3–4 and 3–5 show mean and

TABLE 3–2 Teachers' Comments and Primary Reason for Group Placement, by Students' Race, Grades Four through Six, 1982[a]

Comment/reason	White Students		Black Students	
	Number	Percent	Number	Percent
Comments about students				
Reading ability	1,435	29.1	604	28.9
General ability	848	17.2	317	15.2
Evidence	373	7.6	193	9.2
Work habits	765	15.5	293	14.0
Behavior or personality	869	17.6	382	18.3
Home background	458	9.3	228	10.9
Physical attributes	88	1.8	31	1.5
Miscellaneous	108	2.1	42	2.0
TOTAL	4,938	100.0	2,090	100.0
Primary reason for placement				
Reading ability	238	40.9	89	39.7
General ability	132	22.7	51	22.2
Evidence	40	6.9	28	1.2
Work habits	88	1.5	23	10.0
Behavior or personality	77	13.2	34	14.8
Home background	7	1.2	5	2.1
Physical attributes	0	0	0	0
Miscellaneous	0	0	0	0
TOTAL	582	100.0	230	100.0

Source: Haller (1995, tables 4 and 5).

a. Student sample comprises 667 whites and 267 blacks. For primary reason for placement, chi square is 10.3, $p < 0.07$.

TABLE 3–3 Displacement of Teachers' Group Recommendations Compared with Predictions from Test Scores, by Students' Race, Grades Four through Six, 1982[a]

Displacement	White Students		Black Students		Total	
	Number	Percent	Number	Percent	Number	Percent
Upward	121	18.1	47	17.6	168	18.0
None	434	65.1	167	62.5	601	64.3
Downward	112	16.8	53	19.9	165	17.7
TOTAL	667	100	267	100	934	100

Source: Haller (1995, table 8).

a. Comparison is with placement that would have resulted from using a student's class rank in scores on the Comprehensive Test of Basic Skills as the sole criterion. The chi square is 1.23, $p = 0.54$.

median effect sizes across studies for five categories of grouping: XYZ, within-class, and across-grade grouping, and enrichment and accelerated classes. Table 3–4 shows effects for grouping versus no grouping in each category. Table 3–5 focuses on the XYZ and within-class grouping categories, showing the same effects separately for high-, low-, and middle-ability groups.[29] The effects are not distinguished for particular racial groups.

In XYZ grouping, which represents the largest number of studies, students are assigned to separate classes based on assessments that often include, but are not restricted to, IQ or achievement test scores.[30] Pedagogically, classes differ in terms of the pace of instruction and the amount of material covered, but not the basic curriculum.[31] In contrast, the four other approaches involve more tailoring of curriculum and instruction to students in the group.

Within-class ability grouping needs no special explanation here; but it should be noted that virtually all of the literature on studies using comparison groups is for mathematics.[32] Cross-grade ability grouping combines students from different classrooms, usually for instruction in a single subject for a small part of each day, after which they return to their regular rooms. Enriched and accelerated programs are for students identified as gifted and talented. Typically, enriched programs not only proceed at a faster pace than heterogeneous classes, but also use more challenging and stimulating materials. Accelerated programs cover material in less time than regular classes, and may or may not use standard curriculums.[33]

For XYZ grouping, the basic finding is that it makes no difference. Table 3–4 shows a mean effect size of 0.03 and a median of 0.04 for fifty-one stud-

TABLE 3–4 Estimated Effect Sizes for Selected Types of Ability Grouping[a]

Effect size and summary statistic[b]	XYZ Number	XYZ Percent	Within-Class Number	Within-Class Percent	Cross-Grade Number	Cross-Grade Percent	Enriched Number	Enriched Percent	Accelerated[c] Number	Accelerated[c] Percent
Range										
Less than 0	21	41	2	18	2	14	3	12	0	0
0 to 0.25	25	49	5	44	4	29	4	16	0	0
0.26 to 0.50	5	10	2	18	5	36	9	36	3	13
0.51 to 0.75	0	0	1	9	1	7	7	28	2	9
0.76 to 1.00	0	0	1	9	2	14	1	4	10	43
Over 1.00	0	0	0	0	0	0	1	4	8	35
Summary statistic										
Mean		0.03		0.25		0.33		0.41		0.87
Median		0.04		0.21		0.30		0.40		0.87
Total studies	51		11		14		25		23	

Source: Author's tabulations from Kulik (1992, tables 1 and 3–6).

a. Sample comprises studies using control or comparison classrooms.

b. Denominator for effect sizes is the pooled standard deviation.

c. In order to average across studies that compare accelerated students to older control groups and those that use same-age comparisons, one standard deviation is added to the effect sizes for studies that use older comparison groups; see text and note 38 for further details.

ies, with a distribution centered quite close to zero.[34] About two-thirds of these studies report separate effect sizes for high, middle, and low groups. Table 3–5 shows that the effect is essentially zero for each ability level.[35]

Studies of the other four types of ability grouping find higher scores for students who are grouped than for those who are not. All the effect sizes for within-class grouping are positive and statistically significant, with small to moderate magnitudes of 0.21 (overall median, Table 3–4) to 0.35 (low-ability median, Table 3–5). Similarly, the effect sizes for cross-grade grouping are 0.33 (overall mean) and 0.30 (overall median).[36]

In regard to enriched and accelerated programs, authors disagree, on methodological grounds, about whether research reviews on ability grouping

TABLE 3–5   Estimated Effect Sizes for XYZ and Within-Class Grouping, by Level of Ability[a]

Effect size and summary statistic[b]	Type of Ability Grouping											
	XYZ						Within-Class					
	High Ability		Middle Ability		Low Ability		High Ability		Middle Ability		Low Ability	
	Number	Percent	Number	Percent	Number	Percent	Number	Percent	Number	Percent	Number	Percent
Range												
Less than 0	12	34	15	52	18	51	0	0	1	17	2	33
0 to 0.25	17	49	11	38	14	40	2	33	3	50	0	0
0.26 to 0.50	3	9	3	10	3	9	4	67	2	33	3	50
0.51 to 0.75	3	9	0	0	0	0	0	0	0	0	1	17
Summary statistic												
Mean		0.10		−0.02		−0.01		0.30		0.18		0.16
Median		0.13		−0.02		−0.01		0.26		0.22		0.35
Total studies	35		29		35		6		6		6	

Source: Author's tabulations from Kulik (1992, tables 1 and 4).

a. Sample comprises studies using ungrouped control or comparison classrooms. Note that roughly one-third of the studies in Kulik's meta-analysis that reported overall effect sizes did not report effect sizes separately for different ability groups. Therefore, fewer studies of XYZ and within-class grouping are covered in Table 3–5 than in Table 3–4.

b. Denominator for effect sizes is the pooled standard deviation.

should include such studies. I believe that they should be included, but with the caution that effects may be overstated and that one has no estimated effect sizes for the students left behind in regular classes.[37] Findings support the claim that for the students smart enough, motivated enough, or lucky enough to be selected, enriched and accelerated programs increase achievement. The median effect sizes are 0.40 for studies of enrichment classes and 0.84 for studies of acceleration.[38] Even if these are overestimates, it seems unlikely that they are so overstated as to warrant ignoring the general finding that tailored instruction appears to promote higher achievement.[39]

In summary, XYZ grouping involves very little tailoring to the needs and proficiencies of particular students and produces virtually no effect on test scores. In contrast, when instruction is tailored, for both the top and the bottom of the distribution, all students appear to benefit (and there is not much impact on disparity). However, enriched and accelerated classes probably do increase the test score gap between high and low scorers, since they benefit students who already score high. To estimate the magnitude of this effect, one would need to know how the students who are left in the regular classes are affected by having the top students removed. None of the studies using comparison group methods addresses this question.

Reading Groups.   Ability grouping for within-class reading instruction has not been studied using control or comparison classrooms. Indeed, the practice is so pervasive that comparison classrooms are probably very difficult to find. As an alternative, some studies have used survey data to control for student characteristics that correlate with group placement. This almost invariably leads to the conclusion that all students would benefit from moving to a higher group or be hurt by moving to a lower group. Because such estimates are strongly biased by omitted variables, they are only useful as upper bounds. Small upper bounds can provide assurance that real effects are small, but large upper bounds are not helpful. Unfortunately, the upper bound estimates that I have seen are moderately large.[40]

Slavin is not far off the mark when he writes: "When comparing high- to low-ability groups, pretest or covariate differences of one or two standard deviations are typical. . . . Are the San Francisco Forty-Niners better than the Palo Alto High School football team, controlling for height, weight, speed, and age? Such questions fall into the realm of the unknowable."[41]

Without studies that use control or comparison groups, one simply cannot know how much reading group placement affects student achievement.[42]

Racial Bias in High School Track Placement

Studies of tracking that use nationally representative samples of high schools from the early 1980s through the early 1990s find no statistically significant racial differences in placements or courses studied, after socioeconomic status, test scores, and past performance are taken into account.[43] Socioeconomic status, however, does bias placements, such that students from families with more education and income are more likely to be enrolled in challenging tracks, even after controlling for test scores.[44] Consequently, racial differences in socioeconomic status account for small racial differences in track placement among students with similar test scores.[45]

Figure 3–1 shows black-white patterns in reported track placement in 1982 and 1992. Even without controls for socioeconomic status or past aca-

FIGURE 3–1   High School Seniors in General, Academic, and Vocational Tracks, by Race, 1982, 1992[a]

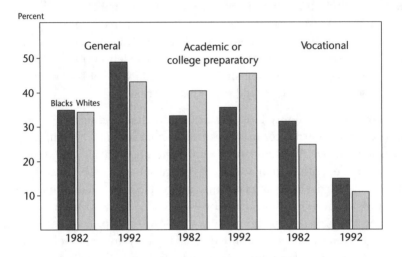

Source: National Center for Education Statistics, *Digest of Education Statistics,* 1996, table 132.

a. Student self-reports. Data for 1982 are from the first follow-up of the High School and Beyond survey; data for 1992 are from the second follow-up survey of the National Educational Longitudinal Study of 1988.

demic performance, differences were relatively small in both years. Over the decade, movement out of vocational tracks was more toward the college prep or academic tracks for whites than for blacks, but even these differences are not large.[46] I suspect, however, that track placements are more racially imbalanced in highly integrated schools. I would also expect to find in the same schools that track placements are more racially skewed within the college prep track, with fewer blacks at the highest levels (honors or advanced placement, for example). The data exist to examine these patterns more carefully than past studies have in order to learn more about whether tracking issues differ depending on the level of racial integration.

Effects of High School Tracking

Blacks are more heavily represented than whites in less academically challenging tracks. So, if track placement affects test performance, tracking could exacerbate the black-white test score gap even if all track placements were based on race-blind criteria, such as past performance. Since most high schools practice tracking, studies that use control or comparison groups from untracked schools are hard to find.[47] Therefore, just as in the ability group-

TABLE 3–6   Differences in Instruction between High School Tracks[a]

Units as indicated

Subject and track	Time in Instruction[b]		Observed Time Off Task[b]	Reported Rating of Class Time Spent On[d]		Expected Homework Time[e]
	Reported[c]	Observed		Learning	Behavior	
English						
High track	82	81	2	2.80	1.48	42
Low track	71	75	4	2.44	1.83	13
Mathematics						
High track	77	81	1	2.77	1.43	38
Low track	63	78	4	2.53	1.81	27

Source: Gamoran and Berends (1987, p. 425), constructed from data in Oakes (1985, pp. 98, 100, 101, 103).

a. Sample comprises 160 classes.

b. Percent.

c. By teachers.

d. By students, on a scale from 1 to 3, where 3 denotes the most time spent.

e. By teachers, in minutes.

ing literature, an alternative methodology is to use survey data to measure the impact of tracking, by simulating the consequences of moving particular students among tracks. For example, Laura Argys, Daniel Rees, and Dominic Brewer examine the effect of tracking on high school mathematics scores using data from the NELS:88.[48] Compared to heterogeneous math classes, they find effect sizes of –0.24 for the below average classes and 0.37 for the honors classes.[49] Because of inadequate controls for selection bias, however, their study undoubtedly overestimates the extent to which tracking helps those at the top and hurts those at the bottom.

Findings from national data probably mask considerable variability across racial and ethnic groups and across different school and community settings. Research on the effects of tracking remains very incomplete.

Observational Differences Are Small.   Jeannie Oakes is probably the most influential writer on the negative effects of grouping and tracking. Oakes concludes that teachers of higher track classes tend to be more enthusiastic, work harder, prepare more, and respond more supportively than do teachers of lower track classes.[50] I believe that this is so. Indeed, Table 3–6, compiled from Oakes's data, shows that time in instruction, time off task, time spent on learning, and expectations of how much time students will spend on homework, all favor the high track. However, only the difference in expected time on homework is impressively large.[51] That most of the differences are surprisingly small may explain why studies of XYZ grouping show few, if any, effects.

Even though Oakes strongly opposes tracking and ability grouping, she acknowledges that instruction is remarkably similar among tracks and groups: "The most significant thing we found is that generally our entire sample of classes turned out to be pretty noninvolving places. As we expected, passive activities—listening to the teachers, writing answers to questions, and taking tests—were dominant at all track levels."[52] Given this similarity of teaching styles and classroom procedures, one should not expect large consequences from alternative grouping and tracking arrangements, except where there are substantial differences in curriculum and courses taken.

Effects Depend on Teachers.   Opponents of tracking also claim that students in lower tracks become resentful and alienated from school, because these tracks confer subordinate status in the school hierarchy. Braddock and Slavin, for example, quote Ollie Taylor, a black eleven-year-old recently assigned to the low track at his school: "The only thing that matters in my life is school, and there they think I'm dumb and always will be. I'm starting to think they're right. Hell, I know they put all the Black kids together in one group if they can, but that doesn't make any difference either. I'm still dumb. . . . Upper tracks? Man, when do you think I see *those* kids? . . . If I ever walked into one of their rooms, they'd throw me out before the teacher even came in. They'd say I'd only be holding them back from their learning."[53]

But is tracking really the problem? Compare Ollie's statement to the following descriptions of life in heterogeneous classrooms, offered in 1996 by black males between the ages of nine and nineteen in the Messages Project in Fort Wayne, Indiana:

> A common message . . . was that teachers . . . favored those kids they believed were smart. Those kids were usually identified as white children. [The black students] reported that they felt unimportant in the classroom and that they were not respected in the classroom. The participants expressed anger and frustration that they were perceived as stupid or of less worth in the classroom. Some suggested that they had been stigmatized by their behavior in a previous grade.

Participants reported an unwillingness to answer questions for fear of appearing stupid. One student reported that his teacher encouraged him in class but then gave him a failing grade. His response to this action: "Makes you want to go home and school not even over and you haven't had lunch yet."[54]

The similarity is evident.

Indications that ability grouping might even make low performers feel better come from Kulik's findings regarding self-esteem. Kulik's meta-analysis of studies with control or comparison groups shows that grouping by ability slightly raises the self-esteem of the lowest groups and slightly lowers the self-esteem of higher groups.[55] Of thirteen studies that estimate the effect of ability grouping on self-esteem, eleven show separate effects for high-ability groups and eleven show separate effects for low-ability groups. Nine of the eleven effect sizes for high-ability groups are negative, with an average of −0.15; nine of the eleven effect sizes for low ability groups are positive, with an average of 0.19. These are small effects, but they clearly run counter to the claim that self-esteem is harmed by ability grouping.

Perhaps more for black children than for whites, teachers play a central role in determining how students feel about their positions in the achievement hierarchy. The focus groups of black students in the Messages Project revealed, for example, that "participants in the College Bridge Program and youth in the younger groups all indicated that they received positive expectations and encouragement from *particular* teachers. Even in situations where participants did not suggest any motivation at home, teacher expectations weighed heavily in their motivation to perform well in school."[56]

There is an extensive literature on the ways in which teachers treat students differently, based on their perceived status as high or low achievers. For low achievers, these include waiting less time for them to answer; giving them the answers or calling on someone else, rather than trying to improve their responses by offering clues or repeating or rephrasing questions; accepting inappropriate behavior or incorrect answers; criticizing them more often for failure; praising them less often for success; failing to give feedback to their public responses; paying less attention; calling on them less often with questions; seating them further from the teacher; demanding less from low achievers (teaching them less, providing unsolicited help); interacting with them more in private than in public, and monitoring and structuring their activities more closely; in grading tests and assignments, not giving them the benefit of the doubt in borderline cases, in contrast to high achievers; less friendly interaction, including less smiling and fewer other nonverbal indicators of support, attention, and responsiveness (such as eye contact); less use of effective but time-consuming instructional methods when time is limited; and less acceptance and use of their ideas.[57] Moreover, students seem to understand the distinctions of status that these behaviors convey.[58] The distinctions will be more important for black students than for whites if, as discussed in chapter 4, blacks are more affected by teacher perceptions than whites, and more represented among students of whom teachers expect less. Unfortunately, researchers know little about the pervasiveness of these practices in classrooms or their consequences for student achievement.

In the end, the fundamental problem is not ability grouping or tracking per se. Instead, for critics and proponents alike, the problem is the expected quality of instruction for the students about whom they are most concerned. If critics could believe that teachers would be assigned fairly, placements would be flexibly based on students' progress, and teaching would really be tailored to children's needs, they might cease to object. Similarly, if proponents felt assured that the quality of instruction for students at the top of the class would not decline under more heterogeneous arrangements, they might lower their defenses.

INSTRUCTIONAL INTERVENTIONS

Few instructional interventions specifically aim to reduce the black-white test score gap. However, many aim to assist children who are at risk of failure— and these children are frequently black.[59] Improving achievement among black students who are at risk of failure is one way to narrow the black-white test score gap.

Credible claims of remarkable progress for a few students, a few classrooms, or a few schools are common enough. Such successes are regarded as special cases, dependent on a few talented leaders.[60] The more interesting and formidable challenge is to replicate success for many students in many classrooms across many schools, by improving the performance of many average teachers and administrators.[61] Recent news reports of small test score improvements for students in several major city school districts suggest that this might be possible. And there is evidence from a current crop of highly touted interventions for students at risk of failure that makes one hopeful. These include Success for All, the Reading Recovery tutoring program, Henry Levin's Accelerated Schools Program, and James Comer's School Development Program.[62] Evidence of effectiveness is most extensive for Success for All.[63]

Success for All

Success for All is the only well-documented widely replicated program to improve elementary school instruction that uses comparison groups and covers large numbers of black children across several states and cities. While most of the children are African American and many others are nonwhite minorities, the program is based on principles that come from general research findings, where race is not a focus. Similar principles underlie many other programs that have not been so carefully evaluated. Hence the findings discussed below are indicative of broader possibilities.

Based at Johns Hopkins University in the Center for Research on the Education of Students Placed at Risk (CRESPAR), and strongly identified with Robert Slavin, the Success for All initiative began in a single Baltimore elementary school in 1987. It currently operates in roughly 300 schools in seventy districts in twenty-four states. It aims to head off later school failure by making sure that students placed at risk have a firm foundation in reading.

Success for All preschool and kindergarten programs emphasize language skills and prereading activities, such as story telling, music, and art. An early reading curriculum based on principles that have been established through research begins in the second semester of kindergarten or in first grade. Students spend most of the day in heterogeneous classes. However, for ninety minutes each day students from first through third (and sometimes up to sixth) grade regroup across classes and grade levels into small classes that are more homogeneous in current reading proficiency.

Regrouping in this way for reading instruction allows all children to receive instruction at the same time. This replaces the typical arrangement for elementary schoolrooms where the teacher works with one reading group at a time while other students work at their seats alone. Students who need help receive an additional twenty minutes of one-on-one tutoring by certified teachers each day. Teachers and tutors assess individual progress every eight weeks and adjust group placement accordingly. While "the particular elements of SFA may vary from school to school," Slavin and colleagues report, "there is one factor we try to make consistent in all schools: a relentless focus on the success of every child. . . . Success does not come from piling on additional services, but from coordinating human resources around a well-defined goal, constantly assessing progress toward that goal, and never giving up until success is achieved."[64] This responsiveness pays dividends when the school receives guidance to ensure the quality of implementation. Schools that attempt SFA without help from CRESPAR tend to witness less student progress.[65]

For measuring effects, schools in the program are matched to comparison schools with students that have similar ethnic profiles, poverty levels, and patterns of past performance on standardized examinations.[66] Further, individual students in the Success for All schools are matched on baseline test scores to individuals in the comparison schools. Table 3–7 shows effect sizes for various examinations for the top 75 percent and the bottom 25 percent of students on pretests.[67] These effect sizes compare scores for Success for All and control students, divided by the pooled standard deviation across all students in the sample, so that the effect sizes for the top 75 percent and those for the bottom 25 percent are directly comparable.[68] All effect sizes are statistically significant at the 0.01 level or better, in favor of Success for All. Moreover, after first grade, effect sizes are larger for the bottom 25 percent of students.[69] In other words, the program not only increases overall performance—it also helps low-scoring students the most.

Aside from the cost of setting up preschool and full-day kindergarten programs, most of the expenses for Success for All can be covered by redirecting funds from existing state and federal programs.[70] Success for All shows that it is possible to produce sustained improvement in students' achievement test scores when schools and communities make the commitment to do so. Commitment alone is not sufficient, however. Success for All draws on years of research on reading instruction, and it also has a well-oiled machine—albeit with less than infinite capacity—to manage dissemination and replication.

Should Instruction Differ for Black and White Students?

For now, I see little reason to believe that different instructional methods or curriculums are required for black and white students—the same work for both.[71] This is not inconsistent with the view that schools should pay special attention to race, ethnicity, and social class, so that students, teachers, and parents from disparate backgrounds might understand one another and collaborate more effectively. Further, it makes sense that some teaching styles and school environments are better suited to children from particular backgrounds. One common hypothesis is that all children learn more when their home and school environments are well matched—that is, when there is cultural congruence. Some black children, especially those from low-income households, come from home environments that differ systematically from the typical white mainstream to which schools and teachers are usually oriented.

Wade Boykin of Howard University, and several of his former students, lead current research on this topic. They find that black children in early ele-

TABLE 3–7   Effects of Success for All on Standardized Test Scores, First through Fifth Grades[a]

Effect sizes

Sample, test, and summary statistic	First Grade	Second Grade	Third Grade	Fourth Grade	Fifth Grade
Top 75 percent					
Durrell Oral Reading	0.46	0.36	0.34	. . .	. . .
Woodcock Passage Comprehension	0.42	0.38	0.44	0.40	0.64
Woodcock Word Attack	0.82	0.68	0.45	0.47	0.70
Woodcock Word Identification	0.51	0.42	0.34	0.42	0.62
Gray Oral Reading Comprehension	. . .	. . .	. . .	0.29	0.48
Gray Oral Passage Reading	. . .	. . .	. . .	0.47	0.73
Summary statistic					
Mean effect size	0.55	0.46	0.39	0.41	0.63
Number of school cohorts	55	36	33	13	6
Bottom 25 percent					
Durrell Oral Reading	0.34	0.43	0.43	. . .	. . .
Woodcock Passage Comprehension	0.41	0.50	0.72	1.29	0.84
Woodcock Word Attack	0.71	0.79	0.46	0.47	0.87
Woodcock Word Identification	0.43	0.66	0.53	1.17	0.99
Gray Oral Reading Comprehension	. . .	. . .	. . .	0.88	0.91
Gray Oral Passage Reading	. . .	. . .	. . .	0.62	0.50
Summary statistic					
Mean effect size	0.47	0.60	0.53	0.88	0.82
Number of school cohorts	55	36	33	13	6

Source: Author's calculations based on Slavin and others (1996, tables 2–6).

a. All effects are different from zero at $p < 0.01$. Note that effect sizes reported for the bottom 25 percent are computed using the overall pooled standard deviation, and therefore differ from those presented by Slavin and colleagues, who use the standard deviation for the bottom 25 percent.

mentary school tend to do better on both memory and reasoning tasks, relative to matched whites, when teachers allow "verve." Allowing verve means mixing or switching back and forth between tasks, rather than focusing on one task at a time for longer periods. Both black and white children tend to improve when tasks are mixed, but black children improve more.[72]

In several other projects, Boykin and Brenda Allen find that black children from low-income backgrounds do better when classes include physical movement, when music plays in the background or is directly part of the instruction, and when they work in teams for group rather than individual rewards.[73] The authors report that these features of the classroom are consistent with the children's descriptions of their home environments. They are careful to say that their findings are context-specific to the children in their samples and may not be applicable to other times and places. This work is in the early stages of development, but it is clearly worth pursuing and broadening.

Do Black Teachers Raise the Test Scores of Black Children?

One version of the cultural congruence hypothesis is that black children should learn more in classes taught by black teachers. The evidence is mixed, however. Richard Murnane studied the learning gains of black students in first through third grade classrooms in New Haven, Connecticut, in 1970–72.[74] He found that black teachers with less than six years of experience were more effective at raising children's reading and mathematics scores than white teachers with the same level of experience. In his multi-variate analysis for gains in both reading and mathematics scores, black teachers were more effective by between a quarter and a half standard deviation, with the greatest difference for reading. Black and white teachers with more than six years of experience were more similar to one another in effectiveness, but black teachers still held a small advantage.

George Farkas and colleagues studied a large school district in the late 1980s.[75] They found that black seventh- and eighth-graders were absent from school less frequently when they had black teachers, other things equal. However, being taught by an African American did not affect students' scores on a social studies test matched to the district-level curriculum. Ronald Ehrenberg, Daniel Goldhaber, and Dominic Brewer use data for eighth- and tenth-graders from the NELS:88 to study gains in tests on history, reading, mathematics, and science.[76] They do not find statistically significant effects of teachers' race on scores for whites, blacks, or Hispanics. Finally, Ehrenberg and Brewer analyze data for 1966 from the Equality of Educational Oppor-

TABLE 3–8   Teachers' Socioeconomic Status and Fall-to-Spring Test Score Gains, by Race of Teachers and Students, First Grade, Baltimore, 1982–83[a]

Teachers' race and measure	Low Socioeconomic Status Teachers		High Socioeconomic Status Teachers	
	Black Students	White Students	Black Students	White Students
Black teachers				
Fall verbal scores	284.5	283.7	280.7	286.6
Gain through spring	54.9	56.2	56.3	85.4
Fall mathematics scores	292.7	298.1	292.5	301.0
Gain through spring	50.4	41.7	39.3	69.1
White teachers				
Fall verbal scores	290.9	274.4	265.6	273.3
Gain through spring	40.7	53.4	61.8	70.0
Fall mathematics scores	274.3	279.3	278.3	289.2
Gain through spring	47.7	61.6	55.5	55.3

Source: Data are from the Beginning School Study for the 1982–83 school year. Data were provided by Karl Alexander, Johns Hopkins University. Sample sizes appear in Table 3–9.

a. Scores are on the California Achievement Test for a random sample of first-graders from twenty Baltimore schools.

tunity study.[77] After controlling for teachers' verbal scores and other characteristics, they find that compared with white teachers, black teachers were associated with lower gains for elementary students and white high school students, and with higher gains for black high school students.

Karl Alexander, Doris Entwisle, and Maxine Thompson analyze data from twenty Baltimore schools in the Beginning School Study in the 1982–83 school year, looking at gains in scores on the California Achievement Test from the beginning to the end of the first grade. They report that "black performance falls short of white only in the classrooms of high-SES [socioeconomic status] teachers."[78] However, Tables 3–8 and 3–9 here show new calculations by Alexander, which suggest that teacher's race and socioeconomic status interact. Compared with all other teachers, high status black teachers are the best at producing gains in both verbal and mathematics scores for white students, but for black students they are average in producing gains in

TABLE 3–9   Effect Sizes of Teachers' Socioeconomic Status on Fall-to-Spring Test Score Gains, by Race of Teachers and Students, First Grade, Baltimore, 1982–83[a]

	Black Teachers		White Teachers	
Item	Black Students	White Students	Black Students	White Students
Effect size for verbal scores	0.03	0.64	0.46	0.37
p value[b]	0.17	0.001	0.05	0.17
Number of students with				
High socioeconomic status teachers	83	42	38	50
Low socioeconomic status teachers	124	102	17	16
Effect size for mathematics scores	−0.37	0.92	0.26	−0.21
p value[b]	0.005	0.0001	0.32	0.44
Number of students with				
High socioeconomic status teachers	83	40	38	49
Low socioeconomic status teachers	120	100	20	28

Source: Author's calculations based on data used for Table 3–8.

a. Scores are on the California Achievement Test for a random sample of first-graders from twenty Baltimore schools. Effect sizes are calculated as the mean gain with teachers of high socioeconomic status minus the mean gain with teachers of low socioeconomic status, divided by the overall standard deviation of student-level gains in verbal or mathematics scores. For both reading and mathematics, the standard deviation in gains (45.4 and 29.9, respectively) is roughly the same as the standard deviation in fall levels (38.2 and 30.4, respectively), so either can be used to compute the effect size.

b. P values are for the within-race effect of teachers' socioeconomic status.

verbal scores and below average for mathematics scores. Only black teachers of low socioeconomic status produce higher gains for black students than for white students, and then only in mathematics, where they produce very low gains for white students.

On the one hand, black teachers of high socioeconomic status may have expected more of white students or worked harder with them than other teachers. On the other, the best results for black students, especially in mathematics, were associated with black teachers of low socioeconomic status and white teachers of high socioeconomic status. It seems quite plausible that low status black teachers and high status white teachers are the most comfortable with black children of low socioeconomic status.[79]

These findings for black teachers of high socioeconomic status are reminiscent of the findings for high status black children by Boykin and colleagues. One might say that in both cases, blacks of high socioeconomic status responded more like whites than whites did: the teachers were the most effective with white students, and the students were the least responsive to teaching practices allowing for verve. Both findings indicate that distinctions of social class may be as important as racial distinctions for understanding the black-white achievement gap and how to reduce it.

THE TEST SCORES OF TEACHERS

Teachers differ greatly in effectiveness. The difference between a good teacher and a bad teacher can be a full grade level of achievement in a school year.[80] But social scientists are unable to identify and measure most of the characteristics that make one teacher more effective than another. No one characteristic is a reliable predictor of a teacher's performance. Nor are most teachers uniformly good or bad in every subject or with all types of students. Nevertheless, research tends to find that teachers who have attended better colleges or scored higher on standardized examinations are more successful at helping their students to score higher.[81] One hypothesis is that teachers who score high on tests are good at teaching students to do well on tests or that they place greater emphasis on test-taking skills. By this reasoning, test score differences overstate differences in how much children have learned. I have found no research that tries to test the validity of this hypothesis or to gauge the magnitude of any associated overstatement of differences in learning.

In this section, I review evidence from Texas in the 1980s showing that teachers' scores were lower in districts where larger percentages of students were black or Hispanic.[82] I also present evidence that this contributed to Texas's black-white test score gap among students. Finally, I use data from Alabama to show that certification testing reduces the number of people who enter the teaching profession with weak basic skills. In the process, it narrows the skill gap between new black and white teachers. I suggest that because rejected candidates would probably have taught disproportionately in black districts, initial certification testing for teachers is probably helping to narrow the test score gap between black and white students.

Teachers' Scores and the Percentage of Black Students

In 1986 the State of Texas tested all of its teachers with the Texas Examination of Current Administrators and Teachers (TECAT), a basic test of literacy skills. Table 3–10 examines teachers' TECAT scores and their students' scores on mathematics achievement tests. Black teachers had lower scores than white teachers by more than one standard deviation, and black teachers were more likely than white teachers to teach in districts with many black students (Table 3–10, column 1).[83] Moreover, white teachers who taught in districts with higher concentrations of black students tended to have lower scores than other white teachers (Table 3–10, column 2). In Texas, as certainly in other states, attracting and retaining talented people with strong skills to teach in the districts where black students are heavily represented is part of the unfinished business of equalizing educational opportunity.[84]

Teachers' Scores and the Black-White Test Score Gap for Students

Estimates using the Texas data and standard econometric specifications for education production functions show that teachers' scores on TECAT are important predictors of their students' mathematics scores (Table 3–10, columns 4 and 6).[85] In addition, teachers' scores help to explain why average mathematics scores are lower in districts with higher proportions of black students.[86] However, one cannot be sure that teachers' test scores affect students' scores, because teachers' scores might be standing in for some omitted variables that are correlated with both teachers' and students' scores. Fortunately, the availability of separate scores for elementary and high school teachers allows me to circumvent this problem.[87] I compare gains in test scores for high school students to those of elementary school students in the same district, and ask whether the difference in gains is larger in districts where the TECAT gap between high school and elementary school teachers is larger.[88] Using this approach, a change of one standard deviation in teachers' TECAT scores predicts a change of 0.17 standard deviations in students' scores over the course of two years.[89]

If the impact of skilled teachers is important and it accumulates, unusually high (or low) TECAT scores in a district should help to pull up (or push down) students' scores, and this impact should become more apparent the longer children are in school. For example, among Texas districts where students do poorly in the early years of elementary school, those in which TECAT scores are unusually high should present much higher scores for students at the end of high school than those in which TECAT scores are unusually low. To test this proposition, I group districts into four sets: unusually high TECAT scores but low first and third grade mathematics scores (sample size is three districts); unusually high TECAT scores and high first and third grade mathematics scores (thirty-seven); unusually low TECAT scores and

TABLE 3–10   Effects of Percent Minority on Teacher Test Scores and of Teacher Test Scores on Student Mathematics Achievement, Texas[a]

	Dependent Variable						
	Tecat Scores		Mathematics Scores, 1988				Differ-ence in Gains[b]
	Black Teachers	White Teachers	Fifth Grade		Eleventh Grade		
Explanatory variable	(1)	(2)	(3)	(4)	(5)	(6)	(7)
TECAT scores							
High school teachers	. . .	. . .	. . .	. . .	. . .	0.128 (3.83)	0.164 (2.09)
Elementary teachers	. . .	. . .	. . .	0.146 (2.96)	. . .	. . .	−0.179 (2.13)
Percent minority students[c]							
Black	−0.031 (3.52)	−0.014 (9.58)	−0.006 (1.81)	−0.0004 (0.12)	−0.019 (7.83)	−0.015 (5.70)	−0.012 (2.07)
Hispanic	−0.013 (2.93)	−0.010 (14.03)	−0.008 (3.35)	−0.007 (2.78)	−0.014 (8.33)	−0.013 (7.73)	−0.007 (1.91)
Mathematics scores, 1986							
Third grade	. . .	. . .	0.394 (12.08)	0.367 (11.41)	. . .	. . .	. . .
Ninth grade	. . .	. . .	. . .	. . .	0.455 (16.92)	0.438 (16.15)	. . .
Additional variables[d]	*	*	yes	yes	yes	yes	yes
Summary statistic							
Number of districts	386	919	884	884	853	853	849
$\overline{R}^2$	0.03	0.19	0.46	0.47	0.72	0.73	0.04

Source: Author's calculations using data from the Texas Education Agency. For a detailed description of the data, see Ferguson (1991a).

a. Observations are for districts and data are district-level averages; Houston and Dallas are not included in the analysis. Teachers' scores on the Texas Examination of Current Administrators and Teachers and students' mathematics scores are measured in standard deviations of the mean scores among districts. In both cases, this standard deviation is roughly one-third the standard deviation of the state-wide distribution of scores among individuals. To correct for heteroskedasticity, each observation in each regression is weighted by the square root of student enrollment. t statistics are in parentheses.

b. Ninth through eleventh grades minus third through fifth grades.

c. Scaled from 0 to 100.

d. Asterisk denotes that constant term is the only control variable. Otherwise, control variables include teachers per student; percent of teachers with master's degrees; percent of teachers with five or more years of experience; percent of adult population with more than high school education; percent of adult population with high school education; log per capita income; percent children in poverty; percent female-headed families; percent in public schools; percent migrant farm worker students; percent English is second language; and indicator variables for city, suburb, town, non-metro city, rural, Mexican border high-poverty district.

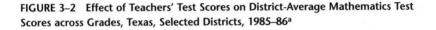

FIGURE 3-2   Effect of Teachers' Test Scores on District-Average Mathematics Test Scores across Grades, Texas, Selected Districts, 1985–86[a]

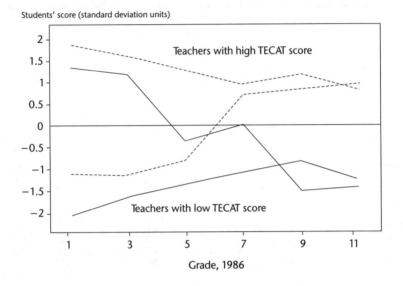

Source: Author's calculations based on data obtained from the Texas Education Agency.

a. Sample comprises three districts with unusually high teacher scores on the Texas Examination for Current Administrators and Teachers and unusually low student scores on mathematics achievement tests; four districts with low teacher scores and high student scores; thirty-seven districts with high scores for both teachers and students; and twenty-five districts with low scores for both teachers and students. For TECAT scores, "high" and "low" mean one standard deviation or more above and below, respectively, the Texas mean; for mathematics scores, the respective criteria are 0.50 standard deviations above and below the Texas mean. Standard deviations for both teachers' and students' scores are from the distribution of district-level means. In each case, the ratio of this standard deviation to that for individuals statewide is 3 to 1.

low first and third grade mathematics scores (twenty-five); and unusually low TECAT scores and high first and third grade mathematics scores (four).[90]

Figure 3–2 graphs the district-average math score for odd-numbered grades from one through eleven for the 1985–86 school year in each of the four sets of districts.[91] Compare the patterns for districts with similar teachers' scores. The dashed lines are districts where teachers' scores are more than a standard deviation above the state-wide mean. Even though they start at opposite extremes for first and third grade scores, the two converge completely by the eleventh grade. The solid lines are districts where teachers' scores are more than a standard deviation below the state-wide mean. Here too, students' scores have converged by the eleventh grade, but at a far lower level. Teachers' TECAT scores seem to dominate outcomes by the eleventh grade.

FIGURE 3–3   Difference between Mean College Entrance Examination Scores of White and Black Teachers by Year of Entry into the Profession, Alabama, 1976–88[a]

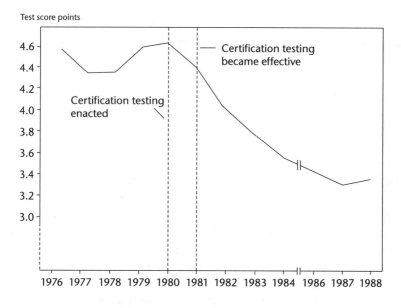

Source: Author's calculations based on unpublished data.

a. Teachers' scores are on the ACT and are not associated with any professional certification tests. The mean score is 20.3, the median score is 20.0, the standard deviation among individual teachers is 3.7, and the standard deviation among district means is 1.4.

Figure 3–2 is not absolute proof of causation, but it is exactly what one would expect under the assumption that teachers' measured skills are important determinants of students' scores. Also, the magnitude of the change from elementary through high school is almost exactly what one would predict with the regression estimates from Table 3–10, column 7. Specifically, for two districts that start with equal student scores but with teacher's scores separated by two standard deviations, the difference in student scores would over ten years accumulate to 1.70 standard deviations.[92] This is a large effect.

Certification Testing and the Black-White Test Score Gap for Students

About twenty-five years ago, working with data from the 1966 Coleman report, David Armor wrote: "Even though black teachers' formal training seems as extensive as that of white teachers, if not more so, their verbal scores indicate that they have far less academic achievement. It is especially ironic that, when schools are concerned with raising black student achievement, the black teachers who have the major responsibility for it suffer from the same disadvantage as their students."[93] Certification testing began in earnest in the early 1980s and, as of 1996, policymakers in forty-three states had enacted some form of initial competency testing for teachers, albeit relying less on research evidence than on their own judgment.[94] Thirty-nine of these states include a test of basic reading, and some also test mathematics skills. This initial testing is usually supplemented by an additional test of professional knowledge, such as the National Teachers Exam, which is used in twenty-one states.

Initial certification testing limits entry into the teaching profession. For example, Figure 3–3 shows that after certification testing was introduced in Alabama in 1981, the test score gap between new black and white teachers fell sharply.[95] Since districts with more black students also have more black teachers in Alabama, a change that increases the average level of skill among incoming black teachers should disproportionately benefit black children.[96] If, as seems likely, this pattern recurs in other states, one should find that black children's scores improve more than do white children's scores after states implement certification testing for teachers.

In the 1980s, certification test passing rates for black teaching applicants in some states were half those for whites.[97] Certainly, some of the black candidates who failed would have become good teachers. However, the relevant question is whether students are, on average, better off with the policy in place. I think that the answer is yes.

CLASS SIZE

Reducing class size is a standard prescription for improving the quality of public education. Currently, the national ratio of pupils to teachers is low by historical standards. Also, as Table 3–11 shows, it is quite similar at schools with a high percentage of black students and those with a high percentage of whites.[98] Despite the strong convictions of many teachers, parents, and advocates of policy that small classes are better, there is no research consensus on whether reducing class size matters, or how much. I summarize this debate briefly and then review recent evidence that reductions in class size may matter more for black children than for whites. If black children have less effective work habits and pose more behavioral challenges, the greater opportunities for individual attention afforded by small classes may be especially important for them.[99]

TABLE 3–11   Mean Class Sizes, by Percent Black Students and Percent Free Lunch Students, 1987–92[a]

Ratio	Percentage Range				
Basis	0 to 20	20 to 40	40 to 60	60 to 80	80 to 100
Black students	17.86	17.40	16.87	16.66	17.55
Free lunch students	17.92	17.37	17.22	17.30	17.32

Source: Author's calculations based on data from the Department of Education's Common Core of Data Surveys, School-Level File.

a. Table reports mean ratio of pupils to full-time equivalent instructional staff. See text for complications in calculating this ratio.

Recent summaries of the research literature on education production functions have reached diametrically opposed conclusions regarding the effect of resources, including class size, on student achievement. This research tries to estimate the effect of class size by comparing student achievement in schools or districts with large and small classes. To obtain valid conclusions, all the correlates of class size that might affect student achievement must be held constant. In a series of influential summaries, Eric Hanushek finds that there is no consistent relationship between class size and student achievement.[100] He reaches this conclusion by counting the number of statistically significant and insignificant, and positive and negative estimates in the literature. However, this "vote counting" method of synthesizing different studies can easily fail to detect effects that actually do exist.

Larry Hedges, Richard Laine, and Robert Greenwald use formal methods of meta-analysis, which have greater statistical power.[101] They analyze most of the same studies as Hanushek and find that several kinds of resources, including class size, have beneficial effects on student outcomes. In the debate that has ensued, each party has applied assumptions that, if correct, favor its own position. However, the pivotal assumptions are not testable, so there is an intellectual standoff.[102]

My own view is that the literature on educational production functions is sufficiently flawed, especially in the way that it treats class size, that neither vote counting nor meta-analysis is reliable. The data are often inadequate and the quality of available studies is variable. Typically, such studies cannot compensate adequately for the possibility of reversed causation. Districts may aim for smaller classes at schools where children are performing poorly, just as individual schools provide smaller classes for children whose past and expected levels of performance are low. Hence classes are sometimes smaller precisely because the children in them have special needs for more individualized attention. This type of reverse causation might obscure any tendency for smaller class size, per se, to produce higher achievement.

Experimental studies offer a more methodologically sound alternative. Tennessee's Project Star (for student-teacher achievement ratio), funded by the state legislature in 1985, is the largest experimental study of class size ever to be conducted.[103] It operated in roughly eighty schools, with 330 classrooms serving 6,500 students. Students were randomly assigned to small classes (thirteen to seventeen students) and large classes (twenty-two to twenty-five students), beginning in kindergarten and continuing through third grade.[104]

Children in small classes gained more in both reading and mathematics achievement than those in large classes from kindergarten through the end of first grade, but the advantage shrank between first and third grades.[105] No one knows what would have happened to the test score advantage if the children in the small classes had shifted to large classes for the second and third grades.[106] However, while the experiment ended at third grade, children who had been in the smaller classes remained at an advantage at least through seventh grade.[107] This was true for both black and white children.

The effect of small classes was larger for black children than for whites, and racial differences in scores were smaller in small classes. Table 3–12 reports effect sizes on the Stanford Achievement Test for kindergarten through third grade. It shows that after kindergarten, the effects for both reading and mathematics were typically twice as large for blacks as for whites. Other analysis shows that the effects for blacks in inner cities were even larger than the average effects for blacks.[108] Recent reanalysis conducted by Alan Krueger has found these results to be robust.[109]

If smaller classes help blacks more than whites in Tennessee, the same is probably true in other states. Nationally, the pupil-to-teacher ratio in elementary schools fell by roughly 25 percent between 1970 and 1990. Therefore, this drop should be reflected in national data on black-white test score differences for elementary students. To examine this hypothesis, I chart the national trend in the black-white gap in test scores, using data from the National Assessment of Educational Progress (NAEP), the only continuing, nationally representative assessment of educational progress for the United States. Its periodic report, *The Nation's Report Card*, shows trends in the performance of nine-, thirteen-, and seventeen-year-olds (or fourth-, eighth-, and eleventh-graders). NAEP scores are standardized, on a scale from 0 to

TABLE 3–12 Project Star, Tennessee: Effects of Small Classes Relative to Large Classes on Reading and Mathematics Test Scores, by Race, Kindergarten through Third Grade[a]

Effect sizes[b]

Test and sample	Grade			
	Kindergarten	One	Two	Three
Reading				
Whites	. . .	0.17	0.13	0.17
Blacks	. . .	0.37	0.33	0.40
Total	0.18	0.24	0.23	0.26
Mathematics				
Whites	0.17	0.22	0.12	0.16
Blacks	0.08	0.31	0.35	0.30
Total	0.15	0.27	0.20	0.23

Source: Nye and others (1993, table 3).

a. Small classes have between thirteen and seventeen children; large classes have between twenty-two and twenty-five children. Scores are on the Stanford Achievement Test.

b. Effect sizes equal differences in scores for small versus large classes, divided by the pooled standard deviation of scores within the respective grade-level cohort.

500, to be comparable not only across time but also across age groups. I discuss only the reading and mathematics trends for nine-year-olds, since this sample is the closest in age to the children in the Tennessee experiment.

Figure 3–4 presents pupil-to-teacher ratios and black-white test score gaps for reading and mathematics for nine-year-olds. It can be seen that nearly all of the inflections in the lines for pupils per teacher are matched in the lines for racial disparity in reading and mathematics scores. Since the NAEP data cover only eight observations for reading and seven for mathematics over a period of twenty-three years, this finding should not be taken as proof of a relationship. However, it seems highly improbable that so many of the inflections match by chance.[110] A simple regression analysis supports this view.[111] Therefore, I strongly suspect that the patterns in Figure 3–4 reflect a systematic causal relationship between class size and the black-white test score gap. One possible explanation is that class size has fallen more in schools that serve blacks. Another interpretation, consistent with the findings from Ten-

FIGURE 3–4   Average Class Size and the Black-White Test Score Gap in Reading and Mathematics, Nine-Year-Olds[a]

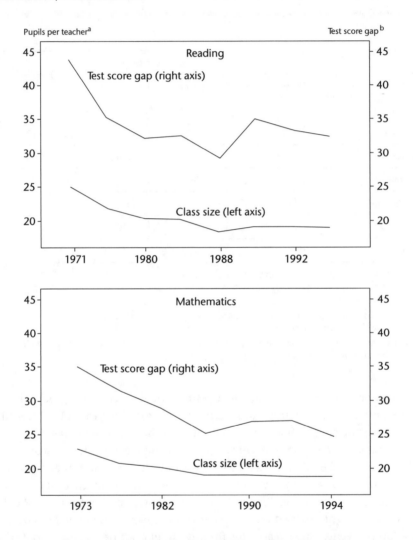

Source: Data on test scores are from National Center for Educational Statistics (1996). Pupils per teacher are from the center's *Digest of Educational Statistics*: data through 1989 are from the 1991 edition; data for 1990–94 are from the 1996 edition.

a. Data up to 1990 were later revised and subjected to smoothing, but this graph represents the original numbers.

b. Average score for whites minus that for blacks from the National Assessment of Educational Progress.

nessee, is that even when the reductions have been equally distributed, their impact has been greater for black students. The effect sizes implied by Figure 3–4 are similar in magnitude to those in the Tennessee experiment.[112]

Given that researchers cannot agree about whether resources such as class size make any difference at all, it is premature to assert that class size affects the black-white test score gap. Nor is it known whether reducing class size does more good for younger or older children. Nevertheless, the matching inflections in trends in the pupil-to-teacher ratio and differences in scores between blacks and whites in Figure 3–4, and the similarity of effect sizes for third-graders in the Tennessee data and those implied by the NAEP data for nine-year-olds, make it quite plausible that much of the reduction in the test-score gap among nine-year-olds in NAEP data may be the consequence of changes in class size after 1971. Smaller classes in the early grades probably help black students more than whites: racial and socioeconomic differences in the effects of class size warrant more research attention than they have received to date.

SUMMARY AND CONCLUSION

The opening section of this chapter strongly confirms that compensatory preschools raise achievement test scores for both blacks and whites by the time they enter kindergarten, but studies disagree on whether the effect is lasting for blacks. I speculate that it might last longer and be more consistent if the primary and secondary schools that blacks attend were more effective. Ironically, if the gains from preschool persist for whites and those for blacks do not, the ideal of universal access to preschool might actually add to the black-white test score gap.

In reviewing the evidence on ability grouping and curriculum tracking, I find no evidence for racial bias in placements, once past performance is taken into account. There is, however, a tendency for children from families of higher socioeconomic status to be in higher ability groups and tracks than measured past performance would predict. In some cases, this contributes to racial differences in placement patterns. The mechanisms that produce these differences should be addressed in future research. In addition, heavily integrated schools should be examined separately from more segregated schools. I suspect that grouping and tracking patterns in heavily integrated schools may have a more distinctly racial component than one sees in the aggregated data.

Because a larger share of black elementary school children are in lower within-class ability groups and lower ability classrooms, any negative effect of ability grouping on children in slower groups adds to the black-white achievement gap. Research shows that grouping children into different classes by ability and varying the pace, but not the curriculum or instructional methods, has little effect on achievement. By contrast, when curriculum or instruction is tailored well to the needs of the different groups, as in cross-grade grouping or enriched and accelerated classes, some children are helped. But it is not known whether it is necessary to separate children in different classes to achieve these positive effects. For within-class ability grouping for mathematics, the little sound evidence that exists suggests that the impacts of ability grouping may be positive for both high and low groups. There is no methodologically sound evidence on the effects of within-class ability grouping for reading. Despite strong opinions on both sides of the debate, the available research yields no general prescription about separating children by ability.

For high schools, black-white differences in curriculum track placement are smaller than in the past, but blacks still remain underrepresented in the most challenging tracks. This is not necessarily evidence of bias. Blacks are represented in rough proportion to what one would predict, given the proficiencies with which they enter high school. The potential consequences of making classes more heterogeneous in terms of student preparation or motivation are unclear.

The most common complaint about ability grouping and curriculum tracking is that students in lower ability groups and in less academically challenging curriculum tracks receive lower quality teaching. Ethnographic research supports this contention. But evidence also indicates that "lows" are taught less well than "highs" when groups and classrooms are heterogeneous. Poor teaching in low ability groups is probably no more harmful than poor teaching to the same students in groups that are less homogeneous. One arrangement appears no better than the other.

When all is said and done, the main concern is quality of teaching. Any instructional regime that is responsive to the needs of individual children and flexible enough not to place ceilings on their progress is likely to benefit all children and, by the very nature of what it means to be responsive, to enhance the opportunities for those who start behind to catch up. Most children in the Success for All program gain relative to comparison groups; those in the bottom 25 percent on baseline measures gain the most. The program mainly serves minorities, most of whom are black. Success for All shows that children can make impressive progress if instruction is good and if problems such as the need for reading glasses or clothing or health care that might interfere with learning are monitored and managed.

Black children do not require exotic instructional strategies that allegedly suit black children better than whites. At the same time, there is some evidence that the fit between home and school learning environments can be improved. A few researchers have identified changes in classroom management for early elementary grades which, compared to standard practices, can help both black and white children, but appear to benefit black children from households of lower socioeconomic status the most. In at least one study, black children from households of high socioeconomic status are the only ones who do not benefit. The school performance of such children receives far less attention than it warrants, since black children are grossly underrepresented among top achievers, whom one would expect mainly to be of high socioeconomic status.

I also consider the evidence on the effects of matching black children with black teachers. On balance, I do not find clear support for the proposition that black teachers are significantly better than white teachers in helping black children to improve their scores on standardized examinations. Indeed, questions about racial differences in teacher effectiveness have not been well researched. The little evidence that we have is mixed. In addition, there is tentative evidence that teachers' social class backgrounds might be as important as race, and in complicated ways. In any case, what surely matters most is that teachers of any race have the skills they need to be effective in the classroom. Some of these skills can be measured by standardized exams. Studies tend to show that teachers' exam scores help to predict students' scores, irrespective of teachers' racial backgrounds.

Teacher certification tests can measure skills that predict student performance and can be effective for screening potential teachers. Most states adopted certification testing for new teachers during the 1980s; Texas and Arkansas are the only states that have tested incumbent teachers for recertification. Scores from Texas suggest that the impact of teachers' basic skills on students' test scores accumulates over time. Texas districts that have more black students have lower scoring teachers, and the latter contribute to lower scores for black students.

In Alabama, testing for new teachers has narrowed the gap in basic skills between incoming black and white teachers. Since black teachers are more often matched with black students, this may gradually increase the quality of teaching in the schools where black teachers tend to be employed—in schools with predominately black student populations. Continued use of certification testing seems warranted, especially if the tests are refined and validated for their ability to identify effective classroom teachers.

Finally, I review evidence from Tennessee's Project Star that class size matters more for black students than for whites, and matters more in the inner city. Like many of the other findings discussed in this chapter, those of Project Star need to be confirmed (or refuted) through replication. Still, the interaction of class size and race is not an especially surprising finding, given the issues discussed in chapter 4. If, as the evidence indicates, black children are more sensitive than whites to teachers' perceptions, and black children's work habits and behavioral problems present greater challenges to teachers, smaller classes that are easier for teachers to manage may have more impact on improving black students' scores than whites'. It is probably correct that having fewer pupils per class can improve learning outcomes and reduce racial disparities. There is no consensus on how small classes should be, but few experts who think that class size matters would condone a pupil-to-teacher ratio much above twenty.

This and the following chapter show that schools can and do affect test scores and the black-white test score gap. Further, both teachers and students have latent aptitudes that can be realized if parents and other stake-holders create the incentives and provide the resources to help elicit these potentials. Whether the black-white test score gap would narrow if schools and teachers became more effective is uncertain. I believe it would. However, if the gap were to remain because *all* children improved, that too would be quite acceptable.

Thanks to Karl Alexander, John Ballantine, William Dickens, James Flynn, Christopher Jencks, Jens Ludwig, Meredith Phillips, and Jason Snipes for helpful discussions and comments on earlier drafts. I am also grateful to Karl Alexander for calculations provided at my request for this chapter. Jason Snipes provided able research assistance.

CHAPTER 4

Teachers' Perceptions and Expectations and the Black-White Test Score Gap

African-American children arrive at kindergarten with fewer reading skills than whites, even when their parents have equal years of schooling. In an ideal world, schools would reduce these disparities. Unfortunately, national data show that, at best, the black-white test score gap is roughly constant (in standard deviations) from the primary through the secondary grades.[1] At worst, the gap widens.[2] Among blacks and whites with equal current scores, blacks tend to make less future progress. This is the second of two chapters on how schools might affect this story. It examines evidence for the proposition that teachers' perceptions, expectations, and behaviors interact with students' beliefs, behaviors, and work habits in ways that help to perpetuate the black-white test score gap.[3]

No matter what material resources are available, no matter what strategies school districts use to allocate children to schools, and no matter how children are grouped for instruction, schoolchildren spend their days in social interaction with teachers and other students. As students and teachers immerse themselves in the routines of schooling, perceptions and expectations both reflect and determine the goals that they set for achievement; the strategies they use to pursue the goals; the skills, energy, and other resources they use to implement the strategies; and the rewards they expect from making the effort. These should affect standardized scores as well as other measures of achievement.

It is a common, if controversial, assumption that teachers' perceptions, expectations, and behaviors are biased by racial stereotypes. The literature is full of seeming contradictions. For example, Sara Lawrence Lightfoot writes: "Teachers, like all of us, use the dimensions of class, race, sex, ethnicity to bring order to their perception of the classroom environment. Rather than teachers gaining more in-depth and holistic understanding of the child, with the passage of time teachers' perceptions become increasingly stereotyped and children become hardened caricatures of an initially discriminatory vision."[4]

Similarly, Reuben Baron, David Tom, and Harris Cooper argue that "the race or class of a particular student may cue the teacher to apply the generalized expectations, therefore making it difficult for the teacher to develop *specific* expectations tailored to individual students. In this manner, the race or class distinction among students is perpetuated. The familiar operation of stereotypes takes place in that it becomes difficult for minority or disadvantaged students to distinguish themselves from the generalized expectation."[5]

On the other side, Jerome Brophy doubts that bias is important: "Few teachers can sustain grossly inaccurate expectations for many of their students in the face of daily feedback that contradicts those expectations."[6] Emil Haller adds: "Undoubtedly there are some racially biased people who are teachers. . . . However . . . the problem does not seem to be of that nature. Conceiving it so is to confuse the issue, to do a serious injustice to the vast majority of teachers, and ultimately to visit an even more serious one on minority pupils. After all . . . children's reading skills are not much improved by subtly (and not so subtly) labeling their teachers racists."[7]

Some aspects of this debate are substantive, but others are semantic. The chapter begins by distinguishing among alternative definitions of racial bias and reviewing evidence on teachers' perceptions and expectations. Later sections address the ways in which teachers' and students' behaviors might be both causes and consequences of racially disparate perceptions and expectations regarding achievement, and might therefore contribute to perpetuating the black-white test score gap.

BIAS IN TEACHERS' PERCEPTIONS AND EXPECTATIONS

Expectations, perceptions, and behaviors that look biased under one criterion often look unbiased under another. However, researchers who study racial bias seldom evaluate their findings by more than a single standard. The discourse that results can be quite perplexing. One body of literature alleges bias and another denies it, but much of this disagreement is really over what is meant by "bias." At least three different conceptions of bias appear in this debate.

Bias is deviation from some benchmark that defines neutrality, or lack of bias. One type of benchmark is "unconditional" race neutrality. By this criterion, teachers who are unbiased expect the same, on average, of black and white students. A second type of benchmark is "conditional" race neutrality—that is, conditioned on observable, measurable criteria. For example, unbiased teachers should expect the same of black and white students on the condition that they have the same past grades and test scores. The third type of benchmark is conditioned not on past performance but on unobserved potential. It requires neutrality—for example, equal expectations and aspirations—in regard to blacks and whites who have equal potential. Insofar as "potential" differs from past performance, however, it is difficult to prove. Assuming that black and white children are born with the same potential (which seems a fair assumption), there is no distinction at birth between unconditional race neutrality and neutrality conditioned on unobserved potential. However, disparities in potential may develop as children grow older; recent literature on brain development, for example, suggests that experience alters potential. Therefore unconditional race neutrality may or may not remain the best approximation to neutrality conditioned on unobserved potential.

Unconditional Race Neutrality

Unconditional race neutrality requires that teachers' perceptions, expectations, and behaviors be uncorrelated with students' race. By this definition, an unbiased perception, expectation, or treatment has the same average value for all racial groups. This benchmark for racial bias is the standard in experimental studies. Such studies typically find that teachers are racially biased.

In experimental studies researchers systematically manipulate information about students. Although race is included, the sample is selected to avoid any correlation between race and the other characteristics noted.[8] In a typical experiment, teachers receive information about students in written descriptions, photographs, videotapes—or occasionally, real children, who act as the experimenter's confederates. The teachers then predict one or more measures of ability or academic performance for each student. If the experiment is run well, the teachers do not discern that race is a variable in the experiment or that the real purpose is to assess their racial biases.

Baron, Tom, and Cooper conduct a meta-analysis of experimental studies that focus on teachers' expectations, sixteen of which deal with race.[9] Teachers have higher expectations for white students in nine of the studies, and for blacks in one study. The differences are statistically significant in five of these studies, all favoring whites. The remaining six studies do not report which group is favored. In these studies, the differences are statistically insignificant. Overall, the hypothesis of identical expectations for black and white students is clearly rejected ($p < 0.002$).[10]

An interesting study by Debra DeMeis and Ralph Turner is not included in Baron, Tom, and Cooper's meta-analysis but supports their conclusion.[11] Sixty-eight white female elementary school teachers, with an average of seven years of teaching experience, were selected from summer school classes at a university in Kentucky during the 1970s. They were played tapes of male fifth-graders responding to the question, "What happened on your favorite TV show the last time you watched it?," and each tape was accompanied by a picture of a black or a white student. DeMeis and Turner asked teachers to rate the taped responses for personality, quality of response, current academic abilities, and future academic abilities. The race of the student in the picture was a statistically significant predictor for each of the four outcomes ($p < 0.0001$).[12]

If the benchmark is unconditional race neutrality, teachers are found to hold racially biased expectations. What should one make of this pervasive racial bias? Consider people who learn from real life that when one flips a coin the odds of getting heads are 60:40. Place these people in an experimental situation where, unknown to them, the odds have been set to 50:50. If each person is then given only one toss of the coin, will their predictions be unbiased? In an environment where real differences in performance between blacks and whites are the norm, if the benchmark for declaring expectations unbiased is unconditional race neutrality, biased expectations are what one should expect.[13] For the same reasons, this type of bias is also pervasive in naturalistic studies—that is, studies in real classrooms, without experimental controls.

Experimental research of this kind establishes that teachers believe certain stereotypes and use the stereotypes in one-time encounters with experimental targets. But it does not establish that the stereotypes would represent biased estimates of the average if they were applied in real classrooms outside the experimental setting. Nor does it prove that teachers in real classrooms treat students inappropriately, or that their stereotypes prevent them from forming accurate perceptions about individual students.

Evidence on Accuracy

For at least two decades, scholars in education have emphasized that teachers' contemporaneous perceptions of students' performance, as well as their expectations of students' future performance, are generally accurate.[14] For example, it has been found that first grade teachers can learn enough about children in the first few weeks of school to predict with some accuracy their rank order on examinations held at the beginning of second grade.[15] Once set, teachers' expectations do not change a great deal. This may be because their early impressions of proficiency are accurate, and the actual rank order does not change much.

There are several possible reasons for stability in rank ordering. First, teachers' perceptions and expectations might be relatively inflexible. Self-fulfilling expectation effects, discussed below, will typically be strongest for the teachers whose expectations are least flexible.[16] For these teachers, correlations between beginning-of-year and end-of-year assessments should be among the highest.[17] A second reason for stability might be that few students try hard to change their positions. A third might be that the pace and style of standard teaching offer few effective opportunities for students who are behind to catch up.[18] Most evidence about the accuracy of teachers' perceptions comes from correlations between teachers' predictions and actual test scores, which typically range between 0.50 and 0.90.[19] At least at the low end of this range, one might alternatively focus on the inaccuracy of the predictions, in "glass half empty" fashion.

I know of only three studies that report separate correlations for blacks and whites. Haller finds that the correlation between teachers' subjective assessments of the reading proficiency of fourth, fifth, and sixth graders and students' scores on the Comprehensive Test of Basic Skills is 0.73 for whites and 0.74 for blacks.[20] Jacqueline Irvine asked teachers to rank 213 fifth, sixth, and seventh graders on general academic ability during the second, tenth, and final weeks of the 1983–84 school year. Correlations between these ratings and scores on the California Achievement Test are similar for blacks and whites.[21] Similarly, Margie Gaines finds that teachers' predictions of performance on the Iowa Test of Basic Skills are as accurate for black students as for whites.[22]

The similarity in correlations for blacks and whites means that the rank order of achievement among blacks is as stable as that among whites, and that teachers achieve similar accuracy in assessing both racial groups. It does not, however, imply that teachers' perceptions or expectations have the same impact on blacks and whites.[23] Neither does it mean that teachers are racially unbiased. In this context, accuracy is not always the opposite of bias. If self-fulfilling prophecy were always perfect, for example, each student's performance would be exactly what the teacher expected. Therefore if expectations were biased, outcomes would be perfectly predicted but biased.

Race Neutrality Conditioned on Observables

The second type of benchmark for measuring bias is race neutrality conditioned on observables. The assumption is that teacher's perceptions and expectations are unbiased if they are based only on legitimate observable predictors of performance, such as past grades, test scores, attitudes about school, and beliefs about personal abilities (for example, as measured by a survey). In this case, the benchmark is only conditionally race neutral: if past performance or another of these predictors is correlated with race, the benchmark will be too. Bias is the difference between the actual perception or expectation and the benchmark for neutrality.

This type of bias can be estimated by regressing a teacher's perceptions or expectations on both race and one or more other explanatory variables that one regards as legitimate predictors of performance. The coefficient of student race then measures the average racial bias among teachers in the sample. This benchmark is probably more appropriate than unconditional race neutrality when considering, for example, whether teachers rely on biased judgments to nominate students for particular curriculum tracks or ability groups. As I show below, it might also be more appropriate for analyzing whether teachers' biases produce self-fulfilling prophecies of poor performance among black students. However, it is not sufficient to distinguish conditional from unconditional race neutrality; the existing literature often makes a further distinction between past performance and future potential.

Race Neutrality Conditioned on Potential

The third type of benchmark—which may or may not equate with either of the two discussed above—is the level of performance that a student could reach at full potential. In this case, bias is found in the perception or estimation of a student's full potential. Full potential equals demonstrated plus latent potential. It is alleged that teachers underestimate the latent potential of blacks more than that of whites.

It is of major concern to African Americans that teachers underestimate the potential of black students, if not necessarily their performance. Consider the following passage from a 1989 report entitled *Visions of a Better Way: A Black Appraisal of American Public Schooling:* "We hold this truth to be self-evident: all black children are capable of learning and achieving. Others who have hesitated, equivocated, or denied this fact have assumed that black children could not master their schoolwork or have cautioned that blacks were not 'academically oriented.' As a result, they have perpetuated a myth of intellectual inferiority, perhaps genetically based. These falsehoods prop up an inequitable social hierarchy with blacks disproportionately repre-sented at the bottom, and they absolve schools of their fundamental respon-sibility to educate all children, no matter how deprived."[24]

An earlier description likewise alleges bias, judged against the benchmark of future potential: "In the middle class white school, student inattention was taken as an indication of teacher need to arouse student interest, but the same behavior in a lower class black school was rationalized as boredom due to limited student attention span. In general, the teachers in the lower class black school were characterized by low expectations for the children and low respect for their ability to learn."[25]

If, as they surely must, perceptions of children's intellectual potential affect the setting of goals in both homes and classrooms, teachers and par-ents who underestimate children's potential will tend to set goals that are too low.[26] Such underestimation is undoubtedly a major problem, irrespective of race. A great waste of human potential and much social injustice results from the fact that teachers are not given the incentives and support they need to set, believe in, and skillfully pursue higher goals for all students, and in par-ticular, for African Americans and other stigmatized minorities. The payoff to searching more aggressively for ways to help children learn would surely be higher than most people imagine.

Reliable estimates of bias related to future potential are not possible, because there is no clear basis on which to measure human potential.[27] Sur-veys find that expressed beliefs in the intellectual inferiority of blacks have moderated over the years.[28] In the General Social Survey, for example, the percentage of whites responding that blacks have less "in-born ability to learn" fell from 27 percent in 1977 to 10 percent in the 1996.[29] There is no way to know the degree to which this reduction is due to changes in beliefs as opposed to changes in social norms. The same survey found in 1990 that when respondents were not constrained to attribute differences to genetic factors, 53 percent agreed that blacks and Hispanics are less intelligent than whites. Indeed, 30 percent of blacks and 35 percent of Hispanics agreed.[30]

Many experts think that genetic differences are at least partially to blame for existing black-white differences in academic achievement. A 1984 sur-vey questioned 1,020 experts on intelligence, most of them professors and university-based researchers who study testing, psychology, and education. Almost half (46 percent) expressed the opinion that black-white differences in intelligence are at least partially genetic. Fifteen percent said that only environment is responsible, 24 percent regarded the available evidence as insufficient, and 14 percent did not answer; in other words, only 15 percent clearly disagreed.[31] With expert opinion slanted so strongly in favor of the genetic hypothesis and widespread media attention paid to books like Richard Herrnstein and Charles Murray's *The Bell Curve,* there is little prospect that "rumors of inferiority" will cease or that racial differences in estimates of students' potential will disappear.[32]

Writers concerned with bias in the estimation of potential often claim that it leads to self-fulfilling prophecies. Their point is that children would achieve more if teachers and other adults expected that they could. In most cases, it might be more appropriate to describe bias of this type as producing expectations that are "sustaining" of past trends.[33] Such an expectation is likely to block the absorption of new information into a decision process, and thereby to sustain the trend that existed before the new information was received.

SELF-FULFILLING PROPHECY

A self-fulfilling prophecy occurs when bias in a teacher's expectation of a student's performance affects that performance. Self-fulfilling prophecies may be associated with any of the three types of bias discussed above, but only those associated with the second type—where the benchmark is conditioned on observables—can be well measured. The basic concept was introduced into social science by Robert Merton in 1948, and Robert Rosenthal and Lenore Jacobson's work on the topic sparked a small industry of studies during the 1970s and early 1980s.[34] The effect shows up (and sometimes fails to do so) in a wide range of experimental studies with animals and with human subjects.[35] Experimental studies in education typically involve the random assignment of students to groups that have been labeled as high or low performing.

The successful instigation of self-fulfilling prophecies by researchers requires that (1) teachers believe false information about students; (2) teachers act on the information in ways that students can perceive; and (3) students respond in ways that confirm the expectation. The effect can fail to appear—and it often does—if any one of these conditions fails.[36] In experiments that confirm the effect, groups labeled as high performing outperform those labeled as low performing. A meta-analysis by Mary Lee Smith identifies forty-four estimates of effect sizes for reading scores, with an average of 0.48 standard deviations distinguishing students with high and low labels.[37] The average across seventeen effects for mathematics is much smaller, at 0.18. Why the effects should be smaller for mathematics than for reading is unclear. Perhaps mathematics instruction is less flexible, and therefore less affected by teachers' perceptions.

Brophy, a leader since the early 1970s in research on teacher expectations, asserts that on average, teachers' expectations in real classrooms probably make only a small difference to their students' achievement.[38] He adds the caveat, however, that teachers who hold rigid expectations and permit these to guide their interactions with students can produce larger effects. It is plausible, but not established in any literature that I have seen, that expectations of black students might be more rigid than those of whites. Moreover, expectation effects might accumulate from year to year. Surprisingly, there appears to be no good evidence on the degree to which expectation effects accumulate. If small effects accumulate, they could make a larger difference over time. In the short run, even a small difference due to expectations could push a score across the boundary between two grade levels, and thereby become consequential.

In naturalistic studies, the magnitude of self-fulfilling prophecy can be estimated as the coefficient on a teacher's expectation measure in an equation where the dependent variable is the student's ultimate performance at the end of a school year. Assuming that the estimated effect of the teacher's expectation is not simply a stand-in for omitted variables, the idiosyncratic contribution of the teacher's expectation is the consequence of bias.[39] In some cases, teacher biases exist but do not affect actual scores or grades, either because teachers do not act on their biases or because student performance does not respond to the biased actions that teachers take. Finally, it is also important to note that a teacher's perception of current performance and expectation of future performance can differ, one showing bias while the other does not.[40]

Testing for Racial Differences in Expectancy Effects

Lee Jussim, Jacquelynne Eccles, and Stephanie Madon are the only researchers who have tested for racial differences in the impact of teachers' perceptions on students' test scores.[41] They collected teachers' perceptions of current performance, talent, and effort in mathematics for 1,664 sixth-graders in October 1982.[42] They then tested for what they call racial stereotype bias—that is, whether a student's race predicts teachers' perceptions after controlling for background factors, including previous grades, previous test scores, self-perception of mathematical ability, self-reported level of effort, and self-reported time spent on homework. This is an example of the second type of bias defined above, using a benchmark of racial neutrality conditioned on observables, including past performance. They find no evidence of racial stereotype bias in teachers' perceptions of current performance, talent, or effort for this sample of sixth-graders.[43] The coefficient on student race is small and statistically insignificant.[44]

If racial differences in teachers' current perceptions are explained by students' past performance and attitudes, then these perceptions can only be an important source of a *future* black-white test score gap if they affect blacks and whites differently. This is precisely what Jussim, Eccles, and Madon find when they analyze the effects of teachers' perceptions of performance, talent, and effort in October on mathematics grades and scores on the mathematics section of the Michigan Educational Assessment Program (MEAP) the following spring semester, in May 1983.[45] For both grades and scores, the estimated impact of teacher perceptions is almost three times as great for African American students as for whites.[46] Effects are also larger for girls and for children from low-income families. Further, the effect is cumulative across disadvantages or stigmas: black children from low-income backgrounds experience the effects of both race and income. Teachers' perceptions of student effort do not affect MEAP scores but do affect grades, even though they are not strongly correlated with self-reports of effort.[47]

What might explain racial differences in the consequences of teachers' perceptions? One possibility is that the result is simply a statistical artifact due to omitted variable bias. This seems unlikely.[48] More plausibly, teachers are less flexible in their expectations of blacks, females, and students from low-income households. Or, as Rhonda Weinstein speculates, "minority status may play a role in the vulnerability with which students respond to teacher expectations. Differences in cultural values (family compared to school) may serve to immunize some children from the impact of teacher views of their performance or alternately to heighten their susceptibility to the dominant viewpoint."[49] Perhaps the behaviors of both teachers and students are affected by the combination of the student's race and the teacher's perception of performance. These possibilities are addressed below.

Table 4–1 shows simulated mathematics scores and grades and teachers' performance ratings, holding all other student characteristics constant. For both blacks and whites, there is a positive relationship between teachers' performance ratings in October and the students' grades and scores in May. However, the effect is stronger for blacks. Blacks who receive the highest performance rating (5) in October are predicted to outperform whites who receive that rating. Conversely, blacks who receive the lowest rating in October lag an estimated half standard deviation behind whites with that rating.

TABLE 4–1   Spring Standardized Grades and Test Scores in Mathematics and Fall Performance Ratings, Sixth Grade, 1982–83[a]

Standard deviation units

Measure and race	Fall Performance Rating				
	1	*2*	*3*	*4*	*5*
Predicted spring grades					
Blacks	−1.00	−0.57	−0.14	0.28	0.71
Whites	−0.43	−0.25	−0.07	0.11	0.28
Difference	−0.57	−0.32	−0.07	0.18	0.43
Predicted spring scores					
Blacks	−0.79	−0.46	−0.13	0.20	0.53
Whites	−0.30	−0.17	−0.04	0.09	0.21
Difference	−0.50	−0.29	−0.09	0.11	0.31

Source: Author's calculations based on data from Jussim, Eccles, and Madon (1996, pp. 308–11).

a. All other student characteristics are held constant. Grades and test scores relate to the mathematics section of the Michigan Educational Assessment Program. Fall ratings are such that 1 denotes the lowest level of current performance and 5 denotes the highest level. The overall mean is zero and the standard deviation is one.

If teachers tend to be accurate both in current perceptions and in expectations of future progress, the findings of Jussim, Eccles, and Madon require that teachers expect the pattern shown in Table 4–1.[50] This would represent stereotype bias for expected progress, even if there is no such bias in the evaluation of October performance. The accuracy of the stereotype might reflect self-fulfilling prophecy in the teacher's expectation, or it might not. Evidence that teacher perceptions affect subsequent performance more for blacks than for whites suggests either that black students respond differently than whites to similar treatment from teachers, or that teachers treat black and white students differently, or both.

DO BLACK AND WHITE CHILDREN RESPOND TO TEACHERS DIFFERENTLY?

The finding that black students respond more strongly to teachers' beliefs has not been replicated, but it is consistent with findings from several other studies that ask related questions. In one recent study, Clifton Casteel asks eighth- and ninth-graders whom they most want to please with their class-work.[51] "Teachers" is the answer of 81 percent of black females, 62 percent of black males, 28 percent of white females, and 32 percent of white males. Whites are more concerned with pleasing parents. Doris Entwisle and Karl Alexander find that teachers' ratings of first-graders' maturity have larger effects for blacks than for whites on both verbal and arithmetic scores on the California Achievement Test (CAT).[52] Judith Kleinfeld finds that high-school students' perceptions of their own ability are more correlated with perceived teacher ratings of ability for blacks, but more correlated with perceived parent ratings for whites.[53] Irvine reaches similar conclusions.[54]

Jussim, Eccles, and Madon suggest, and I agree, that Claude Steele's recent work offers one reason why black and white students might respond differently despite identical classroom conditions.[55] Steele identifies a phenomenon that he calls stereotype threat, and the resulting stereotype anxiety, that can affect members of any stigmatized group. When the stereotype concerns ability, "threatened" individuals are anxious not to perform in ways that might corroborate the stereotype. They fear that the stereotype might become the basis of pejorative judgments by others, as well as of their own self-perceptions.

One effect of this anxiety is "a disruptive apprehension" that can interfere with performance. Under stressful test conditions, Steele finds that women and blacks perform worse when they are primed to be conscious of their race or gender. Steele theorizes that when the anxiety is sufficiently intense, it can provoke a response of "disidentification" with the task at hand or with the general category of tasks. Students decide not to consider performance in that particular domain as important to personal goals or self-perceptions.

Steele has tested this idea only for high-achieving students at highly selective colleges. The degree to which stereotype threat and anxiety might apply to students in primary and secondary schools remains to be investigated. Jussim, Eccles, and Madon's findings were for sixth-graders. Are children this young aware enough of stereotypes to be susceptible to stereotype threat or stereotype anxiety? Perhaps.[56]

Susan Gross studied the mathematics performance of students in a racially integrated suburb of Washington, D.C., during the 1985–86 school year.[57] In fourth grade, 92 percent of blacks and 86 percent of whites who were above grade level on the number of mathematics competencies that they had mastered scored in the eighth and ninth stanines (that is, ninths) of the California Achievement Test for Math (CATM). In the sixth grade, 82 percent of whites who were above grade level in completion of competencies were in the eighth and ninth stanines on the CATM. For blacks, however, the figure was only 68 percent.[58] Gross points out that for the sixth-graders, this pattern of performance on the CATM was inconsistent with in-school performance, and hence she cautions against basing ability group placements on test scores alone.

Gross and her team also conducted focus groups with middle school and high school students. She reports "a deep commitment on the part of high-achieving black students to do well in mathematics so that they could move on to good colleges and professional careers." But the same students felt "deep frustration at the incidents of racism they had experienced in the lower expectations they had perceived from teachers and other students. . . . This was particularly true regarding the honors-level black students who reported that each year they had to prove they were capable of doing honors work."[59] Moreover, it was common knowledge that children in upper elementary grades felt the same types of pressure.[60] If the CATM was regarded as a test of ability for sixth-graders, Steele's theory could well explain why black students who were above grade level on competencies got lower CATM scores than their white peers.[61]

Gross appears to find evidence of the type of disengagement that Steele hypothesizes, which could help to explain the larger negative impact on black students that Jussim, Eccles, and Madon find when their performance is perceived to be low. Teachers told Gross that black students were overrepresented among students who were "least studious" and "did not come to their classes prepared to work or in the proper frame of mind to attend fully to instruction."[62]

Both teachers and administrators reported that black parents were less supportive of the school's mission than white parents. However, when Gross convened parents in focus groups, black parents were more supportive of the idea that their children should strive for the higher level classes in mathematics, even if that meant getting lower grades. White parents tended to say that their children should stay in the top sections only if they were likely to do well. Possibly the black parents were sending a mixed message: "Shoot for the top, but if you don't do as well as the white kids, we'll understand."[63] If black children sense more ambivalence from their parents than do white children, their teachers' opinions might take on a special significance for them, as the statistical evidence appears to show.

In a study inspired by the work of John Ogbu, Roslyn Mickelson distinguishes "abstract" from "concrete" attitudes in twelfth grade students.[64] She finds that concrete attitudes predict cumulative high school grade point averages, but abstract attitudes do not.[65] Her measure of abstract attitudes reflects mainstream ideology, standard optimistic rhetoric about education and the American dream. Respondents were asked to indicate their level of agreement with the following statements:

- Education is the key to success in the future.
- If everyone in America gets a good education, we can end poverty.
- Achievement and effort in school lead to job success later on.
- The way for poor people to become middle class is for them to get a good education.
- School success is not necessarily a clear path to a better life.
- Getting a good education is a practical road to success for a young black [white] man [woman] like me.
- Young white [black] women [men] like me have a chance of making it if we do well in school.
- Education really pays off in the future for young black [white] men [women] like me.

In contrast, her measure of concrete attitudes includes questions that elicit doubt and ambivalence about education as a route to mainstream success:[66]

- Based on their experiences, my parents say people like us are not always paid or promoted according to our education.
- All I need to learn for my future is to read, write and make change.
- Although my parents tell me to get a good education to get a good job, they face barriers to job success.
- When our teachers give us homework, my friends never think of doing it.
- People in my family haven't been treated fairly at work, no matter how much education they have.
- Studying in school rarely pays off later with good jobs.

Students might acquire such concrete attitudes from routine, informal, personal interaction with friends, parents, and other adults, as well as from the broader society.

Mickelson finds that blacks express greater agreement than do whites with the optimistic but abstract beliefs about success and the American dream. However, in their concrete attitudes, which are actually expectations for fairness, blacks are less hopeful than whites. Table 4–2 summarizes the pattern (on both indexes, higher values correspond to higher levels of agreement). This finding suggests why surveys usually find that blacks subscribe to main-

TABLE 4–2   Abstract and Concrete Beliefs about the Importance of Education for Success, by Race and Socioeconomic Background, Twelfth Grade, Spring 1983[a]

Mean score

Socioeconomic status and measure	Males			Females		
	Black	White	Effect Size	Black	White	Effect Size
White collar						
Abstract beliefs	5.50	5.06	0.58	5.27	5.09	0.24
Concrete beliefs	4.38	4.90	−0.53	4.43	5.00	−0.58
Sample size	56	224	. . .	84	241	. . .
Blue collar						
Abstract beliefs	5.28	4.99	0.38	5.34	5.21	0.17
Concrete beliefs	4.19	4.54	−0.36	4.19	4.81	−0.63
Sample size	138	100	. . .	140	93	. . .

Source: Mickelson (1990).

a. Sample is taken from eight Los Angeles high schools. Classification as white collar or blue collar is based on a combination of standard blue collar–white collar distinctions and parental education. On each index, higher values denote higher levels of agreement with the given abstract or concrete beliefs; see text for details. Racial differences in abstract scores are significant with $p < 0.05$; class differences for concrete scores are significant with $p < 0.0005$; racial differences for concrete scores are significant with $p < 0.0001$. Full sample standard deviations are 0.76 for abstract scores and 0.98 for concrete scores. Each effect size equals the black-white gap in the respective measure divided by the full-sample standard deviation for either abstract or concrete beliefs, whichever applies.

stream values as much as do whites, but behave in ways that show less commitment to mainstream success.

DO TEACHERS TREAT BLACK AND WHITE STUDENTS DIFFERENTLY?

I know of only four experimental studies that deal with teachers' treatment of black and white students, all dating from the 1970s.[67] These studies control differences between students by matching or random assignment. As with most of the experimental literature already discussed, the experiments are contrived one-time encounters. All four experiments find that teachers are less supportive of black than white students.

In Marylee Taylor's experiment, for example, a six-year-old student was said to be watching from behind a screen as college students of education undergoing teacher training taught a prescribed lesson.[68] In each case, the phantom student was described as black or white, male or female, and of high or low ability. The teachers were told that the students could see and hear them and would respond to their instructions by pushing buttons to activate ten lights on a panel. In fact, all of the "student feedback" was provided by a single adult, who was blind to the description of the "student" given to any particular teacher. Taylor finds that black phantom students received briefer feedback after mistakes (the standardized effect size is 0.613), less positive feedback after correct responses (0.423), and fewer "helpful slips of the tongue"—that is, unauthorized coaching (0.536). Each of the experimental studies suggests that some teachers may help white students more than blacks, and that the differences may be large enough to have nontrivial effects on performance.

Studies of real classrooms confirm this hypothesis. While some find no racial differences, more find differences favoring white students.[69] The studies that do find differences are probably more likely to be published. Nonetheless, if the benchmark is unconditional race neutrality, there is strong evidence of racial bias in how teachers treat students. It is nearly impossible in naturalistic studies to determine whether teachers would appear racially biased if one controlled racial differences in students' behaviors, work habits, and social skills. But since students and parents cannot read a teacher's mind, they may *think* that differences in treatment reflect favoritism. And when teachers appear biased, trust may be eroded and relationships spoiled.

Evidence on Possible Reasons for Differential Treatment

In general, there is no way of knowing whether teachers' perceptions of students' attitudes and behaviors are accurate. Jussim, Eccles, and Madon's finding that teacher perceptions of effort predict grades but not standardized test scores suggests that teachers' perceptions of effort may not be accurate, as does their finding that teachers' perceptions of effort were only moderately correlated with students' self-reports.

In 1990 the Prospects survey, conducted for the Department of Education, asked a national sample of teachers to rate specific students in their classes on the following criteria: "cares about doing well," "gets along with teachers," and "works hard at school."[70] The three response categories ranged from "very much" to "not at all." Teachers rated black children lower than whites by a statistically significant margin on all three items. To measure the racial differences in these ratings, I subtract for each racial group the percentage with the lowest ranking from the percentage with the highest ranking in

FIGURE 4–1   Teachers' Perceptions of Students' Levels of Effort[a]

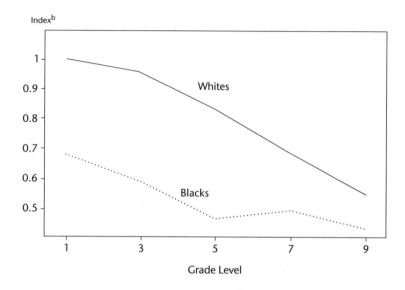

Source: Author's calculations based on data collected in the early 1990s for the Prospects study of educational growth and opportunity; see Puma and others (1993).

a. Teachers rated students on the following criteria: cares about doing well, gets along with teachers, and works hard at school. Data for first-graders represent one cohort (1,979 black; 5,333 white); third- and fifth-graders represent a second cohort (1,276 black; 4,045 white); seventh- and ninth-graders represent a third cohort (393 black; 2,424 white). Numbers are weighted to be nationally representative. Chi-square tests on each item for each grade show that through the seventh grade, all black-white differences are statistically significant at the 0.01 level or better. For the ninth grade, the differences are not statistically significant, but the black sample is quite small.

b. Composite index for black and white students in first through ninth grades, constructed such that white first-graders are equal to 1 and higher index values are better; see text for details.

each grade, and then sum the results for the three questions. Higher values of the index are therefore better. The index is standardized to equal 1 for white first-graders.

Figure 4–1 shows the means for blacks and whites by grade level. As can be seen, teachers perceive the greatest difference between black and white students in the early years of elementary school. After the fifth grade the gap narrows, but it does not completely close. The apparent similarity in how blacks and whites relate to school by ninth grade is consistent with data on eighth graders from the 1988 National Education Longitudinal Study (NELS). Several authors have remarked on the similarity of black and white attitudes in the NELS.[71] But because that survey did not reach students earlier in their school careers (and also because it did not ask the right questions), it may lead people to underestimate the degree to which racial differences in work habits, behavior, and attitudes below the eighth grade affect teacher-student relations and the black-white test score gap.

Reciprocal Effects between Student Behavior and Teacher Performance

Teachers' judgments about how much they enjoy teaching students inevitably affect their own behaviors. This can apply in regard to entire classrooms and in regard to individual students. Teachers may respond to difficult students by withdrawing support.[72] This could help account for Jussim, Eccles, and Madon's finding that teachers' perceptions at the beginning of the school year, although unbiased, are stronger predictors of end-of-year performance for black students than for whites. Specifically, among equally low-performing black and white students, black students might be perceived as more difficult, and therefore receive less teacher support than whites; while among equally high-performing students, black students might be perceived as less difficult, and therefore receive more teacher support than whites.[73] I have not found any quantitative research in naturalistic settings that controls for initial student performance and systematically measures racial differences in how much positive reinforcement students provide to teachers. However, on average black *students* may give *teachers* less positive reinforcement than do white students with similar levels of beginning-of-year performance.

For example, Willis and Brophy asked twenty-eight first grade teachers to nominate three children to each of four groups, with the following results:[74]

> *Attachment:* If you could keep one student another year for the sheer joy of it, whom would you pick?
>
> Regarding boys in the *attachment groups,* the teachers made more positive comments about their clothing . . . more often assigned them as leaders or classroom helpers . . . high ability [student] who is well-adjusted to the school situation, conforms to the teacher's rules and "rewards" the teacher by being somewhat dependent upon her and by doing well in his schoolwork.
>
> *Indifference:* If a parent were to drop in unannounced for a conference, whose child would you be least prepared to talk about?
>
> Boys in the *indifference group* were described as more likely to . . . have a "blank" eye expression . . . to have a disinterested or uncooperative parent . . . to have failed to live up to the teachers' initial expectations. . . . Never-

theless, the Metropolitan Readiness Test scores of these boys did not differ significantly from those of their classmates.

Concern: If you could devote all your attention to a child who concerned you a great deal, whom would you pick?

Boys in the *concern group* were especially likely to be described as . . . having a speech impediment . . . being active and vivacious, seeking teacher attention . . . needing readiness work, having generally poor oral and verbal skills . . . and having generally low abilities. . . . [These children are] perceived as making legitimate demands because they generally conform to classroom rules but are in need of help due to low ability.

Rejection: If your class was to be reduced by one child, whom would you be relieved to have removed?

Boys in the *rejection group* were described as being more likely to be nonwhite than white, coming from intact families in which both parents were living, as being immature and not well-adjusted, as being independent, as being loud or disruptive in the classroom, as being rarely inactive or not vivacious . . . as needing extra help because of generally low ability, as needing readiness work. . . . These children did not differ significantly from their classmates on the Metropolitan Readiness Test scores despite the teachers' comments about low ability.

The rejection group is the only one in which nonwhite boys are overrepresented in teachers' remarks. Clearly, much more was involved in shaping the teacher-to-student relationship than simply the child's initial ability or academic performance, at least in first grade. Children's work habits and behaviors (and sometimes even their parents' behaviors) affected teacher preferences. Figure 4–1 has shown that in the 1990s teachers perceive that blacks rate lower than whites on attitudes, effort, and behavior. Based on these patterns, my guess is that *on average* teachers probably prefer to teach whites, and *on average* they probably give whites more plentiful and unambiguous support.

Mismatches of race between teachers and students do not appear to be the central problem. Even black teachers need help in learning to cope with some of the special demands that black children from disadvantaged backgrounds may present.[75] Paula, a young black teacher enrolled in a program to help teachers understand, manage, and teach difficult students, admitted:

The first thing I knew was that they were just BADD. I know part of the problem was myself because I was saying things that I probably shouldn't have said because they got me so upset and I wasn't able to handle it. . . .

I felt that being black I would automatically know more, and so forth, and in ways I think I do, but [the training program] has helped me to understand things from many perspectives. . . . Black teachers who have been in different programs . . . haven't got this cultural awareness and I know that because they're so negative. . . . A lot of them aren't culturally sensitive to their own culture.[76]

It remains an open question how much difference teachers' preferences about whom they teach make to the educational outcomes of students. In difficult schools there may be many "burned out" teachers, who are simply going through the motions and waiting for retirement. It is also unclear to what degree this pattern of bad student behavior and teacher burnout is racially distinct. In many classrooms, teachers and students are embroiled in conflict and confusion that they lack the skills and external support to resolve. Research to analyze the effectiveness and replicability of programs such as that in which Paula was enrolled should be a priority in order to improve the schooling of black children in settings where behavior is a problem.

Indeed, signals about performance can have racial overtones, and these can interfere with teacher-student relations and with learning. A summary of focus group discussions with black males between the ages of nine and nineteen in Fort Wayne, Ind., in 1996 reports: "Students expressed disappointment in their grades when moving from one class to another, but could not explain the differences from year to year with the exception of saying that the teacher was prejudiced. Racial prejudice of the teachers was a perception that was common in all the groups. . . . The teacher who encouraged and expected more from the students was always mentioned, but only as the exception."[77] Teachers in integrated schools can be "biased" in ways as simple as reinforcing a propensity of white children to speak more often in class.[78] As a result, black students may assume that the teachers think whites are smarter or like the white students better. How teachers communicate about academic ability—especially in integrated schools where the performance of whites is superior—can affect the degree to which black students disengage from the pursuit of excellence, or alternatively, stay engaged and aim for mastery.[79]

RACE AND THE ROLE OF PEER CULTURE

What teachers communicate to students about ability is important, because positioning in the hierarchy of *perceived ability* has social significance for both individuals and groups—and this, in turn, has feedback effects on school performance. Readily observable racial patterns in messages from teachers or black-white differences in actual performance can produce stereotype anxiety and can blur the distinction between racial and achievement-related aspects of students' identities.

Shared stereotype anxiety probably encourages black students to form peer groups that disengage from academic competition. Members may secretly want to *be* "smart," like the students (often disproportionately white) whom teachers favor. Nevertheless, they may also resent any effort by black peers to defect from group norms by *acting* smart. In one school district with which I am currently familiar, it is common to hear that some black students accuse their peers of "acting white" when their personal styles seem to resemble those of the smart white kids. However, the same black students who make the accusations resent any insinuation that they themselves are stupid. There is duality. It seems that being smart is valued, but acting smart—or aspiring to move up in the achievement hierarchy, with the associated peer and teacher relationship patterns—is frowned on, at least in others.

How much these factors help to account for the black-white test score gap is uncertain. Philip Cook and Jens Ludwig (1997) conclude that adolescent peer pressure and the acting white hypothesis bear virtually no responsibility for black-white differences in academic performance. Their study advances the debate, but it leaves the central question unresolved, as I explain in a comment following that chapter. Nevertheless, rather than simply attacking black peer culture, reducing the amount of unresponsive and ineffective teaching is almost surely a more important response to the black-white test score gap.

RESPONSIVE TEACHING

As noted at the outset of this chapter, the average black child arrives at kindergarten with fewer academic skills than the average white child. Schools may then push students along in ways that sustain or add to racial disparities, validating the expectation that black-white differences in achievement are normal, perhaps even inevitable. But if instruction is appropriately stimulating and responsive to children's progress, teachers' expectations may be neither self-fulfilling nor sustaining. The more inviting and responsive instruction is to children's own efforts to improve, the less teachers' initial perceptions and expectations will predict later success.

Research that measures how instructional methods affect the accuracy of teacher expectations is rare. One relevant set of studies deals with "wait time"—that is, how long a teacher waits for students to raise their hands, for students to begin talking, and for students to continue talking after a pause. Minority students in integrated classrooms participate more when wait time is longer. This improves their performance relative to whites and changes teacher expectations.[80]

Corrective feedback is probably more significant than wait time, however. In a study that does not mention race, Thomas Guskey looks at forty-four intermediate and high school teachers who taught various subjects in two metropolitan school systems.[81] Each teacher taught two matched classes, after receiving training. One class was instructed using the teacher's standard methods, and the other was taught with a "feedback and corrective" process learned in the training. Both classes received the same final examination and grading standards. Guskey compared teacher ratings of "probable achievement" from early in the semester with final grades and examination scores, and also with end-of-term ratings of "achievement potential."[82] For ten teachers, the training made no difference to their students' performance. However, for thirty-four others—the "positive change" group—the experimental classes did better than the controls on both grades and scores. Among this group, teachers' early expectations were less predictive of students' later achievement as a result of the improved techniques for feedback and correction. Specifically, as shown in Table 4–3, correlations between teachers' initial ratings of probable achievement and the students' final grades and examination scores were markedly lower for experimental classes than for classes using customary methods; "no-change" teachers had high correlations in both classes. It seems likely that better feedback and corrective methods could also affect the rank order of performance by race, although Guskey does not investigate this issue.[83]

It is worth noting that responsive teaching can take negative as well as positive forms. For example, some teachers may give incentives and assistance to students who want to improve their positions in the class and penalize students who do not. In an often cited study, Karen Brattesani, Rhonda Weinstein, and Hermine Marshall compare fourth, fifth, and sixth grade classes in which student surveys had indicated various levels of differential treatment.[84] In the classrooms with higher levels of differential treatment, more students with below average scores at the beginning of the year made unusually large gains, but fewer students with above average scores made gains.[85]

Both of these studies show that greater responsiveness to individual children can weaken the link between past and future performance, and perhaps

TABLE 4–3   Effects of Improved Techniques in Feedback and Correction[a]

| | Correlation between Initial Rating and | | | | | |
| | Final Rating | | Course Grade | | Final Examination | |
Teacher sample	Experi-mental	Control	Experi-mental	Control	Experi-mental	Control
Positive change	0.53	0.83	0.51	0.80	0.31	0.50
No change	0.92	0.90	0.77	0.79	0.69	0.75

Source: Guskey (1982).

a. Sample comprises forty-four intermediate and high school teachers of various subjects in two metropolitan school systems; see text for details. The positive change group includes the thirty-four whose classes taught using the improved feedback techniques earned higher final examination scores and course grades than their control classes. For the ten teachers in the no change group, either course grades or scores on the final examination were higher in the control classes.

also alter trajectories. Both are silent about race and ethnicity. Unfortunately, statistical studies that deal directly with race do not investigate whether particular teaching practices can change the rank order of performance among students.

THE GREAT EXPECTATIONS INITIATIVE

Great Expectations is a public-private partnership created in 1989 to bring Marva Collins's ideas about teaching into Oklahoma schools.[86] (Collins, an African American, teaches in the inner city in Chicago and is probably the most widely known elementary teacher in the nation.) The initiative includes a range of techniques that Collins has developed over the years. It aims to nurture in all students, not only the most talented, the expectation that they are destined to be important people if they do their best in school to prepare well for the future. Those who misbehave should be reminded regularly that the teacher cares and refuses to give up on them. Teaching methods combine high challenge for students with feedback from teachers *and peers* in forms that make learning fun and emphasize its importance for a happy and effective life. Progress is celebrated, so that every student can earn the opportunity for positive recognition from teachers, peers, and parents. In addition to more standard materials for core subjects, the curriculum includes uplifting, forward-looking poetry, which students memorize and discuss and recite at school and at home. The story of Great Expectations shows real people struggling, with some success, to change teaching practices—and in the process, teachers' expectations—for disadvantaged, mostly minority, children. Whites, blacks, Hispanics, and native Americans are all represented among the poorly performing children that the initiative aims to help. Racial gaps are not an emphasis.

The incentive for the Great Expectations initiative was a threat of takeover of certain Oklahoma schools by the state if test scores for third-graders persisted below the twenty-fifth percentile for three consecutive years on the Iowa Test of Basic Skills. Educators in the schools that joined Great Expectations knew of Marva Collins's reputation for working wonders with children in inner-city Chicago. Her own school had never been independently evaluated, but she appeared to be effective with the types of children that the Oklahoma schools were failing. Although administrators were not certain that these methods could be transferred from Chicago to Oklahoma, they judged it worth a try. For the first training, two teachers from each of twenty-five pilot schools were sent to Collins's Westside Preparatory School in Chicago. There they had a "seeing is believing" experience concerning what children from disadvantaged backgrounds could achieve.

As the initiative spread through the pilot schools in Oklahoma, however, there was substantial resistance from teachers who had not gone to Chicago. The head mentor teacher told me that virtually all of the resistance she encountered represented one or more of the following three perspectives:[87]

- Time: "I just don't have the time to try this. It's too much. I just can't do it."
- Satisfaction with current practices: "I just don't see the need for doing things differently from what I already do."
- Hopeless students: "You don't know my kids. You couldn't do that with my kids. All that positive stuff is treating kids like babies: discipline has to be tough—you can't mix it with being nice."

Some teachers were insecure: their low expectations for students were partly the consequence of low expectations for themselves as teachers.[88] At the other extreme, some teachers thrived using Collins's ideas and felt professionally rejuvenated. Each summer during the 1990s several hundred teachers have been trained or have received refresher courses through free summer institutes at Northeastern State University. Through the work of the Great Expectations Foundation, funding for the institutes and mentor teachers comes from private donors, philanthropic foundations, the State Board of Regents, and the state Department of Education. School-site training by mentor teachers during the school year reinforces the training received at

TABLE 4–4 Teachers' Assessments of Student Progress due to the Great Expectations Program, Oklahoma[a]

Percent

Assessment	Aspect of Classroom Performance			
	Academic Perfor-Mance	Attitudes	Behaviors	Teachers' Job Satisfaction
More than I thought was possible	22.37	31.59	25.00	35.53
A lot	55.26	46.05	44.74	48.68
Some	22.37	19.74	28.95	13.16
None	0.00	2.63	1.32	2.16

Source: Author's tabulations from a survey conducted at the Great Expectations Summer Institute, July 1993.

a. Sample comprises seventy-six teachers with some prior training in Great Expectations methods (representing close to a 100 percent response rate of potential interviewees). Participants were asked to complete the following statement: "Because of Great Expectations, the improvement in [aspect of classroom performance] of my students has been. . . ."

the summer institutes. Staffs for the institutes comprise professors from several NSU departments and elementary school teachers who have distinguished themselves in the classroom using the Great Expectations teaching methods.

In a baseline survey administered at the Summer Institute in July 1993, I asked teachers with some previous Great Expectations training to describe the improvement in their students' performance since they began using these methods. Table 4–4 presents the results.

The two portraits that follow offer "existence proofs" of the proposition that teaching practices and expectations can change dramatically, even for experienced teachers. At the same time, both of the teachers described express reservations.

Greg Robarts, Fourth Grade Teacher, Beehive Elementary School

Greg Robarts's classroom is a roughly even mix of black, white, Chicano, and Native American children, almost all of whom come from very poor families.[89] Before the Great Expectations initiative, Robarts had taught for seventeen years and believed himself to be a good teacher. But seeing what children at Westside Preparatory School in Chicago could do gave him pause: "I didn't really know how to teach reading. After one workshop in phonics I feel that I know more today than I learned in seventeen years teaching."

He describes seeing Westside Preparatory School as "an awakening." "I saw something I'd never seen before; I actually saw education taking place. I saw children interested in learning. After seeing her approach, and seeing that it worked, I thought, 'What I'm doing now isn't working. At best it's just kind of passing.' . . . I had to rededicate myself."

Collins's basic philosophy resonated with Robarts's beliefs about teaching, but he had to unlearn old habits, such as sitting at his desk saying, "Open the book to page 34, here are the instructions. . . ." Even his own principal described Robarts as a "desk sitter" before he changed to the Great Expectations way of running a classroom: "Teach on your feet, not in your seat." Before Great Expectations,

> I was secure with all the books and things. A lot of teachers are where I was. They're embarrassed to say "I don't know." It's that fear of judgment . . . teachers are hesitant to ask. . . . Teaching independently . . . instead of from the book, those are the kinds of things that I wasn't courageous enough to try.

[How long was it before you felt comfortable with this new style?]

> Oh, I think after about the first day. And I made some horrible mistakes. But my kids just hugged me and said, "Oh, Mr. Robarts, you're so different from when you left!" And they would just say, "Oh, you're doing well." And when I would start kind of maybe, "Well, maybe I need to sit down now; I've kind of done the Marva Collins stuff now, so maybe I need to sit down." The kids would say, "Mr. Robarts, we sense that you're being average again." And so, I said, "Okay." So I always asked them to encourage me when they sensed that I was being average or substandard.

Many people who are not familiar with the Great Expectations approach say that it overemphasizes memorization and underemphasizes higher order thinking. Robarts disagrees. He says these functions are complements, not substitutes: memory is the foundation for higher order thinking. He finds that without practice at memorization many children cannot remember a dictated sentence long enough to write it down. After a few weeks of memorizing poetry and other things, he says, the change is remarkable. He thinks that people who dismiss memory work as outmoded are simply uninformed about how children learn, not only because memory supports higher order thinking, but because children can memorize things that are worth knowing. In addition, by reciting what they have memorized, children build self-confidence and motivation. He says: "If you had told me two years ago that

I would have a class of fourth-graders that would know all the states and capitals and would know geographically where things are located, that could spell words, that could read, that could do . . . I would have said, 'Well, maybe if you're in Quail Creek—which is a very affluent area of Oklahoma City—perhaps. But in this area, no, it wouldn't happen. . . . You know, maybe rote memory is not positive in some aspects, but I think that when a child has experienced total failure all through school it can be a major first step."

Much of the memory work in Great Expectations classrooms involves poetry that contains rules for healthy and productive living—messages worth remembering. Robarts reports exciting results from his efforts: "absenteeism is almost nil, refusal to do homework is almost nil, test scores are substantially up." He also describes a "miracle turn-around student" during his first semester using Collins's methods. The student's disciplinary folder was a "blizzard of suspensions." An African-American boy diagnosed as learning disabled, he was "a throw-away child," Robarts says. "He was not supposed to be able to do anything. He came very hostile . . . a tough cracker to break. I didn't understand when Collins said, 'You can look in the eyes of the children when they come, and there's a dullness.' I know what she means now. Children like Jerry have been so programmed to believe that the school is nothing. That *they* are nothing, that the only guarantee they have in school is failure. And it's so exciting to see their eyes brighten, and to see the *child* say that they *can* do." When Jerry transferred to a new school the following year, his classmates teased him for speaking standard English. Jerry persisted, with support from his new teacher. On returning to visit Mr. Robarts, Jerry reported that his new classmates began to change to be more like him, because of the positive responses that he was getting from the teacher.

Robarts realizes that he is not typical. Other teachers need more ongoing support. When I first interviewed him, in December 1991—after the first summer institute but nine months before mentor teachers began working in teachers' classrooms—Robarts was sober about the value of a four-hour demonstration that he and his class were to give the next week for teachers who had not gone to any summer institute: "We'll get them excited. They'll go back to their classrooms, they'll meet with the same failures that they've had. They'll struggle. They'll crash. They'll burn. They'll say, 'To hell with it. It's just another thing that they're doing.' And that will be the end of it. If there is no follow-through, no support person, no person to be supportive and say, 'Well now, this is a possibility,' it will all come to naught." In fact, Robarts was among the teachers who had pushed for the establishment of summer institutes and the use of mentor teachers for ongoing technical assistance.

Currently, both programs remain in place, complemented by an academy for principals.

Gloria Chavers, Third Grade Teacher, Lafayette Elementary School

Gloria Chavers recalls not thinking much about Great Expectations at the time that her school applied to participate in the program. However, when the first two teachers came back from Chicago, "They were excited. There was no doubt about that." The principal asked other teachers to observe in the classrooms of the trained teachers. "So we went to Mrs. Sherrin's [third grade] room. But this excitement that she had, I couldn't pick up on it. Because, and I talked at length with the principal about it at the time, I hadn't experienced what they had experienced. And for them to sit and tell me about what a five-year-old, and they would call these little children's names, you know, they could recite all this. I'd never been around any children who could do this, so it was hard for me to envision."

Chavers also recalls that she saw changes that she did not like in Sherrin's students. She had taught some of these children herself, as a second grade teacher. Now, they were calling themselves "college bound." At that time, Chavers's view was that "in this school system, college is not for everyone. We have a lot of lower socioeconomic people. College is the exception, not the rule."

Finally, the opportunity came to attend the first summer institute. "As it turned out, it was really well worth it," says Chavers. The following semester, she reorganized the way she ran her classroom. "We've gone back to a highly structured way of reading and teaching phonics [using chants]. We'd gotten away from that." She also now teaches the whole class in one group and from one book. She reports that when she first changed, "Some children struggled, but it's surprising when they have their peers reading and reading well, it seems to give them more incentive to read better."

At the summer institute, Chavers learned how to teach addition and subtraction using chants, but the class had not gone on to multiplication and division. So, back at her school, she made up her own chants for multiplication and division. She recalls: "And then I told [the students] one day, I said, 'Well, we'll sing this out.' Well, they didn't know what that was. I told them, 'It's like you're standing on the corner trying to sell something.' And even the children who have more difficulty with math, they have been able to pick up on those multiplication tables. They can not only say them, they can pass their tests! A lot of times after we do them, they'll go out of the room and you'll hear them going down the hall buzzing, singing them. You know, they like to do it. It's really, it's not anything new, it's just the way it's presented."

Chavers talks on about bringing her love of music into the classroom now in ways she never felt authorized to do before. She talks about impressing her friends with her students' written work. She speaks with pride about parents who glow when they see report cards that are better than ever before, who brag that their children are doing work that the parents themselves did not see until junior high school. Parental interest and participation has clearly increased. According to the district superintendent of a rural white community where one of the schools is located, "Some parents here were kind of skeptical about going up and bringing 'this black thing from Chicago,'" into this white, mostly rural section of Oklahoma. The same parents became supporters, however, when they saw the difference that it made for their children.

Chavers says that her children are convinced that they can do anything. When she plays choral music on a tape recorder they beg to learn the songs: "This week they said, 'Oh, won't you play the music?' And, 'Oh, can't we learn the song?'. . . . And they assured me, 'Oh, we can learn it.' So in two afternoons, they pretty well learned it. I was once a music teacher. With this new program I've been able to incorporate it again." When asked who gave her permission to do so, she says, "I just did it. I don't have to feel like this isn't part of my work anymore." Other teachers at other schools expressed similar feelings of a new freedom to bring their personal interests and talents into the classroom.

At the time of our interview, Chavers had been teaching for seventeen years. But, she says, "With the introduction of this program, it's just been different. The whole atmosphere has been different around here. The discipline problems for me have all but just totally disappeared, with this program. And it's not the fact that you're after the kids all the time. It's, 'This is what I expect of you.' You know, 'You are here for a job. This is your job, and my job here is to teach you. Your job is to be the best student you can be. And that is what I expect of you.'"

Robarts and Chavers are examples of what is possible, though perhaps not for all teachers. According to the head mentor teacher, the most important distinction between schools that do very well with Great Expectations and those that do not appears to be having an effective principal who understands the initiative. One characteristic of such principals is that they find ways of removing ineffectual or uncooperative teachers from their schools. The outcomes of the Great Expectations initiative have not yet been rigorously evaluated. However, several teachers bragged during interviews that average test scores in their own classes had risen by 30 or more percentiles in the space of one year.[90] The key for teachers is the apparently effective program of professional development that has helped them to expect more and achieve more for both themselves and their students.

CONCLUSION

Any conception of bias requires a corresponding conception of neutrality. A major reason that no consensus has emerged from scholarship concerning the importance of racial bias in the classroom is that there is no single benchmark for racial neutrality. Instead, there are at least three: unconditional race neutrality, race neutrality conditioned on observables (including past performance), and race neutrality conditioned on unobserved potential. Moreover, racial biases can exist in teachers' perceptions, expectations, or behaviors, or in any combination of the three.

Consider teacher perceptions of current student performance. If the benchmark for bias is unconditional race neutrality, most teachers are biased, but evidence shows that this is mainly because their perceptions of current performance are correct. When their perceptions early in a school year are inaccurate, the inaccuracies may become true through a process of self-fulfilling prophecy, but there is little evidence that initial inaccuracies or prophecies systematically favor either blacks or whites. In fact, where the benchmark is racial neutrality after taking past performance and other observable predictors into account, evidence favors the conclusion that teacher perceptions of current performance are generally unbiased. Whether the same applies to expectations and behaviors is less clear. I have found no clear evidence on whether teachers' expectations or behaviors are racially biased for students whom they perceive to be equal on past or present measures of performance or proficiency. However, taking unconditional racial neutrality as the benchmark, it is clear that teachers' perceptions and expectations are biased in favor of whites and that teacher behaviors appear less supportive of blacks. Clearly, the benchmark chosen for neutrality affects the conclusions.

Robert Schuller says, "Any fool can count the seeds in an apple, but only God can count the apples in a seed."[91] Similarly, tests can measure what children know, but only God can measure their latent future potential. Neutrality conditioned on latent future potential relates to a third type of bias and a third way in which teachers' beliefs can matter. Since potential is unobserved, racial bias of this type is virtually impossible to gauge with any reliability. Still, it does seem especially likely that teachers underestimate the potential of students whose current performance is poor, including dispro-portionate numbers of blacks. Also, blacks are underrepresented among stu-dents with the very highest scores, and potential for greater black repre-sentation at the top of the distribution is unproven. Thus at both ends of the test score distribution, stereotypes of black intellectual inferiority are reinforced by past and present disparities in performance, and this probably causes teachers to underestimate the potential of black children more than that of whites. If they expect black children to have less potential, teachers are likely to search with less conviction than they should for ways to help these children to improve, and hence miss opportunities to reduce the black-white test score gap.

Simply cajoling teachers to raise their expectations for black children—using phrases such as "All children can learn"—is probably a waste of time. However, good professional development programs can make a difference. Recall that some teachers in Oklahoma responded to the Great Expectations program with the assertion, "My kids couldn't do that." If they had gone on teaching as they had always done, that judgment would have been correct. But when they changed their teaching methods, they learned that they were wrong. Similarly, Guskey shows that teachers can learn responsive teach-ing methods that weaken the link between past and future performance.[92] Teachers who have been helped to improve their classroom practices can have "seeing is believing" experiences that challenge their prior biases. More research is needed on how professional development programs affect both test score levels and the black-white test score gap.

Even in the absence of the biases discussed above, teachers' beliefs prob-ably affect black students more than whites. The evidence is quite thin, but the few studies that bear on this hypothesis appear to support it. Jussim, Eccles, and Madon find that teachers' perceptions of sixth-graders' mathe-matics performance in October do not contain a racial bias once they control past performance and attitudes.[93] Nevertheless, the effect of teachers' Octo-ber perceptions on students' mathematics scores in May is almost three times larger for blacks than for whites. Further, the effect is also larger for females than for males, and larger for both black and white students from low-in-come households. Findings from other studies are consistent with these results. Casteel finds that black eighth- and ninth-graders are more eager to please their teachers, but their white peers are more concerned about pleas-ing their parents.[94] These differences may be due to parenting. For example, white parents might exert more consistent pressure for good grades; black parents might be less assertive about grades and more deferential themselves to teachers. Future research should actively pursue these questions, including the implications for policy, teaching, and parenting.

My bottom line conclusion is that teachers' perceptions, expectations, and behaviors probably do help to sustain, and perhaps even to expand, the black-white test score gap. The magnitude of the effect is uncertain, but it may be quite substantial if effects accumulate from kindergarten through high school. The full story is quite complicated and parts of it currently hang by thin threads of evidence. Much remains on this research agenda.

Fortunately, successful interventions do establish that children of all racial and ethnic groups have more potential than most people have assumed. As the evidence accumulates, it should be possible to focus with greater determination on cultivating and harvesting all that youthful minds embody.[95] It would then be no surprise if the black-white test score gap began to shrink again, as it did in the 1980s—and ultimately disappeared.

Thanks to Karl Alexander, William Dickens, James Flynn, Christopher Jencks, Meredith Phillips, and Jason Snipes for helpful discussions and comments on earlier drafts. I am also grateful to Lee Jussim and Meredith Phillips for calculations that they conducted at my request for this chapter. Jason Snipes provided able research assistance.

CHAPTER 5

A Diagnostic Analysis of Black-White GPA Disparities in Shaker Heights, Ohio

This quantitative case study explores how race, family background, attitudes, and behaviors are related to achievement disparities among middle school and high school students in Shaker Heights, Ohio. The purpose is to inform the search for ways of raising achievement and reducing disparities. Until recently, well-to-do suburbs have escaped the spotlight of research and journalism about disparities in achievement among racial groups. Now, however, high-stakes testing and the standards movement are forcing school leaders to acknowledge that, even in the suburbs, students of color are underrepresented among high achievers and overrepresented among students who get low grades and score poorly on standardized exams.

Shaker Heights is an inner-ring suburb on the east side of Cleveland and widely regarded as a model community. Residents have worked over several decades to maintain a relatively stable mix of whites and African Americans as well as a school system that is reputedly among the best in the nation. Graduates go to college in large numbers, many to elite institutions. Even so, as the national movement to raise standards has gained momentum, Shaker Heights, like other districts, is confronting achievement gaps. At one extreme, black and white students in Shaker Heights achieve top scores on college entrance exams. At the other extreme, students are at risk of failing the exam that Ohio now requires for high school graduation. The latter group is disproportionately black.

The focal measure of achievement in this study is the student's grade point average (GPA) from the most recently completed semester.[1] Black and white students have both high and low GPAs. Nonetheless, the black-white GPA gap equals roughly one letter grade. The mean GPA is in the neighborhood of C+ for blacks and B+ for whites.

OVERVIEW

The data for the study come from a survey developed by John H. Bishop at Cornell University, called the Cornell Assessment of Secondary School Student Culture. Virtually all seventh through eleventh graders in Shaker Heights completed the survey at the end of the spring semester in 1999 and are represented in the data for this study. Often, quantitative studies in education use very small data sets constructed for very narrow purposes. Other times, they use large national data sets that include only a small sample from any particular school, and the contextual differences between-schools can make it difficult to interpret findings about within-school processes. Because Shaker Heights has only one middle school and one high school, all students in each grade attend the same school. Therefore, no between-school effects confound the analysis. The sample is large and complete enough to allow for analyses of subgroups, and the questions in the survey are richly textured enough to capture a variety of important distinctions.

The data have a standard set of limitations. First, they are self-reported by students. Therefore, some measures are less reliable than if the data had come from official records or from observations by trained, objective investigators. Second, methodological requirements (for example, longitudinal data and exogenous sources of variation) necessary to distinguish causal relationships from mere correlation could not be met. Therefore, to be cautious, the text will usually say that the explanatory variables "predict" grade point averages, as opposed to "cause" them. Finally, while some of the issues may deserve separate analyses for different grade levels, the analysis of grade-level differences is beyond the scope of this paper.

Six key findings and interpretations resulted from analysis of the data. First, the characteristics of black and white youth in Shaker Heights that predict black-white GPA differences implicate skills, much more than effort, as the main reasons for the GPA gap.

The analysis of the GPA gap in this paper uses a number of explanatory variables as predictors of GPA in a standard statistical procedure called multiple regression analysis.[2] For an explanatory variable to be an important predictor of the black-white GPA gap, the black-white difference in that variable needs to be nontrivial and a significant predictor of GPA, holding other explanatory variables constant. Many variables meet one or the other of these criteria—that is, a nontrivial black-white difference is found or the variable is a significant predictor of GPA—but only a few meet both. The few that do relate most directly to academic skill and social background advantages, as opposed to effort, interest, or behavior.

Second, compared with white classmates, blacks report spending as much (or more) time doing homework, but a lower rate of homework completion. Note also that the amount of time spent doing homework (a measure of effort) does not help in predicting GPA, once the percentage of homework completed (a measure of effort and proficiency) is taken into account.

Overall, the data indicate that blacks on average spend about twenty minutes less time each night on homework than whites do. However, within a given pattern of course taking (in other words, controlling for the mix of regular, honors, and Advanced Placement [AP] courses) black students report more time on homework than white classmates, but lower rates of homework completion.[3] This finding emerges from simple tabulations and also from statistical estimates that control for family background and many other factors.

Teachers see only the rate of homework completion, not the time devoted to trying. They also see behaviors that are difficult to interpret. For example, blacks in the survey are twice as likely to identify "tough" as a characteristic of popular peers, while whites are more likely to identify "outgoing" and "self-confident." Teachers and administrators in Shaker Heights have told me that black-white differences in tough behavior and rates of homework completion make it appear that blacks exert less effort than whites and have more oppositional attitudes about achievement. The analysis here concurs that black students might behave differently and complete less homework than whites, but not that their effort is less than among white classmates or that their peer culture is more opposed to achievement.[4]

Third, attitudes and behaviors are more important for predicting within-race than between-race GPA disparities.

In contrast to comparisons between blacks and whites, attitudes differ greatly between high and low achievers within each racial group. Together, both skill-related and effort-related attitudes play major roles in predicting GPAs of B or better for some black students, but C or lower for others. However, how to interpret such results is not clear, because the direction of causation cannot be measured. Over time, attitudes and behaviors can affect achievement, but achievement can also affect attitudes and behaviors, in a process of cumulative causation.[5] Whatever the pattern of causation might be, attitudes and behaviors are an integral part of the story about within-race disparities.

Fourth, to think clearly about achievement gaps, it is important to distinguish: (a) what children know in terms of their stock of academic knowledge, (b) the pace at which they learn new things to add to the stock, (c) their knowledge of techniques and strategies that help them to learn effectively and efficiently and to manage the pace of new learning, (d) the effort that the individual chooses (or is required) to devote to the process, and (e) how individual-level variations in all of the above depend on group-level characteristics, resources, and processes.

Consider, for example, hypothetical runners from two tribes, the Whites and the Blacks, who are competing as individuals in a single long-distance race to acquire academic knowledge. Each step in the race adds to the knowledge that each runner accumulates. Most runners from the White tribe are ahead of most runners from the Black tribe. Variations in effort and natural ability are evident within each tribe, but no systematic differences between the tribes exist on these dimensions. Therefore, neither effort nor natural ability can account for why members of the White tribe tend to be ahead. Instead, the main reasons are that many in the White tribe had head starts at the beginning of the race and many have also received extensive informal coaching from tribal elders on effective running techniques and racing strategies. Superior techniques allow a runner to maintain a given pace with less effort; and knowledge of racing strategies leads to better decisions. Hence, members of the White tribe tend to be ahead not only in terms of academic knowledge accumulated during the race, but they are also more knowledgeable about running techniques and racing strategies.

Individuals in the Black tribe would like to comply with demands that they should run up closer to where most of the Whites are. But this is a tough challenge. There are no shortcuts, so the only way to catch up is to run faster (that is, learn faster) than most of the Whites. But is this possible? Simply exerting greater effort while using old techniques and strategies might do little to close the gap, thereby leading to disappointment and frustration for all but the most talented Black tribal members. The combination of increased effort together with highly effective coaching to refine techniques and strategies might improve prospects considerably. Therefore, expanding the supply of highly effective coaching is a major priority. Another priority is to address social pressures that might discourage some runners from always doing their best.

Fifth, all segments of the school community report negative peer pressures. Black and white students who never take honors or AP courses seem moderately inclined to hold back effort in response to their peers. Conversely, students who take honors or AP courses seem less prone to allow the peer pressures that they experience to hold them back.

As a gauge of holding back, a question in the survey asks whether the respondent agrees, or not, with the statement "I didn't try as hard as I could in school because I worried about what my friends might think." Other things being equal, a student who agrees with the statement has an estimated grade point average that is one-fifth of a letter grade lower, compared with a student who does not agree. By this measure of holding back, 21 percent of black males, 10 percent of black females, 7 percent of white males, and 3 percent of white females report that at least once a week they hold back. These racial differences are associated mostly with whether students take honors and AP courses. By course level, blacks and whites differ hardly at all in their reported propensity to hold back.

Reports of holding back are highest among students who report negative peer pressure and take no honors or AP classes. For example, among both black and white students, more than four of every ten males who take no honors or AP classes and who agree that "my friends make fun of people who try to do real well in school" also report holding back on their own work effort. If they agree in addition that friends disapprove of grade competition, then the rate of holding back rises to over half.

Students who take any honors or AP courses and who agree with the same statements about peer pressure are much less likely (especially among whites) to say that they ever hold back because of what friends might think. Because the nonhonors and non-AP courses are where black students are concentrated, and also where most of the holding back occurs for both blacks and whites who experience peer pressure, the black-white difference in honors and AP course taking predicts much (though not all) of the black-white difference in reports of holding back. Because only one in five black males and one in ten black females reports holding back, and because some white students hold back, too, holding back predicts only a small fraction of black-white GPA gaps. Still, the issue is important to consider because it could be a drag on improvement as Shaker Heights strives to raise achievement levels among the students who are furthest behind. Also, holding back may be more common than the survey responses imply, if not everyone affected by such impulses reports them.

Sixth, honors and AP courses may be socially isolating for black students, which may diminish the degree to which black students aspire to take such courses.

Avoidance of honors and AP courses can be another form of holding back but may not be reported as such in the survey responses. Black students are far less likely to take honors and AP courses, even controlling for attitudes, behaviors, and family background. This black-white difference cannot be explained with any certainty. Because few black students (aside from those already in honors classes) have GPAs of 3.0 or better, many may not be prepared to enter more advanced courses.[6] Nonetheless, some black students could engage their studies differently, perhaps seeking more help from teachers, if they earnestly aspired to take advanced courses.[7]

Concerns about social isolation might deter aspirations to qualify for honors and Advanced Placement courses, even if values among blacks are no more oppositional to hard work and achievement, per se, than among whites. Recall the racing metaphor. Talented runners in the Black tribe might find it easier and socially more satisfying simply to accommodate the slower pace of their friends, instead of breaking away. Breaking away academically while remaining connected socially may require code switching (for example, to speak black slang at the appropriate times) and navigating back and forth between black and white social groups. Inability or unwillingness to do these things to signal his or her identification with other black students may be the main reason for the occasions when black high achievers get accused of "acting white."

In the end, the black-white GPA gap in Shaker Heights seems to be more a skill gap than an effort gap. However, effort, social pressures, and honors and AP enrollments are certainly part of the achievement story. For black students, their teachers, and their parents, substantial narrowing of the achievement gap may require more effort, a more supportive peer culture, and less ambivalence about honors and AP course taking. However, most important, narrowing the gap will almost certainly require more effective and efficient learning techniques and strategies, so that the pace of new learning can accelerate as the level of effort increases.

STIGMAS, STEREOTYPES, AND MARGINALITY

Prominent ideas about underachievement among African American youth emphasize the importance of stigmas and stereotypes. In her book on black youth culture of achievement, Signithia Fordham writes about the sense that black people feel of being the stigmatized, subdominant minority group opposite the dominant "Other" in the form of mainstream, white society.[8] She reports a common need among black adolescents, especially males, to cultivate a sense of identity that is explicitly distinct from this Other and to signal that identity through an identifiably black persona. Young people have many ways of managing this process. Some methods may detract from school performance while others may promote it. An influential set of ideas about how they might detract concerns oppositional culture.

Oppositional Culture

Anthropologist John Ogbu is the person most identified with the idea that the historical mistreatment and continuing marginality of blacks in the United States foster "attitudes and skills less favorable to white middle-class type school success."[9] He contends that black people born and raised in the United States compare their condition with that of the white majority and feel a sense of resentment and pessimism that helps to foster a reactive, oppositional culture. In Ogbu's thesis, minorities who migrated freely to the United States are "voluntary" as opposed to "involuntary" minorities. Voluntary minorities have not endured as much oppression in the United States as blacks descendant from American slaves. In addition, voluntary minorities are less resentful of their status because their standard of comparison is usually their country of origin, where conditions were worse. The resentment and marginality that involuntary minorities feel is, according to Ogbu, the basis for resistance or incomplete acceptance of school norms and goals, which helps to explain black underachievement.

In contrast, some economists and sociologists have concluded that Ogbu and the school of thought that he represents are wrong about youth in the United States. Economists Philip J. Cook and Jens Ludwig find in nationally representative data for the period around 1990 that black and white youth had essentially equivalent attitudes and behaviors.[10] They find that this is especially true when family characteristics such as education, income, and household structure are taken into account. The attitudes and behaviors that Cook and Ludwig analyzed included indexes of self-perceived popularity tabulated by student GPA and by membership in the honor society, reported time spent on homework, school attendance, and expected years of schooling.

Cook and Ludwig's work has been important because it effectively calls previous, mostly ethnographic, findings into question. They ask: Do African American adolescents report greater alienation from school than non-Hispanic whites? Does academic success lead to social ostracism among black adolescents? Do the social costs or benefits of academic success differ by race? For each question, their answer based on analysis of nationally representative data is, "Apparently not." Further, sociologists James Ainsworth-Darnell and Douglas B. Downey analyzed the same national data and came to essentially similar conclusions, though they found some behavioral differences that Cook and Ludwig did not address.[11] Their findings support the hypothesis that blacks have more problems than whites in a category they call "skills, habits and styles." They find that variables in this category, as distinct from oppositional attitudes about achievement, help in a small way to explain the achievement gap in the data that they analyzed.

Stereotype Threat and Disidentification

Even if research findings accumulate showing that black students seem no more oppositional to schooling than whites, or perhaps even less so, stigmas and stereotypes could still affect achievement. Some black youth are motivated to prove stereotypes wrong or to defy them.[12] However, research in psychology cautions that setting out to challenge a stigma or to prove a stereotype wrong is not easy. Claude Steele and Joshua Aronson have produced laboratory evidence of "stereotype anxiety," which is induced by "stereotype threat."[13] In the context of race, the anxiety is a nervous anticipation induced by the threat that one's performance might confirm a negative racial generalization. Such anxiety can depress performance even among students who value achievement, know that they have the skills to do very well, and are trying to do their best.

Stereotype anxiety may depress performance most when students both fear and expect that their performance might confirm the stereotype. This can produce disidentification, because it may feel better emotionally to fail because of not trying than because of low ability. To fail after an earnest effort would seem to be confirmation of low ability. In extreme cases, disidentification resulting from discouragement is associated with learned helplessness.[14] In learned helplessness, a person stops trying because he or she believes that even his or her best effort will not be enough. In school situations that are ambiguous in this regard, determination to excel might alternate with feelings of helplessness, such that students sabotage their success with fleeting resolves that move them back and forth between working hard and hardly working.

Among males and females, blacks and whites, Shaker Heights has students who consider schoolwork interesting, pay close attention in class, spend a few hours each night on homework, and try to do their best. At the other extreme, students have experienced academic difficulty and lean toward dis-identification as a way of coping.

THE DATA

Data for this paper come from a survey developed by John Bishop that was administered in Shaker Heights at the end of the spring semester in 1999.[15] Shaker Heights has one high school with grades nine through twelve and one middle school attended by seventh and eighth graders. All seventh through eleventh graders in attendance were given the survey to complete during a regular class period. A total of 1,699 students responded to the survey, pro-viding, aside from a few who were absent, virtually complete coverage for the five grade levels. Eighty-three percent of respondents were black or white, which are the two groups in the present analysis.[16] All of the data are self-re-ports. Hence, the usual cautions are in order regarding possible inaccuracies and biases. At the same time, I know of no reason to expect that more accu-rate data would invalidate my basic findings.

A number of variables were used in the study. Some describe the child and others the family. Parents' average years of schooling and household composition variables aim to capture systematic differences among house-holds in the supports that they are able to provide for achievement. For example, parents' years of schooling may indicate income differences that affect resources in the home, as well as parents' academic orientations and aptitudes passed on from parent to child. Similarly, household composition may reflect differences in financial resources per child, parental supervision, and teen's responsibilities for helping to maintain the household. Variables in other categories measure social perceptions, attitudes, and behaviors that I hypothesize affect, and reflect, school engagement. Means and standard deviations for all variables appear in Table A–1 (see p. 192). Most variables are coded as yes = 1 and no = 0, or they have been standardized to have a mean of zero and standard deviation of one across all students in the sample.[17] A few variables are measured in other conventional units such as GPA points (on a four-point scale), hours, or proportions.

Race and Family Background

The race and gender variables in the analysis are indicator variables that identify the race or gender group (that is, black male, black female, white male, or white female) to which each student belongs. The analysis also includes both mother's and father's years of schooling.[18] Preliminary estimates showed no clear evidence that mother's or father's education was a stronger predictor than the other, so the two were combined to form variables for average parental years of schooling: twelve years or fewer, thirteen to fifteen years, sixteen years, and graduate degree.[19] Surprisingly large differences in parental schooling were found between Shaker Heights's black and white students. Mothers and fathers together average at least four years of college in roughly 90 percent of white households, compared with about 45 percent of black households. Parents in one quarter of black households have only twelve or fewer years of schooling. The same is true for less than 5 percent of white households. A larger percentage of parents have postgraduate degrees among whites than have four-year college degrees among blacks.

Household composition is measured by indicator variables for "two parents," "one parent and one stepparent," and "one parent or neither." An unknown number of the "one parent or neither" cases is foster families and children living with relatives. Just as racial differences in parental education are large, so are differences in household composition. The percentage living with "one parent or neither" is 52 percent for black males, 53 percent for black females, 8.6 percent for white males, and 14.6 percent for white females. Black students average between two and three siblings, whites between one and two.

Reasons for Failing to Study or Complete Homework

Items in this category are reasons that students agree are important for why they sometimes do not study or finish their homework:

- Competing time commitments ("Not enough time [to study or finish homework] because of work and/or school activities").
- Could get a good grade without studying.
- Simply decided not to bother.
    I preferred to party or hang out with friends.
    The assignment was boring or pointless.
    I didn't care about the grade in that course.
    Friends wanted to do something else.
    Didn't work hard is usually a reason when I get a bad grade.
- Carelessness and poor planning.
    Started too late, poor planning.
    I got distracted at home.
    I forgot the assignment.

- The work was too difficult.

  The assignment was too long and difficult.
  No one to help me at home.
  I didn't understand the material.
  The class was hard is usually a reason when I get a bad grade.

The first two items are yes/no variables. Each of the others is a composite of the yes/no values of the individual components. Each composite is scaled to have a mean of zero and is measured in standardized (that is, standard deviation) units.[20]

Classroom Attitudes and Behaviors

The category of classroom attitudes and behaviors covers what students think and do while in class. Five items gauge the frequency of particular thoughts and behaviors. The question in the survey asks, "How often?" and the respondent can indicate never, seldom, fairly often, often, usually, or always. The five items are: find studies intrinsically interesting, contribute to class discussion, do homework in one class for another, joke around in class, and really pay attention in class. For this study, each measure is transformed to standard deviation units by setting its mean equal to zero and its standard deviation equal to one. The sixth variable in this category is a yes/no question pertaining to the following statement: "I didn't try as hard as I could at school because I worried about what my friends might think." Below, this variable is called "hold back or hide work effort."

Other Attitudes and Behaviors

Other attitudes and behaviors is a residual category for indexes that do not fit neatly in the categories above. It includes hours of watching television on typical school days, a variable called "aspiration for years of college" measuring the highest level of schooling the student hopes to attain, whether the student copies homework from friends roughly once a week or more, whether the student studies with friends roughly once a week or more, and whether they agree that teachers maintain good discipline in the classroom.[21] It also includes a composite variable called "friends think academic zeal isn't cool." This variable is constructed from indicators of student agreement or disagreement with the following statements. Values are highest for students who agree with the first four and disagree with the last two.

- It's not cool to be competitive about grades.
- It's not cool to frequently volunteer answers or comments in class.

- It's not cool to study real hard for tests and quizzes.
- It's not cool to be enthusiastic about what you are learning in school.
- It's annoying when other students talk or joke around in class.
- It's annoying when students try to get teachers off track.

As a composite of the six items, "friends think academic zeal isn't cool" is a fairly direct measure of peer opposition to expressions of school engagement.[22]

Another variable, "work hard to please adults," measures the degree to which pleasing teachers and parents is among the motivations when the student works hard. Students were asked the following question, "When you work real hard in school, which are important reasons?" Response options included the following:[23]

- I don't want to embarrass my family.
- To please or impress my parents.
- To please or impress my teacher.
- My teachers encourage me to work hard.

Students who score higher on this index care more about pleasing adults.

Perceptions Regarding Popularity

The data also include measures of what students perceive are the determinants, or at least the correlates, of popularity. A central proposition in conventional wisdom about achievement disparities is that peer effects are important determinants.[24] If black and white students differ systematically in what they report are the styles and routines that most characterize popular peers, then it can be inferred that they probably differ also in the styles and routines to which they are trying to conform to be popular.

A question in the survey asked students to complete the following sentence: "During the first year of middle or junior high school, the members of the most popular crowd (my gender) were _____." Respondents could check any characteristic that applied from a list that the survey supplied. Consistent with at least some degree of racial segmentation, both similarities and statistically significant differences, by both race and gender, turned up in their responses.[25]

The correlates of popularity warrant examination. The data in Table 5–1 show that "smart" ranks at the bottom for all but white females and that "cool clothes" ranks at the top for all but white males. "Being funny" ranks second for all but white females. Things that relate most to academic life,

TABLE 5–1   Characteristics of Members of the Most Popular Crowd in the First Year of Middle or Junior High School, According to Groups by Gender and Race

Percent

	Males		Females	
Characteristic	*Black*	*White*	*Black*	*White*
Cool clothes	**77**	**61**	82	81
Funny	73	70	**58**	**46**
Good at sports	72	70	**35**	**55**
Tough	**53**	**27**	**38**	**10**
Self-confident	**47**	**65**	57	62
Outgoing	**44**	**62**	58	64
Not attentive in class	26	24	28	22
Attentive in class	25	22	31	28
Worked hard to get good grades	23	19	31	27
Made fun of kids who studied a lot	16	18	19	17
Smart	**14**	**20**	19	**29**
Number of respondents	307	357	322	356

Note: Boldfaced numbers indicate a statistically significant racial difference at the 0.05 level, by gender.

from "not attentive in class" to "smart," all rate near the bottom of the ranking. Hence, regarding criteria for popularity, both blacks and whites focus mostly outside the classroom.

Alongside the racial similarities are some differences. Numbers in boldface in Table 5–1 indicate when the black-white difference, within gender, is statistically distinguishable from zero at the 0.05 level. Considering only the statistically significant differences, black males are more likely than white males to cite "cool clothes" and "tough" as characteristics of the most popular crowd. White males are more likely than black males to cite "self-confident," "outgoing," and "smart" (although, even among white males, only 20 percent cite "smart"). Black females are more likely than white females to cite "funny" and "tough"; white females more frequently cite "good at sports" and "smart."

Students who appear to be outgoing, self-confident, and not especially tough probably fit better with teachers' own personal styles. Differences in how black and white students carry themselves may foster subtle differences in student-teacher relations for black and white students. Informal discussions with teachers in Shaker Heights and other places tend to support this conjecture.

The characteristics that a student identifies as describing the most popular crowd do not necessarily describe that student. They probably do, however, reveal something about the student's sense of identity and tendencies to affiliate with (or aspire to) particular crowds. The list in Table 5–1 is too long to use for the entire analysis. Therefore, the analysis includes only the four categories for which black-white differences are statistically significant: "tough," "outgoing," "self-confident," and "smart." They are included with other variables introduced above, under the broad heading of "attitudes and behaviors."

PREDICTING ATTITUDES AND BEHAVIORS

In exploring the relationship of race and other background measures to attitudes and behaviors, questions arise about parental education and household structure, oppositional peer culture, holding back in response to peer pressure, and time-use patterns for homework and television watching. The statistical basis of the analysis is a set of multiple regression equations in which the explanatory variables are race and gender, parental education, number of parents in the household, and number of siblings. In all, thirty-eight equations were estimated, two for each attitude or behavior as the dependent variable. This produced too many numbers to report here, so Table 5–2 provides a qualitative summary. All entries in the table (other than "—") represent statistically significant differences at the 0.05 level or better.

Each line of Table 5–2 pertains to a particular attitude or behavior as the dependent variable and summarizes partial results for two estimated equations. For each line, results from a first equation appear in columns 1a and 1b; results for the second appear in columns 2a through 2d.[26] The equation for columns 1a and 1b includes only the race and gender variables as predictors. Hence, the word *black* or *white* simply indicates whether blacks or whites have the higher value (though not necessarily the best value) for that gender. This is a difference-of-racial-means test, done separately by gender. For comparison, the estimation procedure for columns 2a through 2d included (in addition to the race and gender indicators) parental education

TABLE 5–2 Statistically Significant Effects of Family Background and Race, within Gender, for School-Related Attitudes and Behaviors

School-related attitude or behavior	Specification 1: No background controls		Specification 2: With background controls			
	Males (race with the higher value) (1a)	Females (race with the higher value) (1b)	Males (race with the higher value) (2a)	Females (race with the higher value) (2b)	Parents average twelve years schooling (2c)	Live with one parent or neither (2d)
Important reasons when failing to study or complete homework						
Carelessness and poor planning	—	Black	—	—	—	—
Competing time commitments	White	White	White	White	Lower	—
Could get good grade without it	White	White	White	White	Lower	Lower
Simply decided not to bother	White	—	White	White	—	Higher
The work was too difficult	White	White	—	—	—	Lower
Classroom behaviors and attitudes						
Do homework in one class for another	Black	Black	Black	Black	—	—
Hold back or hide work effort	Black	Black	Black	Black	—	—
Really pay attention in class	—	—	—	—	Lower	Lower
Studies intrinsically interesting	—	White	Black	—	Lower	—
Contribute to class discussion	White	White	—	—	Lower	Lower
Joke around in class	—	White	White	White	—	—
Life outside the classroom						
TV hours per school night	Black	Black	Black	Black	Higher	Higher
Aspiration for years of college	White	White	White	Black	Lower	Lower
Copy homework from friends	—	—	—	—	—	—
Study with friends	—	—	—	—	—	—
Friends say academic zeal not cool	White	—	White	White	—	—

TABLE 5–2   Statistically Significant Effects of Family Background and Race, within Gender, for School-Related Attitudes and Behaviors *(continued)*

School-related attitude or behavior	Specification 1: No background controls		Specification 2: With background controls			
	Males (race with the higher value) (la)	Females (race with the higher value) (1b)	Males (race with the higher value) (2a)	Females (race with the higher value) (2b)	Parents average twelve years schooling (2c)	Live with one parent or neither (2d)
What respondent perceives as characteristics of the most popular crowd						
Outgoing	White	—	White	—	Lower	—
Self-confident	White	—	White	—	Lower	—
Smart	White	White	White	White	—	—
Tough	Black	Black	Black	Black	—	—

— = Not significant at the 0.05 level of significance.

levels, the number of parents in the household, and the number of siblings. When the entry in column 2a or 2b differs from that in 1a or 1b, it is because of the influence of including the family background variables in the analysis. Some of what appear to be race effects are instead family background effects.

The word *higher* (or *lower*) in column 2c indicates that students whose parents have only twelve or fewer years of schooling report the attitude or behavior more (or less) than those whose parents have postgraduate degrees. I chose to compare "twelve or fewer years" with "graduate degrees" in Table 5–2, because these are the extreme categories and are most likely to capture whether there is any effect of parental education.[27] Similarly, the *higher* (or *lower*) in column 2d indicates that students who live with one or neither of their parents report the behavior more (or less) than students who live with their mother and father. The vast majority of children whose parents have only twelve years of schooling in Shaker Heights, or who live with one or neither parent, are black. However, the fact that some are white allows for distinguishing statistically the degree to which each attitude or behavior is associated with parental education or household structure, as opposed to racial differences that remain to be explained in other ways.

Parental Education and Household Composition

The estimates summarized in Table 5–2 indicate a clear pattern in the ways that parental education makes a difference. Compared with students whose parents have graduate degrees, those whose parents have only high school degrees report that they pay less attention in class, regard their studies as intrinsically less interesting, and participate less in class discussion. They are also less likely to report that they can get good grades without doing their assignments. Further, they watch more hours of television, have lower college aspirations, and are less likely to say that the most popular crowd is outgoing and self-confident.

Thus, some key advantages of having well-educated parents are that they prepare children to concentrate, to be curious, to enjoy the exchange of ideas, to have high academic aspirations, and to admire people who are outgoing and self-confident. Students most lacking in this type of preparation may be the most prone to disidentify with school, especially when faced with intellectual challenges. These differences probably reflect the child's learning history both at home and at school. In particular, there is residential movement of some households back and forth between Shaker Heights and adjacent neighborhoods in Cleveland, where schools are reputedly not as effective. Children of highly educated parents are more likely to have attended Shaker Heights schools (or similar schools) continuously since kindergarten.

The pattern for students who live with one or neither parent (versus both parents) resembles that for students who live with parents that have only twelve years of schooling (versus graduate degrees), but some differences are related to both interest and effort. First, students from single-parent families appear more often to slack off. They are less likely to say that the work was too difficult and more likely to say that they simply decided not to bother, as explanations for failing to study or complete their homework. This could be face-saving, because it feels better to fail because of not trying than to try and then look or feel stupid. However, if such reports of low effort were face-saving, meant to hide low self-perceived ability, then they would probably appear for children of less educated parents as well, but they do not. Children whose parents have only twelve years of schooling seem the least academically prepared and the most disengaged. Students from single-parent households are just as likely as students from two-parent households to regard their studies as intrinsically interesting. Hence, while the findings for low levels of parental education point to lack of student interest, poor intellectual preparation, and probably some degree of academic disidentification,

TABLE 5–3   Peer Pressure, by Race and Gender

Percent agreeing

School-related attitude or behavior	Black		White	
	Males	Females	Males	Females
Friends think it's not cool to	Panel A			
Be competitive about grades*	33	43	50	58
Frequently volunteer answers or comments in class	18	13	19	8
Study real hard for tests or quizzes	12	6	12	5
Be enthusiastic about what you are learning in school	26	14	30	18
Friends think it's annoying when				
Other students talk or joke around in class*	46	56	34	43
Students try to get teachers off track*	52	63	37	38
Friends make fun of people who try to do real well in school	Panel B			
	24	10	20	11
Number of students	(303)	(351)	(328)	(360)

* Indicates a statistically significant black-white difference at the 0.05 level for both males and females.

the findings for single-parent households point to a problem with effort (perhaps because of less supervision or more family responsibilities) among students who nonetheless find their studies interesting.

No Evidence for Oppositional Culture

A popular proposition in discussions of the black-white achievement gap is that peer culture might be more oppositional to achievement among black students than among whites. The data in Table 5–2 show no support for this (though keep in mind that there may be self-reporting bias). There are a number of attitudes and behaviors for which blacks and whites are not statistically distinguishable, once family background controls are in place (and sometimes even without them). These include "really paying attention in class," "participating in class discussion," "copying homework from friends," and "studying with friends." They also include "carelessness and poor planning" and "the work was too difficult" as reasons for missing homework

TABLE 5–4   Peer Pressure and Holding Back, by Race and Gender

Number of students

Agreement with statements	Black		White		Row total
	Male	Female	Male	Female	
Statement A: Peers make fun of people who try to do real well in school.					
Statement B: Peers think it's not cool to be competitive about grades.					
	Panel A				
Students with no honors or Advanced Placement (AP) courses					
Neither statement A nor B	117	111	22	19	269
Either statement A or B	72	92	14	19	197
Both statements A and B	32	11	8	3	54
TOTAL	221	214	44	41	520
Students with at least one honors or AP course					
Neither statement A nor B	44	71	113	117	345
Either statement A or B	28	59	138	181	406
Both statements A and B	6	7	31	19	63
TOTAL	78	137	282	317	814
	Panel B				
Percent who report that "I didn't try as hard as I could at school because I worried about what my friends might think"					
Students with no honors or AP courses					
Neither statement A nor B	13	12	14	5	12
Either statement A or B	25	8	14	11	15
Both statements A and B	53	36	63	33	50
TOTAL	23	11	23	10	17
Students with at least one honors or AP course					
Neither statement A nor B	5	6	4	1	3
Either statement A or B	14	5	3	3	4
Both statements A and B	17	29	13	0	11
TOTAL	9	7	4	2	4

assignments. Further, compared with white males, black males are more inclined to say that their studies are intrinsically interesting, holding constant family background. Generally, whites express more relaxed, confident, and cavalier attitudes about their studies than blacks express about theirs. Whites are also the most likely to give multiple reasons for failing to study or complete homework. More than blacks, whites report that they have competing time commitments; they sometimes know that they can get a good grade without studying or doing the assignment; and they sometimes simply decide not to bother. Whites also report more than blacks that they joke around in class and that their friends think academic zeal is not cool.

Tabulations for the items that make up the variable named "friends say academic zeal is not cool" are shown in panel A of Table 5–3, under the subheadings "friends think it's not cool to" and "friends think it's annoying when." A larger percentage of whites than blacks report that friends would agree that being competitive about grades is not cool. A larger percentage of blacks report that friends are annoyed when students joke around in class or try to get teachers off track (perhaps because it happens more in their classes). These black-white differences regarding competitiveness and annoyances are statistically significant. Similarly, the survey has a question regarding whether "friends make fun of people who try to do real well in school." Panel B of Table 5–3 tabulates the responses. There are statistically significant differences by gender, but not by race.

Findings here do not support the view that black students' peer culture in Shaker Heights is more oppositional to achievement than whites' (even though behaviors may differ because blacks tend to place a higher value than whites do on appearing tough and so forth).

Holding Back as a Response to Peer Pressure

The variable "hold back or hide work effort" comes from the statement "I didn't try as hard as I could at school because I worried about what my friends might think." The answer is coded as a "yes" if the student marked on the survey that he or she does this "about once a week" or more often. Blacks hold back more than whites, and no statistically significant relationship exists of holding back to parental education or the number of parents in the household.[28]

Table 5–4 focuses on two of the items from Table 5–3 and their relationship to holding back. The panel A of Table 5–4 shows the number of students who agree with neither, one, or both of the following statements from Table 5–3: (A) "Peers make fun of people who try to do real well in school"; and

(B) "Peers think it's not cool to be competitive about grades." Just as in Table 5–3, the numbers in Table 5–4 are tabulated by race and gender. However, in Table 5–4, they are also tabulated by whether the student takes any honors or AP classes.

Panel B of Table 5–4 shows that holding back is concentrated among students who report peer pressure and take no honors or AP classes. For example, of the fifty-four students who take no honors or AP courses and who agree with both statements A and B, half report holding back. Conversely, of the sixty-three students who take at least one honors or AP class and who agree with both statements A and B, only 11 percent report that they hold back.

Simple tabulations for the whole sample show that males hold back more than females, and the black/white ratio of holding back for both males and females is 3:1 (see Table A–1). However, among students who take no honors or AP classes, the 3:1 ratio goes away and no racial pattern emerges. Multiple regression results (not shown here) demonstrate that racial differences in the propensity to hold back are no longer statistically significant, once honors and AP course taking and peer pressures are taken into account.[29] Other things being equal, the black-white difference in holding back predicts only a very small fraction of the black-white achievement gap, because only a minority of blacks report holding back, and some whites hold back, too. Still, the findings should not be ignored as Shaker Heights and other districts organize to raise achievement levels. The same can be said for time-use and television watching.

Time-Use, Television, and "Tribal Differences"

Black students watch television more than whites. The black/white ratio for the number of hours watched on school nights is almost 2-to-1 for males and almost 2.5-to-1 for females. The time students report watching television plus the time they report doing homework are depicted in Figure 5–1. For all four race and gender groups, graphs are shown for students who take mostly honors or AP courses and for others who take none. Graphs for those who take some, but fewer than half honors and AP courses, are not shown. The largest total is almost six hours per day for black girls in honors courses (these hours may overlap if students do homework and watch TV at the same time). White males and females spend an average of 3.5 to 4 hours, with more of it devoted to homework for those who take mostly honors and AP courses. A statistically significant trade-off is evident between watching television and spending time on homework, but it is very small. Specifically, an extra hour watching television predicts only five minutes less on homework.

Watching television could reduce the efficiency of time spent doing homework even though it appears to have very little effect on the amount of time spent. Black students do report lower homework completion rates than white students who report the same amount of time doing homework.[30] However, when a test is conducted to determine whether the lower homework completion rate might be caused by watching television, the result is that the estimated effect of television watching is so small as to be completely inconsequential. Apparently, the lower homework completion rate is not because of television. Neither do differences among individuals in time watching television predict differences in grade point averages. Watching television contributes nothing as a predictor of achievement gaps.

It is difficult to believe that watching television for three or more hours each day can be as inconsequential as these findings suggest. The only effect worth noting is that watching television is part of the explanation for why black students have a greater propensity to do homework for one class in another. I find that black-white differences in time spent watching television account for between one quarter and one-third of the black-white difference in the inclination to do homework in one class for another.[31] Even for this effect, further analysis shows that doing homework for one class in another appears itself to be a benign practice.[32]

Again, it appears from the analysis of individual-level data that the time black students in Shaker Heights spend watching television is, for the most part, not being taken from homework time. Clearly, however, compared with white students, between one and two hours per day is being taken from something that black youth would otherwise be doing and that white youth might already be doing. The following thought experiment suggests a way that the black-white difference in television watching and the achievement gap might be related, even though the findings do not show it.

Imagine a community with two large tribes. One tribe has a required two-hour clinic each night where students learn study- and test-taking skills. The other tribe has no clinic. Assume that children in the tribe without the clinic spend most of their time watching television while the other tribe is in the clinic. Children who attend the clinic watch television during their free time, too, but because of the clinic, they have less of it. In both tribes, family duties and other miscellaneous factors mean that some children watch television more than others, and these factors produce variation within each tribe in the amounts of time that children spend watching television.

In this example, the clinic causes tribal differences in television watching and achievement. Something analogous could be happening in Shaker

FIGURE 5–1   Hours of Homework and Television by Race and Gender and Proportion Honors and Advanced Placement (AP) Courses Taken

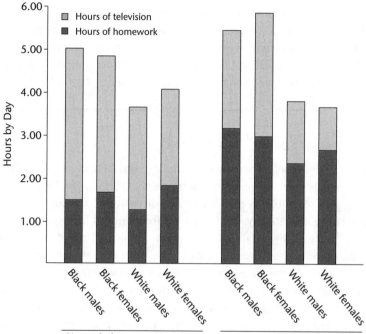

Heights. Not an organized clinic, but nonetheless a system of norms, learning resources in homes, and enrichment activities take time from watching television and benefit achievement. However, in this example, the effects on achievement of tribal-level norms, resources, or activities could not be detected from individual-level data on time watching television.

A final point concerns the social function of television. The data show that no matter whether the student is black or white, those who have more black friends spend more time watching television.[33] During a visit to Shaker Heights's high school, black students were asked why they watched television so much. A high-achieving black male answered, only half jokingly, "You have to watch television to get your material to be funny." He proceeded to explain that much of the social conversation among black youth at the lunch table and after school is about what happens on television. Hence, when young people watch television they are doing their "social homework."[34]

If a student stopped watching television and switched to more high-yield learning activities, the change would have a cost in social terms. That student could not contribute as much to socially important banter about what the group watched or understand shorthand references. Even if friends accepted this, the student would feel more marginal to the group. The social function of television might be why the trade-off between homework time and television time seems so small. If the goal is to have a good day at school, television and homework might be more like complements than substitutes. Both need to get done.

PREDICTING ACADEMIC PERFORMANCE

The impact that particular beliefs, attitudes, and behaviors might have on achievement is more difficult to determine than one might initially expect. One category of problems relates to those discussed in the context of television watching. Specifically, the key causal forces might be group- or community-level instead of individual-level phenomena and not detectable using individual-level data. However, another problem is that some attitudes and behaviors are probably causes and effects of achievement. For example, it is easy to think of reasons that high aspirations at the beginning of the school year might cause higher grades during the year and higher grades might reinforce high aspirations. Therefore, it would be wrong to conclude that a positive correlation between grade point average and aspirations is only because high aspirations cause high grades. Causation operates in both directions and is cumulative over time. Unfortunately, for most, if not all, of the attitude and behavior variables in the analysis, the magnitudes of causal effects in each direction are difficult, if not impossible, to sort out. Please keep this caution in mind below and also when citing findings from this study.[35] Findings of no effect are easiest to interpret. However, findings that particular attitudes or behaviors are strong predictors of achievement should be interpreted cautiously as such correlations may not indicate causation.

The Black-White Gap in GPA

On the survey for this study, students were asked to indicate their GPA for the past semester by marking one letter from among the standard options of A, A–, B+, and so on, down to F. Their responses were later coded in the data as 4.0 for A, 3.67 for A–, and so on, down to 0 for F. In the district's grading scale, grades in Advanced Placement courses receive an extra point, such that an A is worth 5.0 points. Grades in honors courses get an extra half point, making an A worth 4.5. Whether some students inflated the letter grades that they reported, in an effort to reflect the extra points they typically receive for honors or AP grades, could not be determined. If they did, then this is part of what the regression coefficient on the "proportion honors and AP courses" is measuring in the equations predicting GPA.

Measured by grade point averages, an achievement gap exists in Shaker Heights between blacks and whites. On a 4-point scale, the mean GPA in the 1999 data for seventh to eleventh graders is 2.08 for black males, 2.43 for black females, 3.21 for white males, and 3.36 for white females. This amounts to a gap of 1.13 GPA points for males and 0.93 GPA points for females. In attempting to understand the gap, multiple regressions were estimated in which GPA is the dependent variable. I report findings for two specifications. Specification A excludes, but specification B includes, the proportion of courses taken at the honors and AP levels, the rate of homework completion, and the number of hours per day the student typically spends doing homework. Both specifications include the measures of parents' education and household composition and the measures of student attitudes and behaviors.[36] A full set of regression results is reported in the Appendix.

For each explanatory variable, multiplying the black-white difference in mean values times the estimated regression weight for that variable produces an estimate of how much the racial gap in that variable contributes to the gap in GPA. This calculation is performed and then the variables are aggregated into six categories for the purpose of summarizing the results. Table 5–5 has the estimated contribution of each explanatory category to the gap in GPA for both males and females. No evidence exists in the table that attitudes and behaviors are a major explanation for the black-white GPA gap, though they do predict a small part of it.[37] (The reason that estimated effects for parents' education, household composition, and attitudes and behaviors are smaller in specification B than in specification A is that these same variables in specification B are operating partly through their effects on homework completion, hours on homework, and enrollment in honors courses.)

In specification A, black-white differences in attitudes and behaviors account for 0.21 GPA points of the 1.12 point gap for males and 0.18 GPA points of the 0.93 point gap for females. Inside the attitudes and behaviors category, two variables that contribute most to the 0.21 and the 0.18 are "competing time commitments" and "could get a good grade without studying." Both are reasons students give for failing sometimes to do homework. Both are reported more by whites than blacks and by students whose parents have more schooling. The two variables together account for 0.13 of the 0.18

for girls and 0.09 of the 0.21 for males. An additional 0.08 of the 0.21 for males is associated with differences in college aspirations. Hence for males, three variables account for 0.17 of the 0.21. All seem related to GPA primarily as reflections of academic skill and family background advantages.

Even though they do not help much in predicting the black-white gap, other attitudes and behaviors do help in predicting GPA. An inspection of Table A–2 (see p. 194) shows that eleven attitude or behavior variables have statistically significant coefficients at the 0.05 level in specification A, and six in specification B. The reason for their relatively small role in predicting the black-white GPA gap is that racial differences in these other attitudes and behaviors are small. In sum, black-white differences in attitudes and behaviors that help to explain the GPA gap appear to be mostly related to skill. The attitudes and behaviors that differ by race and do not seem related to skill, such as believing that "tough" is popular or watching lots of television, do not help in predicting GPA once other variables are controlled.

The single largest predictor of the black-white GPA gap is the proportion of courses taken at the honors and AP levels. The analysis to predict honors and AP course taking shows that parental education, household composition, attitudes, and behaviors all play some role in why fewer black than white students take honors and AP courses (see Table A–5). Still, half of the racial difference in honors and AP course taking remains unexplained by the variables in the analysis.

The number of black students who do not enroll in honors or AP courses but who report grade point averages of B or better is small. So, for the time being, a strong case cannot be made for pushing students wholesale into honors and AP courses. The biggest single challenge—the core challenge facing the district—is the low performance level among the large number of black students, especially males, who take no honors or AP courses. If some black students are reluctant to move into honors and AP courses and to work at the level required, addressing this reluctance is a worthwhile component of a more general strategy for addressing the achievement gap. However, the more general strategy needs to entail a strong focus on the large numbers who take no honors or AP courses and who will not be candidates for honors in the near-term future.

The GPA Gap among Blacks

An appropriate alternative to comparing blacks with whites is using high- and low-achieving black students as the basis of analysis. Black students for whom the regressions predict GPAs of C (2.00) or lower are compared with

TABLE 5–5   Contribution of Each Explanatory Category to the Black-White Grade Point Average Gap

Explanatory category	Males		Females	
	Specification A (1)	Specification B (2)	Specification A (3)	Specification B (4)
Parents' education	0.17	0.11	0.17	0.11
Household composition	0.10	0.05	0.09	0.05
Attitudes and behaviors	0.21	0.11	0.18	0.08
Proportion honors and Advanced Placement courses	—	0.28	—	0.26
Homework completion rate	—	0.11	—	0.11
Hours per night on homework	—	0.00	—	0.01
Total predicted difference	0.47	0.66	0.43	0.61
Total actual difference	1.12	1.12	0.93	0.93
Predicted/actual	0.42	0.59	0.46	0.66

— = Not included in the estimated regression.

other black students for whom the regressions predict GPAs of B (3.00) or higher (see Table 5–6). Because the comparisons of predicted GPA for these groups are within race and gender, the weights are from regressions on the data for black males or females, respectively. The numbers reported at the bottom of Table 5–6 show that the means of predicted and actual GPAs among students in these categories are very close.

Similar to the black-white comparisons, parental education, household composition, and the proportion of courses taken at the honors and AP levels are among the predictors of GPA gaps. For both males and females, these three categories account for about half a GPA point, roughly one-third of the gap that is being analyzed. However, in contrast to the story for the black-white gap, a full GPA point of the performance gap is related to homework completion, attitudes, and behaviors. Further, when homework completion is not in the equation, most of its influence on the predicted GPA gap is captured by the attitude and behavior variables.

Table 5–7 unbundles the attitude and behavior category for males. Table 5–8 does the same for females. Estimates from specifications A and B appear

TABLE 5–6   Contribution of Each Explanatory Category to the Grade Point Average (GPA) Gap between Black Students with a Predicted GPA of C or Lower versus Those with a Predicted GPA of B or Higher

	Males		Females	
Explanatory category	Specifi-cation A (1)	Specifi-cation B (2)	Specifi-cation A (3)	Specifi-cation B (4)
Parents' education	0.23	0.14	0.24	0.10
Household composition	0.15	0.09	0.26	0.12
Attitudes and behaviors	1.12	0.56	0.94	0.44
Proportion honors and Advanced Placement courses	—	0.23	—	0.32
Homework completion rate	—	0.59	—	0.45
Hours per night on homework	—	0.13	—	0.09
Total predicted difference	1.50	1.74	1.44	1.52
Mean GPA above 3.00: predicted (actual)	3.14 (2.93)	3.35 (3.31)	3.14 (3.24)	3.25 (3.31)
Predicted number of students in high range	11	19	34	44
Mean GPA below 2.00: predicted (actual)	1.64 (1.65)	1.60 (1.56)	1.63 (1.77)	1.72 (1.75)
Predicted number of students in low range	141	147	64	77

in both tables. Numbers discussed below are from specification A, unless otherwise indicated. Both tables identify the top five attitudes and behaviors that contribute to the gap because high achievers report them more than low achievers, and also the top five among negative predictors of GPA that contribute to the gap because high achievers report them less than low achievers do.

As with the black-white gap, some of the most strongly predictive variables in this analysis are probably proxies for accumulated skills and advantages. This seems especially true for "competing time commitments" and "could get a good grade without study." High achievers report both more often than low achievers do as reasons for missing homework. They appear to be proxies for omitted measures of skill and advantage. Together, they account for 0.37 and 0.18 points of the predicted GPA difference for males and females, respectively. Also, by far the most important predictor of the gap among females is the number of years of college that the student hopes to attain.

A number of the other variables measure orientations that affect achievement and do not require skills and family advantages. For example, aside from the variables just mentioned, the third variable that appears in the top five for both males and females is "really pay attention in class." Among things that high achievers do less, two variables appear in the top five for both males and females: "simply decided not to bother" with homework and "holding back or hiding work effort." These things, like paying attention in class, do not require academic skill or family advantages to improve (though they may require social skill). The three—deciding not to bother, holding back, and paying attention—account for about a third of a GPA point among males and a fifth among females. Among males, the other three things high achievers report less are "copying homework from friends," "carelessness and poor planning" (as a reason for missing homework), and "joking around in class." All three connote less seriousness—perhaps more disidentification— among low-achieving than among high-achieving boys.

Engagement

Generally, black students who are low achievers seem less engaged with schooling than the high achievers. However, they are not anti-achievement or oppositional in the sense that they object to school achievement norms (though acting "tough" may violate some behavior norms). Among black males and females whose predicted GPAs are 2.0 or lower, the mean value of the "friends think academic zeal isn't cool" variable is right around the mean for all students in Shaker Heights. At the same time, 32 percent of these males and 21 percent of the females report that they hold back. The same is true for only one male and one female among blacks with predicted GPAs of 3.0 and higher.

Research emphasizes four categories of factors that affect engagement. The first is purposes or goals. Second, a person needs recipes—or strategies—to apply in pursuing the goals or purposes. Third, they need to have (and believe that they have) sufficient ability, personal resources, and help from others to make at least one strategy feasible. Fourth, rewards need to be sufficient to make the effort worthwhile. If there is no goal or no strategy, if skills and resources are insufficient, or if rewards seem too limited or off target, then engagement is likely to be minimal. Most people, including adolescents, face

TABLE 5–7 Contributions of Attitude and Behavior Variables to Grade Point Average (GPA) Gaps between Black Males with a Predicted GPA of C and Lower versus Those with a Predicted GPA of B and Higher

Attitude or behavior variable	Specification A	Specification B
High achievers report these more		
Competing time commitments	0.22	0.12
Could get good grade without study	0.15	0.11
Really pay attention in class	0.12	0.00
Work hard to please adults	0.10	0.05
Schoolwork is intrinsically interesting	0.04	0.00
SUBTOTAL	0.63	0.27
F-test probability value for subtotal	0.000	0.000
High achievers report these less		
Simply decided not to bother	0.12	0.07
Copy homework from friends	0.08	0.03
Carelessness and poor planning	0.08	0.07
Joke around in class	0.08	0.03
Hold back or hide work effort	0.07	0.06
SUBTOTAL	0.43	0.26
F-test probability value for subtotal	0.000	0.003
TOTAL	1.12	0.56

Note: The small difference between the column total and the sum of the listed numbers is the result of rounding.

many competing uses for their time and attention. Choices to pay attention and to engage in one thing instead of another can affect achievement and rewards in each domain toward which attention could potentially be directed. This is not claiming that every action is the result of careful reason. Some actions are habits or impulsive. Nonetheless, implicit purposes, strategies, resources, and rewards (and penalties) can affect even informal behaviors and decisions.[38]

TABLE 5–8   Contributions of Attitude and Behavior Variables to Grade Point Average (GPA) Gaps between Black Females with a Predicted GPA of C and Lower versus Those with a Predicted GPA of B and Higher

Attitude or behavior variable	Specification A	Specification B
High achievers report these more		
Number of years of college hope to attain	0.30	0.16
Could get good grade without study	0.10	0.06
Contribute to class discussion	0.09	0.04
Competing time commitments	0.08	0.04
Really pay attention in class	0.08	0.04
SUBTOTAL	0.65	0.34
F-test probability value for subtotal	0.000	0.115
High achievers report these less		
Simply decided not to bother	0.08	0.01
Hold back or hide work effort	0.05	0.02
Work hard to please adults	0.04	0.03
The work was too difficult	0.04	0.02
The popular crowd is tough	0.04	0.02
SUBTOTAL	0.25	0.10
F-test probability value for subtotal	0.038	0.308
TOTAL	0.94	0.44

Note: The small difference between the column total and the sum of the listed numbers is the result of rounding.

Recall the earlier discussion of holding back and its relationship to peer pressure. Then reflect on the fact that 32 percent of black males and 21 percent of black females with predicted GPAs of 2.0 or lower report holding back. For potential high achievers, there may be a tension between social engagement with low-achieving peers who are seeking ways to cope with their status as low achievers and earnest academic engagement toward high achievement. To the degree that such a tension exists, the challenge for

Shaker Heights as a community is to alleviate it. Many low achievers need help with goals, strategies, supports, and rewards to enable and encourage them to overcome any feelings of academic disidentification, to stop holding back, and to begin taking their studies more seriously.

HIGH ACHIEVERS, BLACK IDENTITY, AND ACTING WHITE

Anthropologists Ogbu and Fordham offer the oppositional culture explanation as a reason that black students often seem to work below their potential. Economists Cook and Ludwig and sociologists Ainsworth-Darnell and Downey indicate that black students seem no more oppositional than white students to school achievement and associated norms. This paper has similar findings. No evidence exists in this paper's findings that black students are any more opposed than white students to achievement norms in Shaker Heights. Still, according to interviews with black youth in Shaker Heights, they occasionally accuse peers of acting white. What is it that they are objecting to when they make such accusations and should any consequences be expected for achievement?

Acting White

Adolescents have many ways of classifying one another. Sociologists who catalogue the distinctions cite such catchwords as brains, druggies, jocks, loners, normals, outcasts, populars, toughs, special interest groups (such as band members or student counselors), and others.[39] In addition to these, there is the category of race. Laurence Steinberg, Sanford M. Dornbusch, and B. Bradford Brown studied students at racially integrated high schools in Wisconsin and California. Within racial groups, students could identify one another as members of one of several crowds—jocks, populars, brains, nerds, and so forth. However, "when presented with the name of an African-American classmate, a white student would typically not know the group that this student associated with, or might simply say that the student was a part of the 'black' crowd."[40] Especially for nonwhites in the United States, race is salient in how youth classify themselves socially and is a standard category that others use as well.

The dominant pattern of school achievement across the United States is that black youth tend to earn lower grades and test scores than whites. Explanations are along a continuum from an emphasis on genetics and heredity at one end, to environmental factors at the other, with many blends in the middle.[41] Few, if any, of the explanations are flattering to black people.

Especially in racially integrated schools, students see the patterns, hear the explanations, and face decisions about how to respond. The present study and those by Cook and Ludwig and Ainsworth-Darnell and Downey suggest that the response is not typically to question the legitimacy or desirability of school success any more than whites do. In light of this evidence, the idea that black students in the United States are part of an oppositional culture in which the core dynamic is a uniquely high level of resistance to achievement appears to be wrong as a general proposition.

However, there is an oppositional culture that is distinctly African American. Further, it may have an effect on whether achievement aspirations are fully acted upon. Among its essential features is the drive to maintain a shared sense of African American identity that is distinct from—that is, in opposition to—the Other that Signithia Fordham writes about in her book *Blacked Out*. The Other is not white people, especially as individuals. Instead, the Other is the cultural system of white superiority within which negative racial stigma is kept alive and out of which insinuations of black inferiority and marginality emanate.[42] Black racial solidarity serves as a mechanism of mutual validation and a shield against "rumors of inferiority."[43] Any apparent attempt by a black person to escape the stigma of race by joining the Other—by speaking and behaving in ways that appear to seek an exemption from the stigma while leaving it unchallenged—may meet the accusation of acting white. (This is not meant to suggest that people are especially skilled at reading one another's motives when deciding who is trying to escape the stigma and who is not.)[44]

It therefore becomes normal to seek ways as a black teenager (or even as an adult) to signal to others that you "know who you are" and have no intention of "leaving the fold." This is especially so if you are striving toward goals that might seem atypical for blacks. The line between being a source of pride for the community (because your successes represent the community) or a target of resentment (because you appear to be disassociating and distancing your successes from the community) can be thin.

In June 1999 the ABC-TV program *20/20* aired a segment on the topic of acting white as it applies among black high school students.[45] The setting was a racially mixed high school in Wisconsin where reporter Charles Gibson interviewed students who had been accused of acting white and others who had made the accusations. Comments by accusers in the segment were especially telling. When Gibson suggested to one young man that trying to hold others back from reaching their full potential was not a good thing to do, the student's response was, "Yeah, but they were kickin' their old friends to the side for new friends, and that's not right either." A young woman in a similar exchange retorted, "Yeah, I'm gonna call you actin' white if you act like you think you're better than me." Another young man, now a record producer and rap recording artist, had gone away to Exeter, the elite private preparatory school, and come back dressing and speaking differently from when he left. He was accused of acting white. His interpretation of why former friends in the neighborhood were a little "put off" or "taken aback" was not that they resented his success. Instead, his interpretation was sensitive to their concern that he might be trying to escape the stigma. He said they wondered if he had "sold out" to the Other part of society that looked down on people like themselves. He responded by finding ways to share his success and "By letting them know that I'm not ashamed. I can still speak slang. I can still rap, even."

Social cohesion among black students in an integrated school provides a haven. It is a place to "fit."[46] Black students who want to be high achievers and remain socially connected to peers have to invest in their studies and also in signals of racial group fidelity. One form of investing in the signal is keeping up with the popular culture. Watching the right television shows and listening to the right music is doing one's social homework. Because my findings suggest no effect of television watching on grade point averages, no evidence shows that maintaining these routines either helps or detracts from school achievement. However, the need for social cohesion—driven in part by the existence of the Other and by a culture of opposition to it—might affect achievement in more subtle ways.

Holding Back and Mock Seriousness

Peer pressure may not be the only reason to hold back. Students who have the skills to perform at high levels sometimes hold back because their friends are struggling and they want to fit in. Signithia Fordham provides an illustration:

> Though Sidney and Max scored higher than most of the high-achieving males on the PSAT, nonetheless their response was to avoid learning what their scores were and, once that was no longer possible, to minimize the importance of what they had done. Since their friends are like them—football players and athletes—they do not want to call attention to themselves in areas other than athletics. Max confesses: "I knew what I was capable of doing, but sometimes I held back. I just held myself from doing it, to make somebody else happy. That's all I was doing, really."[47]

Accommodating less skilled members may depress group performance if more skilled members want to fit in and to avoid making others feel inferior. Consider two friends walking on the street, urgently en route to an important destination. The slower walker is not in good physical condition. He does not appear to be able to keep up if the friend who is more fit were to accelerate. A decision by the faster friend to hold back in this situation—to keep walking slowly—would seem completely reasonable based on feelings of empathy and social attachment. Active peer pressure, stigmas, or stereotypes are not required for such voluntary inclinations toward accommodation to operate. The following example, introducing the concept of "mock seriousness," helps to show how the process can operate in the classroom.

In the winter of 1999–2000, anthropologist Sara Stoutland conducted a series of interviews for a project that she and I were doing in the upper-income, racially integrated schools of Brookline, Massachusetts. The two high school teachers that Stoutland interviewed independently identified behaviors among black students that one of the teachers labeled "mock seriousness." An essential feature of their stories is a social tension that seems to develop when a child is about to reach a higher standard. The child breaks the tension with humor involving a small in-group of black classmates—in other words, they "play it off"—and the moment is lost. It is as if the child calls time out and signals, "We all know that this isn't really serious." The following two passages are illustrative. First, the speaker is a dedicated teacher of social studies. He organized a special elective seminar targeted to African American seniors. Most elected to take it for honors, even though many had never had an honors experience. He said:

They are finding an honors experience a whole other level of hard work. And many are doing well. But there is one kid who is one of the most insightful, perceptive thinkers I've seen in a number of years. And also one of the most courageous in his willingness to take a stand that runs counter to other kids on issues and not having to go along with the crowd. But whenever I congratulate him on what he said, he is so unfamiliar with that experience that he has to showboat or make a joke out of it in some way. And that undermines the seriousness of his accomplishments. And there is a group of guys that he plays off of. And you can tell that they are not used to perceiving themselves as intellectuals. There is a mock seriousness about it, rather than a genuine one. . . . A lot of kids have talked about what it is like to distinguish yourself academically and the potential of isolation. You're not in an environment [that is, the honors classroom] with a lot of other African American kids. And kids do talk about being seen by others as leaving the fold.

Next is a passage from an interview with an experienced teacher of foreign languages. She said:

> In my standard class, there is a group of African American kids and they all want to get good grades. And this is a group of kids that when you call home and their parents get on them, they start to bring in their homework. But then they start to slip. There is the one girl in particular that I think is really, really bright. And she gets it together for awhile and then she just slips. And it's hard for me to push her to the next level. She's in tenth grade. I asked her, "What is going on?" She said, "What I really care about. . . . I just care about my friends. I want to do well and I know that I should, but I'm more interested in my friends. So I don't want to work harder than I have to." So she'll start to be serious and work harder and be right on like my higher achieving kids. But the instant one of the other kids in this group of five African American kids makes some kind of under your breath joke, she is the first one to burst out laughing. . . . She doesn't want to maintain a tone of seriousness for very long. And that is the culture of that group of five or six kids—you don't want to be serious for too long or you're not cool. So they get together and—they are definitely not at-risk kids, I've seen much more at-risk kids. This is a group who could be doing more, but they get it together and get it together and then fall apart. So, they have this dynamic going and they build on it as a group.[48]

Both people quoted are skilled, highly energetic teachers. Both care a great deal about students and have gone far beyond what most teachers do in searching for ways to help black students achieve at high levels. Both believe their students have much potential and both have achieved successes. However, in each of these passages, they identify social processes that interfere with maintaining seriousness at moments when progress seems greatly possible, and they assert that it happens most among black students.

Honors Courses and the Potential for Social Isolation

Black students who take mostly honors and Advanced Placement courses in Shaker Heights are not the norm. Further, they are socially distinctive in their responses to the questionnaire. Table 5–9 contains percentages by race and gender for students who take no honors or Advanced Placement classes, those who take some (but less than half), and those who take at least half their courses at the honors or AP levels. The pattern is almost exactly reversed

TABLE 5–9   Students, by Race and Gender, Taking No Courses at the Honors or Advanced Placement (AP) Level, Taking Less Than Half, or Taking at Least Half

Percent

	Blacks		Whites	
Coursework	Males	Females	Males	Females
No honors or AP courses	73.7	61.9	14.3	11.6
Some, but less than half	17.1	24.9	24.0	25.5
Half or more honors and AP courses	9.2	13.2	61.7	62.9
Number of respondents	(316)	(362)	(334)	(361)

for black and white students. Nonhonors classes primarily serve blacks, while the honors and AP classes serve primarily whites.

Black males who take no honors and those who take mostly honors report essentially the same characteristics of the most popular crowd (see Table 5–10). In contrast, reports from black females are more similar to those from classmates who take the same level courses as they do. Among white students, males who take no honors or Advanced Placement courses appear more similar to other students who take no honors or AP classes. White females have a more mixed profile in which both race and course level seem to be reflected.

The clear impression one gets from the data in Table 5–10 is that at least some black males in honors and Advanced Placement courses are relatively isolated in their classes from their social reference group—other black males. Black females appear to be more socially distinct from black students who take no honors or AP courses. The same impression comes from other numbers, shown in Table 5–11. First, black males in mostly honors and AP courses appear to lack friends from whom to copy homework (because they copy less often than any other group). This may be an important disadvantage. For many students copying homework is a normal academic survival strategy. Second, black males in mostly honors and AP courses are the most likely to report that studying makes you less popular (though the difference from white males at the mostly honors level falls short of statistical significance).[49] And third, black males who take mostly honors courses talk to their friends about what they are learning only about as much as students who take no honors courses at all.

TABLE 5–10 Students Agreeing That "Tough," "Self-Confident," or "Outgoing" Described the Most Popular Crowd of Their Gender in the First Year of Middle or Junior High School, by Race, Gender, and Proportion Honors or Advanced Placement (AP) Courses Taken

Percent

Coursework	Black		White	
	Male	Female	Male	Female
Agreed "tough" described the most popular crowd				
No honors or AP courses	56 (124 of 222)	40 (87 of 218)	34 (15 of 44)	20 (8 of 41)
Some, but less than half	42 (22 of 53)	42 (36 of 86)	38 (30 of 78)	10 (9 of 91)
Half or more honors and AP courses	56 (15 of 27)	19 (9 of 48)	21 (42 of 200)	8 (18 of 223)
TOTAL	53 (161 of 304)	38 (135 of 357)	27 (87 of 322)	10 (35 of 356)
Agreed "self-confident" described the most popular crowd				
No honors or AP courses	46 (102 of 222)	51 (111 of 218)	39 (17 of 44)	49 (20 of 41)
Some, but less than half	55 (29 of 53)	70 (60 of 86)	72 (56 of 78)	58 (53 of 91)
Half or more honors and AP courses	44 (12 of 27)	58 (28 of 48)	68 (136 of 200)	67 (149 of 223)
TOTAL	48 (144 of 304)	57 (202 of 357)	65 (209 of 322)	62 (222 of 356)
Agreed "outgoing" described the most popular crowd				
No honors or AP courses	41 (91 of 222)	51 (112 of 218)	43 (19 of 44)	51 (21 of 41)
Some, but less than half	57 (30 of 53)	64 (55 of 86)	64 (50 of 78)	60 (55 of 91)
Half or more honors and AP courses	44 (12 of 27)	75 (36 of 48)	66 (131 of 200)	69 (153 of 223)
TOTAL	44 (135 of 304)	58 (207 of 357)	62 (200 of 322)	64 (229 of 356)

TABLE 5–11   Students Agreeing about Copying Homework, the Link between School Work and Popularity, and Studying with Friends, by Race, Gender, and Proportion Honors or Advanced Placement (AP) Courses Taken

Percent

Coursework	Black		White	
	Male	Female	Male	Female
Copy homework from friends weekly				
No honors or AP courses	44 (100 of 227)	34 (75 of 221)	35 (16 of 46)	34 (14 of 41)
Some, but less than half	35 (19 of 54)	29 (26 of 90)	40 (32 of 80)	35 (32 of 91)
Half or more honors and AP courses	21 (6 of 28)	46 (22 of 48)	44 (89 of 204)	33 (76 of 227)
Agree that studying a lot tends to make you less popular				
No honors or AP courses	29 (64 of 224)	19 (40 of 215)	24 (11 of 45)	21 (9 of 42)
Some, but less than half	23 (12 of 52)	9 (8 of 90)	20 (16 of 80)	11 (10 of 91)
Half or more honors and AP courses	37 (10 of 27)	13 (6 of 48)	24 (49 of 204)	14 (32 of 224)
Talk with friends about what they learn				
No honors or AP courses	55 (124 of 227)	59 (130 of 222)	52 (24 of 46)	76 (31 of 41)
Some, but less than half	55 (29 of 53)	68 (61 of 90)	64 (51 of 80)	78 (72 of 92)
Half or more honors and AP courses	52 (14 of 27)	77 (37 of 48)	71 (146 of 205)	85 (194 of 227)

These data seem to indicate that concerns about the potential of social isolation is one reason that black students, especially males, might choose to avoid honors and AP courses. Anecdotal evidence is plentiful. For example, at a recent conference of high-achieving minority teenagers from Shaker Heights and a dozen or so similar districts from across the nation, one black male said, "If you're a girl, some guy's always going to talk to you," but if you are a guy, you might end up all by yourself. Hence, when they do enroll in honors and AP classes, black males often take special measures to maintain their standing "within the fold" among other black males. Signithia Fordham writes the following about one of the young men in her ethnographic sample who is bright and whose parents push him to take advanced courses: "He must also repeatedly assure his classmates that though he has to take courses generally identified with the school's brainiacs, he is still very much one of the 'homeboys.' It is not Max's friends who are holding him back. It is, rather, his personal sense of marginality, his desire . . . to maintain his connectedness to the African American community."[50]

Regarding girls, a conversation I had with a young woman at the conference may be instructive. She said, "If you did everything that's required to stay in tight with the other black girls, you couldn't make it in honors or AP courses," because it would be too time-consuming. She indicated that girls like herself, because they are unwilling or unable to comply with some social requirements, are often unwelcome among girls who take no honors or AP classes. Boys, she says, have it easier. However, she echoed the quotation from the young man that "some guy's always going to talk to you" if you are a girl. She said that the main way she and some of her friends stay socially connected with other black students is that the boys bring them in, often to the dismay of the other black girls. She was clear, however, that there is no stigma on high achievement: "The attitude is that if you want to get A's, go on and get 'em." When she gets accused of acting white, it is because of the way she speaks and wears her hair. She lacks the skill to speak slang or to "sound black." However, she has become more socially accepted because now she at least tries (and friends laugh).

To summarize, black students who take mostly honors and Advanced Placement classes risk social isolation. They may find themselves suspended between the black and white communities—feeling fully connected to neither. Rather than be isolated, black high achievers seem to take the necessary measures to feel connected socially. It can be a challenge. However, the answer is only partly to give them more company, by getting larger numbers of black students into higher-level courses. Based on grades, the number currently prepared for such courses appears to be small. The more appropriate response is to improve supports and instruction—ranging from social skills to lessons on learning techniques—at every level of course taking and for all students.[51] As achievement levels rise in the courses where black students are concentrated, more will qualify for higher-level classes and enter them prepared to succeed.

CONCLUSION

Over the past decade, ethnographic researchers and news reporters have popularized the idea that alienation and social marginality among black Americans foster an oppositional culture that devalues academic performance and puts down high achievers by accusing them of acting white. The present study of the achievement disparities in Shaker Heights, Ohio, relies on self-reported survey data from seventh-to-eleventh graders collected in the spring of 1999. Upon first inspection, some patterns in the data seem consistent with the oppositional culture perspective. Among both males and females, black teenagers in Shaker Heights complete less homework on average than whites, participate less in class discussions, and are more inclined than white students to act tough and get into fights.[52] Black students also enroll in honors and AP courses at a much lower rate than whites, and it is well known in Shaker Heights that peers sometimes accuse blacks who enroll in such courses of acting white.

While these patterns seem consistent with the oppositional culture explanation for black-white achievement disparities, this paper tells a more complicated story. First, some things that appear to be elements of black youth culture are best understood nonracially, in terms of socioeconomic background. For example, blacks' lower self-reported propensity to participate in class discussion disappears once I control for parental education and other nonracial measures of family background. Holding family background constant, black males report more interest in their studies than white males and there is no black-white difference among females.

Second, black students report spending as much (or more) time doing their homework each day as white students who take the same classes.[53] This and related findings suggest that the reason blacks complete less homework than whites may be that they have fewer skills and get less help at home, not that they care less or exert less effort.

Third, the percentage of youth who report peer pressure against hard work and academic competition is similar among blacks and whites.

Fourth, blacks and whites seem equally happy with their teachers. For example, 77 percent of black males, 81 percent of white males, 82 percent of black females, and 85 percent of white females agree that teachers grade them fairly.[54]

Fifth, 53 percent of black males but only 27 percent of white males, and 38 percent of black females but only 10 percent of white females, believe that being tough contributes to popularity. However, once other variables are controlled, this belief is not a statistically significant predictor of the student's grade point average and does not help in predicting the black-white GPA gap.[55]

Sixth, whether judged by grades, standardized test scores, or other criteria, the average black student in Shaker Heights is less well prepared than the average white student to do well in honors and AP courses. For example, on the Ohio Sixth Grade Proficiency Test in 1999, 91 percent of white males and 89 percent of white females passed the reading portion as opposed to 51 percent of black males and 41 percent of black females. Math results were similar. (All of these passing rates were above the statewide averages for the respective groups.) Student-level data for this study do not include test scores. However, given the size of the test score gap that exists at sixth grade, it is plausible that skill differences account for most of the black-white difference in honors and AP enrollment from seventh grade on.[56] Any residual difference would most likely reflect the tendency of both blacks and whites to take classes with friends and avoid classes in which the other racial group is in the vast majority. Students attest that there is such a tendency, but my data do not allow me to estimate its effect on enrollment patterns. In addition, the role of the student advising system may be important as well, if racial biases exist in the advice that students get about which classes to take.[57]

Seventh, black students who take mostly honors and AP level courses face difficult time pressures and emotional stresses when they try to meet both academic and social requirements. Academically, honors and AP homework assignments can take several hours each day. Socially, keeping up with other black students can involve watching television for two to three hours nightly to participate in daily lunch-table discussions, staying current with new music releases, playing sports, and staying on pace with changing fads in clothing and hair styles (hair is a major focus among black girls).

Despite the difficulties, some struggle to meet both academic and social demands. Others, most often girls, decide to minimize time-consuming and academically unproductive social involvement with black peers who take no honors or AP courses, in favor of spending time with honors and AP classmates (frequently whites) who can also be study partners. A consequence for the latter youth is that black peers may accuse them of acting white. What blacks who make the accusations find offensive, however, is not academically successful students' accomplishments or ambitions, but their apparent rejection of black friends (and sometimes black identity) in favor of white ones. Given both the time pressures and the potential for social isolation from black peers, it is easy to understand why some black students who have the ability to do higher-level work decide to remain instead in nonhonors, non-AP courses.

In conclusion, the present study finds no clear evidence that black students in Shaker Heights are any more opposed to achievement, any less satisfied with school, or any less interested in their studies than their white counterparts—especially those who have similar family backgrounds.

Even so, the black-white GPA gap among seventh-to-eleventh graders in Shaker Heights is roughly one letter grade and the difference among seniors on the Scholastic Assessment Test (SAT) for college entrance is 200 points.[58] The conclusion most in line with the evidence is that skills and learning techniques, not oppositional culture, should be the focus of efforts to close the achievement gap.

Little or no support for the oppositional culture theory.

I gratefully acknowledge very helpful comments from William Dickens, Roland Fryer, Derrick James, Christopher Jencks, John Kain, Larry Kilian, Jens Ludwig, Jal Mehta, James Paces, Wilbur Rich, and Sara Stoutland. Thanks also go to John H. Bishop, who developed the survey upon which the paper relies for data; to all of the people in Shaker Heights, Ohio, who assisted in getting the survey administered; and to the Cleveland and Gund Foundations for their support of this and other work to bolster achievement in Shaker Heights.

TABLE A–1   Means and Standard Deviations for the Entire Shaker Heights, Ohio, Sample and Means for Black and White Males and Females

Variable name	Mean for the entire sample[a]	S.D. for entire sample[a]	Means for race and gender groups			
			Black males	Black females	White males	White females
	(1)	(2)	(3)	(4)	(5)	(6)
Grade point average (as reported)	2.784	0.934	2.083	2.428	3.211	3.354
Proportion honors and Advanced Placement courses	0.324	0.331	0.110	0.160	0.510	0.527
Homework completion rate (z)	−0.001	0.998	−0.295	−0.115	0.144	0.309
Hours per night on homework (hours)	2.226	1.470	1.879	2.150	2.167	2.588
Parents' average years of schooling[b]						
Twelve years or fewer (0, 0.5, 1)	0.152	0.298	0.250	0.255	0.043	0.047
Thirteen to fifteen years (0, 0.5, 1)	0.191	0.322	0.316	0.319	0.064	0.072
Sixteen years (0, 0.5, 1)	0.325	0.372	0.261	0.263	0.389	0.388
Graduate degree (0, 0.5, 1)	0.332	0.396	0.173	0.163	0.503	0.493
Household composition						
Two parents (0,1)	0.554	0.497	0.355	0.349	0.853	0.760
One birth parent and a stepparent (0,1)	0.102	0.303	0.119	0.134	0.060	0.096
One parent or neither (0,1)	0.311	0.463	0.519	0.518	0.087	0.143
Number of siblings	2.116	1.574	2.394	2.539	1.734	1.802
Important reasons when failing to study or do homework						
Competing time commitments (0,1)	0.479	0.497	0.380	0.388	0.538	0.656
Could get good grade without study (0,1)	0.499	0.498	0.420	0.347	0.650	0.616
Simply decided not to bother (z)	0.000	1.000	0.020	−0.155	0.231	−0.034
Carelessness and poor planning (z)	0.000	1.000	−0.049	0.173	−0.123	−0.024
The work was too difficult (z)	0.000	1.000	−0.294	0.096	−0.108	0.252

TABLE A–1   Means and Standard Deviations for the Entire Shaker Heights, Ohio, Sample and Means for Black and White Males and Females   *(continued)*

Variable name	Mean for the entire sample[a]	S.D. for entire sample[a]	Means for race and gender groups			
			Black males	Black females	White males	White females
	(1)	*(2)*	*(3)*	*(4)*	*(5)*	*(6)*
Other attitudes and behaviors						
Work is intrinsically interesting (z)	0.000	1.000	0.032	–0.066	–0.022	0.084
Contribute to class discussion (z)	0.000	1.000	–0.044	–0.091	0.139	0.091
Do homework for one class in another (z)	0.000	1.000	0.161	0.070	–0.095	–0.159
Joke around in class (z)	0.000	1.000	0.187	–0.306	0.330	–0.115
Really pay attention in class (z)	0.000	1.000	–0.123	0.055	–0.076	0.130
Hold back or hide work effort (0,1)	0.097	0.294	0.207	0.102	0.067	0.033
Copy homework from friends (0,1)	0.370	0.475	0.405	0.341	0.415	0.341
Study with friends (0,1)	0.349	0.467	0.279	0.393	0.311	0.419
Agree teachers maintain discipline (0,1)	0.728	0.440	0.686	0.705	0.776	0.767
TV hours per school night	2.311	2.162	3.234	3.061	1.744	1.273
Number years of college hope to attain (z)	0.000	1.000	–0.505	0.069	0.156	0.224
Work hard to please adults (z)	0.000	1.000	0.157	0.062	–0.226	0.013
Friends think academic zeal isn't cool (z)	0.000	1.000	–0.038	–0.139	0.223	–0.040
Agree popular crowd is "tough" (0,1)	0.309	0.456	0.526	0.378	0.270	0.099
Agree popular crowd is "outgoing" (0,1)	0.565	0.481	0.438	0.579	0.621	0.643
Agree popular crowd is "self-confident" (0,1)	0.556	0.489	0.472	0.566	0.649	0.624
Number of students	(1,699)		(318)	(367)	(334)	(363)

a. The means and standard deviations in columns 1 and 2 for the entire sample include all racial groups, not only blacks and whites.

b. 0.5 = one parent in the category; 1 = two parents.

TABLE A–2   Multiple Regression Results for Grade Point Average

Explanatory variable	Specification A			Specification B		
	Coefficient (1)	Standard error (2)	Probability value (3)	Coefficient (4)	Standard error (5)	Probability value (6)
Proportion honors and Advanced Placement courses	—	—	—	0.697	0.092	0.000
Homework completion rate (z)	—	—	—	0.248	0.025	0.000
Hours per night on homework (hours)	—	—	—	0.016	0.015	0.264
Race and gender						
White female is the base category	—	—	—	—	—	—
Black male (0,1)	−0.704	0.077	0.000	−0.507	0.075	0.000
Black female (0,1)	−0.480	0.066	0.000	−0.306	0.065	0.000
White male (0,1)	−0.062	0.048	0.194	−0.051	0.043	0.237
Parents' average years of schooling[a]						
Advanced degree is the base category	—	—	—	—	—	—
Twelve years or fewer (0, 0.5, 1)	−0.546	0.101	0.000	−0.328	0.095	0.001
Thirteen to fifteen years (0, 0.5, 1)	−0.281	0.083	0.001	−0.180	0.076	0.018
Sixteen years (0, 0.5, 1)	−0.118	0.054	0.029	−0.012	0.048	0.808
Household composition						
Two parents is the base category	—	—	—	—	—	—
One birth parent and a stepparent (0,1)	−0.135	0.073	0.064	−0.043	0.064	0.508
One parent or neither (0,1)	−0.147	0.056	0.008	−0.056	0.051	0.272
Number of siblings	−0.038	0.014	0.008	−0.030	0.014	0.026
Important reasons when failing to study or complete homework						
Competing time commitments (0,1)	0.262	0.040	0.000	0.179	0.036	0.000
Could get good grade without study (0,1)	0.206	0.039	0.000	0.143	0.037	0.000
Simply decided not to bother (z)	−0.096	0.020	0.000	−0.047	0.018	0.011

TABLE A–2 Multiple Regression Results for Grade Point Average *(continued)*

Explanatory variable	Specification A			Specification B		
	Coefficient (1)	Standard error (2)	Probability value (3)	Coefficient (4)	Standard error (5)	Probability value (6)
Carelessness and poor planning (z)	–0.038	0.021	0.066	–0.019	0.019	0.327
The work was too difficult (z)	–0.047	0.021	0.025	–0.042	0.019	0.029
Other attitudes and behaviors						
Work is intrinsically interesting (z)	0.021	0.024	0.374	–0.007	0.022	0.746
Contribute to class discussion (z)	0.056	0.024	0.019	0.030	0.022	0.173
Do homework for one class in another (z)	0.037	0.023	0.112	0.043	0.022	0.055
Joke around in class (z)	–0.068	0.024	0.005	–0.056	0.022	0.011
Really pay attention in class (z)	0.070	0.027	0.010	0.023	0.026	0.379
Hold back or hide work effort (0,1)	–0.216	0.083	0.009	–0.111	0.078	0.155
Copy homework from friends (0,1)	–0.090	0.045	0.045	–0.069	0.041	0.094
Study with friends (0,1)	0.082	0.040	0.039	0.012	0.037	0.744
Agree teachers maintain discipline (0,1)	0.081	0.047	0.085	0.064	0.043	0.138
TV hours per school night	0.001	0.012	0.916	0.008	0.012	0.519
Number years of college hope to attain (z)	0.115	0.029	0.000	0.075	0.027	0.005
Work hard to please adults (z)	–0.013	0.021	0.522	–0.006	0.019	0.760
Friends think academic zeal isn't cool (z)	0.029	0.021	0.167	0.030	0.020	0.139
Agree popular crowd is "tough" (0,1)	–0.081	0.048	0.093	–0.034	0.044	0.449
Agree popular crowd is "outgoing" (0,1)	0.061	0.042	0.149	0.026	0.039	0.501
Agree popular crowd is "self-confident" (0,1)	–0.050	0.042	0.231	–0.053	0.038	0.164
Constant	3.274	0.078	0.000	2.806	0.088	0.000
N = 1,267	R-square = 0.505			R-square = 0.586		

— = Not included in the regression.

a. 0.5 = one parent in the category; 1 = two parents.

TABLE A–3   Multiple Regression Results for Homework Completion Rate

	Specification A			Specification B		
	Coeffi-cient	Standard error	Prob-ability value	Coeffi-cient	Standard error	Prob-ability value
Explanatory variable	(1)	(2)	(3)	(4)	(5)	(6)
Proportion honors and Advanced Placement courses				–0.033	0.091	0.716
Hours per night on homework (hours)				0.128	0.019	0.000
Race and gender						
White female is the base category	—	—	—	—	—	—
Black male (0,1)	–0.162	0.084	0.055	–0.178	0.081	0.028
Black female (0,1)	–0.117	0.071	0.100	–0.128	0.071	0.070
White male (0,1)	0.014	0.060	0.816	0.031	0.060	0.604
Parents' average years of schooling[a]						
Advanced degree is the base category	—	—	—	—	—	—
Twelve years or fewer (0, 0.5, 1)	–0.293	0.104	0.005	–0.243	0.102	0.017
Thirteen to fifteen years (0, 0.5, 1)	–0.072	0.096	0.454	–0.045	0.093	0.627
Sixteen years (0, 0.5, 1)	–0.059	0.070	0.395	–0.034	0.069	0.622
Household composition						
Two parents is the base category	—	—	—	—	—	—
One birth parent and a stepparent (0,1)	–0.046	0.082	0.579	–0.039	0.082	0.632
One parent or neither (0,1)	–0.177	0.063	0.005	–0.170	0.061	0.005
Number of siblings	–0.012	0.015	0.440	–0.006	0.015	0.675
Important reasons when failing to study or complete homework						
Competing time commitments (0,1)	0.182	0.046	0.000	0.148	0.045	0.001
Could get good grade without study (0,1)	0.057	0.047	0.227	0.057	0.047	0.228
Simply decided not to bother (z)	–0.161	0.025	0.000	–0.146	0.025	0.000
Carelessness and poor planning (z)	–0.093	0.024	0.000	–0.098	0.023	0.000

TABLE A–3 Multiple Regression Results for Homework Completion Rate *(continued)*

Explanatory variable	Specification A			Specification B		
	Coefficient (1)	Standard error (2)	Probability value (3)	Coefficient (4)	Standard error (5)	Probability value (6)
The work was too difficult (z)	−0.015	0.023	0.521	−0.020	0.022	0.382
Other attitudes and behaviors						
Work is intrinsically interesting (z)	0.092	0.026	0.000	0.078	0.025	0.002
Contribute to class discussion (z)	0.068	0.027	0.012	0.073	0.026	0.006
Do homework for one class in another (z)	−0.022	0.027	0.413	−0.008	0.027	0.771
Joke around in class (z)	−0.068	0.029	0.020	−0.052	0.028	0.066
Really pay attention in class (z)	0.209	0.032	0.000	0.191	0.031	0.000
Hold back or hide work effort (0,1)	−0.230	0.083	0.006	−0.205	0.083	0.013
Copy homework from friends (0,1)	−0.117	0.050	0.020	−0.108	0.049	0.028
Study with friends (0,1)	0.119	0.046	0.010	0.088	0.046	0.055
Agree teachers maintain discipline (0,1)	−0.043	0.054	0.424	−0.053	0.052	0.314
TV hours per school night	−0.008	0.014	0.550	0.001	0.014	0.962
Number years of college hope to attain (z)	0.049	0.029	0.097	0.024	0.029	0.401
Work hard to please adults (z)	0.043	0.023	0.068	0.032	0.023	0.171
Friends think academic zeal isn't cool (z)	−0.002	0.026	0.952	−0.002	0.026	0.950
Agree popular crowd is "tough" (0,1)	−0.059	0.056	0.286	−0.042	0.055	0.446
Agree popular crowd is "outgoing" (0,1)	0.027	0.049	0.575	0.032	0.048	0.501
Agree popular crowd is "self-confident" (0,1)	−0.024	0.049	0.619	−0.040	0.048	0.406
Constant	0.311	0.095	0.001	0.002	0.109	0.986
N = 1,377	R-square = .328			R-square = .355		

— = Not included in the regression.

a. 0.5 = one parent in the category; 1 = two parents.

TABLE A–4   Multiple Regression Results for Hours per Day Doing Homework

Explanatory variable	Specification A			Specification B		
	Coeffi-cient (1)	Standard error (2)	Prob-ability value (3)	Coeffi-cient (4)	Standard error (5)	Prob-ability value (6)
Proportion honors and Advanced Placement courses				1.384	0.159	0.000
Race and gender						
White female is the base category	—	—	—	—	—	—
Black male (0,1)	0.061	0.141	0.666	0.353	0.143	0.014
Black female (0,1)	0.027	0.131	0.834	0.299	0.134	0.026
White male (0,1)	–0.135	0.104	0.192	–0.123	0.100	0.220
Parents' average years of schooling[a]						
Advanced degree is the base category	—	—	—	—	—	—
Twelve years or fewer (0, 0.5, 1)	–0.433	0.153	0.005	–0.177	0.147	0.229
Thirteen to fifteen years (0, 0.5, 1)	–0.228	0.163	0.162	–0.061	0.154	0.695
Sixteen years (0, 0.5, 1)	–0.228	0.118	0.052	–0.038	0.112	0.738
Household composition						
Two parents is the base category	—	—	—	—	—	—
One birth parent and a stepparent (0,1)	–0.063	0.117	0.593	0.073	0.117	0.534
One parent or neither (0,1)	–0.066	0.096	0.496	0.018	0.093	0.846
Number of siblings	–0.045	0.022	0.046	–0.038	0.022	0.081
Important reasons when failing to study or complete homework						
Competing time commitments (0,1)	0.220	0.073	0.003	0.144	0.071	0.043
Could get good grade without study (0,1)	0.017	0.073	0.815	–0.084	0.072	0.244
Simply decided not to bother (z)	–0.126	0.037	0.001	–0.114	0.036	0.001
Carelessness and poor planning (z)	0.042	0.038	0.265	0.035	0.037	0.345
The work was too difficult (z)	0.037	0.034	0.285	0.038	0.033	0.252

TABLE A–4   Multiple Regression Results for Hours per Day Doing Homework (*continued*)

Explanatory variable	Specification A			Specification B		
	Coefficient (1)	Standard error (2)	Probability value (3)	Coefficient (4)	Standard error (5)	Probability value (6)
Other attitudes and behaviors						
Work is intrinsically interesting (z)	0.110	0.043	0.010	0.102	0.041	0.013
Contribute to class discussion (z)	−0.031	0.042	0.472	−0.040	0.042	0.331
Do homework for one class in another (z)	−0.116	0.039	0.003	−0.116	0.038	0.003
Joke around in class (z)	−0.117	0.043	0.007	−0.133	0.041	0.001
Really pay attention in class (z)	0.138	0.043	0.001	0.153	0.043	0.000
Hold back or hide work effort (0,1)	−0.211	0.129	0.102	−0.111	0.126	0.382
Copy homework from friends (0,1)	−0.055	0.077	0.477	−0.075	0.075	0.313
Study with friends (0,1)	0.251	0.077	0.001	0.185	0.076	0.014
Agree teachers maintain discipline (0,1)	0.076	0.084	0.365	0.033	0.080	0.683
TV hours per school night	−0.072	0.021	0.001	−0.058	0.021	0.005
Number years of college hope to attain (z)	0.190	0.043	0.000	0.138	0.042	0.001
Work hard to please adults (z)	0.079	0.041	0.053	0.114	0.039	0.004
Friends think academic zeal isn't cool (z)	0.003	0.038	0.935	0.008	0.036	0.836
Agree popular crowd is "tough" (0,1)	−0.153	0.084	0.069	−0.083	0.080	0.303
Agree popular crowd is "outgoing" (0,1)	−0.024	0.076	0.753	−0.088	0.075	0.242
Agree popular crowd is "self-confident" (0,1)	0.121	0.076	0.113	0.105	0.074	0.158
Constant	2.546	0.149	0.000	1.854	0.148	0.000
N = 1,376	R-square = .214			R-square = .266		

— = Not included in the regression.

a. 0.5 = one parent in the category; 1 = two parents.

TABLE A–5   Multiple Regression Results for Proportion Honors and Advanced Placement Courses

Explanatory variable	Coefficient (1)	Standard error (2)	Probability value (3)
Race and gender			
White female is the base category	—	—	—
Black male (0,1)	−0.207	0.025	0.000
Black female (0,1)	−0.197	0.023	0.000
White male (0,1)	−0.007	0.020	0.713
Parents' average years of schooling[a]			
Advanced degree is the base category	—	—	—
Twelve years or fewer (0, 0.5, 1)	−0.187	0.030	0.000
Thirteen to fifteen years (0, 0.5, 1)	−0.119	0.029	0.000
Sixteen years (0, 0.5, 1)	−0.138	0.022	0.000
Household composition			
Two parents is the base category	—	—	—
One birth parent and a stepparent (0,1)	−0.100	0.023	0.000
One parent or neither (0,1)	−0.059	0.018	0.001
Number of siblings	−0.005	0.004	0.276
Important reasons when failing to complete homework			
Competing time commitments (0,1)	0.057	0.014	0.000
Could get good grade without study (0,1)	0.073	0.014	0.000
Simply decided not to bother (z)	−0.008	0.007	0.234
Carelessness and poor planning (z)	0.005	0.007	0.486
The work was too difficult (z)	−0.002	0.007	0.823

TABLE A–5   Multiple Regression Results for Proportion Honors and Advanced Placement Courses   *(continued)*

Explanatory variable	Coefficient (1)	Standard error (2)	Probability value (3)
Other attitudes and behaviors			
Work is intrinsically interesting (*z*)	0.004	0.007	0.571
Contribute to class discussion (*z*)	0.008	0.008	0.306
Do homework for one class in another (*z*)	0.000	0.007	0.980
Joke around in class (*z*)	0.011	0.008	0.186
Really pay attention in class (*z*)	−0.009	0.008	0.255
Hold back or hide work effort (0,1)	−0.078	0.023	0.001
Copy homework from friends (0,1)	0.017	0.015	0.252
Study with friends (0,1)	0.047	0.014	0.001
Agree teachers maintain discipline (0,1)	0.034	0.016	0.031
TV hours per school night	−0.010	0.004	0.006
Number years of college hope to attain (*z*)	0.040	0.008	0.000
Work hard to please adults (*z*)	−0.025	0.007	0.000
Friends think academic zeal isn't cool (*z*)	−0.002	0.007	0.814
Agree popular crowd is "tough" (0,1)	−0.051	0.015	0.001
Agree popular crowd is "outgoing" (0,1)	0.048	0.015	0.001
Agree popular crowd is "self-confident" (0,1)	0.010	0.015	0.494
Constant	0.494	0.028	0.000
N = 1,373	R-square = .494		

— = Not included in the regression.

a. 0.5 = one parent in the category; 1 = two parents.

CHAPTER 6

What *Doesn't* Meet the Eye

Understanding and Addressing Racial Disparities in High-Achieving Suburban Schools

INTRODUCTION

On January 8, 2002, President Bush signed into law the federal No Child Left Behind Act of 2001. Among other important features, this legislation dictates that states should publish achievement results separately for racial and ethnic groups and work to alleviate intergroup disparities. Thus, for the first time in the nation's history, raising achievement levels among racial and ethnic minorities and closing achievement gaps are explicit goals of federal policy.[1]

Improving the quality of inner-city schools will be an important aspect of pursuing these goals, but it will not be sufficient.[2] Suburbs must respond as well. The U.S. Census for the year 2000 reports that 33 percent of the nation's African-American children, 45 percent of Hispanic children, 54 percent of Asian children, and 55 percent of white children live in suburban communities.[3] Some attend poor, segregated schools, similar to the poorest in the inner city; others attend racially integrated schools in well-off communities, where resources are relatively abundant and schools are reputedly excellent.

This paper concerns racial and ethnic achievement disparities in places where schools are reputedly excellent.[4] Until recently, large achievement gaps in these districts were seldom discussed in public. (Although all racial groups were represented in all parts of the achievement distribution, blacks and Hispanics were underrepresented at the top and overrepresented at the bottom.) Schools took pride, as they still do, in the numbers of graduates scoring high on college entrance exams and matriculating to prestigious universities. Public officials, parents, and teachers alike considered the latter achievements to be proof-positive that the quality of education was high. Not surprisingly, the idea that schools and teachers should be searching relentlessly for ways to raise achievement—with special attention to African-American, Hispanic, and low-income students—was seldom a focus.

Fortunately, this pattern of apparent neglect and denial is beginning to change. In 1999, 15 middle- and upper-middle-income districts in Ohio, Michigan, Wisconsin, Illinois, Massachusetts, New York, New Jersey, North Carolina, California, and Virginia formed the Minority Student Achievement Network (MSAN). Together, they acknowledged the racial and ethnic achievement disparities in their primary and secondary schools. They resolved jointly to seek ways of narrowing gaps between European-American and Asian-American students, on the one hand, versus Hispanic and African-American students, on the other.

Among their first joint initiatives was an effort to understand better what students of different racial and ethnic groups were experiencing in school that might affect their engagement and achievement. During the 2000–01 school year, 95 schools across all 15 districts surveyed middle and high school students using a survey titled the "Ed-Excel Assessment of Secondary School Student Culture."[5] The present paper reports some of what was learned from the responses of students in Grades 7–11 and discusses some implications.[6] For these grades, the sample includes 7,120 blacks, 17,562 whites, 2,491 Hispanics, 2,448 Asians, and 4,507 mixed-race students.[7] The analysis and associated tables in the paper pertain to this full sample of 7th to 11th graders.[8]

Questions in the Ed-Excel survey cover family characteristics, opinions about the quality of instruction, enjoyment of studies, achievement motivations, course-taking patterns, effort, comprehension, grade-point averages, and more. It is well known that survey data can have self-reporting biases. Further, it is virtually impossible—with data collected at one point in time and with only one observation per student—to distinguish causal relationships among variables from mere correlations. Nonetheless, the data indicate strongly that there are common forces at work across the various states and localities represented. The high degree of similarity among districts underscores the strength and consistency of historically rooted social and economic forces that today produce such similar patterns in so many different places. (Due to space limitations, the tables and discussion in this paper address aggregates, pooled for all 15 districts. However, district-by-district tabulations that show the similarity among districts are available on the MSAN Web site at *www.msanetwork.org/pub/edexcel.pdf*.)

The paper begins with a brief preview of key patterns. Then, the main body of the paper presents the survey findings in greater detail. Sections near the end of the paper discuss implications for schools, communities, and policymakers. There, I emphasize the importance of professional development programs that have a combined emphasis on content, pedagogy, and relationships. Findings concerning encouragement focus attention on the possibility that effective teacher-student relationships may be especially important resources for motivating black and Hispanic students. I argue that when teachers have strong content knowledge and are willing to adapt their pedagogies to meet student needs, adding good teacher-student relationships and strong encouragement to the mix may be key. Such relationships and encouragement may help black and Hispanic students seek help more readily, engage their studies deeply, and ultimately overcome skill gaps that are due in substantial measure to past and present disparities in family-background advantages and associated social inequities.

A Preview of Key Patterns

Racial and ethnic differences addressed in this paper fall primarily into four categories. First, there are self-reported achievement and skill disparities. Black, Hispanic, and mixed-race students indicate lower grade-point averages than whites and Asians (which is consistent with official records). Blacks and Hispanics also report less understanding of their teachers' lessons and less comprehension of the material that they read for school. I take the view in this paper that student problems with understanding lessons and comprehending readings reflect knowledge and skill deficiencies that responsive instructional strategies can help to ameliorate.

Second, there are differences in socioeconomic status (SES) and home learning resources. White and Asian students in MSAN communities arrive at school with greater socioeconomic-background advantages, on average, compared to blacks and Hispanics. These advantages include home learning resources, such as books and computers in the home. Several measures of SES are important predictors of achievement (though the estimates indicate that particular SES advantages boost achievement less among blacks and Hispanics than among whites and Asians).

Third, students were asked, "When you work really hard in school, which of the following reasons are most important for you?" In response, nonwhite students—and especially blacks—identified teacher encouragement more frequently than did whites. Further, nonwhites indicated teacher encouragement substantially more often than they emphasized teachers' demands.

Conversely, white students cited teachers' demands more often than non-whites and about equally as often as they (whites) cited teacher encouragement. The emphasis among nonwhites on teacher encouragement, as distinct from teacher demands, suggests the special importance of teacher-student relationships as a source of achievement motivation for blacks and Hispanics in particular.

Fourth, there are racial and ethnic differences in observable behaviors and homework completion rates. The differences make whites and Asians appear to be more academically engaged and may give teachers the impression that whites and Asians are more interested in their studies and work harder, on average, than black or Hispanic classmates.

There is much that does not meet the teacher's eye, however, including a number of intergroup similarities. Measures of effort and interest are the prime examples. As previously stated, there are differences in reported rates of homework completion. Yet reported times spent studying and doing homework differ very little among blacks, whites, and Hispanics in the same school and grade who take the same level classes.[9] Asians are the only group that stands out with regard to effort, as measured by time on homework. Further, no group—not even Asians—expressed a distinctively high level of interest in schoolwork.

ACHIEVEMENT GAPS IN MSAN DISTRICTS

There are three achievement indicators in the MSAN Ed-Excel data, and all show racial gaps.[10] First, the survey asks, "What was your grade-point average last term?" The respondent chooses one option from among A, A−, B+, and so on, down to D+, D, and D−/F. Although self-reports can sometimes be misleading, comparisons of survey findings with official records for race-by-gender groups indicate only moderate inflation in the self-reports and the same basic rank ordering of grade-point average among groups.[11] A second indicator of achievement is the student's response to the following question: "What percentage of the time do you completely understand the teacher's lesson?" The forced-choice question offers five possible responses, ranging from "10% or less" to "90% or more." The third achievement variable is the student's answer to "How much of the material that you read for school do you understand very well?"[12] The response options were "very little or none," "some," "about half," "a lot," and "all or nearly all of it."

Table 6–1 shows the answers for all three questions and each of five race/ethnic groups. In Panel A of Table 6–1, fully half of whites and Asians report

TABLE 6–1   Racial Distributions for Three Achievement Gap Indicators*

Numbers are percentages in each response category for each racial or ethnic group.

Panel A: What was your grade-point average last term?					
	Black	White	Hispanic	Asian	Mixed Race
D+ or below	9	2	8	3	8
C– to C+	35	12	26	12	22
B– to B+	40	36	45	35	38
A– to A	15	50	21	50	32
COLUMN TOTAL	100	100	100	100	100

Panel B: How much of the material that you read for school do you understand very well?					
	Black	White	Hispanic	Asian	Mixed Race
About half or less	55	29	56	42	41
A lot	30	35	30	31	30
Almost all	15	35	14	27	29
COLUMN TOTAL	100	100	100	100	100

Panel C: What percentage of the time do you completely understand the teacher's lesson?					
	Black	White	Hispanic	Asian	Mixed Race
About half the time or less	48	28	46	31	38
65% to 89%	36	44	36	38	38
90% or more	16	29	18	30	24
COLUMN TOTAL	100	100	100	100	100

* Two districts did not use the version of the questionnaire that included the question covered by Panel B, hence the number of respondents is smaller than in the other two panels. The number of respondents is smaller in Panel A than in Panel C because while 8 percent of students did not respond to the grade-point average (GPA) question, only 2 percent did not respond to the question in Panel C. By race, percentages not responding to the GPA question were 9.0% for blacks, 5.4% for whites, 10.3% for Hispanics, 6.4% for Asians, and 6.8% for mixed-race students. If responses were imputed for missing data, the distributions would change only slightly.

TABLE 6–2   Five Types of Socioeconomic Disparity within and among Racial and Ethnic Groups in the MSAN Ed-Excel Data

	Black	White	Hispanic	Asian	Mixed Race
	Percentages within Racial Groups				
Living Arrangements					
One parent or neither	53	15	35	19	37
One parent and stepparent	11	9	10	5	13
Two parents	36	77	55	76	50
TOTAL	100	100	100	100	100
Mother's Years of Schooling					
12 or fewer	28	11	50	25	22
13 to 15	23	12	15	10	17
Four-year college graduate	27	41	16	33	33
Advanced degree	21	36	19	31	28
TOTAL	100	100	100	100	100
Number of Siblings					
Two or fewer siblings	49	81	60	68	59
Three or more siblings	51	19	40	32	41
TOTAL	100	100	100	100	100
Access to a Computer at Home					
No access to a computer at home	22	3	30	10	13
One computer at home	51	40	50	48	44
Two or more computers at home	27	57	20	42	43
TOTAL	100	100	100	100	100
Books in the Student's Home					
10 or fewer books at home	10	2	20	8	6
Between 10 and 100 books at home	50	18	51	45	29
Over 100 books at home	40	79	29	47	65
TOTAL	100	100	100	100	100

grade-point averages of A or A–, while the same is true for only 15 percent of blacks and 21 percent of Hispanics. Conversely, 44 percent of blacks and 34 percent of Hispanics report grade-point averages of C+ or below while only 14 percent of whites and 15 percent of Asians do. In Panel B of Table 6–1, slightly more than 50 percent of blacks and Hispanics responded "about half or less" concerning how much (or how little) of school-related readings they "understand very well."[13] The corresponding number for whites is 29 percent. For Asians and mixed-race students, the corresponding numbers are 42 percent and 43 percent, respectively. Panel C of Table 6–1 shows data for the percentage of the time that students "completely understand" the teacher's lesson. The distribution of answers is similar to Panel B. Almost half of black and Hispanic students indicate that they understand the lesson about half the time or less. The same is true for between one-quarter and one-third of whites and Asians.

FAMILY BACKGROUND DISPARITIES

Are the disparities in Table 6–1 associated with racial and ethnic differences in the SES of students' families? How large are the SES differences? Table 6–2 shows that about half of all black students in the sample report that they live with one or neither parent, while only 15 percent of whites report the same. Other groups are between blacks and whites on this measure. The consistency across districts on this measure (and others) is remarkable, given that the districts are in nine different states. Separately for each of the 15 districts, the percentages of blacks living with one or neither parent are 46, 50, 54, 57, 52, 52, 46, 49, 59, 49, 48, 50, 51, 54, and 53. At the other extreme, the percentages for whites are 14, 14, 15, 15, 22, 14, 16, 11, 14, 12, 10, 12, 19, 18, and 16, respectively.

There also are differences in parental education levels, as shown by the tabulation of "mother's years of schooling" in Table 6–2.[14] Half of Hispanic students report that their mothers have 12 or fewer years of schooling, while 77 percent of whites report that their mothers have either a four-year college degree (41 percent) or a graduate degree (36 percent). Black mothers have more years of schooling than Hispanics but less than Asians, while Asians have less than whites. Parental education levels for blacks and Hispanics in these districts are quite high, compared even to the national averages for whites. Still, there are gaps inside the districts because the education levels among white and Asian residents are so *very* high.

In addition, black and Hispanic students have more siblings. Half of blacks—but only 19 percent of whites, 32 percent of Asians, 40 percent of Hispanics, and 41 percent of mixed-race students—have three or more siblings. Assuming that most siblings live in the same household, more siblings means more sharing of scarce resources, such as the family computer(s) and parental attention. White households have the fewest children and the most computers, while Hispanic households have more children and the fewest computers. Similarly, white youth report more books in their homes than other groups. Hispanic students report the fewest books; black, Asian, and mixed-race students also report substantially fewer books than whites.

Does Socioeconomic Status Predict Achievement Disparities?

The analysis in this section is designed to answer two related questions. One question is whether SES helps to predict racial and ethnic differences in achievement. Many studies have addressed this question, and the answer is virtually always yes.[15] The other question is whether the magnitude of the achievement gap is different for different levels of SES. For both questions, the answer here is yes. Disparities in SES predict substantial portions of the disparity for each measure of achievement, but not all of it.[16] In addition, the residual "unexplained" disparity, holding SES constant, is greater among students from high-SES households.

For this analysis, the grade-point average from the most recent term is measured on a four-point scale; the other two achievement variables from Table 6–1 are measured now in standard deviation units.[17] Also, it is worth noting that the SES variables here relate conceptually to home intellectual resources (such as books in the home, computers in the home, and parents' education) and number of parents per child (number of siblings and number of parents). The data for this study lack financial-status measures, such as wealth, income, or free and reduced-price lunch status.[18]

The analysis here uses four standardized SES categories: lowest SES, lower-middle SES, upper-middle SES, and highest SES.[19] Table 6–3a shows what percentage of each race/ethnic group is in each of them. Only 2 percent of blacks have SES characteristics in the highest SES category, while only 3 percent of whites have characteristics in the lowest category. Approximately 79 percent of blacks, 78 percent of Hispanics, 56 percent of mixed-race students, 46 percent of Asians, and only 28 percent of whites are in the lowest and lower-middle categories combined. A look back at Table 6–2 shows the types of SES disparities for particular variables that together account for the disparities in Table 6–3a.

TABLE 6–3a   Percentage Distribution of Each Race/Ethnic Group across Four SES Categories

	Black	White	Hispanic	Asian	Mixed Race	Total
SES Category	Percentages					
Lowest SES	24	3	19	7	12	10
Lower-middle SES	55	25	59	39	44	40
Upper-middle SES	19	57	19	41	37	40
Highest SES	2	16	3	12	8	10
COLUMN TOTAL	100	100	100	100	100	100

Table 6–3b uses SES "profiles" constructed from the SES categories mentioned above. For a given SES category, say "lower-middle SES," the SES profile comprises the list of mean SES characteristics across all race/ethnic groups combined. Thus, each profile is identical for all race/ethnic groups in a given SES category.

The "prototypical student" defined by a given SES profile has a different predicted achievement level, depending on race/ethnicity. This situation is true for each of the three achievement variables (grade-point average, comprehension of lessons, and understanding of readings). The lowest SES level shows the least race/ethnic achievement disparity.[20] For this profile, the predicted black-white gap in grade-point average (GPA) is only 0.14 GPA points; the predicted grade-point average for Hispanics is actually 0.09 points higher than for whites (Panel A of Table 6–3b). Similarly, in Panel B and Panel C of Table 6–3b, the other two achievement measures do not show any clear tendency for whites to rank higher than other groups. Generally, these findings show only small race/ethnic achievement gaps in MSAN districts among students with the lowest SES profile.

However, at the highest SES level, the disparity among groups is much greater. Whites rank highest and blacks lowest, with sizable gaps between them. The predicted grade-point average gap at the highest SES level is one-fifth of a GPA point between whites and mixed-race students, one-third of a point between whites and Hispanics, and a full half-point between whites and blacks. The rank order of predicted achievement among groups is the same for the two skill measures in Panel B and Panel C. Note that the predictions for whites and Asians are essentially equal across all three measures.

TABLE 6–3b   Simulations by SES Profile and Race/Ethnicity for Three Achievement Measures*

SES Profile	Black	White	Hispanic	Asian	Mixed Race
Panel A Simulated Mean GPA (4-point scale)					
Lowest SES	2.38	2.52	2.61	2.66	2.30
Lower-middle SES	2.65	2.91	2.88	3.07	2.73
Upper-middle SES	2.88	3.36	3.13	3.36	3.17
Highest SES	3.18	3.68	3.34	3.67	3.49
Panel B Simulated Amount That the Student "Completely" Understands of Teachers' Lessons (Standard Deviation Units)					
Lowest SES	–0.38	–0.54	–0.44	–0.58	–0.59
Lower-middle SES	–0.23	–0.22	–0.21	–0.26	–0.26
Upper-middle SES	0.00	0.20	0.01	0.06	0.22
Highest SES	0.04	0.35	0.11	0.35	0.31
Panel C Simulated Amount That the Student Understands "Very Well" of Material Read for School (Standard Deviation Units)					
Lowest SES	–0.56	–0.59	–0.65	–0.64	–0.57
Lower-middle SES	–0.36	–0.15	–0.39	–0.29	–0.31
Upper-middle SES	–0.07	0.25	–0.06	0.17	0.17
Highest SES	0.06	0.44	0.17	0.41	0.36

* Simulations are for fixed SES profiles, where achievement predictions use regression coefficients estimated separately by race/ethnicity. See text and footnotes for more detail.

High-SES students achieve at higher levels than middle-SES and low-SES students among all racial and ethnic groups. However, findings here indicate that the degree to which SES pays off differs among groups. For all three measures, the difference in achievement between high- and low-SES students is smallest for blacks and Hispanics. The reasons are not entirely clear and will be the subject of ongoing research by this author and others. The differences may simply be artifacts of the (in)accuracy with which students answered the survey. More likely, these differences may reflect race/ethnic differences

TABLE 6–4   Racial and Ethnic Differences in Time Studying or Doing Homework (Panel A) and Homework Completion (Panel B)

Honors/AP Enrollment Status	Black	White	Hispanic	Asian	Mixed Race
	Each Group's Mean Minus Whites' Mean				
Panel A: Gap in Time Studying or Doing Homework (in Hours)					
Not currently in honors or AP courses	–0.02	N/A	–0.08*	0.50*	0.05
In at least one honors or AP course	0.09*	N/A	0.04	0.66*	0.03
Panel B: Gap in the Amount of Homework Completed (in Standard Deviations)					
Not currently in honors or AP courses	–0.26*	N/A	–0.29*	0.06*	–0.28*
In at least one honors or AP course	–0.20*	N/A	–0.21*	0.22*	–0.16*

Note: Differences are multiple-regression coefficients on race/ethnic indicator variables, using multiple regressions with school-grade-level fixed effects.

* indicates significance at the 0.05 level.

in home, peer, and classroom processes among high-SES students. In any case, it appears from this analysis that SES differences (and the differential life experiences that they represent) account for some but not all racial and ethnic differences in student-reported grade-point average, understanding of teachers' lessons, and comprehension of materials read for school. Further, the unexplained racial differences are greatest at the highest SES levels.   *N.B.*

Time Spent Studying and Doing Homework

A common view is that an important reason for achievement gaps may be that black and Hispanic students do not work as hard at their studies as white and Asian students.[21] Therefore, the question is asked: Is there evidence in the data that black and Hispanic students in MSAN districts are not working as hard as whites and Asians?

The best measure of student effort in the Ed-Excel data is the student's report of how much time he or she spends on weekdays after school studying and doing homework. The data show very small racial differences among classmates. Panel A of Table 6–4 shows that only Asians stand out as studying more than other groups. Among students not enrolled in honors or advanced placement (AP) classes, Asians report that they study and do homework for about half an hour more per night than other groups. Among those enrolled

TABLE 6–5 Percentages Completing "Some," "Most," or "All" Homework in Given Amounts of Time on Task, Tabulated by Race/Ethnicity for (A) Students Not Currently Enrolled in Honors/AP Courses and (B) Students Who Are

	Whites and Asians			Blacks, Hispanics, Mixed Race		
	Nightly Hours Studying or Doing Homework					
	~1 Hour	~2 Hours	~3+ Hours	~1 Hour	~2 Hours	~3+ Hours
Amount of Homework Completed	Column Percentages			Column Percentages		
A. Column Percentages for Students Who Take No Honors or Advanced Placement Courses						
Some, or not much of it	26	10	7	34	17	12
Most of it	52	52	47	53	63	60
All of it	22	38	46	12	20	28
COLUMN TOTAL	100	100	100	100	100	100
B. Column Percentages for Students in at Least One Honors or Advanced Placement Course						
Some, or not much of it	18	7	3	29	11	8
Most of it	54	54	46	58	62	57
All of it	28	40	51	13	27	34
COLUMN TOTAL	100	100	100	100	100	100

in at least one honors or AP course, Asians report about two-thirds of an hour more. The differences between Asians and others in this regard are very significant statistically. Conversely, the differences in studying and homework between whites compared to blacks and Hispanics are statistically significant, but they are miniscule—the largest is 0.09 hours per night (about five minutes, which is roughly one-twentieth of a standard deviation). Among blacks, whites, Hispanics, and mixed-race students, racial differences in time on homework come primarily from differences in the degree to which the groups enroll in honors and AP courses, not from differences among students taking the same classes.

Although course-level differences among blacks, whites, Hispanics, and mixed-race students in time studying and doing homework are trivial, blacks, Hispanics, and mixed-race students report lower rates of homework completion than whites for any given amount of time spent studying. Panel B of Table 6–4 shows the differences in standard deviation units. By roughly 0.20 to 0.30 standard deviations, blacks, mixed-race students, and Hispanics complete less homework per night than whites do. These are not huge differences, but they are probably large enough to be noticed by teachers and may cause some teachers to assume that blacks, Hispanics, and mixed-race students put less time and effort into their studies compared to whites and Asians classmates. Evidence here suggests that such assumptions about time and effort would be correct regarding how blacks, Hispanics, and mixed-race students compare to Asians, but incorrect regarding how they compare to whites.

Table 6–5 shows homework completion patterns, cross-tabulated with time on homework. It pools student reports of homework completion for math, science, English, and social studies into a composite index of homework completion. Describing how much homework students complete, the three values of the index are "some or not much of it," "most of it," and "all of it."[22] The time-on-homework data are collapsed into three categories, representing about one hour or less (labeled "~1 hour"), about two hours (labeled "~2 hours") and about three hours or more (labeled "~3 hours").

The first three columns of Table 6–5 show the patterns for whites and Asians combined while the second three columns show the patterns for blacks, Hispanics, and mixed-race students. For each amount of time indicated, blacks, Hispanics, and mixed-race students are less likely than whites and Asians to complete all of their homework and more likely to complete "some, or not much of it." For example, among students not enrolled in honors or AP courses who report about two hours per night doing homework, blacks, Hispanics, and mixed-race students are only about half as likely as whites and Asians (20 percent versus 38 percent) to report that they usually complete all of their homework. It appears that black, Hispanic, and mixed-race students work longer to complete the same amount of homework that whites and Asians complete in a shorter time.

Multiple-regression estimates indicate that differences in family background together with gaps in comprehension of readings and teachers' lessons predict almost all differences in homework completion among black, white, Hispanic, and mixed-race students. This finding—together with findings of equal time on homework among blacks, whites, Hispanics, and mixed-race students taking the same classes—supports the interpretation that levels of effort among these groups are quite similar, but knowledge, skills, and family backgrounds are not.[23]

Why Students Work Hard

An adequately ambitious, multidimensional strategy to close racial and ethnic gaps in academic knowledge and skill would have many components. It would focus relentlessly on ideas and activities geared to produce learning. It would have roles for teachers, parents, administrators, students, and others, including policymakers. Among the things it might ask of black, Hispanic, and mixed-race adolescents is that they should devote more time and effort to their studies than they currently do, even if they already work as much, on average, as white classmates. This increase in effort is unlikely to occur without approaches to instruction that push students toward higher goals and make achieving those goals both feasible and rewarding.

The prospect of needing to increase effort levels brings us to the question of whether particular strategies for eliciting more effort from students are likely to be more effective than others. Some insight in this regard comes from student responses to the following question in the Ed-Excel survey: "When you work really hard in school, which of the following reasons are most important to you? (Mark as many as apply to you.)" For each of 14 items, students could darken a bubble indicating that the item is important or they could leave the bubble blank.

Table 6–6 shows student responses by race/ethnicity, ranked in order from the item that received the most responses to the item that received the least. For most items, the rank order from top to bottom is the same for all race/ethnic groups and the percentage of the group indicating that any given item is important does not differ greatly across groups. For example, the top item among all groups is "I need the grades to get into college." The percentage of students indicating that this reason is important ranges from 71 percent of Hispanic students to 81 percent of Asians. White, black, and mixed-race students are nearly identical in their responses, at 78 percent of whites, 77 percent of blacks, and 77 percent of mixed-race students. The percentage marking "to please or impress my parents" occupies a narrow range from 61 percent of whites to 64 percent of Asians. Regarding the extrinsic goals of preparing for good jobs and tough college courses, whites rank lowest and Asians rank highest. For the more intrinsically oriented purposes—specifically, "I want to learn the material" and "the subject is interesting"—group differences are very small. For most items in Table 6–6, no group stands out. The similarities are remarkable.

However, there are two items that show quite interesting race/ethnic differences, especially when considered together.[24] Specifically, when compared to whites, black and Hispanic students are more likely to indicate "my teach-

TABLE 6–6 Percentage of Respondents, by Race/Ethnicity, That Selected Each Respective Response to the Question: "When you work really hard in school, which of the following reasons are most important to you? (Mark as many as apply to you.)"

	Black	White	Hispanic	Asian	Mixed Race
	Percentages				
1. I need the grades to get into college.	77	78	71	81	77
2. To please or impress my parents.	62	61	62	64	63
3. Help me get a better job.	60	54	63	64	59
4. Prepare for tough college courses.	62	53	59	64	58
5. I want to learn the material.	57	52	57	56	53
6. My parents put pressure on me.	44	47	39	50	49
7. The subject is interesting.	37	41	40	40	40
8. My teachers encourage me to work hard.	47	31	41	31	37
9. The teacher demands it.	15	29	19	20	24
10. I enjoyed doing the assignment.	32	29	33	33	32
11. To please or impress my teacher.	29	28	29	29	29
12. I want to keep up with my friends.	24	27	23	31	28
13. I don't want to embarrass my family.	26	15	27	33	24
14. My friends put pressure on me.	8	7	8	9	10

ers encourage me to work hard" as a motivational factor and less likely to identify "the teacher demands it." Blacks are three times as likely to endorse encouragement as they are to cite teacher demands; 47 percent of blacks identify teacher encouragement as an important motivator, compared to 15 percent for teacher demands. Hispanics are two times as likely to cite encouragement (41 percent) compared to demands (19 percent), and whites are likely to cite each roughly equally (31 percent for encouragement and 29 percent for demands). Asians (31 percent for encouragement and 20 percent for demands) and mixed-race students (37 percent for encouragement and 24 percent for demands) fall between the patterns for whites on one side versus blacks and Hispanics on the other.

Responses regarding demands and encouragement are mostly unrelated to measures of SES.[25] As Table 6–7 shows, no matter how many parents students live with or how many years of schooling the mother has attained, race/ethnic differences in the relative importance of encouragement follow the same basic pattern. Not shown is that responses also are unrelated to the study's other measures of socioeconomic background.

I have not studied precisely what teachers' statements, demeanors, and behaviors are interpreted by students in MSAN districts as demanding or encouraging and whether these differ by race and ethnicity. I have, however, asked a few black and Hispanic students in MSAN schools to help me understand these findings concerning encouragement and demands. Concerning demands, they have very little to say. However, they have a great deal to say about encouragement. One student says, "I find it encouraging when teachers tell me I 'can do it' and when they don't make judgments about why I haven't done something that I was supposed to." Another says, "I find it encouraging when teachers give me full explanations to help me understand things, instead of short 'yes' or 'no' answers." A third student says, "I find it encouraging when teachers stay after school to give me extra help and don't seem like they're in a big hurry to go [home]." Based on these and other anecdotal observations, encouragement seems to entail assurances from teachers that students have the ability to succeed and teacher behaviors that provide active support for success. Conversely, a demand is an order to submit to the power of the person making the demand and carries no assurance that the person making the demand really cares about the student or will offer any special assistance. Especially for students of color, survey responses indicate that teacher demands are probably not very effective.

VISIBLE DIFFERENCES, HIDDEN SIMILARITIES

The Ed-Excel survey asked students to identify the characteristics of the most popular crowd in their first year of middle school or junior high. Black and mixed-race students cited "tough" more than whites, Hispanics, or Asians (see Table 6–8). Conversely, larger percentages of whites, Asians, and mixed-race students reported that members of the most popular crowd were "self-confident" and "outgoing." For example, there are not many differences in the percentages of blacks responding that the most popular crowd is "tough" (35 percent), "outgoing" (36 percent), and "self-confident" (39 percent). However, whites identify "outgoing" (54 percent) and "self-confident" (53 percent) more than twice as often as they identify "tough" (22 percent).

TABLE 6–7 Evidence That Encourage/Demand Responses for MSAN Students Are Mainly Racial/Ethnic Patterns, Not Associated with Socioeconomic Status

Question: "When you work really hard in school, which of the following reasons are most important to you? (Check as many as apply to you.)"

	Black	White	Hispanic	Asian	Mixed Race	Total
	Percentage in Each Cell Who Checked the Response: "My teachers encourage me to work hard."					
Living Arrangements						
One parent or neither	47	31	41	31	41	40
One parent and stepparent	53	33	42	37	45	40
Two parents	45	32	41	31	34	34
COLUMN TOTAL	47	32	41	31	38	36
Mother's Years of Schooling						
12 or fewer	50	33	39	32	42	40
13 to 15	45	32	38	30	41	38
Four-year college graduate	43	30	33	29	36	33
Advanced degree	44	31	42	27	33	33
COLUMN TOTAL	46	31	39	30	37	35
	Percentage in Each Cell Who Checked the Response: "The teacher demands it."					
Living Arrangements						
One parent or neither	16	27	18	22	22	20
One parent and stepparent	17	29	23	18	26	24
Two parents	15	30	19	19	26	26
COLUMN TOTAL	16	29	19	20	24	24
Mother's Years of Schooling						
12 or fewer	13	23	19	17	20	19
13 to 15	15	28	18	16	23	22
Four-year college graduate	17	29	18	19	25	26
Advanced degree	17	33	25	25	29	30
COLUMN TOTAL	16	30	20	20	25	25

TABLE 6–8   Percentages Identifying the Listed Characteristics as Descriptive of the Most Popular Crowd during the First Year of Middle or Junior High School

Characteristics	Black	White	Hispanic	Asian	Mixed Race
	Percentages				
Tough	35	22	24	20	33
Outgoing	36	54	36	47	47
Self-Confident	39	53	33	41	49

TABLE 6–9   How Strongly Friends Agree with the Statement, "It's important to study hard to get good grades."

How Important Friends Believe It Is:	Black	White	Hispanic	Asian	Mixed Race
	Column Percentage				
Very important	56	42	49	54	45
Somewhat important	38	49	40	39	45
Not too important	5	7	8	6	7
Not at all important	1	1	2	1	3
TOTAL	100	100	100	100	100

Although there are no survey responses from teachers, anecdotal reports from teachers suggest that group differences in demeanor continue through high school.

Based on homework-completion rates and the ways that students carry themselves, teachers sometimes assume that black and Hispanic students not only work less hard than white classmates but also place a lower priority on earning good grades and enjoy school less. The MSAN Ed-Excel survey responses, however, do not support such inferences.

The Ed-Excel survey asked students whether their friends believe that working hard to get good grades is "very important," "somewhat important," "not too important," or "not at all important." Table 6–9 shows only modest race/ethnic variation in how students responded. For each race/ethnic group, roughly 90 percent answered that their friends regard studying hard to get

TABLE 6–10   Levels of Agreement with Two Statements about Effort

Statements about Effort	Black	White	Hispanic	Asian	Mixed Race
	Percentages That Agree				
If I didn't need good grades, I'd put little effort into my classes.	42	42	45	43	44
I don't like to do any more schoolwork than I have to.	64	74	62	58	71

TABLE 6–11   Actual and Desired Weekly Hours of Tutoring

Hours of Tutoring	Black	White	Hispanic	Asian	Mixed Race
	Hours per Week				
Mean reported actual hours per week	.83	.47	.78	.63	.67
Mean reported desired hours per week	1.45	.78	1.35	1.20	1.12
Desired minus actual	.63	.32	.53	.57	.46

good grades as either very important or somewhat important. The largest percentage answering "very important" was among blacks (56 percent), while the smallest percentage was among whites (42 percent). This result is the opposite of what many teachers might expect based on what they observe. Similarly, Table 6–10 shows that groups are quite similar in responses concerning effort and motivation. Almost half of each group agrees, "If I didn't need good grades, I'd put little effort into my classes." Roughly two-thirds agree, "I don't like to do any more schoolwork than I have to." Whites are the group that agrees most with the latter statement. Finally, nonwhite students want additional tutoring. Although nonwhites already report more hours of tutoring per week than white peers, Table 6–11 shows that the gap between what they get and what they want also is larger.

Groups also are similar in the percentages reporting that they enjoy their studies. Table 6–12 shows patterns for three variables pertaining to enjoyment of books and math problems and four measures pertaining to the percentage of the time that teachers make lessons interesting. There is no clear pattern indicating that one group enjoys school more or judges teachers differently regarding how frequently they make lessons interesting. Hispan-

TABLE 6–12   Percentages That Agree with Selected Statements about Classes

Panel A: Percentages Reporting That They Enjoy Reading School Books and Doing Math Problems

	Black	White	Hispanic	Asian	Mixed Race
			Percentage		
I like the books and plays we read for English.	53	57	62	58	54
I enjoy doing math problems.	54	45	57	62	47
The history and science books are interesting.	40	35	51	48	37

Panel B: Percentages Reporting That the Teacher Makes the Subject Interesting More Than Half the Time

Subject	Black	White	Hispanic	Asian	Mixed Race
			Percentage		
Math	32	31	39	39	30
English	41	45	47	44	43
Social studies	44	49	51	45	46
Science	42	45	49	49	43

ics, at 62 percent, are the group with the largest percentage saying that they enjoy the books and plays they read for English; percentages among the other groups range from 53 percent of blacks to 58 percent of Asians. Asians (at 62 percent) have the largest percentage who enjoy doing math problems, while the lowest percentage is among whites (45 percent). Whites also are least likely to agree that history and science books are interesting.

Table 6–12 shows a high level of agreement among the groups about the percentage of the time that teachers make lessons interesting. Note that with the minor exception of Hispanics in social studies, fewer than half of each group agree that teachers in any subject make lessons interesting more than half the time. For all of the groups, math ranks lowest and the other three subjects are roughly even with one another.

For all groups, students with higher grade-point averages are more prone to feel close to teachers, more likely to think that grading is fair, and less

TABLE 6–13 Percentages That Agree with Two Statements about Fairness in Grading and Closeness to Teachers, Tabulated by Race/Ethnicity and Grade-Point Average

Student's Grade-Point Average at the End of the Last Term	Black	White	Hispanic	Asian	Mixed Race
Panel A Percentage in Each Cell That Agrees: "My teachers DON'T grade me fairly."					
D+ or below	35	38	35	38	41
C– to C+	30	28	26	26	34
B– to B+	23	22	20	22	26
A– to A	20	12	15	24	21
GROUP TOTAL	26	18	22	19	27
Panel B Percentage in Each Cell That Agrees: "I DON'T feel close to any of my teachers."					
D+ or below	48	50	52	57	50
C– to C+	42	45	45	49	47
B– to B+	38	39	38	37	40
A– to A	39	33	39	34	37
GROUP TOTAL	40	37	41	38	41

likely to think that friends avoid asking for help when they need it. Table 6–13 shows that among students with similar grade-point averages, students of different race/ethnic groups are quite similar in their views regarding whether grading is fair and whether they feel close to their teachers. Table 6–14 shows that students with higher grade-point averages are less inclined to believe that friends avoid asking for needed help.

Finally, one small but nonetheless notable difference is among students with grades in the "A– to A" range. Among these students, whites are consistently the most likely to consider grading fair, to feel close to their teachers, and to say that friends do not avoid asking for help. As with most of what this paper has discussed, this pattern for white students in the "A– to A" range holds not only in the aggregate but also for most individual districts.[26] One plausible explanation that is impossible to prove or disprove with the present data is that teachers are more friendly and supportive to high-achieving white students than to white students with lower grades or students of other racial and ethnic groups.

TABLE 6–14 Percentage of Students Who Agree That Friends Don't Ask for Help Even If They Need It, Tabulated by Race/Ethnicity and Last Term's GPA

Student's Grade-Point Average at the End of Last Term	Black	White	Hispanic	Asian	Mixed Race
	Percentage				
D+ or below	31	36	39	35	38
C– to C+	29	28	31	23	31
B– to B+	25	22	27	21	21
A– to A	22	15	26	16	20
GROUP TOTAL	27	19	29	19	24

IMPLICATIONS FOR POLICY AND PRACTICE

Findings in this paper have implications for schools and communities as well as for state and federal policymakers. For schools and communities, I offer the following four recommendations.

1. Assume no motivational differences. It seems likely that incorrect assumptions about group differences in effort and interest may lead some schools to underinvest in searching for ways to raise achievement levels among African-American, Hispanic, and some mixed-race students. Teachers should assume that there are no systematic, group-level differences in effort or motivation to succeed, even when there are clearly observable differences in behavior and academic performance.

2. Address specific skill deficits. Racial and ethnic disparities in self-reported understanding of lessons and readings call attention to the fact that gaps in standardized test scores and school grades reflect real disparities in academic knowledge and skill. To help raise achievement and close gaps, schools should endeavor to identify and address specific skill and knowledge deficits that underlie comprehension problems for individuals in particular racial and ethnic groups and respond in targeted ways.

3. Supply ample encouragement routinely. Given the importance that black and Hispanic students assign to teacher encouragement, teachers need to be aware of what students regard as encouraging. Using this awareness, they need to provide effective forms of encouragement routinely. Further, as the other recommendations imply, encouragement should be matched with truly effective instruction and other forms of academic support both inside and outside the classroom.

4. Provide access to resources and learning experiences. In response to differences in family-background advantages, schools could supply more educational resources and learning experiences outside the home. They could provide access to books and computers and extracurricular opportunities for intellectual enrichment.

Even in the well-to-do suburban communities examined in this paper, teachers and youth-serving professionals may need targeted professional development in order to follow these recommendations. Professional development requires resources. To be persuaded to provide such resources, policymakers need to understand the rationale. At least initially, these recommendations may seem to conflict with current fashions in education policy. In fact, however, I suggest that there is complementarity.

For the past several years, policymakers have placed a heavy emphasis on standards-based reforms. Promoted most prominently by the No Child Left Behind legislation, such reforms are the centerpiece of a national strategy for raising achievement and closing achievement gaps. At their core, standards-based reforms entail a heavy focus on content and alignment. Specifically, there is to be alignment between content standards (i.e., the prescribed knowledge that students are supposed to learn), the content of the curriculum, the content tested on state assessments, and the content that teachers are trained through their schooling and professional development to understand and teach. With some notable exceptions, the possibility that relationships might affect whether students actually learn the content that teachers are trying to teach seldom enters the policy discourse.

Nonetheless, findings in this paper concerning the importance of encouragement to black and Hispanic students suggest that teacher-student relationships may be quite important resources for raising achievement and narrowing achievement gaps.

Content, pedagogy, and relationships are three legs of what I call the "instructional tripod." If one leg of a tripod is too weak, it falls over. Professional development activities that equip teachers to attend simultaneously to all three legs of the instructional tripod stand a better chance of helping states to meet their education policy objectives. Attending well to all three will affect a teacher's capacity and commitment to engage students effectively in learning and, therefore, students' preparation to reach prescribed performance standards in the domains of particular content standards that state policies have articulated. (Refer to Appendix: The Tripod Project, p. 227.)

CONCLUSION   *Teachers can make a difference.*

There is much that does not meet the teacher's eye but that nonetheless affects how ambitiously and effectively students learn. African-American and Hispanic students in MSAN districts have fewer family-background advantages on average, compared to whites and Asians. In addition, they have lower grade-point averages and report less understanding of their lessons. They have lower homework-completion rates than white classmates but report spending virtually the same amount of time doing homework. Skill gaps and differences in home academic supports—not effort or motivation—appear to be the primary explanations for why they complete less homework and get lower grades than whites. Conversely, part of the reason that Asians complete more homework and get higher grades than other nonwhite groups is that they devote more time to their studies.

Perhaps the most interesting finding here is the distinctive importance of teacher encouragement as a reported source of motivation for nonwhite students, especially African-American students, and the fact that this difference is truly a racial difference, mostly unrelated to measures of SES. The special importance of encouragement highlights the likely importance of strong teacher-student relationships in affecting achievement, especially for African-American and Hispanic students. It also highlights the importance of trying to understand racial and ethnic differences in how students experience the social environments of schools and classrooms.[27]

Across the nation, standards-based reforms have been catalysts for a growing number of professional development initiatives to prepare educators to teach new content standards. However, if the aim of these efforts is to raise achievement and narrow gaps, focusing on content and pedagogy alone may be insufficient. A key implication of the findings in this paper is that even in well-to-do suburbs, professional development strategies might wisely attend to all three legs of the instructional tripod—content, pedagogy, and relationships—not just one or two. In this way, such strategies may better prepare teachers to inspire the trust, elicit the cooperation, stimulate the ambition, and support the sustained industriousness required in order to find success with the No Child Left Behind legislation.

Appendix: The Tripod Project

The Tripod Project is an outgrowth of the research upon which this paper reports. It is a response to the first three of four recommendations listed in the section titled *Implications for Policy and Practice*: (1) assume no motivational differences, (2) address specific skill deficits, (3) supply ample encouragement routinely, and (4) provide access to resources and learning experiences. The Tripod Project is organized to harvest and share teachers' best ideas regarding ways of succeeding in the classroom, especially with nonwhite students and children from low-SES households. It also is consistent with emerging best-practice ideas about professional development and instructional leadership.[28] The goal is to enhance school-level capacity to attend to all three legs of the tripod—content, pedagogy, and relationships—by effectively addressing five generic tasks of social and intellectual engagement in the classroom. In addition, a research component aims to refine one's understanding of the ways that particular classroom conditions affect achievement among students of particular racial, ethnic, and socioeconomic backgrounds.

Literatures as diverse as business marketing, social work, innovation diffusion, child development, and group process have developed theories and descriptions of the tasks entailed in achieving and sustaining cooperation among people who share particular contexts and must work together to achieve their goals. Scholars in each separate literature have discovered the same five tasks.[29] The period during which a particular task seems to be the most salient is the stage identified with that task. However, each task has implications for each stage. In addition, there may be backsliding: A task that was mostly resolved can become the most salient again if conditions unravel.

For the Tripod Project, I have adapted these ideas to characterize five tasks and stages of social and intellectual engagement in primary and secondary school classrooms. The basic idea is that students will be most likely to excel if the following conditions are met:

1. Students begin the semester feeling trustful of the teacher and interested (instead of feeling mistrustful and uninterested).
2. Students experience a good balance between teacher control and student autonomy (instead of too little or too much of either).
3. Students are ambitiously goal-oriented in their learning (instead of feeling ambivalent).

4. Students work industriously in pursuing their goals for learning (instead of becoming discouraged in the face of difficulty or disengaged due to boredom).
5. Teachers help students consolidate their new knowledge and, thus equipped, students are well prepared for future classes and life experiences.

The Tripod Project is organized around a series of five schoolwide faculty meetings—one for each stage—all of which have the same basic structure.[30] Each schoolwide meeting leads to work in smaller groups of volunteers where teachers share ideas to expand and refine their repertoire of strategies for succeeding with each respective task and stage. The volunteers seek and find opportunities to report their ideas and experiences to teachers who are not yet as involved in the search for ways of improving.

The next few paragraphs describe briefly how the project addresses all three legs of the tripod and responds to the three recommendations listed above (i.e., assume no motivational differences, address specific skill deficits, and supply ample encouragement routinely).

Stage 1: Trust and Interest versus Mistrust and Indifference. This stage begins on the first day that students arrive in the classroom if not before. Teachers try to signal to students that the year is going to go well, with respect to all five tasks, while students begin developing impressions regarding the teacher's caring, competence, consistency, and respect for students. At this stage, teachers share ideas on establishing good initial rapport with the class and getting off to a good start in which students feel respected, encouraged, and optimistic.

Stage 2: Balanced versus Imbalanced Teacher Control and Student Autonomy. This stage begins soon afterward, as students focus on how seriously to take the teacher and the class and how much autonomy to relinquish in compliance with the teacher's rules and regulations. If the teacher seems firm but also caring, competent, consistent, and respectful, the class should find it easier to achieve a good balance between teacher control and student autonomy. At this stage, teachers share ideas concerning ways of being firm enough to establish and maintain order in the classroom without using heavy-handed methods that might make students fearful and withdrawn or oppositional. These ideas include ways of giving students incentives and choices that promote their dignity and foster a sense of responsibility for helping the class to work well as a community.

Stage 3: Ambitiousness versus Ambivalence. This stage comes on gradually as perceptions develop regarding how feasible, useful, and enjoyable success is likely to be. All three legs of the tripod (content, pedagogy, and relationships) are important, and all four of the recommendations listed above are useful for teachers to keep in mind. Concerning the first two legs of the tripod (content and pedagogy), the feasibility of success depends upon the teacher's content knowledge and pedagogic skill to explain the material so that each student can understand it, given the student's current skill level.

Feasibility also depends upon the student's willingness to ask for help, which is key if the student needs personal assistance from the teacher in order to be successful. A student who views the teacher as uncaring, incompetent, inconsistent, disrespectful, or too controlling is likely to be ambivalent about seeking help from the teacher; a teacher who feels emotionally disconnected from a student or class may send discouraging signals regarding the willingness to provide help. Let me emphasize again that the teacher's knowledge of content and pedagogy is important. However, because of the way that relationships and encouragement affect motivation, help seeking, and help giving, ambitiousness may be difficult to achieve if teacher-student relationship issues that should have been resolved in Stage 1 and Stage 2 remain largely unsettled.

Assuming that such issues are largely settled, sharing among teachers during Stage 3 concerns ways of helping students to understand both teacher and student roles in making success feasible and enjoyable. Teachers share ideas with one another about ways of helping students to make plans, develop strategies, set goals, and adopt generally ambitious orientations toward achievement in particular subjects and classrooms.

Stage 4: Industriousness versus Disengagement.   This stage is the period for following through on the ambitiousness cultivated during Stage 3. The challenge during this stage is to sustain a high level of industriousness and, if this fails, to recover from whatever discouragement or disengagement setbacks might cause. Ideally, the ambitiousness cultivated during Stage 3 will persist through this period when the focus now is on industriously performing the work to make success real. However, if there are setbacks that cast doubt on whether success is truly feasible, if the lessons seem irrelevant or excessively boring, or if relationships among students or between students and the teacher deteriorate in the classroom, students may become discouraged and disengaged. The Tripod Project embodies the presumption that capacity to recover—to be resilient—depends on how deeply students and the teacher care for and trust one another and how well the balance of teacher control and student autonomy is being maintained. It also depends on the level of commitment to success that the teacher and students together achieved during Stage 3.

The sharing among teachers at Stage 4 focuses on ways of making success feasible, enjoyable, and relevant for all students. Some teachers review student work together and talk about patterns of misunderstanding and ways of responding to such patterns, including ways of explaining particular concepts that students find difficult. Some teachers collaborate in reviewing detailed data from standardized exams that may hold clues for where instruction needs to focus. Some teachers trade ideas about ways of structuring lessons and homework assignments and share ideas about ways of showing students that particular topics really do connect to real life. Some teachers talk about ways of diagnosing classroom dynamics, so that peer pressures do not interfere with each individual student's industriousness and commitment. In addition, some teachers share ideas about ways of spotting students who are becoming discouraged because of failure or disengaged because of boredom; teachers also discuss ways of helping such students to recover their industriousness.

Stage 5: Consolidation versus Irresolution.   Coming toward the end of the school year, this final stage is the period for helping students to truly own what they have learned. Ideally, teachers will help students understand the scaffolding by which their learning in the class builds upon what they knew before and also the ways that various facts, ideas, and concepts in their lessons relate to one another. Teachers will talk more than before about the ways that the lessons can help students in real life and the reasons that trying to digest and remember what they have learned is important. Sharing among teachers at this stage concerns ways of motivating and helping students to see connections. Like Stage 3 and Stage 4, much of this sharing is among teachers who have very similar teaching assignments and face similar challenges and opportunities in the classroom.

In the process of sharing ideas and searching for new insights, teachers will find themselves strengthening each leg of the tripod in their own classrooms. This year is the pilot year for the project. Progress is under way, and mechanisms are being designed for sharing ideas among schools and across districts.[31]

The author acknowledges helpful comments from John Diamond, Tom Kelly, Sarah McCann, Sara Stoutland, members of the Research Practitioner Council of the Minority Student Achievement Network, and four anonymous reviewers. Thanks also to John Bishop, who developed the survey upon which the paper relies, to the students who responded to it, and to the teachers and administrators who helped to administer it. The North Central Regional Educational Laboratory (NCREL), the Rockefeller Foundation, the Cleveland Foundation, and the Gund Foundation provided financial support for data collection and analysis.

Afterword to Chapter 6

One of the main themes in chapter 6 is that students of different racial and ethnic groups—Asians, blacks, Hispanics, and whites—have a similar desire to do well in school. When they are in the same classes, students from the different groups on average complete different percentages of their homework, but students from nearly all groups devote about the same amount of time to working on it. Only Asians report spending more time on homework than their classmates.

Since completing this chapter, I have crafted new surveys and collected subsequent rounds of data from schools in the Tripod Project. Most items on Tripod Project surveys are specific to the classroom in which the student takes the survey. They are designed to measure targeted dimensions of academic engagement and classroom practice and to provide information on the ways classrooms differ from one another. Each student may complete the survey for two different classrooms to help distinguish classroom differences from student differences. In addition to classroom-level issues, the surveys have recently probed a number of issues concerning the school climate more generally—issues related to racial identity and peer support for achievement.

The patterns in student responses to these surveys tend to support the finding described in chapter 6 that students in the same classes devote similar amounts of time to homework, even though they have different rates of homework completion. Furthermore, these recent survey responses confirm that, as reported in this chapter, black, white, and Hispanic students give similar reports of how important their friends think it is to work hard to get good grades in school. (Asians give their friends a higher rating than students from the other groups do.)

Similarities among racial and ethnic groups in the effort devoted to homework and in beliefs about the importance of school achievement are often invisible to teachers and peers—hence the chapter title, "What Doesn't Meet the Eye." The things that do meet the eye often include group differences in behavior, which can create the impression that some groups care less than others about achievement. Moreover, some behaviors are dysfunctional in the school environment in that they can interfere with learning. Therefore, behavioral differences can be consequential. They may also represent subtle differences in students' perception of racial bias, which can give rise to feelings of alienation, and in attitudes about compliance with authority. These differences are important to understand and address in order to raise achievement levels and close gaps.

The Tripod Project surveys investigate two behavioral issues that are recurrent in discussions of racial achievement gaps—"acting white" and "acting ghetto." Both are complex issues that we are only beginning to understand through research. The Tripod Project survey for secondary school students asks students to respond on a scale of 1 to 5 (i.e., "never," "usually not," "sometimes," "usually," or "always"), to the statement, "At this school, students like me get accused of 'acting white.'" The survey also asks students whether their behavior style could be described as "acting ghetto." The specific statement is, "People would probably describe my behavior style as 'ghetto.'" The five response options are the same as for "acting white," ranging from "never" to "always."

Table A6–1 shows response patterns among high school students for these two items. The responses come from students in more than four dozen high schools spread across seven states. These include schools in large inner cities as well as from suburbs and a few small towns. The responses characterized as "at least sometimes" include students responding "sometimes," "usually" or "always." (The alternative responses are "usually not" or "never.")

There are several important patterns to observe. First, the "acting white" accusation and the "ghetto" behavior style are not restricted to black youths. Both issues are salient for all four racial and ethnic groups, although not to the same degree. Having one's behavior perceived as "ghetto" seems more prevalent for blacks and Hispanics than accusations of "acting white," while the reverse is true for whites and Asians.

Second, both issues are relevant for students at all four grade-point average (GPA) levels. The "acting white" accusation is not limited to students at the high end of the achievement spectrum, nor is the perception of "acting ghetto" restricted to low-achieving students.

Third, as the percentage of white students in the school rises, accusations of "acting white" decrease for whites but increase for blacks (with a mixed picture for Hispanics and Asians). In other words, white students in schools with a majority of black students are more likely to be accused of "acting white" than in schools where most students are white. For black students, the reverse is true. In an environment where the majority of students are white, black students are more likely to face this accusation.

Fourth, the percentage of blacks who agree that people would at least sometimes describe their behavior style as "ghetto" is never less than 40

TABLE A6–1   Acting White (Acting Ghetto): The first number of each pair is the percentage within that race/GPA cell who agree that people like themselves at least sometimes get accused of "acting white." The numbers in parentheses are the percentages agreeing that people would, at least sometimes, "probably describe my behavior style as 'ghetto'." All respondents represented are high school students.

Race	D-Range GPA	C-Range GPA	B-Range GPA	A-Range GPA
In Schools 0–25 Percent White				
White	55 (28)	58 (30)	54 (28)	48 (17)
Black	27 (54)	34 (52)	37 (45)	34 (40)
Hispanic	28 (53)	27 (47)	27 (38)	31 (28)
Asian	30 (55)	33 (30)	32 (29)	29 (28)
In Schools 25–50 Percent White				
White	42 (39)	47 (30)	46 (18)	43 (11)
Black	37 (66)	36 (57)	36 (46)	46 (52)
Hispanic	28 (49)	28 (39)	22 (29)	22 (22)
Asian	n.a.	36 (42)	23 (30)	8 (24)
In Schools That Are Majority White				
White	34 (27)	36 (21)	30 (15)	25 (9)
Black	46 (78)	40 (67)	42 (46)	45 (45)
Hispanic	36 (59)	29 (47)	26 (32)	20 (13)
Asian	31 (15)	26 (29)	27 (23)	18 (11)

Numbers of Respondents in Table A6–1	White	Black	Hispanic	Asian
Schools 0–25 Percent White	697	2,748	1,998	354
Schools 25–50 Percent White	1,588	791	542	94
Schools Majority White	8,020	665	372	767

percent (for A-range students in schools with fewer than 25 percent whites) and it rises to 78 percent among D-range GPA students in majority white schools. For these latter students in particular, "acting ghetto" may be a way of asserting power in environments where the student feels otherwise powerless. Such behaviors should be studied as institutionally and socially contingent, not as immutable features of youth identity and behavior.

Chapter 6 also points out that there are strong similarities across racial groups in the perception that friends think working hard for high grades is important. Table A6–2 shows patterns in responses to a similar item used in the Tripod Project surveys. Here, the statement is: "My friends think it's important to work hard to get high grades." The table distinguishes responses from students belonging to different racial groups based on their responses to the "acting white" and "acting ghetto" survey items.

Clearly, there is a tendency for students to perceive their friends as more academically committed (they "think it's important to work hard to get high grades") when they also report that they would "seldom" or "never" be accused of "acting white" or be perceived as "acting ghetto." These patterns are strikingly similar across racial and ethnic groups.

The relationships among "acting white," "acting ghetto," academic commitment, and academic achievement will receive much more extensive treatment in future work. For now, the bottom line is that all of these issues and relationships affect students from all racial groups.

Finally, my work with Tripod Project survey data shows that the strongest predictors of the "acting white" accusation are musical preferences (listening to rock music) and personal style (using standard English in informal settings and having a trusting attitude toward strangers), not GPA or academic aspirations. This is consistent with recent findings by other researchers. Nonetheless, the surveys also indicate that the "acting white" accusation is associated with holding back academically. Students who agree that they might be accused of "acting white"—particularly black males—also tend to agree more with the following statement: "I sometimes hold back from doing my best in this class because of what others might say or think." More than 40 percent of black male respondents who say that students like themselves might "sometimes," "usually," or "always" be accused of "acting white" also say that the statement about holding back is at least somewhat (i.e., "sometimes," "usually," or "always") true for them.

Students need help understanding the social pressures that they face and learning to respond in ways that increase their chances of reaching their full potential in all phases of life. The "acting white" and "acting ghetto" phenomena are more complex issues than they are usually considered to be. With deeper understanding of these issues in the future, we will become better able to help young people to cope effectively with the pressures they face and to make better choices concerning both social and academic pursuits.

TABLE A6–2   Row Percentages for Responses to "My friends think it's important to work hard to get high grades," by Race and Ethnicity, for Different Responses to the "Acting White" and "Acting Ghetto" Survey Items

	Never or Usually Not	Sometimes	Usually or Always	Row Total
If Sometimes, Usually, or Always Accused of "Acting White"				
White	15.4	36.1	48.5	100% (N=3,503)
Black	15.0	38.3	46.7	100% (N=1,560)
Hispanic	14.6	40.7	44.7	100% (N=913)
Asian	12.4	37.6	50.0	100% (N=306)
If Never or Usually Not Accused of "Acting White"				
White	13.4	29.7	56.9	100% (N=7,103)
Black	16.1	29.5	54.4	100% (N=2,806)
Hispanic	16.4	30.6	53.0	100% (N=2,415)
Asian	8.6	22.3	69.1	100% (N=975)
If Sometimes, Usually, or Always Accused of "Acting Ghetto"				
White	20.1	43.3	36.6	100% (N=1,627)
Black	15.5	38.1	46.4	100% (N=2,259)
Hispanic	16.7	37.7	45.6	100% (N=1,376)
Asian	14.8	36.3	48.9	100% (N=278)
If Never or Usually Not Perceived as "Acting Ghetto"				
White	12.9	29.6	57.5	100% (N=9,264)
Black	15.8	27.2	57.1	100% (N=2,184)
Hispanic	15.4	30.1	54.5	100% (N=2,044)
Asian	8.2	22.5	69.3	100% (N=1,013)

CHAPTER 7

Five Challenges to Effective Teacher Professional Development

Imagine entering a school as a new principal in the footsteps of others before you who endeavored with various degrees of success to raise student achievement. The experiences and outcomes of those earlier efforts will influence the expectations people have for you. In turn, community expectations for your success or failure will affect the enthusiasm and optimism with which teachers and other stakeholders will greet and assist you as you begin the job. In many ways and for multiple reasons, what you achieve as principal may depend importantly on historically grounded *predispositions* that are already part of the social context, predating your arrival.

Ideas matter too. Whatever the context, the details of the specific *approaches, programs, and proposals* leaders introduce affect how people respond. For example, a new principal might introduce a plan such as the following for professional development to improve instruction and raise students' test scores:

1. Engage teachers in groups to analyze student work and to identify particular weakness.
2. Based on these analyses, select a limited number of skills or topics as priorities for improvement.
3. Identify resources to expand time and funding support and shop around to find (or eventually craft) instructional resources and models to address the instructional priorities.
4. Work in groups to learn the new teaching materials and procedures, sometimes with professional development support from outside the school.

237

5. Plan and confirm the various logistics, especially scheduling, necessary to follow through with implementation.

6. Monitor implementation, make midcourse corrections, assisting teachers who need help, and putting collegial pressure on teachers who seem not to be trying.

7. Monitor student progress and repeat the cycle with other targets for improvement.

Ask the leaders what they did in any school or district where test scores have risen dramatically, and some part of the answer will often resemble this strategy.[1] What determines whether teachers are receptive to such a strategy and whether they work hard to make it successful?

Leadership is a major part of the answer. There are plenty of examples where school principals have introduced and promoted perfectly reasonable and detailed plans and strategies that many teachers never embraced or implemented in their classrooms. So, building on the importance of context and strategy, the focus in this paper is on five challenges to achieving and sustaining social and intellectual engagement in the *implementation* of professional development for school improvement. The challenges concern introducing new activities in ways that inspire buy-in; balancing principal control with teacher autonomy; committing to ambitious goals; maintaining industriousness in pursuit of those goals; and effectively harvesting and sustaining the gains. Together, these challenges are the core of the Engaging Professional Development (EPD) framework.[2]

I consider these challenges from two vantage points. First, they represent categories of *predisposition* that are essentially *features of the context:* individuals and communities in particular contexts tend to be predisposed to address these five challenges in particular ways due to their personalities and histories. Second, for any given context with its various predispositions, challenges arise in specific ways during the introduction and implementation of any particular plan or strategy.

After introducing the five challenges, I show teacher survey findings suggesting that failure to successfully address the first three challenges is among the reasons professional development programs fail. Next, I present a case study in which the focus is on a school's predisposition toward challenges in the framework. A progression of seven principals in twelve years had fostered mistrust and control/autonomy imbalances in the relationships of teachers to administrators and hindered the capacity of administrators to lead the school into a period of ambitiousness and industriousness. Finally, a second case study portrays a school where the predisposition was more accommodating to new leadership and a talented principal led the faculty to a new plateau of high achievement. The case study describes how that principal addressed each of the five challenges in the EPD framework.

In most discussions of "what works" in education, the focus is on rules (for example, for class size) or on programs and their various components. These are clearly important. But no matter what the reform, implementation is key.[3] The central purpose of this paper is to suggest a manageable way to think systematically about the challenges school leaders face as they introduce new ideas and strive for effective implementation. The paper is part of a growing literature on teacher professional learning communities and factors that affect their successes and failures.[4]

FIVE CHALLENGES OF SOCIAL ENGAGEMENT: AN INTERDISCIPLINARY CONSENSUS

Group dynamics in schools involve the interplay of students, teachers, and administrators with a range of differing capabilities, personalities, and aspirations. Still, despite their differences, all of these actors share some very basic motivations. A short but very useful list includes the urge to belong and be accepted by others; the drive for autonomy (freedom, impact, power, personal "agency"); the compulsion to grow in competence, thereby expanding in capacity to achieve important goals; and the opportunity to feel efficacious. Human beings—administrators, teachers, students, and others alike—are attracted instinctively to opportunities that promise such rewards.

How ambitiously and relentlessly people work in social settings depends at least in part on the supply of such payoffs. Moreover, studies in seemingly unrelated literatures contend that which aspect of motivation is peaking in salience at any particular time tends to follow a logical sequence within the life cycle of a particular project or school year. With only slight variation, the sequence has appeared in multiple literatures (including child development, business marketing, social work, innovation diffusion, and organization theory) where writers have independently rediscovered the same progression of social challenges to engaging people in collective work.[5] I argue in this paper that by distinguishing among the challenges in the EPD framework but also understanding their interdependence, school leaders will be prepared to engage teachers more effectively in the work of teaching and learning.

Challenge One: Establishing trust and garnering interest.   When a group initially forms, say a classroom at the beginning of the school year or a school faculty on the first day of a new professional development program, *the need to feel trustful and secure and interested* in the agenda is paramount. For example, students on the first day of class are preoccupied with assessing whether the teacher is going to be "nice" or "mean" and (secondarily) whether the class is going to be "fun." Similarly as adults, say teachers on a school faculty, we seek to feel comfortable with our colleagues and to identify ways that our goals might be met (or not) through participation in any given professional activity. In our efforts to fit well with others and to scope out the agenda, first meetings and first class days are occasions on which people tend to be on their best behavior as they "get a feel" for the people and the agenda.

Challenge Two: Balancing external control and personal autonomy. Typically, the honeymoon is short lived. As the real work begins, forces grow upon individuals to accommodate to leadership directives or group pressures to make personal sacrifices or accommodations. Because there is a natural urge to resist control and maintain autonomy, there is *a need for balance between individuals' desires to be autonomous and the requirements of groups and organizations to align activities for coordination and synergy.* In a classroom, it is often the case that some students resist the rules. Then, teachers' responses teach students what the *real* rules of the classroom are going to be (versus those announced on day one) and students decide in what ways they will or will not try to comply. Similarly, teachers respond to pressures and make decisions to balance their own needs for autonomy, as against the rules, norms, and procedures that school leaders and professional peers try to encourage or enforce.

Challenge Three: Fostering ambitiousness. For students in classrooms and teachers in schools, resolution of challenge 2 helps clarify which rules, rewards, and resources are likely to be stable features of the environment. Possible goals take on greater focus. Judgments concerning which personal goals are likely to be truly achievable become easier to make; students refine earlier impressions into more codified expectations for classroom life and, based on these expectations, *focus their aspirations for personal achievement* (for example, grades); teachers experience an analogous process in the school professional community. For example, they may commit to participate ambitiously in particular professional development activities to improve their instructional practices, or lean toward ambivalence, abstention, or resistance.

Challenge Four: Sustaining industriousness and resilience. Goals, however ambitious they might be, are only unrealized intentions. Achieving goals requires follow-through. The feelings of trust and interest, relations of power and autonomy, and goals for personal achievement developed through tasks 1, 2, and 3 above become the backdrop for a period during which to *work industriously toward goals and resist discouragement or disengagement due to boredom or setbacks* is the central challenge. This period during which challenge 4 is peaking is probably the longest period of most program, project, or school-year cycles. The intensity and relentlessness with which people stay on track during this period determines what they ultimately achieve.

Challenge Five: Achieving mastery and consolidation.   Finally, project, program, or school-year cycles end and the time comes for consolidation. Leaders and participants alike tend to focus on *bringing appropriate closure*. Sustaining positive gains and making connections through which those gains might be the basis for further progress at later times is a central focus. Students write end-of-term papers and study for final exams, helping to consolidate understanding. Teachers finishing a professional development program review materials and make plans for integrating new ideas into future instructional routines. In various ways and to varying degrees, students and teachers take stock and celebrate achievements, consider implications for future endeavors, and pass along resources to other uses.

For each of the five challenges defined above, school leaders take strategic actions and hope people will respond in ways likely to foster success. With rows numbered to correspond to the five challenges, Exhibit 7–1 summarizes actions that school leaders might take to engage teachers in professional development work (column A). In addition, it summarizes actions that teachers take (column B) in their efforts to engage students. Column C summarizes ways that teachers and students might respond. Each response has an upside and a downside possibility. On the upside are trust, balanced autonomy, ambitiousness, industriousness, and consolidation of positive gains. On the downside are mistrust, imbalanced autonomy, ambivalence, discouragement, and squandered potential. The degrees to which these upside versus downside potentials are realized depend upon many things, including leadership.

School leaders play out their roles amidst idiosyncratic local conditions that set the stage for how people respond. Exhibit 7–2 reminds us of the complex chain of events that begin when a leader introduces an idea for instructional improvement. In Exhibit 7–2, the arrows from circles i, ii, and iii to circle B remind us that beliefs, capacities, responsibilities, and community conditions in place before a leader introduces a proposal can affect the ways

EXHIBIT 7–1   Leadership Actions That School Leaders (Column A) and Teachers (Column B) Might Take in Relationship to the Five Challenges Defined in the Text And Ways That Followers Might Respond (or Not) with Regard to Positive Engagement (Column C)

	A	B	C
	School Leaders' Actions (re: a professional development program)	*Teacher's Classroom Leadership (over the course of a school year)*	*Engagement Responses (by school teachers and students)*
1.	Select and engagingly introduce ideas for professional development.	Begin the school year with effective classroom icebreakers.	Feel trustful and interested, versus mistrustful, insecure, or uninterested.
2.	Assign associated responsibilities and define accountability for participation. Design effective feedback and clear, effective monitoring mechanisms.	Establish clear and fair rules and classroom management routines.	Achieve a balance (versus imbalance) of personal autonomy in relationship to the power and control of the leader, teacher, or group.
3.	Refine and clarify feasible and exciting school and personal goals for instructional improvement.	Define challenging but feasible and exciting goals for learning.	Resolve to be ambitious about achieving goals, versus ambivalent, lacking commitment.
4.	Implement activities and help teachers to be successful; monitor and assist the unsuccessful or disengaged.	Implement teaching and learning activities and work with students to help them succeed.	Be relentlessly industrious and resilient, versus discouraged and disengaged.
5.	Codify, celebrate, and reward accomplishments.	Recognize, celebrate, and reward accomplishments.	Achieve, consolidate, and sustain positive changes, versus getting lost in confusion and lack of coherence, and thus squandering gains.

people respond to it. What leaders need to say or do in order to introduce an idea successfully can be very sensitive to such details.

WHY IS PROFESSIONAL DEVELOPMENT OFTEN INEFFECTIVE?

For the past several years the Tripod Project for School Improvement has surveyed students and teachers regarding the five challenges. Table 7–1 presents the findings from one question. Specifically, the spring 2005 survey included

EXHIBIT 7–2 How Leadership and Teacher Engagement Mediate the Link from Instructional Improvement Proposals to Improved Student Learning

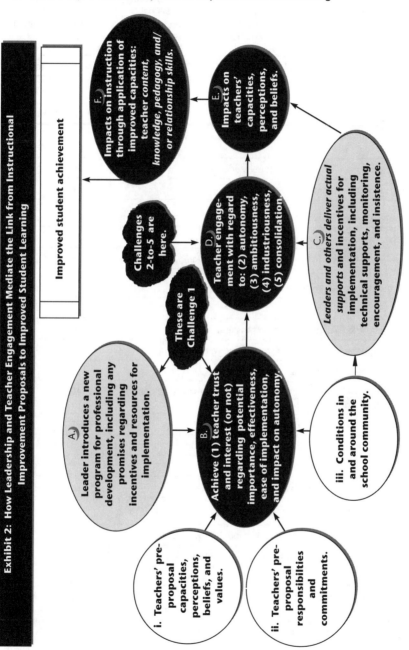

Exhibit 2: How Leadership and Teacher Engagement Mediate the Link from Instructional Improvement Proposals to Improved Student Learning

Improved student achievement

F. Impacts on instruction through application of improved capacities: teacher content, knowledge, pedagogy, and/or relationship skills.

E. Impacts on teachers' capacities, perceptions, and beliefs.

Challenges 2-to-5 are here.

D. Teacher engagement with regard to: (2) autonomy, (3) ambitiousness, (4) industriousness, (5) consolidation.

These are Challenge 1

C. Leaders and others deliver actual supports and incentives for implementation, including technical supports, monitoring, encouragement, and insistence.

A. Leader introduces a new program for professional development, including any promises regarding incentives and resources for implementation.

B. Achieve (1) teacher trust and interest (or not) regarding potential importance, effectiveness, ease of implementation, and impact on autonomy.

iii. Conditions in and around the school community.

i. Teachers' pre-proposal capacities, perceptions, beliefs, and values.

ii. Teachers' pre-proposal responsibilities and commitments.

TABLE 7–1   Reasons for Ineffective Professional Development

Percentages of elementary and secondary school teachers checking each listed statement, in response to the following direction: "Recall the last professional development program at your school that had little or no effect on teaching or learning in your class. With that program in mind, please check all of the following responses that apply."

	Elementary	Secondary
I. Trust & Interest vs. Mistrust & Disinterest		
The way it was introduced didn't inspire me to try it.	18	31
Too many other things were going on, so I didn't pay a lot of attention to it.	19	19
I never thought it could work with my students.	6	10
The goals of the program were not clear.	21	29
II. Balanced vs. Imbalanced Administrator Control & Teacher Autonomy		
Teachers were not held accountable for doing it.	27	29
It was going to infringe too much on my way of doing things.	1	4
III. Ambitiousness vs. Ambivalence		
* A. Feasibility of Success*		
There was too little support and training.	28	36
The people responsible for training me weren't very good.	19	21
* C. Enjoyment/Difficulty*		
It was just too much, on top of everything else the school was trying to do.	40	42
It didn't fit well with other things I was doing.	13	19
Doing it well would have been too much work.	3	8
* D. Supervisor Support & Press*		
Our principal never really took it seriously.	4	10
IV. Industriousness vs. Discouragement & Disengagement		
I really tried to make it work, but it just didn't help my students.	5	8
I started trying to implement it, but then lost interest.	14	9

Sample: 212 teachers from 17 secondary schools and 78 teachers from 19 elementary schools who completed this section of the Spring 2005 Tripod Project Teacher Survey. Teachers represent roughly one quarter of secondary classrooms and one third of elementary school classrooms where students were surveyed. Since responses were voluntary, the numbers here are only suggestive of what a truly representative tally would show. The teacher survey was to be completed online, so nonrespondents are those who, for whatever reason, did not go online to complete the survey.

a set of items after the following prompt: "Recall the last professional development program at your school that had little or no effect on teaching or learning in your class. With that program in mind, please check all of the following responses that apply."

Table 7–1 classifies the items under the first four challenges in the EDP framework. The subheadings under challenge 3 represent three of five "conditions that promote ambitiousness and industriousness" in the EPD framework (the two conditions not shown are "relevance" and "peer support"). Numbers in the table are percentages of elementary and secondary teachers, respectively, who checked any given item in response to the prompt concerning the last program that "had no little or no effect on teaching or learning in your classroom."

Notice that only 5 percent of elementary and 8 percent of secondary teachers responded that the program had little or no effect because "I really tried to make it work, but it just didn't help my students." Similarly, very few teachers indicated that the program failed because "It was going to infringe too much on my way of doing things," or because "Doing it well would have been too much work." No more than 10 percent responded that "I never thought it could work with my students." Generally, there is nothing in the answers to suggest most teachers tried to make the programs work and failed or believed that the programs could not have affected teaching and learning in their classrooms if implemented well.

Instead, it appears the programs had little or no effect because they were never really implemented. First, related to challenge 1 *(trust & interest),* 18 percent of elementary teachers and 31 percent of secondary teachers indicate that "The way it was introduced didn't inspire me to try it." Second, related to challenge 2 *(autonomy/control),* 27 percent of elementary and 29 percent of secondary teachers responded that "Teachers were not held accountable for doing it." Third, related to challenge 3 *(ambitiousness),* 28 percent of elementary and 36 percent of secondary teachers checked, "There was too little support and training." Finally, fully 40 percent of elementary and 42 percent of secondary teachers checked, "It was just too much, on top of everything else the school was trying to do." The teacher surveys suggest that professional development fails not primarily because the ideas do not work when implemented or because teachers reject the approaches outright, but instead because the ideas are not implemented.

The implications are straightforward, at least in principle. Programs that have minimal impact have not been implemented because leaders have failed to do the following:

- Select and introduce ideas in ways that *foster trust (feelings of security) and interest, not mistrust or lack of interest.*
- Assign responsibilities and manage accountability in ways likely to *achieve a balance of leadership control and follower autonomy, not too much or too little of either control or autonomy.*
- Plan, initiate, and monitor implementation in ways that *inspire ambitious goals, not ambivalence and lack of commitment.*
- Support ongoing implementation in ways that *motivate industriousness in the face of setbacks, not discouragement and disengagement.*
- Recognize, celebrate, and reward accomplishments in ways that *sustain and consolidate positive changes, not squander them through confusion and incoherence.*

Of course, to assert that these things are important is much easier than to explain how to do them. As the example of Revolving-Door Middle School (see below) and the issues on Exhibit 7–2 (above) illustrate, local preconditions can pose substantial barriers both to the introduction of new ideas and to their implementation.

TWO CASE STUDIES

This paper is part of a larger project using the Engaging Professional Development framework as a lens for understanding leadership differences in very successful versus less successful schools. As such, we have visited a number of schools over the past year, speaking to administrators and groups of teachers about successes and failures in professional development. The following pages describe two of these schools. The first is a school where recent history has predisposed it toward a balance of too little administrator control and perhaps too much teacher autonomy, discouraging administrators from introducing ideas around which improvement efforts might be organized. The second example is a school that has improved over the past several years because of a strong principal whose leadership has effectively attended to the challenges in the EPD framework.

Case One: Revolving-Door Middle School

Revolving-Door Middle School [obviously, a pseudonym] sits in a blue-collar suburb of Cleveland, Ohio. Two-thirds of the students qualify for free or reduced-price lunch. Roughly one-third are African American and most of the rest are whites. When we visited, it was the third straight year the school experienced a complete turnover of administrators. Indeed, there had been seven principals in twelve years. Student performance on state tests of reading, writing, and science was similar to other districts with comparable student populations, but in math it was lower. For all these subjects, scores at the end of 2004–05, around the time that we visited, were lower than in recent years. The school's rating on the state report card was "academic watch," the second lowest designation, and the school had not made adequate yearly progress (AYP). Nonetheless, teachers expressed pride in their stability as a staff and in their strong sense of commitment to one another and students. One says, "What am I most proud of? We try to build a family instead of just professionalism." Another says, "Everyone on this staff says they are a family and that's what we feel. People leave and come back."

In this school, capacity to achieve trust and interest in new ideas varies depending upon the messenger: teachers trust peer leaders who have been at the school for a long while, but they do not trust that administrators will stay long enough to follow through on new initiatives or enforce new directives. Peers, not administrators, are the sources of influential ideas. A teacher says, "How do I find out about new ideas? Teachers bring them in. I walk across the hall to see what works. We're willing to admit when things aren't working [which she says administrators have not been willing to do]. We all do the same things."

The vice principal believes that suggestions from new administrators would be unwelcome. She says, "This year has been a difficult year for administration. We have all come in here new and have not at this point tried to implement very many new initiatives. We are new folks, and they are sick and tired of relearning new people." She continues, "This year was just to get to know you and it was not successful. We took on a lot of extra burdens trying to build relationships. Especially regarding discipline, we took too much on. A student not doing a writing assignment should not be a referral to the principal. It's a classroom issue. But we took it on this year. It's been completely ineffective—constant referrals, more of the same, an unbelievable amount. And yet, we still have the reputation of being unsupportive." For this school, turnover in administration has produced too little administrator control with perhaps too much teacher autonomy, and the strategy of the current administrators has even further undermined administrators' influence.

Consequently, teachers' responses to control-autonomy questions focus on control *by peer leaders:* "Buy-in regarding a new program? If someone introduces a new idea and I get into it, or even if I don't *but the majority of the school does,* then I realize there has to be a unified front. We can't even have five or six teachers in the building who don't buy in—that can undermine the rest of the building. If I am in the minority on an issue, I still realize I have to support the majority in the building. It's detrimental to have some people doing this thing, and others doing something else." As another explains it, "We do things as a collective. There's not peer pressure, but people go along—if everyone agrees, then everyone else agrees. Kind of go with the flow."

The administrators seem not to understand the key role of peer leaders. When asked about plans for the next year, the vice principal said that a key strategy would be to work with teachers who seem likely to resist things that the administration plans to introduce. This perspective seems blind to the fact that individual teachers in this school are part of a strong community, beholden to the power of *curriculum leaders* and *team leaders* who make the major decisions, both formal and informal, on behalf of other teachers. Curriculum leaders and team leaders are well positioned to deal with resisters, once they themselves accept a new administration proposal.

At the same time, some teachers yearn for administrative leadership. Commenting on the lack of leadership influence from administrators, a teacher says: "Administration needs to be available, in the hallways, in the classrooms, popping in, saying hi—we don't have that here, so people feel, if no one is going to watch me, why should I care?" Continuing, "The last principal tried to get teachers to walk kids to class. We did it for the first couple of weeks, and there were few fights in the hallway. But teachers didn't want to do it. [So some stopped] and nothing ever happened. This sets a tone for the rest of the staff that if you don't do what you don't want to do, nothing is going to happen to you. This was an effort introduced by the principal, but not with buy-in originally from leaders."

Concerning challenges 3, 4, and 5—ambitiousness, industriousness, and consolidation—there is not much professional development activity to report. Aside from a curriculum mapping exercise the previous year that teachers say went well because it was very unrestrictive, the school lacks a coherent, well-directed strategy for raising student achievement. Teachers have instructional routines and the curriculum leaders and team leaders support these in various ways. Leaders maintain the social structure, including a strong sense of community. Moreover, they profess to care deeply about students. But as teachers without administrative leadership or outside support, they do not have the wherewithal to set the school on a strong upward trajectory of improvement.

Among the main things they lack is stable leadership that is capable of attending effectively to the five challenges upon which we are focused here in this chapter. For example, if the administration chose this year to push for literacy instruction across the curriculum, could they introduce it effectively? Could they achieve accountability with a balance of control and autonomy for teachers? Inspire teachers to embrace ambitious goals and to implement the new program relentlessly, resisting discouragement? Would teachers take seriously administrators' overarching vision for school improvement? Without leadership that can meet these challenges, Revolving-Door Middle School seems unlikely to harvest more fully its potential as a professional community that educates children well.

Case Two: Relentless Elementary School

Relentless Elementary School [a pseudonym] is a small elementary school in Northern Ohio where almost 80 percent of students are nonwhite and more than that percentage qualify for free and reduced-price lunch. Similar to Revolving-Door Middle School, the staff prides itself on a strong sense of "family." However, different from Revolving-Door Middle School, they accept their principal as their leader. She arrived four years ago to lead a faculty that she largely inherited. For the first two years, she worked hard to dismiss two teachers she regarded as problems, and ultimately succeeded. A strong leader of professional development, she has focused the staff on particular instructional challenges and been supported by several programs that the district has provided. Test scores rose significantly in the year after she arrived and have stayed high for the past three years, though reading scores dropped a bit in the year before our visit.

Challenge One: Establishing trust and garnering interest. How does this principal introduce ideas to get buy-in (trust and interest)? The principal and teachers independently emphasized the importance of the way professional development is introduced in the school. When a new initiative is one being promoted by the district, the principal takes two lead teachers with her to the district trainings, and then creates two-hour slots where the three educators present the new material to the rest of the staff. The teacher-to-teacher nature of this presentation—with the principal in the mix—is seen as particularly effective. As one teacher reported, "It's expected that the administration will bring in new things. We may not adopt all of it. . . . The bottom line is getting kids to learn. That's our philosophy. If the principal says it's a good idea, 'This is what colleges and universities around the country are doing,' we try it. Usually there are some good points we can keep with us. . . . We've always been a group that assesses the children. Teach and assess. We've adapted to what the district is doing. One of the keys to our success is to ask, 'Is this working?' We're quick to change when we need to." Thus, the culture of the school is one where teachers expect the principal to introduce new and useful ideas and are mostly predisposed to be open, but all agree they will not persist with ideas that do not prove effective.

Challenge Two: Balancing external control and personal autonomy. How does this principal balance leadership control with teacher autonomy? As indicated above, much of her first two years at the school was consumed by a battle to replace two resistant teachers; she has a low tolerance for teachers who refuse to participate appropriately as members of the staff. The primary mechanism for enforcing accountability is frequent, very purposeful communication. The principal says, "We're expected to comply with the district. I have to embrace it; model it; be enthusiastic. I walk them through it. I reinforce what we are supposed to be doing in weekly [grade-level] meetings and also when doing classroom observations." A teacher says, "Our leader works hard herself. She has high standards. You know she is also working. She models for us. The enthusiasm she shows." The principal pays attention to individual teachers, "You have to know your people. Which buttons to push. For some people I might write a note and put it in their box. Others I might approach verbally: 'Please make sure you're there.'" A teacher says, "We get lots of feedback from the principal—for example, the new standards—she makes sure we're really using them." Concerning autonomy, teachers are invited to offer opinions and to expect their opinions will be taken seriously. In addition, the principal agrees implicitly not to strictly enforce some rules, such as the rule that rubrics should be posted in classrooms and reflected in the comments on student work. She says, "You have to pick your battles."

Challenges Three (Fostering ambitiousness) and Four (Sustaining industriousness and resilience). How does this principal support ambitiousness and industriousness? In the EDP framework, we say that people are more likely to be ambitious and industrious when the five conditions that support ambitiousness and industriousness are satisfied. Specifically, (1) success seems feasible on goals that are clearly defined, (2) the goals seem important, (3) the experience is enjoyable, (4) supervisors are both encouraging and insistent, and (5) peers are supportive. The professional climate in this school satisfies all five conditions.

The principal is an enthusiastic proponent of improvement through targeted programs, rigorously implemented. She and teachers agree on the value of weekly meetings where she participates with each grade level team. Together, they examine student work, discuss student progress, and discuss new initiatives. She works one-on-one with some teachers to keep them focused on new instructional approaches. She works hard to keep morale up by convincing them that success is within their control and the work is important.

Much attention is paid to sustaining the school's reputation for high scores on state tests. When asked about the source of their determination to achieve high scores, teachers respond, "Partially us, partially the principal. We are being judged. We want to do well. We all have a competitive streak. Have to keep up our reputation. They keep upping the bar. We've scored 100 percent proficient in some areas. Now you have to get more advanced. We do better than many suburban schools (but they look down on us in a way). We experience joy in seeing our children succeed."

In general, the teachers feel that although there are too many new approaches each year and that they would rather see the results from one before starting something new, the new programs have been very well-supported by the district and the principal both in terms of professional development, and importantly, materials. They emphasize that this was very much not the case in their previous jobs. At this school, they are not expected to just figure things out for themselves after one workshop.

Other than the somewhat spotty use of rubrics, the only examples identified of "failed" programs are the use of computers in instruction (there was very little support until recently) and a teacher evaluation program that required an enormous amount of bookkeeping and was scrapped after one year.

Challenge Five: Achieving mastery and consolidation.   How does this principal achieve coherence and consolidation? Under this principal's leadership, teachers at the school have a clear understanding of their mission and also of the methods by which they work together to achieve it. Coherence with regard to particular programs comes from the ways that programs are managed and monitored during implementation and from the ways that the effective elements from programs are ultimately integrated into the school's core instructional regime. Describing the principal, one teacher says, "She has a lot of enthusiasm and goals in her mind. She reminds us that when you get tired this school doesn't sleep." Then, when working through the fatigue leads ultimately to high test scores, this principal remembers to celebrate with cookouts and other events.

CONCLUSION

This paper concerns the interplay of trust, accountability, ambitiousness, and persistence in the *implementation* of almost any strategy for school change or teacher professional development to improve instructional practice. It proposes an *Effective Professional Development* (EPD) framework built around five challenges that principals and other school leaders face when trying to improve instruction. Leaders can use the framework to diagnose, anticipate, or plan for implementation challenges. The paper demonstrates the utility of the framework first in classifying teacher survey responses concerning failed professional development programs. Teachers' responses suggest that when new initiatives founder it is due less to the initiatives' merits or characteristics, and more to the ways in which the initiatives are introduced, managed, and supported. Too many initiatives are poorly introduced, not embedded in systems of accountability, poorly supported with training, and crowded by competing demands on time and attention.

In the background of the EPD framework, issues associated with all five challenges "hang in the air" as part of the local environment. To various degrees, school communities are predisposed to be trustful or mistrustful; cooperative or caught up in power struggles; ambitious or uncommitted; persistently industrious or easily discouraged; cohesive or chaotic. When historically rooted predispositions foster mistrust and reluctance to submit to control by new administrators, a school may be in a posture to stagnate.

The case of Revolving-Door Middle School illustrates how preconditions that include years of high turnover by administrators can distort the climate for school change in ways that discourage administrators from being leaders. Teachers at Revolving-Door Middle School trust one another but not their new administrators. They are accountable to one another but very autonomous as a group in relationship to administrative control. Historically rooted mistrust of administrators and lack of administrator control (versus collective teacher autonomy) intimidates the administrators against even trying to lead for change. Professional development projects that administrators in other schools might have proposed as contexts for ambitious instructional improvement were not proposed at Revolving-Door. The reasons, it appears, include that mistrust and control/autonomy imbalances seemed insurmountable barriers to the school's new administrators.

In contrast to Revolving-Door Middle School, the principal at Relentless Elementary School faced fewer obstacles when she arrived. The case study describes conditions in her school and how she attends to the challenges in the EPD framework. From five years under her tutelage, teachers are now predisposed to trust not only that this principal will introduce useful new ideas, but also that she will respect their views about whether to adopt particular programs and when to stop using them. She learns new programs along with the teachers so that she can help them with implementation. She meets weekly with grade-level teams to review student work, discuss instructional issues, and make clear her expectations. In terms of the EPD framework, she introduces new ideas (challenge 1) in ways that teachers find appealing; imposes control (challenge 2) in ways that show respect for teachers; inspires ambitiousness (challenge 3) by training teachers well and showing enthusiasm for their work; maintains industriousness (challenge 4) by actively helping teachers succeed as a professional community and refusing to compromise in reaching for high standards; and (challenge 5) manages the school in ways that sustain gains and foster a sense of coherence and integrity for both individual programs and the school as a whole.

Support for this paper and related work was provided by LearningPoint Associates of Naperville, Illinois, and the North Central Regional Educational Laboratory (NCREL). Sarah McCann and David Jacobson conducted interviews for the larger project of which this paper is one product and provided very helpful feedback on an earlier draft. Sara Stoutland also provided helpful feedback. The usual disclaimers apply.

CHAPTER 8

Toward Excellence with Equity

The Role of Parenting and Transformative School Reform

Closing the achievement gap between children of different racial and ethnic backgrounds is a long-term challenge with long-term implications for the United States. There are reasons to be hopeful. Progress has been made in narrowing racial test-score gaps since the early 1970s, when the National Assessment of Educational Progress (NAEP) began tracking test scores at the national level by racial group.[1] For example, the black-white reading score gap for 17-year-olds narrowed by more than 60 percent between 1971 and 1988 (although it then widened slightly), and evidence exists that the black-white IQ gap is narrowing.[2] Further, recent national data show virtually no racial differences in measured ability among children approaching their first birthday.[3] The nation's long-term experience establishes clearly that progress is possible. Now, progress needs to continue and even accelerate. A social movement is developing to meet this challenge.

I believe that skillful parenting and deeply transformative, community-level school reforms are two important and feasible goals to pursue within the broader national movement for "excellence with equity"—a movement aimed relentlessly at high standards of achievement among children from all racial, ethnic, and social class backgrounds. In this chapter I first look briefly at the "movement" idea and introduce some basic principles. Next I review evidence on socioeconomic inequalities, disparities in parenting practices (some of which help predict achievement gaps), and the effectiveness of parenting interventions. Some aspects of this discussion are unflattering to blacks and Latinos, and as a black American I am aware that bigots may cite these findings for racist purposes. However, I believe scholars must not allow bigots to intimidate them into silence on issues that need to be addressed. The point is to look forward with hope at opportunities and responsibilities for progress, not to look backward in order to craft excuses or assign blame. Parenting should be a serious focus of strategies for raising achievement and closing gaps, even for college-educated households, among whom gaps are also large.

Finally, I discuss ways of improving schools by transforming whole school systems from within. Whole-school reform models and other types of programs that originate outside school systems have their roles to play. Experimental evaluations show they often have positive effects. But if achievement gaps are to close dramatically across the nation, school systems will need their own internal capacities and supportive political constituencies for long-term excellence.

WHY A MOVEMENT?

A movement is a diffuse collection of people mobilized by a common sense of purpose to change the world in a particular way. In the United States, female suffrage and civil rights were the pivotal movements of the twentieth century. Now, early in the twenty-first century, there is an emergent movement to raise academic achievement and close skill gaps between children from different racial, ethnic, and social class backgrounds. Universities, governments, and civic organizations around the country are changing policies, launching institutes, developing projects, and conceiving campaigns. In every instance, raising achievement and closing gaps are the goals.

The focus on achievement gaps is inspired by concern for the nation's future. By 2050, racial, ethnic, and socioeconomic groups that are overrepresented among low achievers and underrepresented among high achievers will make up the majority of the population and the workforce. Even more than today, technology and trade will pit workers head-to-head in competition with others around the world. The elderly will be more numerous. When young parents lack reading, math, and job skills to avoid poverty, they will compete with the elderly poor for public supports. Tax burdens on working-age adults are likely to be high. Meanwhile, internationally, the most elevated standards of living will obtain in nations where workers are most skilled and politics most stable. Where the United States will rank in this mix is uncertain. It depends on us. More than we might like to acknowledge, the social stability and vitality of the nation we leave our children depends fundamentally upon how relentlessly and effectively we pursue excellence with equity now and over the next several decades.

Social movements depend upon people who frame and debate ideas and endeavor to mobilize others to embrace particular images of the cause. The movement to raise achievement and narrow gaps is no different. Framing and mobilization are key. In crafting the strategies, policies, programs, and projects that such a movement entails, movement leaders should target adults in all the many roles in which they influence child learning and development. In effect, we need to mobilize across the entire socioecological system that supports child and youth development.

At base this system includes people in their roles as parents, teachers, and leaders in homes, in classrooms, on playgrounds, and even in doctors' and nurses' offices—places where face-to-face experiences most directly produce learning and development.[4] Beyond individual settings, adults affect the ways in which multiple settings connect, in order to achieve consistency and synergy for the children who move back and forth between them.[5] Adults make decisions in workplaces, in central administration offices, and on committees of various kinds, venues in which children typically do not participate but where adults shape many of the rules, resources, and routines that apply in the settings where children do participate.[6] Finally, adults craft and maintain the nation's shared "cultural blueprint," which comprises the laws, languages, religions, property relations, and norms by which Americans live. Important norms include the ways in which race, ethnicity, and social class affect access to power and privilege.[7] Adults in all their many roles affect the way our schools operate and the way our children grow and develop. Leaders in the movement for excellence with equity should seek ways to enlist them all.

SOME BASIC PRINCIPLES

A movement for excellence with equity should aspire to high quality learning opportunities for children and adults alike. Fortunately, substantial agreement exists on the types of experiences children and adults need in order to learn and thrive and on the conditions most likely to produce those experiences. The National Research Council (NRC) Committee on Community-Level Programs for Youth reviewed a wide range of youth development studies—quantitative, qualitative, and theoretical—and found broad commonality in frameworks and findings.[8] Semantics varied, but the ideas were consistent. The following eight "features of positive developmental settings" synthesize a great deal of research. Although the committee was focused on youths, the list is universal, and a movement for excellence with equity would do well to promote these features for every home, classroom, and workplace in which people learn and develop.

1. *Physical and psychological safety* (to prevent feelings of fear and anxiety that might interfere with concentration or motivate withdrawal from participation)
2. *Appropriate structure* (for example, rules that make clear which forms of individual initiative are to be rewarded or penalized and that provide boundaries within and around which individuals can set and pursue goals)
3. *Supportive relationships* (to foster positive emotional states and willingness to take risks that might require social support)[9]
4. *Opportunities to belong* (with an emphasis on accommodating individual skills and interests)
5. *Positive social norms* (to induce healthy behaviors and aspirations, avoiding incentives to be self-destructive or do harm to others)
6. *Support for efficacy and mattering* (to inspire and enable initiative and persistence toward individual and group goals and provide opportunities to make contributions that others value)
7. *Opportunities for skill building* (to support development of physical, intellectual, social, psychological, and emotional skills)
8. *Integration of family, school, and community efforts* (to reduce inconsistencies and promote supportive synergies across settings)[10]

The more consistently children and adults encounter these conditions across multiple settings, the more they will develop the skills and proclivities that prepare them for success. Beware, however, against thinking that the list is a blanket endorsement of peace and harmony under all conditions. As every parent knows, conflict and stress are sometimes necessary. Moreover, conflict and stress are to be expected during periods of dramatic change, when vested interests or attachments to old ways pose resistance in homes, schools, and communities. Indeed, some substantial share of people's work in the movement for equity and excellence will entail challenging social and structural conditions in the society that bias the allocation of public resources and access to opportunity.[11]

Nonetheless, my focus in this chapter is on the two institutions that interface most directly with children and young people as they develop—families and schools. Even before major changes take place in broader social and structural conditions, participants in the excellence with equity movement can take advantage of unexploited opportunities to improve parenting and schooling in ways that raise achievement. We can exploit these opportunities more effectively if we make doing so a priority.

PARENTING

Especially when children are young, home is an important place and parents are extremely important people. Parents have profound influence over the way homes rate on the features just listed, some of which ratings turn out to be correlated with race and socioeconomic status (SES). Within racial groups, research is clear that higher SES parents provide more opportunities at home for academic skill building (item 7) and tend to have greater resources for integrating family, school, and community efforts (item 8).

Similar differences obtain between racial groups, for whom home literacy practices are among the factors contributing to higher achievement by whites and Asians relative to blacks and Hispanics. In this section I report on racial and SES patterns in parenting practices, review key findings on the relationship of parenting to achievement, and summarize evidence on the effectiveness of parenting interventions.

Resources

Resource disparities are important to the story of why parenting practices and opportunities for effective parenting differ across groups. In comparison with typical white parents, poor whites and nonwhites on average have lower incomes. They have fewer years of schooling and fewer academic skills for any given length of schooling.[12] They work fewer weeks per year, at lower average wages, and have accumulated less wealth.[13] They are more stigmatized by assumptions of inferiority and have fewer social network ties to people and institutions that control information or have the capacity to provide other forms of assistance.[14]

Resource disparities do predict achievement gaps. Further, policies and programs that raise income for very poor households have been found to boost achievement among young children. On the basis of a variety of studies, Duncan and Magnuson concluded that socioeconomic resource disparities predicted about 0.5 standard deviation of the test score gap between whites, on the one hand, and blacks and Hispanics, on the other.[15] This magnitude is robust across a number of studies covering different age groups.

One-half standard deviation is typically between one-half and two-thirds (occasionally more) of the total racial achievement gap in any given study.

Although causation can never be completely proved, many mechanisms have been suggested to explain why income and other socioeconomic resources are such strong predictors of student achievement. For example, parents with greater resources have access to safer neighborhoods with better schools and more studious peers.[16] Teachers are more likely to welcome input from high-SES parents and treat them respectfully.[17] High-SES parents can afford more learning tools and materials in the home, may be less stressed by survival pressures and therefore have more patience in helping their children, and may have better and more reliable health services.[18] The list goes on.

To help redress these inequities, policymakers and administrators of programmatic interventions over the years have endeavored to improve school quality in poor areas, increase access to better neighborhoods, improve parent-teacher communication, supplement home learning resources, help parents with stress management, provide access to health care services, and more. All these things are expected to complement or substitute for parental resources. Experience has produced both successes and failures, with no magic bullets but many helpful lessons to build on.[19]

Learning-at-Home Disparities

In an authoritative review of the literature on the contribution of preschool parenting to racial and ethnic gaps in school readiness, Brooks-Gunn and Markman identified racial and ethnic differences on five dimensions of preschool parenting.[20] All involved learning at home, and research has established that all five are contributors to school readiness.[21] The dimensions were nurturance (expressions of love, affection, and care); discipline (responses to behaviors that parents regarded as inappropriate); teaching (strategies for transmitting information or skills to the child); language (amount and characteristics of verbal communication with the child); and materials (books, recordings, and other materials to support learning). These variables resemble the eight features of positive developmental settings summarized from the NRC report. There is more evidence on which to base black-white than Hispanic-white comparisons, but when the average for blacks or Hispanics differs from that for whites in any given study, whites almost always rate higher on the measured practices. Generally, the best studies find racial differences in preschool parenting ranging from one-fifth to three-fifths of a standard deviation, depending on the particular parenting practices.[22] Programming that reduces these differences can shrink achievement gaps at kindergarten entry.

But should middle-class whites be the models? Many people question the validity of using standards from one group to draw conclusions or prescriptions for another. Brooks-Gunn and Markman recounted the way their black graduate students resisted using the two-way contrast between *authoritative* parenting (warm but with firm control) and *authoritarian* parenting (negative, lacking warmth, harsh control) that had become the standard for differentiating parental styles. The students suggested that some very effective black parents might be misclassified under this scheme, and they were correct. Brooks-Gunn and Markman explained:

> We did an exploratory analysis using a sample of about 700 black and white mothers of toddlers, attempting to identify clusters of mothers based on our videotaped ratings on both domains [authoritative and authoritarian]. We identified not two but four groups of mothers—those who were high in warm, firm control and low in negative, harsh control (the classic authoritative behavior); those who were high in negative, harsh control and low in warm, firm control (the classic authoritarian behavior); those who were relatively high in both (what we termed "tough love"); and those who were low in both (what we termed "detached").[23]

Teenage mothers of both racial groups dominated the standard authoritarian group, and many were high school dropouts. In contrast, the "tough love" group was mostly older black mothers with at least a high school education. The standard formulation would have cast them as authoritarian—a less effective form of parenting. But the children of these "tough love" mothers had higher IQ scores and larger vocabularies than the children of detached or authoritarian mothers.[24]

"Tough love" is an example of a practice that differs in prevalence and effectiveness across racial groups. Nonetheless, the general finding in the literature is that there are more similarities than differences regarding which practices predict positive child outcomes. Closing racial and SES gaps in the prevalence of practices that are positively associated with learning can help close achievement gaps.

Whereas much of the literature focuses on low-income and poorly educated parents, learning-at-home gaps appear at all levels of parental education and for students at all grade levels. In the nationally representative Early Childhood Longitudinal Survey–Kindergarten (ECLS-K), numbers of children's books in the home for kindergarten children reported by college-graduate African American mothers were more similar to numbers reported by high-school-educated whites than by college-educated whites (Table 8–1). Findings were similar for records, audiotapes, and compact discs.

The survey also found black-white differences in the frequency with which parents read to children, discussed nature and science, sang, and played games. Whites reported more reading and conversations about nature; blacks reported more singing, playing games, and doing puzzles (Table 8–2).[25] Fryer and Levitt used the ECLS-K to explore how SES, books in the home, and other measures predicted scores as children entered kindergarten. After controlling for an index of standard SES measures, they found that adding the number of children's books to the equation reduced the residual black-white gaps in arithmetic and reading readiness scores by an additional 0.13 standard deviation—equal to one-fifth of the black-white arithmetic gap and one-third of the black-white reading gap.[26] Obviously, this does not mean that buying more books should in itself be a prescription for any group to raise achievement. Surely, the associated literacy practices are what matter— including the ways books are read *and discussed.*[27]

Fryer and Levitt noted that when patterns were examined separately by racial group, the payoff to higher SES in the form of higher school readiness scores was somewhat lower for blacks than for whites, but the basic patterns in the findings remained.[28] Similarly, Selcuk Sirin used seventy-four independent samples in which the relationship of SES to achievement had been estimated and published in journal articles between 1990 and 2000. The meta-analysis he conducted found, as expected, that nonwhites had fewer resources than whites, and this predicted lower achievement among their children. Like Fryer and Levitt, however, he found that parental SES tended to be a stronger predictor of achievement for white students than for minorities. Why? Sirin suggested that "neighborhood and school SES, not family SES, may exert a more powerful effect on academic achievement in minority communities, particularly in African American communities."[29] This is one possibility, but not the only one.

For example, differences in the payoff to higher SES can exist among students of different racial groups living in the same community and attending the same school. Studies would tend to find this result if, for instance, there were differences in course placements, peer culture, or learning-at-home environments among students from different racial groups who had the same measured SES.

I have estimated the relationship of SES to achievement for almost 40,000 middle and high school students from the fifteen suburban districts (across

TABLE 8–1   Numbers of Children's Books (Panel A) and Records, Audiotapes, or CDs (Panel B) (Standard deviation and sample size in parentheses)

Mother's Years of Schooling	African Americans		European Americans	
	Median	Mean	Median	Mean
Panel A: "About how many children's books does your child have in your home now, including library books?"				
12 Years or Fewer	20	30 (33, 1,304)	50	76 (55, 3,099)
13 to 15 Years	30	46 (40, 826)	100	97 (59, 3,042)
16 or More Years	50	65 (51, 258)	100	114 (59, 2,777)
Panel B: "About how many children's records, audiotapes, or CDs do you have at home, including any from the library?"				
12 Years or Fewer	4	8 (13, 1,306)	10	15 (18, 3,114)
13 to 15 Years	8	13 (16, 827)	12	18 (18, 3,072)
16 or More Years	10	16 (16, 260)	20	22 (19, 2,814)

Source: Author's tabulations using ECLS-K Base Year Public Use File.

six states) of the Minority Student Achievement Network (MSAN).[30] On average, white and Asian students in these communities arrive at school with greater socioeconomic background advantages relative to blacks and Hispanics. But they also attend the same schools and live in similar neighborhoods. These are not bad neighborhoods. Nonetheless, the MSAN data, like Sirin's meta-analysis, show a stronger relationship of SES to achievement for whites and Asians than for non-Asian students of color. SES measures here include parents' years of schooling, household structure (two parents, step-parents, and so forth), number of siblings, and numbers of books and computers in the home.

Table 8–3 shows the distribution of households by SES category in the MSAN data.[31] Most whites and Asians are in the upper-middle and highest SES categories, whereas most blacks, Hispanics, and mixed-race students are in the lower-middle and lowest categories.[32] These disparities alone would

TABLE 8–2 Selected Family and Child Learning Practices, by Mother's Years of Schooling, Fall 1998 (Row percentages)

Mother's Years of Schooling	Never	Once or Twice a Week	Three to Six Times a Week	Daily	Total Row Percent	Sample Size
Panel A: Family Members Read Books to the Child						
African American						
12 Years of Fewer	2.0	38.0	29.1	30.9	100	1,313
13 to 15 Years	0.6	25.5	36.6	37.4	100	828
16 or More Years	1.2	14.2	37.3	47.3	100	260
European American						
12 Years or Fewer	1.0	19.4	38.1	41.6	100	3,118
13 to 15 Years	0.3	11.5	41.4	46.8	100	3,074
16 or More Years	0.1	5.7	34.1	60.1	100	2,815
Panel B: Adults Discuss Nature or Do Science Projects with the Child						
African American						
12 Years or Fewer	37.0	40.1	13.1	9.8	100	1,311
13 to 15 Years	24.8	47.6	17.8	9.9	100	828
16 or More Years	16.5	53.9	20.0	9.6	100	260
European American						
12 Years or Fewer	22.2	48.4	20.2	9.2	100	3,116
13 to 15 Years	14.6	51.2	23.7	10.6	100	3,071
16 or More Years	8.5	49.5	31.0	11.0	100	2,814
Panel C: Family Members Sing Songs with the Child						
African American						
12 Years or Fewer	5.5	21.5	19.2	53.9	100	1,313
13 to 15 Years	3.1	18.0	24.4	54.5	100	829
16 or More Years	2.3	18.9	24.6	54.2	100	260

TABLE 8–2   Selected Family and Child Learning Practices, by Mother's Years of Schooling, Fall 1998 (Row percentages)   *(continued)*

Mother's Years of Schooling	Never	Once or Twice a Week	Three to Six Times a Week	Daily	Total Row Percent	Sample Size
European American						
12 Years or Fewer	5.5	25.3	25.8	43.4	100	3,118
13 to 15 Years	3.6	21.9	30.7	43.8	100	3,075
16 or More Years	2.6	21.5	33.3	42.7	100	2,815
Panel D: Family Members Play Games or Do Puzzles with the Child						
African American						
12 Years or Fewer	6.5	36.3	27.0	30.2	100	1,313
13 to 15 Years	3.9	33.3	36.3	26.5	100	829
16 or More Years	4.6	29.3	38.5	27.7	100	260
European American						
12 Years or Fewer	3.6	36.7	39.8	20.2	100	3,118
13 to 15 Years	2.4	34.2	44.0	19.4	100	3,076
16 or More Years	1.7	30.4	48.6	19.3	100	2,815

Source: Author's tabulations using ECLS-K Base Year Public Use File.

TABLE 8–3   Percentage Distribution of Each Race/Ethnic Group across Four SES Categories in Secondary Schools from 15 MSAN Districts

SES Category	Black	White	Hispanic	Asian	Mixed	Total
	Percentages					
Lowest SES	24	3	19	7	12	10
Lower-middle SES	55	25	59	39	44	40
Upper-middle SES	19	57	19	41	37	40
Highest SES	2	16	3	12	8	10
COLUMN TOTAL	100	100	100	100	100	100

TABLE 8–4   Simulations by SES Profile and Race/Ethnicity for Three Achievement Measures*

SES Profile	Black	White	Hispanic	Asian	Mixed
Panel A: Simulated Mean GPA (4-Point Scale)					
Lowest SES	2.38	2.52	2.61	2.66	2.30
Lower-middle SES	2.65	2.91	2.88	3.07	2.73
Upper-middle SES	2.88	3.36	3.13	3.36	3.17
Highest SES	3.18	3.68	3.34	3.67	3.49
Panel B: Simulated Amount That the Student Reports "Completely" Understanding Teachers' Lessons (Standard Deviation Units)					
Lowest SES	−0.38	−0.54	−0.44	−0.58	−0.59
Lower-middle SES	−0.23	−0.22	−0.21	−0.26	−0.26
Upper-middle SES	0.00	0.20	0.01	0.06	0.22
Highest SES	0.04	0.35	0.11	0.35	0.31
Panel C: Simulated Amount That the Student Reports Understanding "Very Well" Material Read for School (Standard Deviation Units)					
Lowest SES	−0.56	−0.59	−0.65	−0.64	−0.57
Lower-middle SES	−0.36	−0.15	−0.39	−0.29	−0.31
Upper-middle SES	−0.07	0.25	−0.06	0.17	0.17
Highest SES	0.06	0.44	0.17	0.41	0.36

*Simulations are for fixed SES profiles, where achievement predictions use regression coefficients estimated separately by race/ethnicity.

predict differences in achievement. But in addition, Table 8–4 shows that achievement disparities in MSAN communities are greatest at the highest SES levels. Other data sets, too, have shown greater racial disparities at higher SES levels.[33] Equalizing SES, at least by standard measures, would go only part of the way toward equalizing school achievement among racial groups if racial differences exist in parenting practices or peer dynamics even within SES categories.

In 2005 I surveyed elementary school students in twenty-nine public schools across a dozen school districts. Most were suburban districts similar

TABLE 8–5 Percentages of "Advantaged" and "Disadvantaged" First through Sixth Graders Responding "Yes" to Selected Statements about Home Life, by Race/Ethnicity*

Survey Items		Asian	Black	Hispanic	White
		Percentages Responding "Yes" (Advantaged, Disadvantaged)			
Panel A:					
1.	At home, someone is always there to help me with my homework if I need it.	52, 34	78, 76	80, 73	80, 74
2.	My parents want me to tell them what I learned in school.	46, 45	65, 62	61, 61	62, 61
3.	Someone reads with me almost every night before I go to sleep.	9, 18	17, 20	19, 32	22, 23
4.	At home, we try to make learning fun.	50, 44	60, 59	56, 59	50, 56
Panel B:					
5.	I read almost every day at home.	66, 56	45, 42	50, 54	59, 52
6.	I have a computer in my bedroom.	45, 29	30, 18	33, 15	23, 20
7.	I have a television in my bedroom.	36, 46	81, 83	70, 69	39, 53
8.	At home, I watch television more than I do anything else.	13, 22	30, 36	14, 27	13, 22
9.	At home, I watch rap videos on television.	11, 19	55, 61	35, 50	15, 24
10.	On many days, I get very sleepy at school.	11, 19	35, 35	18, 30	25, 32
11.	Sometimes my teacher says I don't pay attention as I should.	24, 27	41, 45	28, 45	25, 37

Source: Author's tabulations using Tripod Project student surveys from spring 2005.

*KEY: "Advantaged" students have (by my definition) at least one computer in the home AND are not from single parent households; others are labeled "Disadvantaged." Advantaged: Asian, N = 458; black, N = 659; Hispanic, N = 152; white, N = 1,364. Disadvantaged: Asian, N = 63; black, N = 409; Hispanic, N = 71; white, N = 187

to the MSAN districts already mentioned, but some were inner city. Survey items included several pertaining to learning conditions at home. Table 8–5 shows the percentages of Asian, black, Hispanic, and white students who responded "yes," instead of "maybe" or "no," to selected items. All were first through sixth graders in May 2005. The table shows responses for both "advantaged" and "disadvantaged" students. The "advantaged" were defined as those who reported at least one computer and two adults in the home;

the "disadvantaged" lived in single-parent homes, lacked a computer in the home, or both.

Table 8–5 shows interesting differences in learning-at-home environments.[34] Blacks, Hispanics, and whites appear to have more supportive home conditions than Asians (items 1–4). In comparison with Asians, larger percentages of blacks, Hispanics, and whites reported that help with homework was always available if needed, that parents expressed curiosity about what they were learning at school, and that parents tried to make learning fun. These are all conditions one assumes would support learning.

However, upon inspecting items 5–11, one suspects that Asians (and whites) nonetheless have the net advantage. These items seem more related to the amount of time children spend on academic learning activities at home. Asians agreed most that "I read almost every day at home." Advantaged Asians were the only students more likely to have a computer than a television in their bedrooms. Both advantaged and disadvantaged Asians indicated less television watching than blacks and Hispanics (and far less watching of rap videos). Moreover, a smaller percentage of Asians than of other groups reported becoming sleepy at school. This might partly explain why a smaller percentage of Asians than of other groups agreed that "Sometimes my teacher says I don't pay attention as I should." Whites responded similarly to blacks and Hispanics on items 1–5 and similarly to Asians on items 5–11.

This constellation of findings should cause those of us who are parents of school-age children to take notice. We might respond in any of several ways. One is simply to await more evidence. Another is to campaign against presenting such data in public because they might stigmatize and contribute to stereotypes. A more constructive response is to consider whether there are things we should be changing in our own homes and then act on what we decide while joining with others to more fully explore the potential of parenting.

Preschool Parenting and School Readiness Interventions

According to Brooks-Gunn and Markman, "when researchers measuring school readiness gaps control for parenting differences, the racial and ethnic gaps narrow by 25 to 50 percent. And it is possible to alter parenting behavior to improve readiness."[35] Brooks-Gunn and Markman reported that center-based preschool programs that had parenting components tended to improve both parenting and school readiness among poor children. They reported that family literacy programs could improve school readiness as well. Home-based parenting programs without a center-based child-care component tended to benefit the mother but not the child, at least over the time span covered by most studies.

These encouraging findings for preschool programs with parenting components came mainly from high quality experimental studies. The authors of an NRC review in 2001, titled *Eager to Learn: Educating Our Preschoolers,* concluded, as Brooks-Gunn and Markman did, that *high quality* preschool programs with parenting components could have positive and lasting effects. They added, however, that the parenting components of most current programs needed to be improved in order to be comparable to those shown by evaluations to be most effective. They wrote: "The extent to which program effects on children could be enhanced by improved parent involvement is unclear. Although the theoretical basis for efficacy is clear, many current efforts to work with parents do not appear to be effective. Given this apparent discrepancy, rigorous research aimed at identifying highly effective parent involvement strategies would be extremely valuable."[36]

Interventions with Parents of School-Age Children

Policies and programs to involve parents in support of their school-age children's learning have proliferated since the 1960s, encouraged by findings from research.[37] In the early 1990s a publication of the U.S. Department of Education proclaimed: "Three decades of research have shown that parental participation improves students' learning. This is true whether the child is in preschool or the upper grades, whether the family is rich or poor, whether the parents finished high school [or not]."[38] In the often-cited report *A New Generation of Evidence: The Family Is Critical to Student Achievement,* Henderson and Berla went so far as to claim that "the evidence is now beyond dispute. When schools work together with families to support learning, children tend to succeed not just in school but throughout life."[39]

While optimistic that parent involvement can help raise student achievement, some researchers are more cautious.[40] Baker and Soden critically analyzed hundreds of studies and found that a "lack of scientific rigor in the research informing practice and policy" had contributed greatly to the confusion faced by those attempting to understand the field of parent involvement.[41] One reason research on parental involvement is often "messy" is that programs cover a broad range of activities and most have multiple components. Complexity is compounded when programs are embedded in comprehensive school reform initiatives such as the Accelerated Schools Project, Success for All, and the School Development Program. Isolating the effects of parent involvement in complex interventions is extremely difficult and seldom attempted.[42]

A well-known saying by the late evaluation expert Donald Campbell exhorts one to "evaluate no program before it is proud." Appropriately, the vast majority of books and articles on parent involvement are focused not on the evaluation of parental involvement programs but on what it takes to make them work—to help them become "proud." Challenges to becoming proud include limited skills and knowledge on which to build collaboration; lack of resources (of all types); misperceptions between parents and teachers about each other's motives and beliefs; low expectations and negative attitudes; cultural differences between families and schools; lack of interest; lack of trust; lack of systemic support; and problems in parent-professional interactions, such as negative communication around poor student performance. Implementation can be profoundly challenging, especially for schools serving middle and high school students in low-income neighborhoods.[43] William Jeynes reported on findings from a meta-analysis of fifty-three studies of parental involvement. All of them measured effects on secondary school students' academic achievement. The researchers used a variety of methodologies, so the analyses are most accurately understood as showing a pattern of associations—the estimated effects might or might not be causal. The expected positive correlation between parental involvement and student achievement was confirmed for most aspects of parental involvement covered by the studies, although relationships were statistically significant more often for grades than for standardized test scores. Jeynes reported that effect sizes for "overall educational outcomes, grades, and academic achievement" averaged on the order of 0.5 standard deviations. The magnitude was similar for whites and racial minorities.[44]

Jeynes concluded: "Parental involvement programs . . . influenced educational outcomes, although to a lesser degree than preexisting expressions of parental support."[45] He found that activities such as communication about school and participation in school functions had smaller estimated relationships to achievement than did measures of parental style (for example, authoritativeness and warmth) and expectations (for example, for grades and years of schooling).

Turner, Nye, and Schwartz reported on a meta-analysis of parental involvement and academic achievement for students in grades K–5.[46] To be included in their analysis, an intervention had to meet the following criteria: the treatment had to involve parental activities outside of formal schooling aimed at enhancing student achievement; academic achievement had to be measured as an outcome; and treatment and control groups had to be selected using random assignment. By the end of an exhaustive search they had identified nineteen such studies among hundreds of books and articles. Results were mixed, but the overall effect-size estimate was statistically significant and quantitatively meaningful, at 0.43 standard deviations. The average duration of programs in these studies was less than half a year of schooling. Because the studies were all randomized field trials, this effect size can be interpreted as causal.

My research assistant spent much of 1999 searching for studies that used random assignment or good quasi-experimental designs to test whether it was possible to change parenting in ways that enhanced achievement. She found only five studies that used these methodologies. They showed the following:

- In comparison with a control group that received extra help neither at school nor at home, students' first- and second-grade reading achievement increased when parents listened to their children read school books at home two to four times each week. In comparison with an alternative treatment group given extra reading help at school, however, no improvement was found.[47]
- An intervention including parental involvement for at-risk, urban fourth- and fifth-graders improved scholastic and behavioral self-concept ratings but not academic achievement.[48]
- A homework intervention for sixth graders entailed three alternative treatments: (1) neither the student nor the family received guidance on involving family members in mathematics assignments; (2) the student received guidance on how to involve a family member; (3) both the student and the family received guidance on how to involve family in math assignments. The study found that such guidance did not increase student achievement.[49]
- Low-achieving, inner-city seventh graders assigned for ten weeks to a reading group that included parents showed the largest gains in fundamental reading skills six months later, in comparison with a control group that received no treatment, a reading class without parent involvement, and a school-based tutoring group.[50]
- Inner-city elementary school students whose parents participated in a program designed to teach tutoring skills in reading and mathematics demonstrated positive effects, with experiment students showing a significant increase in achievement over students in the control group.[51]

The strongest support for the value of parental involvement came from the three studies that focused on parents' involvement in reading.[52] Balli, Demo, and Wedman found that efforts to involve parents did not significantly affect mathematics achievement (estimated effects were positive but not statistically significant).[53] Evidence from a correlational study by Joyce Epstein lends support to the differential effect of parental involvement on reading versus mathematics achievement. Specifically, on the basis of a survey of teachers and principals and using achievement test scores of 293 third and fifth graders, Epstein found a positive correlation between teachers' efforts to achieve parent involvement and students' reading achievement, but no such correlation for mathematics.[54]

Because experimental studies randomly assign people to be treated or not, there is no systematic difference at baseline between the treated and the untreated. This makes it very likely that any post-treatment differences are due to the treatment and not to something else. People trained in evaluation research tend to dismiss non-experimental studies as unreliable. I usually count myself among them, but some non-experimental studies are worth taking seriously. Operation Higher Achievement, for example, was aimed at helping the parents of 826 African American children in one inner-city elementary school to create conditions in the home to promote academic learning. Results showed that students intensively exposed to the program gained a 0.5 to 0.6 grade equivalent more during the year than those who were less intensively exposed.[55]

In the end, evaluation studies find that some parenting interventions produce achievement gains and some do not. No one program model produces the same effects in every application. Nonetheless, enough interventions have produced gains with at least moderately large effect sizes, even in rigorously conducted experimental trials, that further consideration of parenting programs as achievement-gap interventions is warranted.

A great deal of activity focused on helping parents to be effective is already in motion around the Unites States. It is worth learning more about them and making them more central to both research and intervention efforts aimed at helping children achieve at higher levels. Strategies should differ depending upon the populations involved and their capacity to help themselves. Future work with middle-class households, especially among blacks and Latinos, might best be pursued by asking organizations that blacks and Latinos control to take lead roles in designing, implementing, and monitoring new efforts.

TRANSFORMATIVE SCHOOL REFORM

Over the past few decades, educators have designed and implemented a huge number of programs to help teachers become more effective. Few of them have been widely replicated. Among those that have, a small number have been evaluated rigorously for effect, and among these some have proved effective enough to justify broader replication. Although no program is guaranteed to work under all conditions, and findings are almost always mixed, evaluation results have been encouraging for Success for All, Direct Instruction, Comer's School Development Program, First Things First, Talent Development, Job Corps, and several others. Those with more finely specified components, better training for teachers, and professionally managed implementation tend to show the most consistent results. Generally, implementation tends to be stronger when the program developer and his or her organization are directly involved. I believe, however, that state and local leaders in the movement for excellence with equity should depend on such programs only as a means toward the longer-term goal of institutionalizing excellence in the people and social networks embedded in the everyday lives of their districts.

There is plenty of evidence that interventions can have positive effects on achievement in schools and communities.[56] Whether or not they actually do in any particular case depends on a number of factors. For example, in a survey of teachers that I conducted in the spring of 2005, I listed seventeen reasons that a program might have little, if any, effect on teaching or learning. The survey instruction read: "Recall the last professional development program at your school that had little or no effect on teaching or learning in your class. With that program in mind, please check all the following responses that apply."[57] The four items teachers checked most often were:

- It was just too much on top of everything else the school was trying to do (37 percent)
- There was too little support and training (30 percent)
- Teachers were not held accountable for doing it (25 percent)
- The way it was introduced didn't inspire me to try (25 percent)

Altogether, 67 percent of elementary school respondents and 88 percent of secondary school respondents checked at least one of these four responses. In contrast, only 7 percent checked "I really tried to make it work, but it just didn't help my students." Only 8 percent responded that "I never thought it could work with my students." Instead, the pattern of responses suggests that the main reasons the programs did not work was that the teachers did not implement them. This highlights the importance of capacity and leadership in the selection, introduction, scheduling, provision of support and training, and overall management of professional development programs.

If school systems could keep talented leaders in curriculum and instruction jobs for as long as a decade, with stable political support for long-term strategic planning and implementation, including frequent reviews and midcourse corrections, might the result be the wholesale transformation of teaching and instruction? Might labor relations function more smoothly? Might teachers be better trained and instruction better differentiated to meet the needs of all students? Might people hold one another more accountable for giving their best effort? Would achievement rise? Would gaps become narrow? Could districts become highly effective design and implementation organizations for achieving excellence with equity? We should try to find out. Some large cities are making a start.

Large Cities

The Council of Great City Schools is the membership organization for most large city school districts in the United States.[58] In 2001 the council convened an advisory committee of school superintendents and education researchers to help design a study. The committee would identify cities making the most impressive progress in narrowing racial gaps while raising overall average scores and would try to understand the reasons for their successes. The research and evaluation firm MDRC would help design the study, conduct the site visits, and write the main report.

The advisory committee scanned the data looking for districts that met the following three criteria: improvement in both reading and math in all or nearly all grades from the beginning of their state's testing program through the spring of 2001; faster rates of improvement than their respective states had achieved for at least three years; and simultaneous narrowing of racial-ethnic achievement gaps. The districts selected for case studies were Charlotte-Mecklenburg, North Carolina; Houston, Texas; and Sacramento, California. For these three districts, positive trends in elementary school scores were evident and better than the respective state averages. Progress was greatest for the lowest scoring groups, so gaps had narrowed. Middle schools had achieved some progress as well, although less than elementary schools, and high schools had made no progress at all.

The study was admittedly exploratory—it would not be definitive. Some members of the advisory committee (including me) thought there would be no valid basis for judgments about which district actions or policies might be contributing to achievement. Still, the committee selected two anonymous comparison districts that had experienced little improvement and proceeded. The MDRC researchers would look for political and managerial differences between the case study districts and the comparison districts and would offer judgments concerning whether some of those differences might help explain why the case study districts had done better.

What the MDRC researchers found was more coherent than anyone had a right to expect. All three case study districts had begun from very low levels. Each had a chaotic political history before the reforms that led to improvement. There had been political factionalism on the school boards, infighting among school departments, and bad relations between schools and central administration. District-level operations were sometimes managed by people who had been promoted into their positions because of seniority instead of qualifications. There was no coherent focus on teaching and learning. Teacher recruitment and retention were difficult. The curriculum was undemanding, instruction was unaligned with state standards, and professional development was in disarray.

By the time MDRC arrived in the case study districts, conditions had changed. In a summary of the report, Casserly and Snipes distinguished what they called "preconditions for reform" and "district strategies for reform." They wrote that they found in place the following preconditions for reform:

- A new role for the school board, whereby a new board majority (or other governing unit) focused on policy-level decisions that supported improved student achievement rather than day-to-day operations of the district
- A vision shared by the chief executive or superintendent of the school district and the school board regarding the goals and strategies of reform
- An ability to sell the leadership's vision for reform to city and district stakeholders
- A focus on revamping district operations to serve and support the schools, including a capacity to diagnose instructional problems
- Resources to support reform and improvement

Grounded in the foregoing preconditions, the case study districts were pursuing the following district strategies for reform:

- Specific goals for student achievement had been set at the school and district levels, and these were associated with fixed schedules and consequences for failure; accountability systems held district and building-level staff personally responsible

- District-level curricula and instructional approaches were developed and adopted, aligned with state standards
- Districtwide professional development supported the reforms, striving for consistent, districtwide implementation of the curriculum and instructional approaches
- A commitment had been made to data-driven decisionmaking about instruction, and the district was investing in the capacity to follow through on that commitment
- Lower-performing schools received special attention, including extra resources and an infusion of qualified teachers[59]

The emphasis in the early stages of reform was on elementary schools, which may help explain why progress at the high school level had not occurred.

Officials in the two comparison districts said they were implementing many of the same reforms seen in the case study districts. But as Casserly and Snipes described it:

- They lacked consensus among key stakeholders about district priorities or an overall strategy for reform
- They lacked specific, clear standards, achievement goals, time lines, and consequences
- The districts' central offices took little or no responsibility for improving instruction or creating a cohesive instructional strategy throughout the district
- The policies and practices of the central office were not strongly connected to intended changes in teaching and learning in the classrooms
- The districts gave schools multiple and conflicting curriculum and instructional expectations, which they were left to decipher on their own.[60]

Progress in the case study districts was not achieved easily. There was resistance. Principals and teachers complained as jobs became more demanding and stressful. Parents and students complained as more time on reading and math meant less time for music, art, and field trips. Experienced teachers complained that the new approaches to instruction were inferior to what they already were doing, although test scores provided no justification for continuing old practices. Advocates for the gifted and talented complained that devoting so much attention to low achievers was causing the highest achievers to be neglected. District officials responded to such complaints in a number of ways, some more effective than others. Some complaints had merit. But with strong preconditions for reform in place, the superintendent and other leaders had the incentives and clout to push ahead with the district strategies for reform that were beginning to make a difference in student achievement.

School-Level Transformation without the District

The preceding focus was on districts because transformative, district-level reform may be the only way to make progress at the scale the nation needs. Currently, most districts, whether city, suburban, or rural, are only steps from the starting line—and some seem to stand behind it. In the meantime, many schools have not waited for their districts but have pushed ahead, guided by the same strategic practices and principles that the Council of Great City Schools examples have in common.

For example, David Jacobson and I selected several schools from the Ohio State Department of Education's "Ohio Schools of Promise" list.[61] These were schools that ranked high on Ohio's state standardized exams. From the longer list we chose schools with relatively large concentrations of racial minority and free-lunch-eligible students. What we saw in site visits to these high-performing, high-poverty schools was the same basic pattern for achieving improvement that other researchers have reported in recent years. Specifically:

- Teachers and administrators analyze student work to identify particular weaknesses
- On the basis of these analyses they select a limited number of skills or topics as priorities for improvement
- They shop around to find (or eventually craft) instructional resources and practices to address their chosen priorities (for some schools, these resources and practices come from whole-school-reform vendors)
- They work in groups to learn the new teaching materials and procedures, sometimes with professional development support from outside the school
- They plan the logistics, especially scheduling, necessary to follow through with implementation
- They monitor implementation, make midcourse corrections, assist teachers who need help, and put pressure on teachers who seem not to be trying
- They monitor student progress and repeat the cycle.

Whether or not a school can initiate and follow through on this type of process depends on the professional climate in the school and the available resources. It also depends on leadership. Recall the top four reasons from my survey for the failure of professional development to be effective: "It was just too much," "There was too little support and training," "Teachers were not held accountable," and "The way it was introduced didn't inspire me to try." Considering each in turn, one would not be surprised to discover that effective school leaders manage professional development in ways that make time in the schedule for new work, provide adequate support and training, monitor teacher participation for accountability, and from the outset introduce and develop ideas in ways geared to attract and sustain participation.

It would be ideal if every school principal were able and inclined to achieve excellence for students from all backgrounds and with minimal district interference. There would be no need for districtwide reforms that restrict school-level autonomy. After all, autonomy restrictions on schools that are already highly effective could do more harm than good. But if many schools need help and districts lack the capacity to support multiple school-level approaches to professional development, then district-level approaches make a great deal of sense.[62] It follows that efforts to build a political movement to mobilize and sustain the will to develop and protect such district-level reforms and associated leadership make a great deal of sense as well.

CONCLUSION

The United States is at the cutting edge of a dramatic shift in national identity. There will be no racial majority group in the country by the middle of the present century. The economic vitality and social stability of the nation that future generations will inherit will depend upon how effectively Americans now alive help all their children, beginning now, to reach their academic potential. Great progress is possible. Earlier I recounted how more than 60 percent of the reading score gap between blacks and whites disappeared between 1971 and 1988. For fourth graders in the NAEP series, recent evidence indicates that gaps are narrowing even as scores for all groups are rising. Working through all the many roles in which they operate, adults today have a duty to help these fourth graders and their contemporaries continue making progress as they pass through high school and college and eventually into the workplace.

Success will require more than changes in policy. Individuals, families, communities, school systems, and nations have *lifestyles*—routine ways of allocating time, effort, attention, and resources to activities. Progress in a national movement for excellence with equity will require lifestyle changes in the ways in which the nation does schooling. Similarly, for most parents, of any racial or social class background, it is not difficult to imagine lifestyle changes likely to raise their children's achievement. Examples are required daily leisure reading, discussions in which children explain their homework answers to parents, and appropriate bedtimes, routinely enforced.

No such changes will happen consistently without adults who take steps to commence and sustain them, often against initial resistance. Sometimes adults can be induced by public policies that provide incentives or persuaded by the information gleaned from special programs or public information campaigns. Multiple means of influencing adults should be tried and studied for their effectiveness. In the end, developing and sustaining the collective will, skill, and discipline of adults to effectively prioritize learning by children, *including other people's children,* is the central challenge we face in a long-term, nationwide movement for building excellence with equity.

Afterword to Chapter 8

Since writing this chapter, I have conducted a number of presentations for black and Hispanic parents about the roles parents can play in helping to raise achievement levels and reduce gaps. Some of the data that I discuss at these presentations come from the National Assessment of Educational Progress (NAEP) and concern black-white and Hispanic-white gaps in reading, math, and science scores, by parental education level. The data show clearly that achievement gaps are large enough to be concerned about at all levels of parental education, including among the children of college graduates.

Some of my presentations are to audiences in which most black and Hispanic parents are college graduates. The evidence that such audiences find most disturbing concerns the fact that reading, math, and science scores among twelfth-grade children of black and Hispanic college graduates are, on average, no higher than scores among children of white high school graduates who never attended college, and sometimes are closer to the scores among children of white high school dropouts (see, for example, Table A8).

Many black and Hispanic parents regard the data in Table A8 as a call to action. They have encouraged me to include the data in this book so that it can motivate others, as it has motivated them, to find ways of responding. The responses that seem warranted include not only searching for ways to improve the services that schools and other institutions provide, but also ways to enrich home life, beginning in early childhood. There is a growing body of research showing that early childhood experiences differ across racial groups and have long-term effects. Similar evidence is growing that parenting styles matter as children get older. Most parents appreciate information on how to do the best they can for their children, and many can be effective consumers of research-based evidence even in the absence of formal programs. We need to support the continuing development of research that can inform parents of all racial and ethnic groups and to create better mechanisms for translating findings into forms that parents can use.

TABLE A8   National Assessment of Educational Progress Reading, Math, and Science Scores (and Gaps) for 12th Graders, by Race/Ethnicity and Parental Education Level

Parental Education Level	Less Than High School Graduate	High School Graduate	Some College	College Graduate	Column D minus Column B
Column	A	B	C	D	E
Mean NAEP Reading Scores in 2005 (Range: 0–500)					
Black	256	256	271	274	18
Hispanic	270	267	280	279	12
White	267	280	292	302	22
White-Black Gap	11	24	21	28	4
White-Hispanic Gap	−3	13	12	23	10
Mean NAEP Math Scores in 2000 (Range: 0–500)					
Black	267	267	276	282	15
Hispanic	277	279	290	294	15
White	279	294	306	317	23
White-Black Gap	12	27	30	34	7
White-Hispanic Gap	2	15	16	23	8
Mean NAEP Science Scores in 2005 (Range: 0–300)					
Black	110	107	124	127	20
Hispanic	123	123	136	138	15
White	133	144	156	163	19
White-Black Gap	23	37	32	36	−1
White-Hispanic Gap	10	21	20	25	4

Source: U.S. Department of Education, Institute of Education Sciences, National Center for Education Statistics, *National Assessment of Educational Progress (NAEP), 2005 Science Assessment, 2005 Reading Assessment, 2000 Mathematics Assessment.* Data come from nationally representative samples. Downloaded from the Internet in September, 2007, using the online NAEP Data Explorer. This table does not include high school dropouts or students who did not take the test because of language problems or other issues. It also does not include students for whom parental education levels were not available.

Urgency and Possibility

A Call for a National Movement

Social and cultural movements succeed when a critical mass of stakeholders—potential activists in neighborhoods, cities, states, and the nation—develop a sense of urgency for change of a particular nature and rise to meet the challenge. Some set out to persuade in ways that change priorities and routines, while others do the strategic design and implementation work upon which effective event management, organizational transformations, and stable new institutional arrangements depend.

The urgency that drives a movement may come from perceptions of threat, possibility, or both. Accordingly, the title of this book, *Toward Excellence with Equity*, is inspired by both threat and possibility. One quite serious threat is that *if we fail to create* a successful movement for excellence with equity, one that is aimed at raising achievement levels for all racial and ethnic groups while narrowing gaps between groups, the nation's economic prosperity and domestic tranquility could decline over the next half century as the United States becomes a majority nonwhite nation.[1] Conversely, *if we do create* such a movement we can conceivably sustain and increase our prosperity and move closer to becoming the Great Society that President Lyndon B. Johnson envisioned in 1964 when he said:

> You can help build a society where the demands of morality, and the needs of the spirit, can be realized in the life of the Nation.
>
> So, will you join in the battle to give every citizen the full equality which God enjoins and the law requires, whatever his belief, or race, or the color of his skin?
>
> Will you join in the battle to give every citizen an escape from the crushing weight of poverty?

Will you join in the battle to build the "Great Society?"

We have the power to shape the civilization that we want. But we need your will, your labor, your hearts, if we are to build that kind of society.[2]

This speech was mainly a call to action, to the embrace of a lofty vision involving people's *will, labor,* and *hearts.*

President Johnson's speech was part of a social movement for fairness and prosperity that was interwoven with the civil rights movement. In the 1960s, the civil rights movement and the vision of the Great Society achieved a break with the past—a historic discontinuity, both culturally and structurally. Structurally, the legislative record of that period included new programs such as Head Start, higher education loans and scholarships, Medicare, Medicaid, clean air and water legislation, civil rights laws, and more.[3] Culturally, the ideas of the Great Society helped change race relations, expectations of social mobility, and other important norms. Building on the hopefulness that John F. Kennedy inspired, Johnson's vision of the Great Society cultivated a national sense of collective efficacy, shared destiny, and social responsibility—a sense that is not entirely gone today but clearly needs renewal.

At one point in his Great Society speech, Johnson spoke directly to younger members of the audience, saying, "Within your lifetime, powerful forces, already loosed, will take us toward a way of life beyond the realm of our experience, almost beyond the bounds of our imagination." This was true in 1964 and is even truer today. In order to prepare as best we can, we need a movement to achieve excellence with equity.

To achieve success, improvements in the design and implementation of public policies are certainly necessary, but they will not be sufficient. We need reforms in what children and youth, from birth through young adulthood, experience in their homes, schools, afterschool programs, and in other settings where they live and develop. We need to focus the nation on the idea that we share responsibility for the changes that need to occur. As adults, we need to focus on the children whose lives we can reach not only through the public policies we enact, *but also in our private lives.*

THE RACIAL EQUITY GOAL

Academic excellence is difficult to achieve but it is not a controversial goal. Widespread excellence in academic achievement can enhance the quality of life that we enjoy as a nation. It can cultivate a well-informed citizenry that is capable of understanding and coping with scientific advancements and other complex social changes. It can build capacity for managing coming challenges, including an aging population, global climate change, and increasing diversity. Most Americans will agree with the goal of raising all groups toward excellence.

Racial test-score gaps among teenagers are as large among the children of college graduates as among the children of high school graduates and dropouts (see the Afterword to chapter 8). Hence, closing the achievement gap between blacks and Hispanics on the one hand and whites and Asians on the other is a racial challenge, not simply a socioeconomic one. We need *racial* equality goals. As all groups pursue excellence, a compelling goal for racial equity is that lagging groups should rise faster until race and ethnicity cease to be predictors of grades, test scores, or any other measure of academic skill or knowledge. If this were to happen, remaining achievement disparities would be within racial groups but not between them, and our national prospects for both prosperity and social tranquility would surely be enhanced.

(*Group-proportional racial equality in achievement*) is a condition in which each racial/ethnic group in society is represented equally in the distribution among low, middle, and high achievers. With group-proportional equality, race and ethnicity are unrelated to accomplishment, so knowing a person's race tells you nothing about his past, present, or future achievements. Recent findings for nine-year-olds in the National Assessment of Educational Progress Long-Term Trend Assessment indicate that scores rose for all groups from 1999 to 2004, but more rapidly for blacks and Hispanics than for whites. So at least during this period, nine-year-olds moved closer to group-proportional equality, even though all groups improved. A similar trend obtained in math for teenagers during the 1980s, but then reversed slightly.

Aspiring to group-proportional equality between racial groups does not require indifference to within-group disparity. Indeed, children should have equal life chances, regardless of their family backgrounds. At the same time, we can reasonably expect that there will always be individual-level differences in academic achievement and that some of these may be impossible to overcome. However, if we refuse to assume that there must always be differences in academic achievement between racial and ethnic groups, then group-proportional equality is a compelling goal for the nation.

Of course, setting racial, ethnic, and socioeconomic goals is much easier than achieving them, when deeply engrained social biases affect the goals we set for ourselves and others, our insecurities when undertaking challenging work, and our comfort zones of social interaction and exchange. Chapter 4 of this book reviewed the literature on teacher expectations. Teachers' beliefs concerning their own potential effectiveness with children from particular racial, ethnic, and socioeconomic backgrounds can either raise or depress the aspirations they set for student achievement outcomes and how hard they search for ways of improving. Social perceptions related to race, ethnicity, and socioeconomic status also affect student confidence. Research on stereotype threat (see chapter 5) shows that student performance can be depressed when fear of confirming a negative stereotype interferes with concentration and distracts students from doing their best. Outside of education, research on subconscious racial biases and on racial discrimination between job applicants with equal apparent qualifications shows that racial biases remain firmly entrenched.[4] The conclusion is unavoidable that working to perceive and treat one another as equals across racial, ethnic, and socioeconomic boundaries must be an important part of the nation's social movement to achieve excellence and group-proportional equality.

A COLLECTIVE-ACTION CHALLENGE

There is a recurring debate in social-change discourse about whether people have the power to change taken-for-granted routines in ways that improve their condition. The observer who believes that people do have this power interprets their condition as cultural, and thus tends to judge them responsible for both their condition and for any improvement that is to be achieved. Conversely, if the observer perceives that they do not have this power, then their condition is interpreted as being constrained by structural conditions, and the observer tends to assign responsibility for change to whatever entities have the power to change the structures that constrain. To blame individuals for conditions beyond their control is often said to be blaming the victim.

However, attempts to neatly classify conditions as either structural or cultural can be simplistic and even misguided. Historical sociologist Orlando Patterson (2002) has written the following concerning the difficulty of distinguishing between cultural and structural conditions:

> Some attitudes, and patterns of thought and behavior among some groups— some of which may be problematic, some desirable—may be cultural continuities, or they may simply be associated structural continuities pure and simple, or they may be associated structural continuities in the process of becoming dissociated and institutionalized into cultural continuities. Deciding what they are is a matter for empirical verification . . . not something to be decided by theoretical or ideological fiat. (p. 30)

Here Patterson has given us a reason not to get stuck in the trap of debating whether cultural or structural phenomena are to blame for conditions we wish to change. It is hard to know the difference, and we may often be wrong. When strategizing to raise achievement and close gaps in the absence of definitive evidence, allowing for the possibility that key outcomes reflect both structural and cultural factors seems to me a wise approach.

Furthermore, even if a behavior pattern is known to be purely cultural, unconstrained by laws or other absolute impediments, assigning responsibility for change to unsupported individuals may be expecting too much. Let us assume for the sake of illustration that a particular behavior (for example, excessive time socializing) is cultural and also dysfunctional in relationship to some important purpose such as academic excellence. Should we expect large numbers of individuals to escape that cultural condition unassisted? Even if they perceive the dysfunctionality and have the self-control to change, they may decide not to if they expect the social penalties to be too high to make the change worthwhile. Social penalties can come in many forms, from disapproving relatives, friends, or colleagues who may regard the norm violation as an ethical transgression or simply "not cool."

For most readers, the prototypic image of persistent cultural dysfunctionality is not an adult in a professional role. However, as an example, consider the culture of teaching English literature in American high school classrooms. There are cultural norms of teaching that may seem right because they are well-established, standard practice and congruent with norms in the broader society. One such practice is to insist that classroom discussions of English literature be conducted in formal English, with one person speaking at a time. These norms—that is, formal English and one speaker at a time—could be best for students from some backgrounds but dysfunctional, or at least not optimal, for others.

For example, Carol Lee (2007) maintains that students who are more fluent in black English dialect than in formal English often participate in class more thoughtfully and with greater energy when allowed to use their regular speech patterns and interaction styles—including sometimes talking over other speakers—in discussions of literature. As a teacher, Lee finds this style of classroom discourse an effective way to elicit and refine students' critical-thinking skills and to engender a love of literature. Furthermore, it can focus attention on learning formal English, which Lee agrees is important.

Lee's ideas are prominent in contemporary discourse about culturally competent instruction for African American students, but some of them are quite different from standard practices in many classrooms. Even though it could be a highly effective way of teaching, condoning dialects other than formal English in English literature classrooms might violate cultural norms on many high school campuses. Even teachers who are attracted to Lee's methods might hold back, feeling constrained by their own sense of propriety or by the prospect of disapproval from colleagues.

The fact that one person's violation of a cultural norm imposes psychic and perhaps also nonpsychic costs on other people puts cultural change in the realm of problems that require collective action—that is, problems best solved by collectives, not individuals alone. This is not to say that the collective will necessarily make the right decision, but only that norms are more likely to change in stable ways when the decisions to change them are undertaken collectively.[5] Teachers inspired to test new approaches are more likely to do so when colleagues formally condone their deviations from established practice. Changes in parenting and peer cultures may benefit similarly from collective processes.

Concerning the stability of cultures, Patterson (2002) proposes that cultural norms usually are not single beliefs or practices but webs of beliefs and practices, or what he calls "cultural complexes." He writes, "Cultural complexes are causally self-perpetuating. What this means in practical sociological terms is that they are normative, taken-for-granted, social processes that are believed in, valorized and acted on simply because they have always been there, or are believed to have always been there, and are among the social things that make life meaningful and 'real'" (p. 21).

There are cultural complexes associated with teaching, parenting, socializing, and participating in popular culture. In the context of a movement for excellence with equity, it is important to view the changing of cultural norms in schools, homes, and youth peer groups as collective action projects requiring organizers and leadership, not adjustments that individuals will carry out in isolation without regard for others' responses. Similarly, structural conditions are seldom under the control of a single person and changing those will also require organizing and leadership.

FOUR INPUT GOALS AND ASSOCIATED CHALLENGES

An economist by training, I find it useful to think in terms of inputs, production processes, and associated outputs and outcomes, including spillover effects, in the context of scarcity and, therefore, tradeoffs. Four main categories of social and material "inputs" produce the experiences through which children learn and develop from birth through early adulthood. Those inputs are themselves produced and modified by a range of institutions and actors, each of which has limited time and resources and faces tradeoffs in how their time and resources are deployed. A movement for excellence with equity will affect the resources people have at their disposal, especially information about how to serve children most effectively. Furthermore, it will affect the choices people make in allocating their time and attention to children—the amount of time, the quality of their attention, and the kinds of activities they engage in—which will in turn increase the social and economic payoffs gained from this investment of time and attention.

Children experience learning in four major types of settings: at home, in school, with peers, and in out-of-school activities and programs. If more parents, teachers, peers, and out-of-school service providers had the proper resources, information, and incentives to both enable and induce high-quality developmental supports for children, we would more often achieve the type of redundancy in developmental supports that Edmund W. Gordon (2005) calls for in the following passage:

> Most complex systems that achieve effectiveness and stability are characterized by redundancy—that is, systems in which all critical mechanisms have back-up or alternative components in case of failure in the primary system. It is possible that the educative systems of human societies also require redundancy—multi-layered mechanisms by which the developmental tasks of human learning are engaged, supported, and mastered. (p. 333)

The following four input goals are central to child and youth learning and development. They are quite standard; none is controversial. All are justified by the types of research discussed in this volume. They are the proximal conditions through which less proximal societal forces help shape developmental outcomes. They constitute key purposes toward which leadership, institution-building, and public policy should ultimately be directed in a movement for excellence with equity. They are: *proximate determinants*

1. *High-quality parenting* that nurtures social, emotional, and intellectual growth by balancing warmth and responsiveness with structure and demands, and by providing other key supports, including strong connections in the world beyond the family from infancy forward.
2. *High-quality teaching* in preschools, K–12 schools, and colleges that engages and challenges students of all ages, and functions effectively to help students experience the joys and rewards of reaching for excellence.

3. *High-quality youth peer cultures* that support behaviors conducive to academic learning and the pursuit of excellence and that reflect norms conducive to healthy relationships and lifestyles.
4. *High-quality community supports* during out-of-school time—operating through both formal programming and informal social ties—to supplement parents' and teachers' efforts with high-quality, high-yield learning experiences for children and youths.

Each input goal has implications within each major developmental period through which children grow—from early childhood on to preschool and early elementary school, on to the primary grades and middle school, through high school and into college, and, ultimately, into adulthood. There are already social-movement-type activities and organizations targeted at these developmental periods, with preschool and early childhood education probably currently the strongest.

Our society has many mechanisms through which to increase both the quantity and the quality of these inputs, including the great variety of communication tools now available through print and electronic media. We need to use these mechanisms to reduce the disparities in the quality of developmental inputs. While some children have warm and demanding parents, excellent teachers, positive peers, and engaging high-yield out-of-school activities in communities with strong leadership, many others do not. The following pages highlight key issues to consider in pursuing these input goals.

Input Goal No. 1: High-Quality Parenting

High-quality parenting that nurtures social, emotional, and intellectual growth by balancing warmth and responsiveness with structure and demands, and by providing other key supports, including strong connections in the world beyond family from infancy forward.

The best available evidence indicates that children of different racial and socioeconomic backgrounds come into the world equally equipped to excel. There are within-group differences, but differences between groups are miniscule. However, by age three, between-group skill differences are clearly in evidence. Later, gaps in school readiness are firmly established by the first day of kindergarten. If the differences are not genetic, then it must be concluded that early childhood experiences are fundamentally important to these learning outcomes. Parents and others in the extended family are the main providers of early childhood experience. In chapter 8, I present evidence that parenting styles and practices differ by parental education and income, by race and ethnicity, and by other family background characteristics. Parenting is far from the only thing that matters. Nevertheless, however difficult it might be to accept, parenting should be addressed as part of the answer to reducing achievement disparities at all levels of parental education.

A movement for excellence with equity must include well-conceived, respectful, and culturally sensitive mechanisms for reaching parents with information and ideas about parenting and for supporting them as they strive to do the best they can for their children. The specifics of what parents need may vary tremendously from one household to the next, so the informational and support mechanisms need to be appropriately flexible and varied. At the same time, in accordance with the discussion in chapter 8, there are common themes in human development and learning that every parent should be encouraged to understand and apply. These themes should be discussed and debated in settings ranging from church basements to university lecture halls, in the context of a concerted national campaign.

There currently is no concerted national effort to provide information or supports for parenting. There are many organizations that focus on parental support and the dissemination of information about parenting, but as a nation we treat parenting as beyond the scope of what organized civic discourse should address. Furthermore, unsolicited suggestions for changing parenting practices are sometimes difficult to deliver and accept, especially because there are racial and ethnic differences in parenting norms and practices. Racial and social-class prejudice on the part of the agents who might deliver the advice is a major concern. Another concern is the negative psychological effect on children and parents alike of an open critique of their family lifestyles.

For example, at a recent conference of the Achievement Gap Initiative at Harvard University, there were several research presentations about parenting as a predictor of achievement outcomes. During the discussion that followed these presentations, speakers expressed concern that our discussions sometimes emanate from a stance of superiority, without proper sensitivity and respect for families' actual experiences. Mary Bacon, a diversity consultant from California, expressed the situation well: "It is clear that there are some parenting styles, some behavioral styles, some learning styles, some world views that are dysfunctional in our world—that are unacceptable in the kind of world that we would like to have." Bacon went on to distinguish between perceiving others' ways as "deviant [or] . . . dysfunctional," suggesting that dysfunctional is almost always the more appropriate perception. She continued, "Because all of us are products of our individual journeys, even with the best intentions we bring our own prejudices to the table [and they] color our perceptions of others. To be effective educators, we must continue to try to suspend judgment about how other people have been shaped by their respective journeys."

Bacon was right to remind us that we are shaped by our journeys and that we should be careful to keep the focus on helping people understand ways they can achieve the goals that they would choose for themselves.

Still, no matter what their backgrounds, it is often difficult for parents to accept that some of their ideas and practices are inconsistent with what research suggests might produce superior outcomes for our children. Furthermore, when it comes to violation of family or community norms, it can be difficult for a parent to be the only one in their family or social network to change their parenting methods. Nonetheless, as chapter 8 discusses, there are parenting practices for all racial groups associated with higher achievement for children. The research is still evolving and some of the details may change, but the general patterns are likely to become even more solidly established over time. To the degree that this is true, it seems that we have a moral responsibility to assemble the evidence as it exists and as it continues to develop, and to make it available to parents in ways that will help convince them to take it seriously. In addition, we should develop more ways to support parents in their efforts to change.

Input Goal No. 2: High-Quality Teaching

High-quality teaching in preschools, K–12 schools, and colleges that engages and challenges students of all ages and that functions effectively to help students experience the joys and rewards of reaching for excellence.

There is growing evidence that students are most motivated when teachers are strong on all three legs of the instructional tripod: content knowledge, pedagogic skills, and relationship skills. Regarding content knowledge, teachers need to know the concepts and content of the curriculum they teach well enough to formulate rigorous lessons and to craft multiple alternative explanations when students find things difficult to understand. Regarding pedagogy, teachers need the skills and dedication to differentiate lessons effectively for students with different levels of preparation, to craft lessons that have relevance to students, and to deliver those in ways that students find intellectually stimulating. Regarding relationships, teachers need to be caring, sensitive, and supportive, but they also need to insist, even demand, that students work hard, not give up in the face of difficulty, and strive for excellence. Furthermore, teachers need to monitor students' relationships with one another, insisting that students avoid teasing or otherwise distracting or discouraging one another from being ambitious and hard working. If we truly care about excellence with equity, we need as a society to give children from all backgrounds access to teaching that has these characteristics.

Teachers differ a great deal in their effectiveness. The evidence is clear that some teachers produce much larger achievement gains than others do and that differences in teacher effectiveness tend to persist from year to year in the absence of effective professional development. The importance of high-quality instruction is highlighted in chapter 3 in the context of evidence that racial differences in access to highly effective teachers are sometimes a contributing factor to persistent black-white achievement gaps. Furthermore, chapter 4 indicates that some teachers' low expectations for what they and their students together are capable of achieving can keep them on established achievement trajectories because searching for ways to improve may not seem worth the effort. A movement for excellence with equity cannot allow any school or teacher to stand apart from the search for ways to improve.

The paramount importance of high-quality instruction is what prompted authors of the No Child Left Behind Act of 2001 (NCLB) to stipulate that placing a highly qualified teacher in every classroom was a requirement for which states would be held accountable. As I write this, NCLB is being revised for reauthorization. Public debates about ways to reformulate the law are in full swing. Research findings on the impact of the bill have been mixed. There seems to be a consensus that the progression of incentives and corrective measures in the bill is not working well, because states and local districts often lack the capacity (and sometimes the will) to implement it effectively.

Furthermore, the goal of universal proficiency by 2014 is widely understood to have been a political calculation—a compromise that many believed from the outset to be overly ambitious. Some even speculate that the deadline was never meant to be met, but was instead meant in a sinister way to show once and for all the futility of erasing racial differences and, thereby, the wastefulness of using public resources in any attempt to do so. However, I do not doubt that most supporters of the NCLB legislation had the best of intentions and understood that the specifics of the bill would evolve over time, through various reauthorizations.

Whatever one thinks of NCLB, it has spurred change in school and district cultures. The attention paid to achievement among poorly performing students in schools with which I have been involved has markedly increased since the law went into effect. At the same time, this sometimes frantic attention has been slow to translate into coherent, sustained, district- and school-level strategies. Many schools and districts need greater capacity for effective labor negotiations and strategic planning. In addition, like the districts described in latter part of chapter 7, they need more visionary, courageous leadership by principals and superintendents who have the knowledge and confidence to be assertive leaders in the context of well-conceived theories of change for school improvement.

Accordingly, serious and sustainable measures to improve teaching in ways that help raise achievement and narrow achievement gaps must attend not only to getting the incentives right on paper but must also, as my colleague Richard Elmore emphasizes, put in place the capability to help school personnel respond effectively. Weak schools need more ambitious cultures, more effective teachers, and stronger leaders. Leaders in weak schools need streamlined authority to dismiss teachers who are chronically ineffective and the capacity to recruit and retrain skilled, committed replacements.

Beyond formal authority and various material resources, leaders also need the sensitivity to nurture teachers and the courage to insist that teachers participate earnestly as members of professional learning communities. Recall from chapter 7 that when professional development training for teachers does not translate into improved instruction, it is often because teachers never implemented what they were supposed to have learned. Working in professional learning communities and taking advantage of various technical supports, teachers can do the difficult job of learning to differentiate instruction more effectively for children of different racial, linguistic, and socioeconomic backgrounds. In so doing, they can become better equipped to raise achievement among students at all levels of preparation and from all social origins.

Input Goal No. 3: High-Quality Youth Peer Cultures

High-quality youth peer cultures that support behaviors conducive to academic learning and the pursuit of excellence and that reflect norms conducive to healthy relationships and lifestyles.

One would be hard pressed to find a young person who prefers low grades to high grades or who would prefer being stupid to being smart. Nonetheless, in any school on any day, it is not difficult to find some youths whose behaviors suggest that they are, at best, indifferent to learning. There may be many reasons, including failure and discouragement at school or family problems at home, but routine distractions associated with peer cultures that—although they are not opposed to high achievement—prioritize values other than school achievement may penalize peers who get the tradeoffs "wrong."

Humans of all racial, ethnic, and social-class backgrounds enjoy feeling accepted, important, successful, and secure. We might say that opportunities to experience these feelings are like social "magnets." Conversely, it is human nature to avoid or resist the people, places, and purposes that make us feel rejected, unimportant, unsuccessful, or insecure. As they reach adolescence, and even before, most young people rely on peers to provide much of the warmth, validation, challenge, and instrumental support that constitute social nourishment, especially if adult sources are ineffective or unavailable.

From a number of sources, we know that young people value success in the domain of academic achievement but that they value acceptance and importance among peers, too. When the quality of performance in school and popularity with peers must be traded off against each other, the desire for social acceptance often carries a great deal of weight and reduces devotion to excellence.

There are a number of issues relating to peer culture worth targeting in a movement for excellence with equity. None is confined to a single racial or ethnic group, although manifestations across groups sometimes differ, and therefore activities should often be race and gender differentiated. All are reasonable targets for a broadly inclusive social and cultural movement in which all racial and gender groups aspire to improve.

Large numbers of middle and high school students admit that trying to be popular distracts them from their work in class.[6] Manifestations of the problem seem worse for boys than for girls, and somewhat greater for blacks than for other groups. Unfortunately, academic attitudes, behavior, and achievement rank low as determinants of popularity.[7] If peer norms heavily favored academic excellence, efforts to be popular would not be an important distraction from schoolwork. There might even be a popularity penalty for students who distracted one another in class. Students would be mutually supportive, eager to help one another if needed. Currently, in both inner-city and suburban classrooms and across all racial groups, many students do not perceive their peers as eager to help.[8]

Perhaps the most discussed topic in the popular media on the issue of peer supports for achievement is the idea that some students perceive working hard in school and seeking to achieve at high levels as "acting white." The Afterword to chapter 6 summarizes evidence that the "acting white" accusation is an issue for all racial groups and that students need help understanding it. Students who say they are likely targets for the accusation are more likely to report that they hold back from doing their best in class because of what others might say or think. The strongest predictors of the "acting white" accusation against students of color are not grade-point averages but elements of personal style, such as speaking proper English in informal settings with friends, liking rock music, and trusting strangers—things that are sometimes more characteristic of high achievers than of low achievers, but not unique to high achievers. The bottom line is that youth from all backgrounds need help understanding and responding in healthy ways to this and other peer pressures that interfere with learning.

Finally, no matter what we think about youth cultures, they are products of our own society, and societal responses are required when they go awry. All youth rebel to some extent during adolescence. However, as Cathy Cohen's (2007) work at the University of Chicago is showing, many young black males in particular believe that society does not care about black males as a group. When young people feel neglected, when they witness injustice, and when they feel demeaned and disrespected they express themselves in oppositional ways that can be misunderstood as senseless rule-breaking. When they feel locked out of opportunity, they may mock the system instead of going through the motions of preparing themselves for opportunities they expect they will never have. Furthermore, young people from relatively well-off families and school systems who face no serious constraints may identify with those who do, mimicking their personal styles and behavior patterns and failing to prepare themselves for opportunities that are well within their reach.

As a society, we need to support youth with our time and attention, push them to excel, give them viable images of future selves toward which to aspire, and help them feel valued for their current and future contributions. We also should help young people draw their understandings from reliable sources—especially sources that avoid confusing entertainment with reality—as they struggle to set their aspirations and present themselves to the world.[9] In addition, because of "cultural complexes," working with one young person at a time on one issue at a time is important, but it's not enough. We must find ways to engage whole peer groups and to bring them along together toward lifestyles conducive to their future vitality. Out-of-school settings are important places to do this work.

Input Goal No. 4: Community Supports during Out-of-School Time

High-quality community supports during out-of-school time—operating through both formal programming and informal social ties—to supplement parents' and teachers' efforts with high-quality, high-yield learning experiences for children and youths.

I first studied out-of-school supports during the early 1990s, when the positive youth development (PYD) movement was beginning.[10] This period coincided with a flurry of comprehensive community initiatives (CCIs), which, supported by large foundations and governmental programs, were influenced deeply by PYD ideas. The idea that motivated them all, now captured in the literature under a variety of labels, is that young people need a variety of supports and experiences to develop to their full potential, and these supports need to be provided across multiple settings, including but not limited to schools and families.[11] Also, influenced deeply by Urie Bronfenbrenner's (1979) work on social ecologies, there is an emphasis in the youth development field on the importance of consistency of norms and values from one setting to the next. There is also explicit attention being given to the idea that developmental needs differ in different developmental periods (age ranges) and that some developmental needs, such as the need for guided autonomy during adolescence, might best be served through community-based, out-of-school programs. In 2002, the National Research Council Committee on Community Youth Programs published a volume (Eccles & Gootman, 2002) that summarized the basis in research for the out-of-school time programming field.

Like schooling studies, studies of out-of-school time programs have found great variability in their quality. However, again like findings regarding schools, the research shows that well-designed and well-implemented programs do improve the outcomes that they target, both academic and nonacademic.[12]

Out-of-school supports can include a range of less formal activities, such as field trips and informal mentoring with neighborhood adults in volunteer roles. However, consistency and dependability in the provision of such supports will often require systematic programming, which costs money for staff and oversight for quality control. In some cases, parents have the resources to pay. In other cases, public and charitable subsidies are required. Some communities have created dedicated revenue streams to cover these expenses, but they represent a only small minority of the communities where such services should be provided, along with high-quality support and monitoring to ensure program capacity and quality.

Progress with regard to the input goals above will be affected by how earnestly citizens organize to hold one another accountable by measuring and monitoring performance and by influencing which visions of living and learning get shared through mass media and other forms of communication. The challenges entailed with meeting goals, and even the details of the goals, will differ between racial and ethnic groups, by levels of parental education and income, and by the types of communities and social networks within which people are embedded. Nonetheless, each of the input goals that I emphasize here is important for every child, no matter what his or her background might be. Some of these things are well-known already, but there is a large "knowing-doing gap" to be overcome.

CIVIC LEADERSHIP AND INSTITUTIONAL CAPACITY

Civic leadership is in large measure the work of people who take responsibility outside of their professional roles for making sure that efforts and resources are directed in thoughtful and potentially effective ways to achieve the civic outcomes that they consider to be priorities.

We need civic leadership to mobilize the collective will and institutional clout to alter the cultural and structural conditions that impede our progress toward achieving excellence with equity. Those of us who believe in the importance of a movement for excellence with equity need to disseminate messages in ways that reach adults in all the many roles through which, directly or indirectly, they influence child learning and development. We need to inform and inspire a commitment to improve routines and practices across the entire socio-ecological system that affects academic and other forms of intellectual competence. We need to assist one another, but also to hold one another accountable.

We need sophisticated, well-funded, and accountable institutional mechanisms. In every city and state, resources and talent need to be devoted to this challenge in proportion to its tremendous importance. The plausibility, morality, and, indeed, the necessity of the proposition that every region of the United States can achieve both excellence and equity—equity with regard to racial outcomes in particular—need to be deeply impressed on the American people, using all available means of communication. There should be a sense of urgency and possibility to achieve both the cultural and the structural changes that seem warranted.

The movement needs to engage every segment of society, including the corporate sector. A promising sign is that the U.S. Chamber of Commerce, the largest national business organization, has recently taken note of the problem. In 2007, the Chamber released an education report card for every state in the nation, along with a statement that included the following:

> The United States in the 21st century faces unprecedented economic and social challenges, ranging from the forces of global competition to the impending retirement of 77 million baby boomers. Succeeding in this new era will require our children to be prepared for the intellectual demands of the modern workplace and a far more complex society. Yet the evidence indicates that our country is not ready.[13]

The Chamber promises to become more involved in education reform:

> For too long the business community has been willing to leave education to the politicians and the educators—standing aside and contenting itself with offers of money, support, and goodwill. But each passing year makes it clear that more, much more, is needed. America's dynamic, immensely productive private sector is the envy of the world. Are there ways in which business expertise, dynamism, accountability, and problem solving could improve our schools? What would a business plan for reform include?

Regional economic development organizations such as the Southern Growth Policies Board are getting involved too. In fact, the list of national and regional organizations that would consider themselves as active in the movement for excellence with equity is already quite long. It includes national business organizations, membership organizations of state and local elected officials, national teachers unions, networks of education intermediaries, civil rights organizations, and a host of think tanks and university research centers. One might say that the movement already exists and simply needs to be named and declared a movement.

However, without capacity-building and leadership on the ground in local communities, pronouncements by national and regional organizations will have limited impact. In every state and metropolitan region, a small number of high-profile organizations are needed outside of government in which private sector corporations, foundations, and other philanthropists pool their resources in order to provide independent *excellence-with-equity "engines"* for the movement.

While no organization that I know is exactly what I have in mind, a number come close. For example, Philadelphia Safe and Sound might be considered a regional "engine" in the field of youth development, although it does not focus explicitly on academic affairs. The organization describes itself as[14] a leading independent non-profit organization that improves the health, safety, and well-being of children and youth through research, technology, program management, and advocacy. We accomplish this in collaboration with government, foundations, corporations, and community groups through the integration and leveraging of resources, research, policy analysis and program development. Throughout Philadelphia, our work spans a broad spectrum of partners including law enforcement, the court system, social service agencies, public and private schools, nonprofits, faith-based organizations and corporations.

Philadelphia Safe and Sound is "a thought leader and agent of change" with three interlocking divisions: a research division that is a think tank on children's issues; a best-practice incubator for new ideas; and a policy and advocacy division to influence policy. Similar to the role that an "engine" for excellence with equity would play, Philadelphia Safe and Sound is a major driver of improvement in how Philadelphia as a civic community takes care of its children and youth. It is an organization through which major actors in the region pool their resources and shape and manage their collective agenda.

Smaller cities and towns will often lack the capacity to create large enough "engines" and will need to rely on state or regional entities. For example, The Prichard Committee for Academic Excellence in Kentucky is a prominent "engine" for academic affairs serving a whole region. It lists its functions as the types of responsibilities that this discussion is advocating. The committee describes its role and functions as follows:

- The Prichard Committee for Academic Excellence is an independent, nonpartisan group of volunteers dedicated to improving education in Kentucky.
- The Prichard Committee receives no government funding. We are funded by foundations, corporations, and individuals in Kentucky and across the country.
- We speak out for progress in education, inform the public, legislators, governors, and other education officials, and work with local parents and citizens.
- We help to solve problems through public statements, meetings, publications, and recommendations made by task forces of our own volunteer members.
- We have commissioned studies by nationally known experts and worked with education officials and concerned citizens to solve problems.

- We inform the public through publications including guide books . . . a quarterly newsletter, a monthly newspaper column, and a Web site.
- We work with local parents and citizens through our regional staff and the Commonwealth Institute for Parent Leadership.

The committee was founded in 1980 as a 30-member citizen panel to plan for the future of higher education in Kentucky. Three years later, members of this group reorganized into a new, independent organization and dedicated themselves to advocating for improved education for all Kentuckians.[15]

"Engines" might take many forms, depending on the characteristics of the places where they develop and the existing division of labor for performing particular functions. For example, the Chicago Consortium for School Research based at the University of Chicago has conducted a great deal of practical research for the Chicago public schools and has been quite helpful as a source of informed expertise in that city's school improvement efforts. Other examples that resemble what I have in mind include the many local education funds around the nation for which the Public Education Network (PEN) is the national organization:[16]

PEN and its members are building public demand and mobilizing resources for quality public education on behalf of 11 million children in more that 1,600 school districts in 33 states, the District of Columbia and Puerto Rico. PEN has expanded its work internationally to include members in the Philippines, Peru and Mexico. . . . Independent community-based organizations must play a central role in building and sustaining broad support for quality public education and for achieving significant reform in the nation's public schools.

State and local nongovernmental "engines" should be staffed by people who are as talented as the staff members of other major institutions and who are diverse enough to be representative of, and trusted by, local stakeholders. Every "engine" should hire or develop staffers who become repositories for information and expertise about issues, activities, organizations, and practices of importance to the success of the movement. These staffers can then be major resources for other organizations.

There is sure to be resentment when "engines" overshadow smaller organizations and soak up resources that might have been spread more thinly, but the economies of scale and scope to be achieved and the possibility for sustainability and depth of impact are a strong justification for their existence. Indeed, if well-funded "engines" that have highly competent staffs make local systems more effective—which, after all, is their purpose—then more resources for smaller organizations are likely to become available. In any case, there is no doubt that some power will shift if such "engines" become more common. However, without large organizations to which major funders are committed, the movement will lack the heft it needs to be highly effective.

Communities need balance in their strategies for addressing the multiple sources of low achievement. A community fully engaged in the movement for excellence with equity, propelled perhaps by the work of one or more local "engines," would address both academic and nonacademic youth-development issues and invite participation from as broad a range of actors as possible. There would likely be "critical friends" site visits to local organizations;[17] community report cards; extensive involvement from print, broadcast, and Internet media; many options for youth involvement; options for parental enrichment; other adult learning activities; accountability through visibility;[18] celebrations balanced by efforts to improve; lots of behind-the-scenes negotiation on behalf of children; a focus on professionalism—and the list could go on.

need to scale up to national level. There are many examples around the nation where some of the above is already in place. However, I know of no examples where the scale, scope, and saturation of the effort is what it needs to be in order to have as great an impact as the nation's children and their future children deserve.

OUR GENERATION'S RESPONSIBILITY

Race-conscious discourse throughout U.S. history has focused mainly on group interests and associated issues of equity; it has emphasized denying or providing opportunity to particular groups, rather than benefits to society as a whole. Slave owners, to protect their caste and material interests, asserted that slavery was morally righteous. Abolitionists disagreed. Later, people who fought Jim Crow laws and leaders of the mid-twentieth-century civil rights movement asserted that the descendents of slaves, as a group, were morally entitled to full participation in the social, political, and economic institutions that stood on the foundations slave labor helped build. Many of us, black Americans in particular, benefit profoundly from the ongoing work of leaders whose primary claims rest on principles of fairness and equity.

Nonetheless, principles of fairness and equity provide too narrow a frame for the work that remains to be done. As a nation, we need narrative frames—ways of telling our stories, expressing our aspirations, and justifying our claims—that help unify us in the face of growing diversity and build our capacity to prevail together in the face of complex challenges. Racial equity needs to be integrated with other themes—including prosperity and excellence themes—in our vision of who we want to be as a nation. Fairness and justice matter in combination with other values, including the self-interest each of us has in building a stable, economically secure nation for our children.

New technologies have increased the economic importance of reading, math, and problem-solving skills for the entire population, not just racial minorities. Communication and transportation advances have intensified competition for jobs from workers around the world for all classes of Americans. Carbon dioxide emissions are changing the global climate for everyone. And millions of immigrants continue to arrive in the United States from Asia, Latin America, Europe, and Africa to be woven into a rapidly changing national fabric. Meanwhile, over a quarter of young adult males who are native-born blacks with less than a high school education are in prisons at any point in time. Black-white and Hispanic-white test-score gaps are as large among the children of college graduates as among the offspring of children whose parents have never attended college. This is the world in which a social and cultural movement for excellence with equity is of paramount importance.

There is a tremendous need for leadership, ranging from informal neighborhood roles to major leadership functions at the national level. We need to flood U.S. society with images of adults in their multiple roles—parents, teachers, ministers, community members, workers, employers, entertainers, policymakers—acting in ways that support high achievement among youth. We need to build civic oversight and intermediary organizations—state and local "engines"—to make and maintain the connections that this movement will require over the next several decades of what some are saying is the Chinese century. Let us make it the American century as well—the century when the American rhetoric about excellence and equality come together in a new American reality—a Great Society.

We can do this. Racial, ethnic, and socioeconomic gaps in mental ability in the United States appear not to exist among infants.[19] Furthermore, for school-age children, test scores are higher and racial gaps are smaller than they were in 1971, when the National Assessment of Educational Progress launched the first systematic effort to track test-score trends for the nation.[20]

Sixty-two percent of the black-white reading score gap among 17-year-olds disappeared between 1971 and 1988; a third of the math score gap vanished over the same period. While too many high school "dropout factories" remain, high school graduation rates are much higher for all groups than at the middle of the last century. Success is achievable. We need to redouble our efforts to make it happen. The stakes are high.

Notes and References

Introduction

Notes

1. From "Bercovitch wins Bode-Pearson Prize" (Gewertz, 2007). Sacvan Bercovitch is the Powell M. Cabot Professor of American Literature *Emeritus*, Harvard University.
2. The chapter covers 1971 through 1996, the years for which test scores from the Long Term Trend Assessment of the National Assessment of Educational Progress were available at the time the chapter was written.
3. Later, John Ogbu (2003) published a book based on several months of school and classroom observations conducted by his research assistant, Astrid Davis. The conclusions that Ogbu and Davis reached about student behaviors and academic performance patterns were consistent with the survey findings. However, the differences in students' family backgrounds were much larger than Ogbu indicates. In addition, black-white differences in student attitudes and beliefs were smaller than one would conclude based on Ogbu's book, which focuses almost exclusively on the black students. In making causal judgments, my reading of the evidence places more weight on the importance of skill gaps developed before students arrive at middle school. Unfortunately, John Ogbu passed away before we had the opportunity to talk through our differences of interpretation.

References

Gewertz, K. (2007, September 20–26). Bercovitch wins Bode-Pearson Prize. *Harvard University Gazette*, p. 3.

Jencks, C., & Phillips, M. (1998). The black-white test score gap: An introduction. In C. Jencks & M. Phillips (Eds.), *The black-white test score gap*. Washington, DC: Brookings Institution Press.

Ogbu, J. (2003). *Black Americans in an affluent suburb*. Mahwah, NJ: Lawrence Erlbaum Associates.

CHAPTER 1 Shifting Challenges: Fifty Years of Economic Change toward Black-White Earnings Equality

Notes

1. Gunnar Myrdal, *An American Dilemma* (New York: Harper & Row, 1962), 222.
2. On oppositional behaviors by stigmatized minorities, see, for example, John Ogbu, *Minority Education and Caste: The American System in Cross-Cultural Perspective* (New York: Aca-

demic Press, 1978). On discouraging and demeaning messages, see Ronald F. Ferguson and Mary S. Jackson, "Black Male Youth and Drugs: How Racial Prejudice, Parents, and Peers Affect Vulnerability," in Peter J. Venturelli, ed., *Drugs in America* (Boston, Mass.: Jones and Bartlett Publishers, 1994).

3. Developing this point is beyond the scope of the present paper. See Ronald F. Ferguson, "Racial Patterns in How School and Teacher Quality Affect Achievement and Earnings," *Challenge: A Journal of Research on Black Males* 2 (1) (May 1991); Ferguson and Jackson, "Black Male Youth and Drugs"; and Ronald F. Ferguson, "How Professionals in Community Based Programs Perceive and Respond to the Needs of Black Male Youth," in Ronald B. Mincy, ed., *Nurturing Young Black Males* (Washington, D.C.: The Urban Institute Press, 1994).

4. This section goes through 1975 because that is roughly the time when improvement ceased to occur. However, much of the actual discussion goes through 1980 because 1980 was a census year. This section relies on the work of a number of authors. Most important among these are James P. Smith and Finis R. Welch, "Black Economic Progress After Myrdal," *Journal of Economic Literature* XXVII (2) (June 1989): 519–64; John H. Donohue III and James Heckman, "Continuous Versus Episodic Change: The Impact of Civil Rights Policy on the Economic Status of Blacks," *Journal of Economic Literature* XXIX (4) (December 1991): 1603–643; and David Card and Alan B. Krueger, "School Quality and Black-White Relative Earnings: A Direct Assessment," *The Quarterly Journal of Economics* CVII (1) (February 1992): 151–200.

5. The data for this graph come from Smith and Welch, "Black Economic Progress After Myrdal." See Ibid., 522, n. 5 for details on the way that they drew this sample from the census public use data files.

6. Decreases in labor force participation have been larger for blacks than for whites and this may lead to an over estimate of progress in relative earnings. Donohue and Heckman, "Continuous Versus Episodic Change," citing studies reviewed in James Heckman, "The Impact of Government on the Economic Status of Black Americans," in Steven Shulman and William Darity, Jr., eds., *The Question of Discrimination* (Middletown, Conn.: Wesleyan University Press, 1989), 50–80, report estimates that "selective attrition of low wage blacks from the labor force likely accounts for 10–20 percent of black measured wage gains from the mid 1960s through the mid-1970s." Also, Smith and Welch, "Black Economic Progress After Myrdal," attempt to correct the estimated ratio of black-to-white male wages for selective attrition and conclude that it "explain[s] at most a minor part [roughly 5 percent] of the observed increase in black-white male wages between 1970 and 1980." William Darity and Samuel Myers were among the first to raise this concern that changes in labor force participation might distort simple black-white economic comparisons. See William A. Darity, Jr. "Illusions of Black Economic Progress," *Review of Black Political Economy* XX (2) (1980): 153–68, and William A. Darity, Jr. and Samuel L. Myers, Jr., "Changes in Black-White Income Inequality, 1968–78: A Decade of Progress?," *Review of Black Political Economy* XX (3) (1980): 355–79.

7. Smith and Welch, "Black Economic Progress After Myrdal," table 15.

8. Based on Donohue and Heckman, "Continuous Versus Episodic Change," fig. 6. Note that these percentages are for gaps in hourly wages holding constant years of schooling, while those in Figure 1–2 are for weekly wages and *do not* hold years of schooling constant.

9. This spike appears in Ibid., table 6, which represents twenty to sixty-four year old males. A similar but smaller spike appears in the numbers from John Bound and Richard B. Freeman, "What Went Wrong? The Erosion of Relative Earnings and Employment Among Young Black Men in the 1980s," *The Quarterly Journal of Economics* CVII (1) (February 1992): 201–32, for men with zero to nine years of experience. These numbers from Bound and Freeman appear in this paper in Figures 1–4 and 1–5. Figure 1–4 shows a huge spike

for black college graduates between 1973 and 1976. Relative earnings for young black males jumped from an average of 4 percent below that for whites in 1973 to an average of 11 percent above that for whites in 1976.

10. Donohue and Heckman, "Continuous Versus Episodic Change."

11. See Ibid., table 2 which is constructed from James P. Smith and Finis R. Welch, *Closing the Gap: Forty Years of Economic Progress for Blacks* (Santa Monica, Calif.: The Rand Corporation, R-3330-DOL, 1986), tables A.1 and A.2.

12. Reynolds Farley and Walter Allen, *The Color Line and the Quality of Life in America* (New York: Russell Sage Foundation, 1987), table 5.1.

13. Donohue and Heckman, "Continuous Versus Episodic Change," n. 13, using data from US Commission on Civil Rights, *The Economic Progress of Black Men in America* (Washington, D.C.: US Government Printing Office, 1986), table 5.2.

14. Smith and Welch, "Black Economic Progress After Myrdal," table 20.

15. Ibid., 215.

16. Card and Krueger, "School Quality and Black-White Relative Earnings," fig. 1.

17. Convergence along other dimensions, including the quality of teachers' preparation to teach, may still be some distance from being achieved. See Ronald F. Ferguson, "Paying for Public Education: New Evidence on How and Why Money Matters," *Harvard Journal of Legislation* 28 (1) (Summer 1991), and Ferguson, "Racial Patterns in How School and Teacher Quality Affect Achievement and Earnings."

18. In 1980, the percentage of twenty-five to thirty-four year old males who were high school graduates or better was 87.2 percent for white males and 75.3 percent for black males. By 1992, the percentages changed to 82.2 percent for black males and 86.3 percent for white males. See U.S. Bureau of the Census, *The Black Population in the United States: March 1991*, Current Population Reports, Series P20–464, September 1992.

19. Smith and Welch, "Black Economic Progress After Myrdal," tables A.1 and A.2.

20. According to Heckman and Donohue, this is also true after accounting for a possible upward bias in estimates of black progress, due to the disproportionate decrease in labor force participation during this period by blacks who would have had lower earnings if they had worked.

21. See, for example, Orley Ashenfelter and James Heckman, "Measuring the Effect of an Anti-Discrimination Program," in Orley Ashenfelter and James Blum, eds., *Estimating the Labor Market Effects of Social Programs* (Princeton, N.J.: Princeton University Industrial Relations Section, 1976), chap. 3, 46–84; Jonathan S. Leonard, "Anti-Discrimination or Reverse Discrimination: The Impact of Changing Demographics, Title VII, and Affirmative Action on Productivity," *Journal of Human Resources* 19 (2) (Spring 1984): 145–72; and Jonathan S. Leonard, "Employment and Occupational Advance Under Affirmative Action," *Review of Economics and Statistics* 66 (3) (1984): 377–85.

22. See Donohue and Heckman, "Continuous Versus Episodic Change," fig. 6 and Bound and Freeman, "What Went Wrong?"

23. This different pattern by age level is discussed in Michael A. Boozer, Alan B. Krueger, and Shari Wolkon, "Race and School Quality Since Brown v. Board of Education," *Brooking Papers: Microeconomics* (1992): table 13.

24. For an extensive review of why young black men are doing worse in the labor market see Philip Moss and Chris Tilly, "Why Black Men are Doing Worse in the Labor Market: A Review of Supply-Side and Demand-Side Explanations" (New York: Social Science Research Council, 1991).

25. See, for example, Chinhui Juhn, Kevin M. Murphy, and Brooks Pierce, "Accounting for the Slowdown in Black-White Wage Convergence," in Marvin H. Kosters, ed., *Workers and Their Wages: Changing Patterns in the United States* (Washington, D.C.: American Enterprise Institute Press, 1991); William M. Rodgers III, "Black-White Wage Gaps, 1979–1991: A Dis-

tributional Analysis," unpublished paper, Harvard University, 1993; Bound and Freeman, "What Went Wrong?"; Smith and Welch, "Black Economic Progress After Myrdal"; and Card and Krueger, "School Quality and Black-White Relative Earnings."

26. "Potential experience" is the number of years during which a person could "potentially" have been working and accumulating experience. Most researchers measure it as the smaller of age minus years of schooling minus six, or age minus eighteen. Hence, experience for years when the respondent was under age eighteen or enrolled in school does not count.

27. The data for Figures 1–4 and 1–5 are from Bound and Freeman, "What Went Wrong?," table 1. The data for Figure 1–6 were provided directly by John Bound.

28. White college graduates were also the only group that did not experience a decline in the real purchasing power of its earnings.

29. Juhn, Murphy, and Pierce, "Accounting for the Slowdown in Black-White Wage Convergence," were among the first to construct an indirect test of this hypothesis. They compared the pattern from 1963–1987 in average earnings for blacks relative to those for a particular category of whites—whites at the years-of-schooling level that put them at the same percentile in the overall earnings distribution as the average black worker in 1963. They found that blacks' earnings tracked closely on those of the white comparison group. The results of their empirical test suggest that the forces responsible for blacks' average earnings falling behind whites' average earnings may be the same as the forces responsible for the increasing earnings disparity among whites. This force, they suggest, is the increasing demand for skill and the growing differential in pay that employers are willing to offer to more skilled workers.

30. See Ina V. S. Mullis and Lynn B. Jenkins, "The Reading Report Card, 1971–88: Trends from the Nation's Report Card" (Princeton, N.J.: National Assessment of Educational Progress at Educational Testing Service, 1990), and John A. Dossey, Ina V. S. Mullis, Mary M. Lindquist, and Donald L. Chambers, "The Mathematics Report Card, Are We Measuring Up? Trends and Achievement Based on the 1986 National Assessment" (Princeton, N.J.: National Assessment of Educational Progress at Educational Testing Service, 1988).

31. Bound and Freeman, "What Went Wrong?," n. 6, report that the gap in earnings during the 1980s was roughly the same with or without controls for years of education. This was not because blacks did not continue to close the gap in schooling. Instead, it was because the rate of return to additional years of schooling (especially post-high school) was increasing. This offset the positive relative earnings effect of increased years of schooling, because it made the remaining gap in schooling more important as a source of earnings disparity between black and white males.

32. For more on the growing inequality in the economy during the late 1970s and 1980s see Lawrence F. Katz and Kevin M. Murphy, "Changes in Relative Wages, 1963–1987: Supply and Demand Factors," *The Quarterly Journal of Economics* CVII (1) (February 1992): 35–78; Kevin M. Murphy and Finis Welch, "The Structure of Wages," *The Quarterly Journal of Economics* CVII (1) (February 1992): 285–326; Frank Levy and Richard Murnane, "US Earnings Levels and Earnings Inequality: A Review of Recent Trends and Proposed Explanations," *Journal of Economic Literature* XXX (September 1992): 1333–381; Lawrence Mishel and Ruy A. Teixeira, "The Myth of the Coming Labor Shortage: Jobs, Skills, and Incomes of America's Workforce 2000" (Washington, D.C.: Economic Policy Institute, 1991); Robert Moffit and Peter Gottschalk, "Trends in the Covariance Structure of Earnings in the United States: 1969–1987," Institute for Research on Poverty, discussion paper no. 1001–93 (Madison, Wis.: University of Wisconsin, 1993); McKinley Blackburn, David E. Bloom, and Richard B. Freeman, "The Declining Economic Position of Less Skilled American Men," in Gary Burtless, ed., *A Future of Lousy Jobs? The Changing Structure of US Wages* (Washington, D.C.: The Brookings Institution, 1990); John Bound and George Johnson, "Changes

in the Structure of Wages in the 1980s: An Evaluation of Alternative Explanations," *The American Economic Review* 82 (3) (June 1942): 371–92; and Alan B. Krueger, "How Computers Have Changed the Wage Structure: Evidence from Microdata, 1984–1989," *The Quarterly Journal of Economics* CVIII (1) (February 1993): 33–60.

33. Boozer, Krueger, and Wolkon express skepticism that an increase in the value of skill is responsible for the increase in disparity between young black and white males. The gap in skill between older blacks and whites is greater than that between younger blacks and whites. Boozer, Krueger, and Wolkon argue that one should expect an increase in the value of skill to cause the disparity among older workers to increase by more, but in fact it changes hardly at all.

34. See, for example, Richard J. Murnane, John B. Willett, and Frank Levy, "The Growing Importance of Cognitive Skills in Wage Determination," Harvard University Graduate School of Education and M.I.T., unpublished paper, March 1994. See also Ronald F. Ferguson, "New Evidence on the Growing Value of Skill and Consequences for Racial Disparity and Returns to Schooling," Working Paper #H-93-10, Malcolm Wiener Center for Social Policy, John F. Kennedy School of Government, Harvard University, 1993. In this working paper I show that for twenty-three year old males the measured impact of test scores on wages grew during the 1980s and that this helps to explain the increase in racial earnings disparity. However, I have refined these estimates and now find higher coefficients on test scores in the early 1980s than I had previously estimated. It is clearly true that test scores in the NLSY predict racial earnings differences that are difficult to predict without test scores. However, if the effect was already strong in the early 1980s, it may not explain the trend in earnings disparity during the 1980s. Resolution on this question concerning the trend is difficult given the character of available data.

35. Employers are reporting these changes in a project that I am conducting with John Ballantine.

36. Bound and Freeman, "What Went Wrong?"

37. George J. Borias, Richard B. Freeman, and Lawrence F. Katz, "On the Labor Market Effects of Trade and Immigration," Harvard University, Department of Economics, unpublished paper, 1989. Also see George J. Borias, Richard B. Freeman, and Kevin Lang, "Undocumented Mexican-Born Workers in the United States: How Many and How Permanent," in Richard Freeman and J. Abowd, eds., *Immigration, Trade and the Labor Market* (Chicago: University of Chicago Press and NBER, 1991).

38. Jonathan S. Leonard, "The Impact of Affirmative Action Regulation and Equal Employment Law on Black Employment," *Journal of Economic Perspectives* 4 (4) (Fall 1990): 47–64.

39. Reported in Bound and Freeman, "What Went Wrong?," 215, n. 13. Also see Jeremiah Cotton, "The Gap at the Top: Relative Occupational Earnings Disadvantage of the Black Male Middle Class," *Review of Black Political Economy* 18 (3) (Winter 1990): 21–38, for a related discussion.

40. Ibid.

41. Michael Fix and Raymond J. Struyk, eds., *Clear and Convincing Evidence* (Washington, D.C.: Urban Institute Press, 1993).

42. See extensive interview findings in Joleen Kirschenman and Katherine Neckerman, "We'd Love to Hire Them, But . . . : The Meaning of Race for Employers," in Christopher Jencks and Paul E. Peterson, eds., *The Urban Underclass* (Washington, D.C.: The Brookings Institution, 1991).

43. Ronald F. Ferguson and Randall Filer, "Do Better Jobs Make Better Workers? Absenteeism from Work Among Inner-City Minority Youth," in R. Freeman and H. Holzer, eds., *The Black Youth Employment Crisis* (Chicago: University of Chicago Press and NBER, 1986), report higher absenteeism rates for blacks than for whites in the Current Population Sur-

vey. Blacks have higher quit rates than whites in the National Longitudinal Survey of Youth.

44. See June O'Neill, "The Role of Human Capital in Earnings Differences Between Black and White Men," *Journal of Economic Perspectives* 4 (4) (Fall 1990): 25–45; Derek A. Neal and William R. Johnson, "The Role of Pre-Market Factors in Black-White Wage Differences," unpublished paper; Nan L. Maxwell, "The Effect on Black-White Wage Differences of Differences in the Quantity and Quality of Education," *Industrial and Labor Relations Review* 47 (2) (January 1994): 249–64; Ferguson, "New Evidence on the Growing Value of Skill and Consequences for Racial Disparity and Returns to Schooling"; and Ferguson, "Racial Patterns in How School and Teacher Quality Affect Achievement and Earnings." The findings reported in Ferguson, "New Evidence on the Growing Value of Skill and Consequences for Racial Disparity and Returns to Schooling" have since been modified to reflect larger estimated returns to test scores even in the early 1980s than the paper originally found. Hence, the trends in the "price of skill" that the paper reports are too steep, but the finding that test scores account for much of the racial difference in earnings by the late 1980s still stands.

45. The AFQT score here is standardized to have a mean of zero and a standard deviation of one for each individual age group. The score used is a measure of each respondent's proficiency at the test date relative to his same-aged peers. Since the youngest person at the time of the test was fourteen years old, and little reason exists to expect that the *rank order* of basic skills changes much among a population after age fourteen, the age-standardized AFQT score that we use is probably a good measure of young adults' proficiencies relative to their peers. For a discussion of why academic test scores are related to earnings and of the stability of the relationship between test scores and earnings even if scores are measured at young ages, see Christopher Jencks, *Who Gets Ahead? The Determinants of Economic Success in America* (New York: Basic Books, Inc., 1979), chap. 5. If these test score data collected in 1980 are not accurate measures for the late 1980s and early 1990s, then the measurement error will cause the findings to underestimate the effect of the measured skills in explaining wages.

46. In order to do the most representative analysis, we exclude the supplemental samples of poor whites, identified by sample identification numbers two and nine in the NLSY. Including these would cause blacks to appear more well-off relative to whites than they actually are. We also exclude members of the special military sample identified by sample identification numbers of fifteen and over. To avoid distortions due to student or military status, we exclude men who were enrolled in school as of May 1 of any survey year from 1988–1992 or who had military income during this period. Men with reported hourly earnings of less than $1 or more than $75 were dropped (these constituted less than 1 percent of the sample).

47. Wages are in 1988 dollars. The natural logarithm of the average real wage for the five years is the dependent variable and each man in the analysis contributes one observation to each estimated regression equation.

48. Years-of-schooling controls are dummy (0,1) variables for individual years of schooling. This allows the effect of years of schooling to be nonlinear. Potential experience is essentially a measure of age. We measure it in the standard way: it equals age minus years of schooling minus six, if years of schooling exceeds twelve; and it equals age minus eighteen if years of schooling is less than twelve. The location controls are individual 0, 1 variables for each of the four major census regions, and 0,1 variables to measure rural versus central city versus suburban location.

49. In other analyses we have tested the importance of other family background variables. Generally, once test scores are in the analysis, contributions of family background variables to equations for employment outcomes are small and statistically insignificant.

Including other variables does not change the bottom-line conclusions of the simpler analysis reported here. Where family background measures are most important, in a more extensive analysis, is in predicting the test scores. Mothers' and fathers' years of schooling, characteristics of the fathers' occupation, and the number of educational resources in the home are all important predictors of the AFQT test score that we use.

50. This discussion of results is intended to be accessible to a general audience. Some of the technical details are in the footnotes, but the full pattern of results is not shown. Readers may write to the author for a copy of the full regression results.

51. We estimated four equations to construct Panels A and B of Figure 1–7: one that used the data for whites only and excluded the AFQT from the explanatory variables; a second that used the data for whites only but included the AFQT; a third that used the data for blacks only without the AFQT; and, a fourth that used the data for blacks only and included the AFQT among the explanatory variables. Again, all estimates include controls for years of schooling, census region, central city versus suburban versus rural residence, and years of potential experience.

52. Differences between Panels A and B are due to differences in blacks' and whites' average characteristics, not to differences in their treatment. Differences in *treatment* are reflected in the length of each bar, since each bar represents the difference between being treated as black or white.

53. Statistical tests do not reject the null hypothesis that these two approaches are equivalent.

54. The t-statistic on the 16.1 percent is 8.21; the t-statistic on the 4.8 percent is 2.08. The adjusted R-square statistic is 0.2845 for the regression that excludes the AFQT and 0.3302 for the regression that includes it.

55. Pooling the regions together in regressions and using 0,1 variables to capture the black-white differential for each region produces essentially the same pattern in estimates of racial differences. We report results from separate regressions primarily to assure readers that the estimated patterns really do apply separately to each region. Results for the West are not shown because the sample size for blacks in the West is too small to make the estimates reliable. We find that the AFQT score in the West matters as much for predicting wages as for the other regions, but the estimated black-white difference has a very large standard error because of the small number of blacks in the NLSY's Western sample. Men from the West are, however, included in estimates that pool all regions, such as those in Figure 1–7 and in Panels D and E of Figure 1–8.

56. We cannot know for sure whether this difference represents unequal treatment. It may be that blacks are different in a way that our estimates do not measure, that they live in lower-wage cities, or that their referral networks do not contain information about the same quality of jobs as for whites. Analogous statements apply for estimates that suggest nearly equal treatment.

57. The –3.6 has a t-statistic of 0.87, such that this estimate of –3.6 is not statistically distinguishable from zero.

58. The research paper that presents these findings more formally is currently in progress. What follows is simply a summary of findings.

59. All of the regression results for total weeks worked are from Tobit regressions that take account of truncation at both zero and fifty-two weeks per year.

60. Racial bias does not appear to be important in the interviewer's rating: race is not a predictor of the interviewer's rating once test scores, years of schooling, and social background factors are controlled. The occupational complexity measure comes from the occupation that the respondent had in 1985, not the occupation that he has during any of the three years from 1986 to 1988 for which the analysis aims to explain the number of weeks worked.

61. It seems reasonable to speculate that youths who engage in early sexual activity, especially boys, may be distracted away from other more developmentally appropriate activities by the increased preoccupation with finding more opportunities to repeat the experience.

62. The occupational complexity ratings come from a factor analysis of job characteristics, conducted as part of a study for the Dictionary of Occupational Titles. The rating is a composite measure of a number of different distinguishable characteristics of jobs, constructed in the early 1980s using 1970 standard occupational classification codes.

63. The Russell Sage Foundation is currently supporting a cluster of research projects among which are both quantitative and qualitative studies that may shed light on these issues.

64. Myrdal, *An American Dilemma,* 1024.

Afterword to Chapter 1

1. David H. Autor, Lawrence F. Katz, and Melissa S. Kearney, "The Polarization of the U.S. Labor Market." National Bureau of Economic Research working paper 11986. January 2006. Also see: Eileen Appelbaum, Annette D. Bernhardt, and Richard J. Murnane, eds., *Low Wage America: How Employers Are Reshaping Opportunity in the Workplace.* New York: Russell Sage Press, 2003.

2. Derek Neal shows patterns in wage inequality computed from data in several U.S. Censuses. See Derek Neal, "Why Has Black-White Skill Convergence Stopped?" In Erik Hanushek and Finis Welch, eds., *Handbook of the Economics of Education.* New York: Elsevier, 2006. Also see: U.S. Department of Education, National Center for Education Statistics, "The Condition of Education 2007" (NCES 2-7-064). Washington, D.C.: U.S. Government Printing Office, 2007.

3. For recent racial comparisons of employment status, see U.S. Department of Labor, "The Employment Situation: September 2007." News, Bureau of Labor Statistics, USDL 07-1492, 2007. For an extensive treatment of incarceration trends and impacts, see Bruce Western, *Punishment and Inequality in America.* New York: Russell Sage Press, 2006. For discussion of the implications of incarceration trends, see Glenn C. Loury, "Racial Stigma, Mass Incarceration and American Values" (Tanner Lectures in Human Values). Delivered at Stanford University, April 4 & 5, 2007. Available at http://www.econ.brown.edu/fac/Glenn_Loury/louryhomepage/

CHAPTER 2   Test-Score Trends along Racial Lines, 1971 to 1996: Popular Culture and Community Academic Standards

Notes

1. As a check on the accuracy of NAEP trends reviewed, Hedges and Nowell (1998) assembled all other nationally representative data sets since 1965 that have race-specific test scores for black and white children. Most of these data sets are cross-sectional, not longitudinal. Hedges and Nowell focus on the difference between blacks' and whites' scores, measured in standard deviations (SD). Examining the gap across exams administered in different years, they found a narrowing of the gap, just as NAEP does.

2. See Ferguson (1998b, Table 9–11) for the author's calculations for 1987–1992 using the U.S. Department of Education's Common Core of Data Surveys, School-Level file. Nationally, the pupil-to-teacher ratio was between 17 and 18, independent of the percentage of black students or the percentage qualifying for free-and-reduced lunch subsidies. (Note that actual class sizes tend to be about 25 percent larger than pupil-to-teacher ratios because teachers have periods off during the day for planning and lunch.) Some authors (e.g., Boozer and Rouse, 1995) suggest that this apparent parity masks differences in class size among students with similar needs. Though a distinct and important possibility, this remains to be established in nationally representative samples.

3. The phrase "acting white" in the academic literature is most associated with the work of Signithia Fordham and John Ogbu (see, for example, Ogbu, 1978; Fordham & Ogbu, 1986; Fordham, 1988; and Belluck, 1999). In two highly influential papers, Philip Cook and Jens Ludwig (1997, 1998) present evidence they believe is inconsistent with the "acting white" hypothesis as an explanation for the black-white achievement gap. Using nationally representative data for high school students, they find few black-white differences across several measures of school effort. Further, they find that high-achieving black students seem to feel just as popular, perhaps even more popular, than do low achievers. Hence, they conclude, the focus of efforts to improve the performance of black students should be on equalizing educational opportunities, not on trying to overcome the fear of acting white. I agree. At the same time, Cook and Ludwig agree that their work has no bearing on the question of whether fear of acting white prevents black students from working harder than whites, which might be required to narrow the black-white achievement gap. For a much more detailed and subtle discussion of these and related issues, see Ferguson (2001).

4. The numbers in Figure 2–4 come from a multiyear project by Laurence Steinberg, B. Bradford Brown, and Sanford Dornbusch. The project produced a number of papers, but many of their findings are summarized in a book by Steinberg (1996). The tabulations in Figure 2–4 are my own, using the raw data graciously provided by Steinberg.

References

Ainsworth-Darnell, J., & Downey, D. (1998). Assessing the oppositional-culture explanation for racial/ethnic differences in school performance. *American Sociological Review, 60,* 536–553.

Belluck, P. (1999, July 4). Reason is sought for lag by blacks in school effort. *New York Times,* p. 1.

Berry, V., & Looney, H., Jr. (1996). Rap music, black men, and the police. In V. Berry & C. Manning-Miller (Eds.), *Mediated messages and African American culture: Contemporary issues.* Thousand Oaks, CA: Sage.

Boozer, M., & Rouse, C. (1995). *Intraschool variation in class size: Patterns and implications* (Working paper No. 5144). Cambridge, MA: National Bureau of Economic Research.

Brophy, J. (1985). Teacher-student interaction. In J. Dusek (Ed.), *Teacher expectancies.* Hillsdale, NJ: Lawrence Erlbaum.

Casteel, C. (1997). Attitudes of African American and Caucasian eighth grade students about praises, rewards, and punishments. *Elementary School Guidance and Counseling, 31,* 262–272.

Coleman, J., Campbell, E., et al. (1966). *Equality of educational opportunity.* Washington, DC: U.S. Government Printing Office.

Commission on Minority Participation in Education and American Life. (1988). *One-third of a nation.* Washington, DC: American Council on Education, Education Commission of the States.

Cook, P., & Ludwig, J. (1997). Weighing the burden of "acting white": Are there race differences in attitudes toward education? *Journal of Policy Analysis and Management, 16,* 656–678.

Cook, P., & Ludwig, J. (1998). The burden of "acting white": Do black adolescents disparage academic achievement? In C. Jencks & M. Phillips (Eds.), *The black-white test score gap.* Washington, DC: Brookings Institution Press.

Du Bois, W. E. B. (1903). *The souls of black folk.* Chicago: McClurg.

Dyson, M. (1996). *Between God and gangsta rap: Bearing witness to black culture.* New York: Oxford University Press.

Ferguson, R. (1998a). Teachers' perceptions and expectations and the black-white test score gap. In C. Jencks & M. Phillips (Eds.), *The black-white test score gap.* Washington, DC: Brookings Institution Press.

Ferguson, R. (1998b). Can schools narrow the black-white test score gap? In C. Jencks & M. Phillips (Eds.), *The black-white test score gap*. Washington, DC: Brookings Institution Press.

Ferguson, R. (2001). A diagnostic analysis of black-white GPA disparities in Shaker Heights, Ohio (*Brookings papers on education policy, 2001*). Washington, DC: Brookings Institution Press.

Fordham, S. (1988). Racelessness as a factor in black students' success: Coping with the burden of "acting white." *Harvard Education Review, 58,* 54–84.

Fordham, S., &. Ogbu, J. (1986). Black students' school success: Coping with the burden of "acting white." *The Urban Review, 18,* 176–206.

Gardner, D. et al. (1983). *A nation at risk: The imperative for educational reform*. Washington, DC: U.S. Government Printing Office.

George, N. (1998). *Hip hop America*. New York: Viking Press.

Good, T. (1987). Two decades of research on teacher expectations: Findings and future directions. *Journal of Teacher Education,* (July–August), 32–47.

Greenwald, R., Hedges, L., & Laine, R. (1996). The effect of school resources on student achievement. *Review of Educational Research, 66,* 361–396.

Grissmer, D., Flanagan, A., & Williamson, S. (1998). Why did the black-white test score gap narrow in the 1970s and 1980s? In C. Jencks & M. Phillips (Eds.), *The black-white test score gap*. Washington, DC: Brookings Institution Press.

Hanson, C. (1995). Predicting cognitive and behavioral effects of gangsta rap. *Basic and Applied Social Psychology, 16*(1, 2), 43–52.

Hanushek, E. (1998). *The evidence on class size* (Occasional Paper 98–1). Rochester, NY: University of Rochester, W. Allen Wallis Institute of Political Economy.

Hedges, L., & Nowell, A. (1998). Black-white test score convergence since 1965. In C. Jencks & M. Phillips (Eds.), *The black-white test score gap*. Washington, DC: Brookings Institution Press.

Howard, J., & Hammond, R. (1985). Rumors of inferiority. *New Republic, 72*(9).

Jencks, C., & Phillips, M. (1998). *The black-white test score gap*. Washington, DC: Brookings Institution Press.

Jencks, C., & Phillips, M. (1999). Aptitude or achievement: Why do test scores predict educational attainment and earnings? In S. Mayer & P. Peterson (Eds.), *Learning and earning: How schools matter*. Washington, DC: Brookings Institution Press.

Johnson, J., Jackson, L., & Gatto, L. (1995). Violent attitudes and deferred academic aspirations: Deleterious effects of exposure to rap music. *Basic and Applied Social Psychology, 16*(1, 2), 27–41.

Jussim, L., Eccles, J., & Madon, S. (1996). Social perception, social stereotypes, and teacher expectations: Accuracy and the quest for the powerful self-fulfilling prophesy. *Advances in Experimental Social Psychology, 28,* 281–387.

Kleinfeld, J. (1972). The relative importance of teachers and parents in the formation of Negro and white students' academic self-concepts. *Journal of Educational Research, 65,* 211–212.

Krueger, A. (1997). *Experimental estimates of education production functions*. Unpublished manuscript, Princeton University and National Bureau of Economic Research.

Martinez, T. (1997). Popular culture as oppositional culture: Rap as resistance. *Sociological Perspectives, 40,* 265–286.

McLaurin, P. (1995). An examination of the effect of culture on pro-social messages directed at African-American at-risk youth. *Communication Monographs, 62,* 321–325.

Mickelson, R. (1990). The attitude-achievement paradox among black adolescents. *Sociology of Education, 63,* 44–61.

Muuss, R. (1988). Friendship patterns and peer-group influences: An ecological perspective based on Bronfenbrenner, Kandel and Dunphy. In *Theories of adolescence* (chapter 14). New York: McGraw-Hill.

National Center for Education Statistics. (1991). *Digest of education statistics 1991*. Washington, DC: Government Printing Office.

National Center for Education Statistics. (1992). *NAEP trends in academic progress*. Washington, DC: U.S. Department of Education.

National Center for Education Statistics. (1996a). *Digest of education statistics 1996*. Washington, DC: Government Printing Office.

National Center for Education Statistics. (1996b). *NAEP trends in academic progress*. Washington, DC: U.S. Department of Education.

National Center for Education Statistics. (1998). *Digest of education statistics 1998*. Washington, DC: Government Printing Office.

Nelson, H. (1991). *Bring the noise: A guide to rap music and hip-hop culture*. New York: Harmony Books.

O'Day, J., & Smith, M. (1993). Systemic reform and educational opportunity. In S. Fuhrman (Ed.), *Designing coherent education policy: Improving the system*. San Francisco: Jossey-Bass.

Ogbu, J. (1978). *Minority education and caste: The American system in cross-cultural comparison*. New York: Academic Press.

Orange, C. (1996). Rap videos: A source of undesirable vicarious empowerment for African-American males. *High School Journal* (April/May).

Phillips, M., Brooks-Gunn, J., Duncan, G., Klebanow, P., & Crane, J. (1998b). Family background, parenting practices, and the black-white test score gap. In C. Jencks & M. Phillips (Eds.), *The black-white test score gap*. Washington, DC: Brookings Institution Press.

Phillips, M., Crouse, J., & Ralph, J. (1998a). Does the black-white test-score gap widen after children enter school? In C. Jencks & M. Phillips (Eds.), *The black-white test score gap*. Washington, DC: Brookings Institution Press.

Public Agenda. (1997). *Getting by: What American youth really think about their schools. Summary report of survey and focus group results*. Washington, DC: Author.

Rose, T. (1991). "Fear of a black planet": Rap music and Black cultural politics in the 1990s. *Journal of Negro Education, 60,* 276–290.

Rose, T. (1994). *Black noise: Rap music and black culture in contemporary America*. Middletown, CT: Wesleyan University Press.

Southern, E. (1997). *The music of black Americans: A history* (3rd ed.). New York: W. W. Norton.

Steinberg, L. (1996). *Beyond the classroom*. New York: Simon and Schuster.

Taylor, M. (1979). Race, sex, and the expression of self-fulfilling prophecies in a laboratory teaching situation. *Personality and Social Psychology, 6,* 897–912.

Zillmann, D., Aust, C., Hoffman, K., Love, C., Ordman,V., Pope, J., et al. (1995). Radical rap: Does it further ethnic division? *Basic and Applied Social Psychology, 16*(1, 2), 1–25.

Afterword to Chapter 2

Notes

1. Perie, M., Moran, R., and Lutkus, A. D., *NAEP 2004: Trends in Academic Progress: Three Decades of Student Performance in Reading and Mathematics* (NCES 2005–464). U.S. Department of Education, Institute of Education Sciences, National Center for Education Statistics. Washington, DC: Government Printing Office, 2005.

2. For more on this point, including graphics, see: Ferguson, Ronald F., "What We've Learned about 'Stalled Progress' in Closing the Black-White Achievement Gap." In Katherine Magnuson and Jane Waldfogel, eds., *Inequality and the Black-White Test Score Gap*. New York: Russell Sage, manuscript under review.

3. Phillips, Meredith, "Can Changes in Adolescent Behavior or Students' Home Environments Help Explain Why the Black-White Test Score Gap Stopped Narrowing in the Late
1980s?" In Katherine Magnuson and Jane Waldfogel, eds., *Inequality and the Black-White
Test Score Gap.* New York: Russell Sage, manuscript under review.
4. Ferguson, op. cit. Also, see: Ferguson, Ronald F., "Parenting Practices, Teenage Lifestyles,
and Academic Achievement among African American Children." *Focus* 25, no. 1 (Spring-
Summer 2007).

CHAPTER 3   Can Schools Narrow the Black-White Test Score Gap?

Notes

1. The fact that I focus on black and white Americans is not an indication that these issues
are any less important for other races and ethnicities. The need for research addressing
the special patterns and circumstances that apply to Latinos, Native Americans, and Asian
Americans remains largely unmet. Similarly, while I focus on test scores, I do not deny
that other aspects of children's development may at times be much more important. If
there are trade-offs between strategies that would improve scores and those that would
benefit children in other ways, great care should be taken to operate in the best interest
of the children being served; on this point, see Darling-Hammond (1991, 1994, 1996);
Darling-Hammond and McLaughlin (1995); Ford (1996).
2. Whenever possible, I present results in terms of "effect sizes" measured in standard deviation units; see chapter 4, note 3.
3. Barnett (1992).
4. Dickens, Kane, and Schultz (forthcoming) point out that the IQ effect of Perry Preschool
had not "gone" by the time the children were nine, it just was not statistically significant.
The point estimate is positive and the standard error is large enough to allow a fairly large
effect. Further, the point estimate is large enough to justify a substantial share of the cost
of the treatment. These authors also reanalyze data used for a large meta-analysis of preschool studies by Lazar and Darlington (1982), who conclude that IQ effects disappear by
the time children are in their teens. Based on the reanalysis, Dickens, Kane, and Schultz
suggest that so strong a conclusion is not warranted.
5. For example, children who attend different schools may be given tests that cannot be fully
equated; children retained in grade are seldom tested with their birth cohort; and in many
cases, children in special education are not tested at all. Moreover if, as is likely, retention
in grade or assignment to special education is greater for the control group, studies based
on tests that schools administer are almost certainly biased against finding that preschool
has lasting effects.
6. Altogether, across the five cohorts, fifty-eight children were chosen as participants and
sixty-five for the control group.
7. Barnett (1992, table 8) gives the mean scores and sample sizes for the treatment and control groups for each age level; these numbers come from the appendixes of Schweinhart
and Weikart (1980) and Berreuta-Clement and others (1984). Barnett's table also gives
probability values for the differences in means. As a rough approximation, I take the usual
formula for the z value for a test of difference in means, assume that the standard deviation is the same in the treatment and control groups, and using the z value corresponding
to the probability value given in the table, solve for the sample standard deviation. I then
divide the difference in means by this standard deviation to obtain the effect size. This calculation is only approximate, because the probability values that I use in fact come from
an analysis of covariance that controls for several covariates, including gender, mother's
employment, and initial IQ. Also, the test taken at age nineteen was not a regular academic achievement test, but the Adult Performance Level test, which measures skills and

knowledge associated with educational and occupational success in several domains that are important in adult life.

8. Reynolds and others (1996).

9. Currie and Thomas (1995).

10. They treat other preschool programs analogously, estimating the difference in PPVT scores between siblings who attend preschool and those who do not. Further, they use a difference-in-difference approach to distinguish the impact of Head Start from other types of preschool program.

11. The benefit of other preschool is zero for whites, but for blacks the point estimate for five-year-olds is 43 percent as large as that for Head Start and almost reaches statistical significance (the coefficient is 1.60 times its standard error). However, this effect for African Americans also dies out, and at roughly the same rate as that of Head Start.

12. Indeed, Currie and Thomas (1995) discuss the necessary assumptions listed here.

13. If parents who have good experiences of Head Start with their first children are more likely to send later children, these families are less likely to be among those with a stay-at-home child. The effective sample will therefore be biased toward households that had a less favorable experience with the program.

14. Currie and Thomas (1995, p. 359). This might result, for example, from positive spillovers from older to younger siblings in black households; or from overrepresentation in the sample of families who had bad experiences—and presumably lower gains than average—with their first-born children in Head Start, and as a consequence, chose not to enroll their later children (see previous note).

15. The total sample in the National Longitudinal Survey of Youth's Child-Mother file includes 329 African-American children who attended Head Start; see Currie and Thomas (1995, table 3). Of these, 57.1 percent have a sibling who attended Head Start, 14.2 percent have a sibling who attended another type of preschool, and 28.6 percent have a sibling who did not attend any preschool. This gives 94 African-American sibling pairs (0.286 x 329). The sibling sample for whites is only slightly larger: 134 pairs.

16. In an unpublished critique of Currie and Thomas (1995), Barnett and Camilli (1996) compare the PPVT to intelligence tests for which even the Perry Preschool sample shows fading gains. They write, quoting Schweinhart and others (1993), that the results of the Perry Preschool experiment "were consistent with the findings of Currie and Thomas in that initial effects on the PPVT and other intelligence tests faded away by age eight, and there were no significant effects on grade repetition" (p. 27). In a response, Currie and Thomas (1996b, p. 8) reject the assertion that the PPVT is essentially an intelligence test: "In contrast to Barnett and Camilli, Currie and Thomas are careful to *not* call PPVT a measure of 'cognitive ability' (which it is not) and refer to it as an indicator of 'academic performance'." It is unclear which interpretation is the most appropriate. On the one hand, it seems at least plausible that if the National Longitudinal Survey of Youth's Child-Mother file had used the achievement test instruments used in the Perry Preschool experiment, Currie and Thomas might have discovered more persistent gains for black children. On the other hand, Currie and Thomas report that when they used the Peabody Individual Achievement Test, the results were similar to, but weaker than, those for the PPVT.

17. Currie and Thomas (1996a).

18. Their equations also include controls for gender, family income, whether a foreign language is spoken in the home, number of siblings, and whether the child is the first born.

19. Students and parents often participate in the choice of track. Lee and Eckstrom (1987) report data from the nationally representative High School and Beyond survey, which asked sophomores at public high schools in 1980 how they had ended up in their particular tracks. Only 33 percent of students in academic tracks, 43 percent in general tracks,

and 37 percent in vocational tracks reported that they had been "assigned." The proportions of students who chose their tracks without help from anyone else—parents, friends, or counselors—were 25 percent, 23 percent, and 25 percent, for the three options respectively. Only 3 percent of students attended schools where there was no choice to make.

20. Kulik (1992, p. 15).
21. An extended discussion about the interaction of teaching methods and grouping arrangements is beyond the scope of this chapter. However, see Bossert, Barnett, and Filby (1984) for a useful discussion.
22. Braddock and Slavin (1993, p. 55); Haller (1985).
23. Haller collected data from teachers in forty-nine self-contained classrooms serving 934 fourth, fifth, and sixth grade students in five school districts. Two of the districts are in the Northeast, one is in Appalachia, one in the deep South, and one in a relatively affluent, racially integrated suburb of an East-Central state. In interviews averaging 1.5 hours, teachers constructed the reading groups that they would recommend to the following year's teacher. In addition, Haller collected teachers' perceptions of students, using a written survey instrument. She finds that they perceived white students as having more ability, better work habits, and fewer behavioral problems than blacks. The students completed the Comprehensive Test of Basic Skills.
24. From Table 3–2, the only notable difference relates to "work habits," which is the primary reason for placement for 10 percent of black students but for only 1.5 percent of whites. There is also a (smaller) racial difference for "evidence": 6.9 percent for whites compared with 1.2 percent for blacks.
25. As discussed in chapter 4, the correlations between teachers' perceptions of student reading ability and the test scores are 0.73 for whites and 0.74 for blacks.
26. Sorensen and Hallinan (1984); Pallas and others (1994); Dreeben and Gamoran (1986).
27. Sorensen and Hallinan (1984) do not control for socioeconomic status. While Pallas and others (1994) and Dreeben and Gamoran (1986) do control for socioeconomic status and find that it is a statistically significant predictor even after controlling for test scores, neither study shows the relationship of race to placement when this factor is not controlled. Haller and Davis (1980) report no effects of children's or teachers' socioeconomic status; they do not use race as a variable in their analysis. Thus evidence is mixed on the importance of social class as a predictor of group placement. Moreover, since most studies do not correct for measurement error in prior scores, students' socioeconomic status may simply be proxying aspects of ability or proficiency that are poorly measured by initial test scores, rather than exerting a true "effect" on group placement.
28. Kulik and Kulik (1982, 1984a, 1984b, 1987, 1989); Kulik (1992). Although Kulik (1992) is published by an organization that focuses on the gifted and talented, his objectivity should not be questioned: he is thorough and shows no particular propensity for advocacy. See also Slavin (1987, 1990b). The main difference between the reviews by Slavin and the Kuliks is that the former do not include studies of enriched and accelerated classes for the gifted and talented, because Slavin claims that the selection of their comparison groups is biased (see note 37 below). In addition, Slavin's conclusions emphasize the lack of general impact of standard grouping practices, rather than the presence of effects in cases where instruction is adapted to specific students. Slavin's own prescriptive ideas are perfectly consistent with tailoring instruction to students' needs (see the discussion of the Success for All program later in this chapter). His main complaint about standard grouping practices is that they are rigid and can trap children in particular trajectories. Substantively, there is not much difference between Slavin's meta-analytic findings and those based on Kulik's 1992 review of the evidence.
29. XYZ and within-class grouping are the only categories for which separate effects for high-, low-, and middle-ability groups are available from more than one or two studies.

30. XYZ grouping arrangements are typical in upper elementary schools, middle schools, and junior high schools. Of the fifty-one studies of XYZ classes reviewed in Kulik (1992), only four involve grades ten through twelve; only seven involve grade three or below.
31. For example, of the fifty-one studies of XYZ classes in Kulik (1992), only nine involve any curricular adjustment. For these, the average effect size is 0.08, as compared with 0.02 for the others.
32. All but three of the eleven studies of within-class grouping reviewed in Kulik (1992) are for mathematics. Of these three, one is for reading; written in 1927, it is also an outlier historically. The second is for "other," and the third is for reading and mathematics combined. Grade levels range evenly from 2 through 8.
33. Roughly half the accelerated programs reviewed in Kulik (1992) cover a single subject, usually mathematics. Others shortened the time spent at particular grades, enabling students to complete grades seven through nine in two years, for example.
34. Thirty-one studies are from the 1960s, twelve are earlier, and eight are later. Thus most of the evidence here is old.
35. Kulik (1992) examines subsets of these studies, broken down by grade level and a number of other criteria. In no case is the effect size different from zero.
36. Not shown on the table, only two of 14 studies for cross-grade grouping present effect sizes by ability level. One shows no effect for any level of ability, the other finds effect sizes of 0.28 for the high group and 0.50 for the low group. Most of the studies of cross-grade grouping were for various combinations of grades 3 to 8. Two studies began with first grade and ran for three years, with effect sizes of 0.33 and 0.81.
37. Slavin's (1987) main complaint concerns selection bias: "Much of this research (e.g, Howell, 1962) compares students in gifted programs to students in the same schools who were not accepted for the gifted program, usually matching on IQ or other measures." But even with careful matching, students who are selected probably differ systematically from those who are not. In response, Kulik (1992, p. 19) writes: "Like many other reviewers, we believe that the methodological weaknesses in studies of enriched and accelerated classes are not great enough to warrant their wholesale dismissal." I am inclined to agree with Kulik when students' baseline scores are relatively similar. However, for assessing the effects of moving children among ability groups that differ by one standard deviation or more, I think that Slavin is correct in dismissing such estimates as useless.

    The effect sizes for enriched and accelerated groups are not comparable to those of other groups because the standard deviation typically only includes students in gifted and talented classes and their comparison group. Kulik reports, in personal communication, that an earlier effort to replace this with the standard deviation for all students made surprisingly little difference. The reason is that students are selected for gifted and talented programs on criteria (for example, effort and motivation) much broader than the test scores used to measure the impact.
38. Roughly half of the effect sizes for accelerated students reported in Kulik (1992) are measured relative to comparison groups one or more grade levels ahead. For accelerated students compared to control groups of the same age, the Kuliks' typical effect size is about one plus the effect size for accelerated students compared to older control groups. In order to average across studies, Table 3–4 adds one standard deviation to the effect sizes for studies that use older comparison groups.
39. Eight of the twenty-five studies of enriched classes reviewed in Kulik (1992) and five of the twenty-three studies of accelerated classes cover grade nine or higher. For these eight enriched classes, the median effect size is 0.40, the same as for enrichment studies overall. The five studies of accelerated classes have a median effect size of 1.1 and a mean of 1.02. In comparison with studies of lower grade levels, these give the most plausible approximations to the possible effects of enriched and accelerated curricular tracking in high

school. Five of the enrichment studies reviewed and two of the acceleration studies cover grade three or below. The rest are concentrated in upper elementary, middle, and junior high school.

40. For example, Dreeben and Gamoran (1986) use data from thirteen first grade reading classes in the Chicago area in 1981–82. Shifting a student to a group where the mean aptitude is a standard deviations higher increases the number of words learned by 0.53 standard deviations and reading achievement by 0.45 standard deviations. Similarly, Weinstein (1976) finds that information on reading group placement adds 25 percent to the explained variance in mid-year reading achievement for first-graders, controlling for reading readiness scores. For methodological reasons I describe in the text, I would not draw any conclusions from such estimates. However, see Eder (1981) for a defense, based on classroom observations, of the proposition that such effects are real.

41. Slavin (1990a, p. 505).

42. It is worth noting that the real purpose of Dreeben and Gamoran's (1986) study, cited in note 40, is to isolate the effects of instructional practices by comparing similar students who attend different schools; see also Gamoran (1986). Their bottom-line conclusion is that instruction, not grouping, explains why black children in the sample learned fewer words and gained less in reading achievement than did whites.

43. See Garet and Delaney (1988); Gamoran and Mare (1989); and Argys, Rees, and Brewer (1996). Even without taking scores into account, racial differences are small. In the nationally representative High School and Beyond sample of tenth-graders in 1980, for example, the simple correlation between track placement and black or Hispanic status is only –0.13, with minorities in lower tracks. The simple correlation between advanced mathematics courses and minority status is –0.20. Moreover, differences in courses taken are predictable by academic background and prior test scores in multivariate equations, with no residual difference due to race. (See Lee and Bryk, 1988, table 6, p. 86.)

44. Studies conducted in the 1960s and 1970s also find higher track placements than measured ability would seem to warrant for students from families of higher socioeconomic status; see Brophy and Good (1974), who cite Douglas (1964); Goldberg, Passow, and Justman (1966); Husen and Svensson (1960).

45. The possibility also exists that the estimated effect of socioeconomic status is in fact due to measurement error in initial test scores; see note 27 above.

46. A related fact is that the number of mathematics and science courses taken by blacks and whites converged between 1982 and 1992, even as both groups increased courses taken in both subjects; see National Center for Education Statistics, *Digest of Education Statistics, 1996*, table 133.

47. As noted above, however, Kulik (1992) reviews thirteen such studies of enriched or accelerated high school classes; see note 39 and related text.

48. Argys, Rees, and Brewer (1996). For our purposes, the NELS:88 data are special both because they pertain to the 1990s and, more important, because teachers rather than students identified the track levels. Earlier studies from survey data rely mostly on students' self-reports, which are known to be less accurate.

49. These effect sizes are my calculations, using the numbers reported by the authors.

50. Oakes (1985). See also Finley (1984); Schwartz (1981); Metz (1978). All of these sources are discussed in Gamoran and Berends (1987).

51. Oakes (1985) does not give the standard deviations from which to calculate effect sizes. Neither does she report comparable numbers from the heterogeneous classes that she observed, which would be the logical comparison if one were considering the effect of abolishing tracking. Finally, it is not possible from data such as these to know what consequences the observed differences might have for disparities in achievement.

52. Oakes (1985, p. 129). Gamoran and Berends (1987) quote this passage in support of the point that similarity of instruction between tracks may be the reason why the literature is uneven in its findings.
53. Braddock and Slavin (1993, p. 51).
54. Jones (1997, p. 9). Jones is the director of the Messages Project, which was established in Fort Wayne, Indiana, in 1996. It began by convening young black males between the ages of nine and nineteen in small focus groups in community-based institutions around the city to discuss "things that make you feel good" and "things that make you feel bad" in interactions with parents, teachers, police officers, store clerks, and ministers. This quote is from a summary of the first meetings, in which a total of seventy-three boys participated in ten groups. Each group had ten or fewer participants and was moderated by an adult familiar to the youth. Three groups were aged nine to twelve; two were aged thirteen to fifteen; two were aged thirteen to seventeen, and three were aged sixteen to nineteen.
55. Kulik (1992, table 2).
56. Jones (1997, p. 8).
57. Multiple references for each of these items are available in Good (1987).
58. See, for example, Weinstein and others (1987).
59. For a review of interventions that focus specifically on African-American students see Levine (1994). For interventions focused on at-risk students in general, see Slavin, Karweit, and Madden (1989); Slavin and Madden (1989).
60. A case in point is Marva Collins, whose apparent success with inner-city children in Chicago has been the subject of the CBS television program "Sixty Minutes" and presented in a biographical movie, in which she is portrayed by Cicely Tyson. Collins's work is widely regarded as idiosyncratic. However, in chapter 4 I discuss an effort to spread her ideas to schools in Oklahoma.
61. For an interesting journalistic account of how difficult this can be, see Sara Mosle, "Public Education's Last, Best Chance," *New York Times Magazine,* August 31, 1997, pp. 30–61.
62. Ross and others (1995) compare the success of Reading Recovery with that of Success for All and find that Success for All is more effective overall, but Reading Recovery appears to have a stronger effect on passage comprehension (one of four measures of reading progress). This is especially true for students who received individualized tutoring. See also Farkas and Vicknair (1995) for a report on another tutoring program that seems to be having some success with disadvantaged students at relatively low cost; and Wasik and Slavin (1993) for a comparison of five tutoring programs. For the Accelerated Schools Program, see Levin (1991a, 1991b); Hoffenberg, Levin, and associates (1993); cited in Barnett (1996). For the School Development Program, see Haynes and Comer (1993); Becker and Hedges (1992). More extensive reading lists are available from the national offices of these programs.
63. Further, it seems likely that effects on test scores will be smaller for programs that are less directive about the organization of learning and what teachers should do in the classroom.
64. Slavin and others (1996, p. 66).
65. Based on a talk that Robert Slavin gave at Harvard's Graduate School of Education, September 26, 1997.
66. For purposes of analysis, each grade-level cohort of students at a school is considered a replication of the program. The summary assessment of twenty-three schools in Slavin and others (1996) includes fifty-five such replications. Some of these cohorts started the program in kindergarten and some in first grade.
67. Hanushek and others (1994) point out that early testing using the California Achievement Test gave less encouraging results, and the test was not used in later evaluations. It is pos-

sible that the tests currently used (see Table 3–7) are better measures of the specific skills emphasized in Success for All.

68. Thus for the bottom 25 percent, the effect sizes shown in Table 3–7 differ from those reported by Slavin and others (1996), who use the standard deviation only among the bottom 25 percent. Their procedure facilitates direct comparison with other programs that serve students similar to those in the bottom 25 percent, but the results may be misleading when compared with effect sizes computed using the overall standard deviation.

69. This tendency for effect sizes to be larger at higher grade levels may be due to the fact that the older cohorts tend to be at schools that start Success for All in kindergarten or pre-kindergarten, while the younger cohorts more often started the program in first grade. In addition, schools that have been implementing the program longer produce larger effect sizes, which suggests that schools improve with practice.

70. See Barnett (1996) for an assessment of the cost-effectiveness of Success for All, the Accelerated Schools Program, and the School Development Program. Hanushek (1994) points out that an effective tutoring program, such as Reading Recovery, may be more efficient for some schools and some students than the more elaborate schoolwide programs like Success for All.

71. Admittedly, scholars continue to disagree about which "traditional" approaches do in fact work. For example, whole language instruction in reading (whereby children learn to read whole words in context, instead of using phonics) is currently under attack because recent research finds that it is not effective; see the exchange of views in *Education Week*, March 20, 1996. Indeed, the value of this approach has been questioned for some time, because it does not normally give students the word attack skills that they need to become good readers. For a review of many meta-analyses of techniques of instruction in education, see Wang, Haertel, and Walberg (1993). See also Tomlinson and Walberg (1986); Waxman and Walberg (1991); Slavin, Karweit, and Madden (1989).

72. Boykin and others (1997). They report one exception: they find that black children of high socioeconomic status do not improve under the verve condition.

73. See Allen and Boykin (1991); and Allen and Boykin (1992). Although the research varies in quality, other writers also suggest that the learning styles of black children are more holistic (Cooper, 1989; O'Neil, 1990; Venson, 1990), and that black children are helped by verbal communication and cooperative social arrangements (Hale-Benson, 1982, 1990; Madhere, 1989; Boykin, 1986; Clark, 1990; Nelson-LeGall and Jones, 1990; Patchen, 1982; Shade, 1989).

74. Murnane (1975).

75. Farkas and others (1990).

76. Ehrenberg, Goldhaber, and Brewer (1995).

77. Ehrenberg and Brewer (1995).

78. Alexander, Entwisle, and Thompson (1987, p. 674). Two points are important here. First, the Beginning School Study is unusual in that the black and white students are much more similar academically than in most other studies. Second, in the analysis, teacher's socioeconomic status is based on the occupation of the head of household when the teacher was a child.

79. To explain this point in more detail would require venturing on quite delicate and speculative ground in psychoanalyzing teachers. Here, let me simply suggest that these particular groups of teachers might feel the least "threatened" by black children of low socioeconomic status, and be the most inclined to believe that such children can achieve at high levels.

80. See Hanushek (1992).

81. See the meta-analysis in Greenwald, Hedges, and Laine (1996, table 1). In a response in the same journal, Hanushek (1996a) disputes their interpretation of the evidence, but he

does not question the findings regarding teachers' test scores. For other evidence on college training and test scores for teachers, see Ehrenberg and Brewer (1994, 1995); Ferguson (1991a, 1991b); Ferguson and Ladd (1996); Hanushek (1972); Straus and Sawyer (1986); Winkler (1975).

82. For additional statistical estimates using these data, see Ferguson (1991a, 1991b). Also, John Kain is currently assembling a large data set for Texas with which to study student performance at the individual level; see Kain (1995); Kain and Singleton (1996).

83. The standard deviation in the text is for the statewide distribution of scores among individual teachers.

84. Arkansas is the only other state that has tested all of its teachers. In Texas, not many teachers lost their jobs as a result of this initiative, because most passed the test with second and third chances; see Shepard and Kreitzer (1987).

85. For a detailed description of the data, see Ferguson (1991a). Houston and Dallas are not included in my analysis.

86. Compare the coefficient on "percent black among students" in column 3 with that in column 4; and the same coefficient in column 5 with that in column 6.

87. Assuming that unmeasured factors affecting differences between the test score gains of elementary and high school students are not positively correlated with differences between the TECAT scores of elementary and high school teachers.

88. The dependent variable in Table 3–10, column 7 is the difference between two differences: that is, the district's mean gain in mathematics scores between the ninth and eleventh grades minus the district's mean gain between third and fifth grades. TECAT scores for elementary teachers and high school teachers are included as separate variables.

89. This number is the average of 0.164 (the coefficient on high school teachers' scores) and 0.179 (the absolute value of the coefficient on elementary school teachers' scores), both from column 7.

90. For teachers' scores, I define "unusually high" (or low) as a district-average TECAT score of more than one standard deviation above (or below) the statewide mean, where the relevant standard deviation is that among district-level means. For students' scores, "low" first and third grade mathematics scores are more than one-half standard deviation below the statewide mean for both years. Again, the relevant standard deviation is that among district-level means. For both students' and teachers' scores, the ratio of this standard deviation to that of individuals statewide is about 3 to 1. Districts with high scoring teachers and low scoring students or low scoring teachers and high scoring students are rare; from roughly 900 districts, I could identify only a few.

91. Reading scores exhibit the same general pattern, as do equivalent data for Alabama, albeit less dramatically (results not shown).

92. That is, 0.17 times two standard deviations times five two-year intervals. This is not simply regression to the mean for student scores. Note that there are two sets of districts whose student scores are far below the mean as of the first and third grades. Only those with high teacher scores have student scores above the mean by the end of high school. Scores do regress toward the mean for the districts with low teacher scores, but these student scores nevertheless remain substantially below the mean. These statements apply correspondingly to the districts with first and third grade scores above the mean.

93. Armor (1972).

94. National Center for Education Statistics, *Digest of Education Statistics,* 1996, table 154. The number of states that implemented certification testing increased from three in 1980 to twenty in 1984 and to forty-two in 1990.

95. The data are calculated from teachers' ACT scores when they applied to college. For more detail on the ACT data for Alabama, see Ferguson and Ladd (1996).

96. The simple correlation between "percent black among students" and "percent black among teachers" is 0.91 among 129 districts in Alabama.
97. "In California, the passing rate for white test takers was 76 percent, but 26 percent for blacks; in Georgia, 87 percent of whites passed the test on the first try, while only 34 percent of blacks did; in Oklahoma, there was a 79 percent pass rate for whites and 48 percent for blacks; in Florida, an 83 percent pass rate for whites, 35 percent for blacks; in Louisiana, 78 percent for whites, 15 percent for blacks; on the NTE [National Teachers Exam] Core Battery, 94 percent of whites passed, compared with 48 percent of blacks"; Irvine (1990, p. 39) based on Anrig (1986).
98. It is in fact rather complicated to obtain accurate black-white comparisons for class size. Hence, the numbers in Table 3–11 are only approximate. Classes of different types (for example, regular, special education, gifted and talented, remedial) have different standard sizes. If blacks are more often in those classes that are typically smaller, such as special education classes, it may still be the case that within any given type of class, blacks are in larger classes. Boozer and Rouse (1995) find this to be so in New Jersey.
99. See chapter 4 for the greater sensitivity of black children to teachers' perceptions, and the discussion of behavioral issues and teachers' assessments of work habits above. Also in chapter 4, see Figure 4–1.
100. Hanushek (1986, 1989, 1991, 1996a, 1996b).
101. Hedges, Laine, and Greenwald (1994a, 1994b); Greenwald, Hedges, and Laine (1996); Hedges and Greenwald (1996).
102. Greenwald, Hedges, and Laine interpret their findings to mean that resources are used productively in most schools, but they feel that individual studies do not have enough statistical power to establish this. Hanushek rejects their interpretation and asserts that they merely answer the uninteresting question of whether resources "might matter somewhere." He points out that they would obtain the same results if resources were used effectively only in a small minority of schools—but a larger number than would occur merely by chance—which Hanushek believes is closer to the truth.
103. See Word and others (1990); Nye and others (1993, 1994); Mosteller and others (1995); Boyd-Zaharias and others (1994).
104. Note that even these "large" classes may be below the level at which large class size is most harmful to performance. Ferguson (1991a) and Glass and Smith (1979), for example, suggest that class size may have threshold effects. The existence of these effects has not been widely explored, however, and once again, problems of obtaining appropriate data make it difficult to be certain of the levels of such thresholds. Perhaps a more dependable method is to ask teachers. Surveys by the Educational Research Service have repeatedly found, over the years, that teachers report that class size shifts from being a minor problem to a more important one in the range of twenty-four students per class; see Robinson and Wittebods (1986). If this is the case, the Tennessee experiment may have missed some of the effect.
105. Analysis of these data is ongoing. It appears that class sizes were not consistently maintained: some of the small classes became larger, and some of the large classes became smaller. This drift may partially account for the slight downward drift in the measured advantage of small classes in the second and third grades. For a discussion of this issue, see Boyd-Zaharias and others (1994). Indeed, Krueger (1997) reanalyzes the data adjusting for the drift in class sizes and finds a slight additional annual gain of 1 percentile for each successive year after the first year in a small class.
106. Hanushek and others (1994b, p. 144) assert that in the second and third grades, smaller classes "made no difference in achievement." The experiment did not test this.
107. Nye and others (1994a).

108. Krueger (1997, table 11).
109. Krueger has reanalyzed the Tennessee Star data to test the sensitivity of the results to each of several limitations. He concludes: "Adjustments for school effects, attrition, re-randomization after kindergarten, nonrandom transitions, and variability in actual class size do not overturn the main findings: Students in small classes scored higher on standardized tests than students in regular-size classes" (Krueger 1997, p. 26).
110. Some might argue that the appropriate class size variable is some combination of class sizes from each of the years that the nine-year-olds have been in schools. I have tried, for example, using the average class size from the years that the students were in grades one through four. In that case, the line for pupils per teacher mirrored the disparities in test scores almost, but not quite, as well as the concurrent pupil-to-teacher ratio (that is, for grade four alone) shown in the figure. Specifically, with the average ratio for grades one through four there is no inflection at 1975, and there is a slight downward slope between 1988 and 1990—otherwise, the picture is essentially the same.
111. Regressions using the eight observations for reading and the seven mathematics observations separately each produce an adjusted R^2 of 0.99. This is true both with and without the inclusion of a simple time trend. The coefficient on pupils per teacher in the reading regressions has t statistics of 5.29 with the trend variable and 4.91 without it; for mathematics, the corresponding t statistics are 2.16 and 7.91, respectively.
112. For example, the ratio of pupils to teachers in the national data dropped from 24.9 in 1971 to 18.0 in 1988. Assuming that teachers only spend about 80 percent of their time in the classroom, this change represents a drop of about 8.6 in average class size: from roughly 31.1 pupils in 1971 to 22.5 in 1988. (In translating pupils per teacher into average class size, it is commonly assumed that teachers spend 80 percent of their time in the classroom, because they have periods off during the day for class planning and administrative responsibilities. I find this assumption confirmed in data for Alabama, where measures of both class size and pupils per teacher are available.) The difference in class sizes in Tennessee's Project Star, between the midpoints of the "large" and "small" ranges, is 8.5. For Tennessee, this change reduced the black-white difference by 0.23 standard deviations (0.40 minus 0.17 standard deviations) in third grade reading scores (see Table 3–12). In Figure 3–4, the change in the national black-white gap from 1971 to 1988 is 14.7; the standard deviations in NAEP reading scores among all nine-year-olds are 41.2 in 1971 and 42.1 in 1988. Using the standard deviation from 1971, a change of 14.7 produces a national black-white difference in effect sizes of 0.36 (14.7 divided by 41.2). This is comparable to the differential effect size of 0.23 from the Tennessee experiment. The difference between 0.36 and 0.23 could easily be accounted for if class sizes nationwide decreased more for blacks than for whites.

References

Alexander, K. L., Entwisle, D. R., & Thompson, M. S. (1987). School performance, status relations, and the structure of sentiment: Bringing the teacher back in. *American Sociology Review, 52,* 665–682.

Allen, B. A., & Boykin A. W. (1991). The influence of contextual factors on Afro-American and Euro-American children's performance: Effects of movement opportunity and music. *International Journal of Psychology, 26,* 373–387.

Allen, B. A., & Boykin A. W. (1992). African American children and the educational process: Alleviating cultural discontinuity through prescriptive pedagogy. *School Psychology Review, 21,* 586–596.

Anrig, G. R. (1986). Teacher education and teacher training: The rush to mandate. *Phi Delta Kappan, 67,* 447–451.

Argys, L. M., Rees, D. I., & Brewer, D. (1996). Detracking America's schools: Equity at zero cost? (Working Paper 9501). Denver: University of Colorado, Denver, Center for Research on Economic and Social Policy.

Armor, D. (1972). School and family effects on black and white achievement: A reexamination of the USOE data. In F. Mosteller & D. P. Moynihan (Eds.), *On equality of educational opportunity.* New York: Random House.

Barnett, W. S. (1992). Benefits of compensatory preschool education. *Journal of Human Resources, 27,* 279–312.

Barnett, W. S. (1996). Economics of school reform: Three promising models. In H. F. Ladd (Ed.), *Holding schools accountable: Performance-based reform in education.* Washington, DC: Brookings.

Barnett, W. S., & Camilli, G. (1996). *Definite results from loose data: A response to "Does Head Start make a difference?"* Unpublished manuscript, Rutgers University.

Becker, B. J., & Hedges, L. V. (1992). *A review of the literature on the effectiveness of Comer's school development program* (Report to the Rockefeller Foundation). New Haven, CT: Yale University, Child Study Center School Development Program.

Berreuta-Clement, J. R., & others. (1984). *Changed lives: The effects of the Perry Preschool Program on youths through age 19.* Ypsilanti, MI: High/Scope Press.

Boozer, M., & Rouse, C. (1995). *Intraschool variation in class size: patterns and implications* (Working Paper 5144). Cambridge, MA: National Bureau of Economic Research.

Bossert, S. T., Barnett, B. G., & Filby, N. N. (1984). Grouping and instructional organization. In P. L. Peterson, L. C. Wilkinson, & M. Hallinan (Eds.), *The social context of instruction: Group organization and group processes.* New York: Academic Press.

Boyd-Zaharias, J., & others. (1994). *Quality schools build on a quality start.* Nashville: Tennessee State University, Center of Excellence in Basic Skills.

Boykin, A. W. (1986). The triple quandary and the schooling of Afro-American children. In U. Neisser (Ed.), *The school achievement of minority children.* Hillsdale, NJ: Erlbaum.

Boykin, A. W., and others. (1997). Social context factors, context variability and school children's task performance: Further explorations in verve. *Journal of Psychology, 131,* 427–437.

Braddock, J., II, & Slavin, R. E. (1993). Why ability grouping must end: Achieving excellence and equity in American education. *Journal of Intergroup Relations, 20*(2), 51–64.

Brophy, J. E., & Good, T. L. (1974). *Teacher-student relationships: Causes and consequences.* New York: Holt, Rinehart and Winston.

Clark, M. L. (1990). Social identity, peer relations, and academic competence of African-American adolescents. *Education and Urban Society, 24,* 41–52.

Cook, M., & Evans, W. N. (1997). *Families or schools? Explaining the convergence in white and black academic performance* (Working Paper).

Cooper, G. C. (1989). Black language and holistic cognitive style. In B. R. J. Shade (Ed.), *Culture, style and the educative process.* Springfield, IL: Charles C. Thomas.

Currie, J., & Thomas, D. (1995). Does Head Start make a difference? *American Economic Review, 85,* 341–364.

Currie, J., & Thomas, D. (1996a). *Report on definite results from loose data: A response to "Does Head Start make a difference?"* Los Angeles: University of California at Los Angeles.

Currie, J., & Thomas, D. (1996b). Does subsequent school quality affect the long-term gains from Head Start? Los Angeles: University of California at Los Angeles.

Darling-Hammond, L. (1991). The implications of testing policy for quality and equality. *Phi Delta Kappan, 73,* 220–225.

Darling-Hammond, L. (1994). Who will speak for the children? *Phi Delta Kappan, 76,* 21–34.

Darling-Hammond, L. (1996). The quiet revolution: Rethinking teacher development. *Educational Leadership, 53*(6), 4–10.

Darling-Hammond, L., & McLaughlin, M. W. (1995). Policies that support professional development in an era of reform. *Phi Delta Kappan, 76,* 597–604.

Dickens, W., Kane, T., & Schultz. C. (1995). Does the bell curve ring true? *Brookings Review, 13* (Summer).

Douglas, J. (1964). *The home and the school.* London: MacGibbon and Kee.

Dreeben, R., & Gamoran, A. (1986). Race, instructions, and learning. *American Sociological Review, 51,* 660–669.

Eder, D. (1981). Ability grouping as a self-fulfilling prophecy: A micro-analysis of teacher-student interaction." *Sociology of Education, 54,* 151–162.

Ehrenberg, R. G., & Brewer, D. J. (1994). Do school and teacher characteristics matter? Evidence from *High School and Beyond. Economics of Education Review, 13,* 1–17.

Ehrenberg, R. G., & Brewer, D. J. (1995). Did teachers' verbal ability and race matter in the 1960s? Coleman revisited. *Economics of Education Review, 14,* 1–21.

Ehrenberg, R. G., Goldhaber, D. D., & Brewer, D. J. (1995). Do teachers' race, gender, and ethnicity matter? Evidence from the National Education Longitudinal Study of 1988. *Industrial and Labor Relations Review, 48,* 547–561.

Farkas, G., & Vicknair, K. (1995). *Reading 1–1 program effect, 1994–95.* Dallas: University of Texas at Dallas, Center for Education and Social Policy.

Farkas, G., & others. (1990). Cultural resources and school success: Gender, ethnicity, and poverty groups within an urban district. *American Sociological Review, 55,* 127–142.

Ferguson, R. F. (1991a). Paying for public education: New evidence on how and why money matters. *Harvard Journal on Legislation, 28,* 465–498.

Ferguson, R. F. (1991b). Racial patterns in how school and teacher quality affect achievement and earnings. *Challenge, 2,* 1–26.

Ferguson, R. F., & Ladd, H. F. (1996). How and why money matters: An analysis of Alabama schools. In H. F. Ladd (Ed.), *Holding schools accountable.*

Finley, M. K. (1984). Teachers and tracking in a comprehensive high school. *Sociology of Education, 57,* 233–243.

Ford, D. Y. (1996). *Reversing the underachievement among gifted black students.* New York: Teachers College Press.

Gamoran, A. (1986). Instructional and institutional effects of ability grouping. *Sociology of Wisconsin, 59,* 185–198.

Gamoran, A., & Berends, M. (1987). The effects of stratification in secondary schools: Synthesis of survey and ethnographic research. *Review of Educational Research, 57,* 415–435.

Gamoran, A., & Mare, R. G. (1989). Secondary school tracking and educational inequality: Compensation, reinforcement, or neutrality? *American Journal of Sociology, 94,* 1146–1183.

Garet, M. S., & Delaney, B. (1988). Students, courses and stratification. *Sociology of Education, 61,* 61–77.

Glass, G. V., & Smith, M. L. (1979). Meta-analysis of research on class size and achievement. *Educational Evaluation and Policy Analysis, 1,* 2–16.

Goldberg, M., Passow, A., & Justman, J. (1966). *The effect of ability grouping.* New York: Teachers College Press.

Good, T. L. (1987). Two decades of research on teacher expectations: Findings and future directions. *Journal of Teacher Education, 38*(4), 32–47.

Greenwald, R., Hedges, L. V., & Laine, R. D. (1996). The effect of school resources on student achievement. *Review of Educational Research, 66,* 361–396.

Hale-Benson, J. E. (1982). *Black children: Their roots, culture and learning styles.* Provo, UT: Brigham Young University Press.

Hale-Benson, J. E. (1990). Visions for children: Educating black children in the context of their culture. In K. Lomotey (Ed.), *Going to school: The African-American experience.* Albany: State University of New York Press.

Haller, E. J. (1985). Pupil race and elementary school ability grouping: Are teachers biased against black children? *American Educational Research Journal, 22,* 465–483.

Haller, E. J., & Davis, S. A. (1980). Does socioeconomic status bias the assignment of elementary school students to reading groups? *American Educational Research Journal, 17,* 409–418.

Hanushek, E. (1972). *Education and race.* Lexington, MA: Heath-Lexington.

Hanushek, E. (1986). The economics of schooling: Production efficiency in public schools. *Journal of Economic Literature, 24,* 1141–1177.

Hanushek, E. (1989). The impact of differential expenditures on school performance. *Educational Researcher, 18*(4), 45–62.

Hanushek, E. (1991). When school finance "reform" may not be good policy. *Harvard Journal on Legislation, 28,* 423–456.

Hanushek, E. (1992). The trade-off between child quantity and quality. *Journal of Political Economy, 100,* 84–117.

Hanushek, E. (1994a). *Making schools work: Improving performance and controlling costs.* Washington, DC: Brookings Institution Press.

Hanushek, E. (1994b). Money might matter somewhere: A response to Hedges, Laine, and Greenwald. *Educational Researcher, 23*(4), 5–8.

Hanushek, E. (1996a). A more complete picture of school resource policies. *Review of Educational Research, 66,* 397–409.

Hanushek, E. (1996b). School resources and student performance. In G. Burtless (Ed.), *Does money matter? The effect of school resources on student achievement and adult success.* Washington, DC: Brookings Institution Press.

Haynes, N. M., & Comer, J. P. (1993). The Yale School Development Program: Process, outcomes, and policy implications. *Urban Education, 28,* 166–199.

Hedges, L. V., & Greenwald, R. (1996). Have times changed? The relation between school resources and student performance. In G. Burtless (Ed.), *Does money matter? The effect of school resources on student achievement and adult success.* Washington, DC: Brookings Institution Press.

Hedges, L. V., Laine, R. D., & Greenwald, R. (1994a). Does money matter? A meta-analysis of studies of the effects of differential inputs on student outcomes. *Educational Researcher, 23*(3), 5–14.

Hedges, L. V., Laine, R. D., & Greenwald, R. (1994b). Money does matter somewhere: A reply to Hanushek. *Educational Researcher, 23*(4), 9–10.

Hoffenberg, W. A., Levin, H. A., & Associates. (1993). *The accelerated schools resource guide.* San Francisco: Jossey-Bass.

Howell, W. (1962). Grouping of talented students leads to better academic achievement in secondary school. *Bulletin of the NASSP, 46.*

Husen, T., & Svennson, N. (1960). Pedagogic milieu and development of intellectual skills. *Schools Review, 68,* 36–51.

Irvine, J. J. (1990). *Black students and school failure.* Westport, CT: Greenwood.

Jones, J. (1997). *The Messages Project, Fort Wayne Urban League, Phase I.* Fort Wayne, IN: Urban League and Taylor University.

Kain, J. F. (1995). *Impact of minority suburbanization on the school attendance and achievement of minority children.* Cambridge, MA: Harvard University, Department of Economics.

Kain, J. F., & Singleton, K. (1996). Equality of educational opportunity revisited. *New England Economic Review,* (May–June), 87–111.

Krueger, A. B. (1997). *Experimental estimates of education production functions.* Princeton, NJ: Princeton University.

Kulik, C.-L. C., & Kulik, J. A. (1982). Effects of ability grouping on secondary school students: A meta-analysis of evaluation findings. *American Educational Research Journal, 19,* 415–428.

Kulik, C.-L. C., & Kulik, J. A. (1984a). *Effects of ability grouping on elementary school pupils: A meta-analysis.* Paper prepared for the annual meeting of the American Psychological Association.

Kulik, C.-L. C., & Kulik, J. A. (1984b). Effects of accelerated instruction on students. *Review of Educational Research, 54,* 409–426.

Kulik, C.-L. C., & Kulik, J. A. (1987). Effects of ability grouping on student achievement. *Equity and Excellence, 23,* 22–30.

Kulik, C.-L. C., & Kulik, J. A. (1989). Meta-analysis in educational research. *International Journal of Educational Research, 13,* 221–340.

Kulik, J. A. (1992). An analysis of the research on ability grouping: Historical and contemporary perspectives. Storrs, CT: University of Connecticut, National Center on the Gifted and Talented.

Lazar, I., & Darlington, R. (1982). Lasting effects of early education: A report from the Consortium for Longitudinal Studies. *Monograph of the Society for Research in Child Development, 196*(47), 2–3.

Lee, V. E., & Bryk, A. S. (1988). Curriculum tracking as mediating the social distribution of high school achievement. *Sociology of Education, 61,* 78–94.

Lee, V. E., & Ekstrom, R. B. (1987). Student access to guidance counseling in high school. *American Educational Research Journal, 24,* 287–310.

Levin, H. M. (1991a). *Accelerating the progress of ALL students.* Paper prepared for the Nelson A. Rockefeller Institute of Government Educational Policy Seminar.

Levin, H. M. (1991b). Learning from accelerated schools. In *Policy perspectives.* Philadelphia: Pew Charitable Trusts, Higher Education Research Program.

Levine, D. L. (1994). Instructional approaches and interventions that can improve the academic performance of African American students. *Journal of Negro Education, 63,* 46–63.

Metz, M. H. (1978). *Classrooms and corridors: The crisis of authority in desegregated secondary schools.* Berkeley: University of California Press.

Madhere, S. S. (1989). Models of intelligence and the black intellect. *Journal of Negro Education, 58,* 189–201.

Mosteller, F. (1995). The Tennessee study of class size in the early school grades. *Future of Children, 5,* 113–117.

Murnane, R. (1975). *The impact of school resources on the learning of inner city children.* Cambridge, MA: Ballinger.

National Center for Education Statistics. (1996). *NAEP 1994 trends in academic progress.* Washington, DC: Department of Education.

National Center for Education Statistics. (1996). *Digest of Education Statistics.* Washington, DC: U.S. Goverment Printing Office.

Nelson-LeGall, S., & Jones, E. (1990). Classroom helpseeking behavior of African-American children. *Education and Urban Society, 24*(1), 27–40.

Nye, B. A., & others. (1993). Tennessee's bold experiment: Using research to inform policy and practice. *Tennessee Education, 22*(3), 10–17.

Nye, B. A., & others. (1994a). *The Lasting Benefit Study: A continuing analysis of the effect of small class size in kindergarten through third grade on student achievement test scores in subsequent grade levels: Seventh grade, 1992–1993* (Technical Report). Nashville: Tennessee State University, Center of Excellence for Research in Basic Skills.

Nye, B. A., & others. (1994b). *Project Challenge, fourth-year summary report: an initial evaluation of the Tennessee Department of Education "at-risk" student/teacher ratio reduction project in sixteen counties, 1990 through 1993.* Nashville: Tennessee State University, Center of Excellence for Research in Basic Skills.

Nye, B. A., & others. (1994c). *The Lasting Benefits Study, seventh grade: Executive summary.* Nashville: Tennessee State University, Center of Excellence for Research in Basic Skills.

Oakes, J. (1985). *Keeping track: How schools structure inequality.* New Haven, CT: Yale University Press.

O'Neil, J. (1990). Making sense of style. *Educational Leadership, 48,* 4–9.

Pallas, A. M., & others. (1994). Ability-group effects: Instructional, social, or institutional? *Sociology of Education, 67,* 27–46.

Patchen, M. (1982). *Black-white contact in schools: Its social and academic effects.* Ashland, OH: Purdue University Press.

Reynolds, A. J., & others. (1996). Cognitive and family-support mediators of preschool effectiveness: A confirmatory analysis. *Child Development, 67,* 1119–1140.

Robinson, G. E., & Wittebods, J. H. (1986). *Class size research: A related cluster analysis for decision making* (Research brief). Arlington, VA: Educational Research Service.

Ross, S. M., & others. (1995). Increasing the academic success of disadvantaged children: An examination of alternative early intervention programs. *American Educational Research Journal, 32,* 773–800.

Schwartz, F. (1981). Supporting or subverting learning: Peer group patterns in four tracked schools. *Anthropology and Education Quarterly, 12,* 99–121.

Schweinhart, L. J., & Weikart, D. P. (1980). *Young children grow up: The effects of the Perry Preschool Program on youths through age 15.* Ypsilanti, MI: High/Scope Press.

Schweinhart, L. J., & others. (1993). *Significant benefits: The High/Scope Perry Preschool Study through age 27.* Ypsilanti, MI: High/Scope Press.

Shade, B. R. J. (1989). Afro-American cognitive patterns: A review of the research. In B. R. J. Shade (Ed.), *Culture, style and the educative process.* Springfield, IL: Charles C. Thomas.

Shepard, L. A., & Kreitzer, A. E. (1987). The Texas teacher test. *Educational Researcher, 16*(6), 22–31.

Slavin, R. E. (1987). Grouping for instruction in the elementary school. *Educational Psychologist, 22,* 109–127.

Slavin, R. E. (1990a). Ability grouping in secondary schools: A response to Hallinan. *Review of Educational Research, 60,* 505–507.

Slavin, R. E. (1990b). Achievement effects of ability grouping in secondary schools: A best-evidence synthesis. *Review of Educational Research, 60,* 471–499.

Slavin, R. E., Karweit, N.L., & Madden, N. A. (1989). *Effective programs for students at risk.* Boston: Allyn and Bacon.

Slavin, R. E., & Madden, N. A. (1989). What works for students at risk: A research synthesis. *Educational Leadership,* (February), 4–13.

Slavin, R. E., & others. (1996). Success for all: A summary of research. *Journal of Education for Students Placed at Risk, 1,* 41–76.

Sorensen, A. B., & Hallinan, M. (1984). Effects of race on assignment to ability groups. In P. Peterson, L. C. Wilkinson, & M. Hallinan (Eds.), *The social context of instruction.* New York: Academic Press.

Straus, R. P., & Sawyer, E. A. (1986). Some new evidence on teacher and student competencies. *Economics of Education Review, 5*(1), 41–48.

Tomlinson, T. M., & Walberg, H. J. (Eds.). (1986). *Academic work and education excellence: Raising student productivity.* Berkeley, CA: McCutchan.

Venson, S. (1990). *Let's education together.* Chicago: Alternative Schools Network.

Wang, M., Haertel, G. D., & Walberg, H. J. (1993). Toward a knowledge base for school learning. *Review of Education Research, 63,* 249–294.

Wasik, B. A., & Slavin, R. E. (1993). Preventing early reading failure with one-to-one tutoring: A review of five programs. *Reading Research Quarterly, 28,* 179–199.

Waxman, H. C., & Walberg, H. J. (Eds.). (1991). *Effective teaching: Current research.* Berkeley, CA: McCutchan.

Weinstein, R. S. (1976). Reading group membership in first grade: Teacher behaviors and pupil experience over time. *Journal of Educational Psychology, 68,* 103–116.

Weinstein, R. S., & others. (1987). Pygmalion and the student: Age and classroom differences in children's awareness of teacher expectations. *Child Development, 58,* 1079–1092.

Winkler, D. R. (1975). Educational achievement and school peer group composition. *Journal of Human Resources, 10,* 189–204.

Word, E., & others. (1990). *Student/Teacher Achievement Ratio (STAR): Tennessee's K–3 class size study, final summary report, 1985–1990.* Nashville: Tennessee State Department of Education.

CHAPTER 4   Teachers' Perceptions and Expectations and the Black-White Test Score Gap

Notes

1. The black-white gap in skills at the beginning of primary school is smaller for more recent cohorts.

2. Existing evidence on group-level disparity at the mean across grade levels within a cohort is not entirely clear, because of measurement issues and data problems.

3. Whenever possible, I present results in terms of "effect sizes" measured in standard deviation units. For example, if one group of students experiences a particular treatment and an otherwise equivalent control or comparison group does not, the effect size of the treatment on test scores is the difference between average scores for the two groups after the treatment, divided by the pooled standard deviation of scores. For an outcome that is normally distributed, an effect size of 0.20 moves a student from the fiftieth to the fifty-eighth percentile; an effect size of 0.50 moves the student to the sixty-ninth percentile; and an effect size of 0.80 moves the student to the seventy-ninth percentile.

4. Lightfoot (1978, pp. 85–86).

5. Baron, Tom, and Cooper (1985, p. 251).

6. Brophy (1985, p. 304).

7. Haller (1985, p. 481) is commenting on racial disparity in ability group assignments. See chapter 3 for more discussion of ability grouping, including Haller's findings.

8. This immediate discussion concerns experiments. However, this first type of benchmark is also used in naturalistic settings. Specifically, in the absence of reliable information *about individuals* on which to base a benchmark that is not unconditionally race neutral, unconditional racial neutrality may seem the only morally defensible alternative.

9. Baron, Tom, and Cooper (1985).

10. Baron, Tom, and Cooper (1985) report that effect sizes could be retrieved for only six of the sixteen studies. In these six studies the black-white differences in teacher expectations average half a standard deviation. If nine of the other studies are assumed to have effect sizes of zero and the one with a significant result but no effect size is assumed to have an effect size of 0.36, then the average effect size across all sixteen studies is 0.22.

11. DeMeis and Turner (1978).

12. To compute the effect sizes for each outcome, I use the standard deviation among blacks as the denominator, since the pooled standard deviation is not reported. The standard deviation among whites is virtually the same as that among blacks. Among students speaking standard English, effect sizes for the black-white differences in personality, quality of response, current academic abilities, and future academic abilities are 0.57, 0.52, 0.55, and 0.44 standard deviations, respectively. For black English, the analogous numbers are 0.34, 0.44, 0.23, and 0.14 standard deviations. The fact that effect sizes are smaller for tapes on which students spoke black English is not surprising, since speaking black Eng-

lish would be an especially negative signal for a white student. Across the four outcomes, within-race effect sizes for black English versus standard English range from 0.23 to 0.45 for blacks and from 0.55 to 0.74 for whites, in all cases favoring standard English. All effect sizes reported in this footnote are calculated from numbers in DeMeis and Turner (1978, table 2).

13. For whatever reasons, average scores on standardized examinations tend to be lower for blacks than for whites. Hence in general the most accurate prediction is that whites will have higher scores.

14. See, for example, Good (1987); Egan and Archer (1985); Mitman (1985); Hoge and Butcher (1984); Monk (1983); Pedulla, Airasian, and Madaus (1980).

15. See Brophy and Good (1974, table 6.1), which presents correlations from Evertson, Brophy, and Good (1972).

16. Eccles and Wigfield (1985), for example, provide a line of reasoning that might support this outcome. Essentially, in order to deviate from a previously established trajectory, the student may need support from the teacher in begining the process of change. If the teacher continues to treat the student as he or she did before the change, the student may decide that the environment is not sufficiently responsive to attain the new goal, feel a lack of control, and return to the old ways.

17. Experimental studies that expose teachers to different sequences of facts show that their expectations are sufficiently flexible to remain accurate as new information becomes available; see, for example, Shavelson, Cadwell, and Izu (1977). The pattern of flexibility among teachers in real classrooms is not known.

18. Indeed, Guskey (1982) finds that improvements in teacher responsiveness reduce the accuracy of teachers' early predictions for end-of-semester performance; see discussion in text below.

19. See Egan and Archer (1985); Irvine (1985); Brophy and Good (1974); Evertson, Brophy, and Good (1972); Willis (1972).

20. Haller (1985, note 4). This study covers forty-nine teachers and 934 fourth, fifth, and sixth graders in five cities across four census regions.

21. See Irvine (1990, p. 77), discussing findings presented first in Irvine (1985). The correlations between second-week rankings and end-of-year test scores are 0.63 for white males and 0.62 for black males. The correlation for black males dipped in the tenth week, but had returned to the same range as for whites by the end of the school year. Irvine emphasizes this difference in the pattern for black and white boys. It seems to me, however, that similarity is the more salient finding: of three comparisons for boys, in only one (boys at the tenth week) is the racial difference notable; and there is no significant racial difference in the three comparisons for girls. Some teachers in Irvine's study were consistently more accurate than others. For the least accurate teacher, the correlations moved from 0.11 for the second week to 0.56 for the end of the year. At the high end, one teacher had correlations of 0.91, 0.92, and 0.89 for the second week, tenth week, and end of the year, respectively.

22. Gaines (1990).

23. Recall that two lines with different slopes can each represent a correlation of one between the variables on the x and y axes. Similarly, teachers' early perceptions or expectations could have a much larger impact on performance for one race than for the other (as represented by a steeper line), even though the correlation between teachers' perceptions or expectations and end-of-year performance is the same for both groups. The possibility of different slopes is explored by Jussim, Eccles, and Madon (1996), as discussed below.

24. Committee on Policy for Racial Justice (1989), quoted in Miller (1995, p. 203). The task force that produced the report included a number of noted black scholars at major uni-

versities, including Sara Lawrence Lightfoot of Harvard (the principal author), James P. Comer of Yale, John Hope Franklin of Duke, and William Julius Wilson, then at the University of Chicago.

25. Leacock (1969), quoted in Brophy and Good (1974, p. 10).

26. Goals are not determined by teachers' expectations alone. The curricular materials that are handed down to teachers from the administration, as well as students' actual behavior, also matter.

27. See Ford (1996) for a useful discussion of the issue in light of theories of multiple intelligences. In the terminology of the present chapter, those who think that potential is very distinct from performance and that ability is equally distributed among the races will favor an unconditionally race-neutral proxy in place of race neutrality conditional on observables. Those who believe that racial differences in performance are good approximations of racial differences in potential might favor a proxy of race neutrality conditional on observables, perhaps augmented by a positive shift factor for all students.

28. Miller (1995, chapter 8) presents a useful review of trends in surveys regarding beliefs about black intellectual inferiority. He points out that numbers in the Harris poll tend to produce smaller percentages because they ask more directly about whether any black-white difference in intelligence is genetic.

29. Kluegel (1990, pp. 514–15, 517).

30. Miller (1995, p. 183), based on Tom Smith (1990, p. 6).

31. Miller (1995, pp. 186–87), based on Snyderman and Rothman (1986, 1987).

32. Herrnstein and Murray (1994); Jeff Howard and Ray Hammond, "Rumors of Inferiority," *New Republic*, September 1989.

33. See, for example, Good (1987).

34. Merton (1948); Rosenthal and Jacobson (1968).

35. See Rosenthal (1994) for a review.

36. The most frequent explanation for failure is that the teachers do not believe information about the students. Sometimes teachers figure out the purpose of the experiment. Other times, teachers have their own sources of credible information or have known the students long enough to form opinions before the experiment begins. In a meta-analysis of eighteen experiments in which IQ or a similar measure of ability was the outcome, Raudenbush (1984) shows very clearly that evidence of the effect was primarily found in studies where teachers had no opportunity to form an independent impression of students before the experiment began.

37. Smith (1980). She does not say what percentage of these effect sizes are calculated from the standard deviation of test score levels as opposed to test score gains.

38. Brophy (1985, p. 304). Specifically, he estimates that teachers' expectations make about a 5 percent difference, but he does not say whether he means the difference in gain over a school year or the difference in total achievement (as in the level on a test). Brophy's statement is based on his own review of the literature, where individual studies seldom cover more than a single school year.

39. This multivariate equation includes controls for predictors of performance, such as past performance and socioeconomic background. Typically, the estimate of self-fulfilling prophecy may tend to be statistically biased upward, because of omitted variables that are positively associated with both teacher expectations and student performance. Hence any findings of this sort must be taken as suggestive, not definitive.

40. It is not unusual, for example, for a teacher to say, "Betty is doing well now because she is repeating the grade and has seen some of this material before. I don't expect she will do as well for the rest of the year." This teacher might be accurate in the current evaluation of the student, but still biased in the expectation. Or the example might be reversed,

with the expectation more positive than the evaluation of current performance. In either case, the expectation might or might not be biased when judged from the perspective of what past performance and attitudes would predict.

41. Jussim, Eccles, and Madon (1996, pp. 350–51). They speculate that the void in the literature stems from the political risk of studying groups that do, in fact, differ. Instead, researchers have tended to focus on experimental studies that assume away differences. See also Jussim (1989) and Jussim and Eccles (1992), which use the same data to study the accuracy of teachers' expectations without emphasizing racial differences.

42. Of the total student sample, seventy-six are African Americans—ideally, a larger number would be preferable for such a study. The data are taken from the Michigan Study of Adolescent Life Transitions, which was not initially designed to study racial differences; for more on the Michigan study, see Wigfield and others (1991).

43. Although they do not report raw means by race, they do report that the correlations of race with grades and standard test scores were –0.12 and –0.14, respectively (in both cases, $p < 0.001$), with black studentss having the lower scores and grades. These correlations are probably smaller than in the typical national sample of (black and white) sixth-graders.

44. Jussim, Eccles, and Madon (1996) perform separate calculations to determine whether the residual variance in teachers' perceptions left unexplained by the background factors is similar for blacks and whites. They find it to be slightly higher for blacks, but by a margin so small as to be inconsequential: "The correlations of ethnicity with the absolute values of the residuals from the models predicting teacher perceptions were 0.06 ($p < 0.05$), 0.07 ($p < 0.05$), and –0.02 (not significant) for performance, talent, and effort, respectively" (p. 355). While two of the three are statistically significant, these suggest only a very small difference in accuracy, and less accuracy for blacks than for whites.

Regarding other effects, they find a small positive relationship between parental education (a proxy for socioeconomic status) and teacher's perception of a student's talent. There are also some small gender effects. Teacher perceptions of performance and effort are higher for girls, after controlling for the factors listed in the text. Hence it appears that teachers relied somewhat on a gender stereotype, although not necessarily a false one.

45. As background variables, the equation to predict scores and grades includes race, mathematics grades from the end of fifth grade, mathematics scores from the end of fifth or beginning of sixth grade, self-perception of ability, self-reported effort at mathematics, self-reported time spent on homework, and indexes of the intrinsic and extrinsic values of mathematics to the student. Interactions of student race with teacher perceptions of effort and talent were tried, but were found to produce strange results, because of collinearity with the interaction for race and performance. The result for performance might best be interpreted as the interaction of race with all aspects of a teacher's perceptions.

46. The effect size for MEAP scores is only 0.14 for whites, but 0.37 for African Americans ($p < 0.001$). This effect size for whites is quite close to that of 0.17 for mathematics achievement scores reported by Smith (1980). For grades, the effect size for African Americans is 0.56, compared with 0.20 for whites ($p < 0.01$).

Calculations conducted by Jussim after the paper was published use a specification that includes additional interaction terms, including interactions of race with past grades and scores. The effect size for MEAP scores rises from the original 0.37 to 0.58 for African Americans and drops from 0.14 to 0.13 for whites. Moreover, the coefficients on past grades and scores are estimated to be somewhat smaller for African Americans than for whites. Hence it appears that the performance of these black students was more dependent on teachers' current opinions and less anchored in measures of past performance than that of whites. One might speculate that this is because past grades and scores were less accurate measures of the knowledge or potential of the black students than of the whites, but one cannot be sure from the information available.

47. It is not clear what to make of absence of any relationship between self-reports and teachers' perceptions of effort. If teachers' assessments really are grossly inaccurate, this fact could contribute to the disengagement of children who are believed not to be trying when in fact they are. It could also contribute to a lack of challenge for students who are slacking off—even though they might appear to be working hard—and who would work harder if asked.

48. The fact that teacher perceptions are also strong predictors for females and for whites from low-income households makes it more likely that this is a real effect for blacks. Further, since Jussim, Eccles, and Madon (1996) find no unexplained racial differences in the October performance ratings for blacks and whites after controlling for background factors, and only a trivial difference in unexplained variation, it seems unlikely that the ratings have very different interpretations or different implicit scalings for blacks and whites. Still, these results need to be replicated several times in order to be firmly established.

49. Weinstein (1985, p. 344).

50. Jussim, Eccles, and Madon (1996) assume that current perceptions are good estimates of expectations for the future and they use "perceptions" and "expectations" interchangeably. Jussim has argued in personal communication that this is a reasonable assumption, based on other research regarding the processes by which people form expectations. It might, however, be inappropriate in the present context, for the reasons explained in the text. I do not know of any research that generates data on teachers' perceptions of current performance along with expectations for future performance for both blacks and whites.

51. Casteel (1997). The sample includes 928 whites and 761 African Americans, from twelve classes in nine schools in two public school districts.

52. Entwisle and Alexander (1988).

53. Kleinfeld (1972).

54. See the discussion in Irvine (1990, pp. 46–49). In support of her conclusion that "researchers have found that black and other minority pupils are more negatively affected by teacher expectations than white students are," Irvine cites Baker (1973), Krupczak (1972), and Yee (1968). I have not found any studies that contradict these few.

55. Claude Steele, "Race and the Schooling of Black Americans," *Atlantic Monthly,* April 1992, pp. 68–78.

56. As informal but reliable evidence, I offer my personal experience. As a fifth-grader, I moved from a segregated school to one that was integrated. In my new classroom, the top reading group was white, with one or two exceptions; the middle group was mixed, but mostly black; and the slow group was all black. While I did not believe that this pattern was unfair, I wanted the teacher to know, and I wanted to know for myself, that I was an exception. The teacher placed me in the middle group. I could not understand why she could not see from my records that I belonged in the top group, despite the fact that I was black. I recall being driven to establish myself as an exception to the racial pattern in the classroom and fearing for a while that my performance in the middle group might not be good enough to do so: I might be trapped in the middle group! After a few weeks the teacher moved me up, and my anxiety abated. However, my constant awareness of racial patterns in group memberships remained.

57. Gross (1993).

58. These fourth and sixth grade results are from a single year for two different cohorts, hence while the differences appear consistent with a trend, they do not clearly establish one. Also, Gross does not report sample sizes broken down into those who were above, at, or below a given grade level. Hence it is not clear how many children these percentages represent.

59. Gross (1993, p. 282).

60. Susan Gross, personal communication.

61. Gross reports, in personal communication, that in a regression analysis using students' classroom performance as a predictor, she found that the CATM test scores of the black high-achievers were below those predicted. These calculations were not published, however, and are no longer available.

62. Gross (1993, p. 281).

63. And this, in turn, might have contributed to the ambivalence that seems to be expressed in the work habits of the black schoolchildren, as shown in Figure 4–1.

64. Ogbu (1978, 1983, 1987); Fordham and Ogbu (1986); Mickelson (1990).

65. Mickelson studied 1,193 seniors from eight high schools in the Los Angeles area during the 1982–83 school year. She analyzes only the responses of blacks and whites, who compose 41 and 59 percent, respectively, of her working sample. In predicting grade point averages, the standardized coefficients on concrete attitudes in the full specification are 0.111 ($p < 0.05$) for blacks and 0.190 ($p < 0.01$) for whites. These are not large effects. Still, the facts that such a rough index of beliefs is statistically significant at all, and that the distinction between abstract and concrete attitudes is demonstrated so clearly (see Table 4–2), are important. The coefficient for abstract attitudes was about a fifth as large as that for concrete attitudes. The t statistic is about 1 for whites and less than 0.5 for blacks. The regressions control for mother's and father's occupation and education, a locus of control index, student's weekly hours worked, percentage of close friends planning to attend a four-year college, and an indicator variable for each of the eight schools in the sample. Mickelson notes that regressions using standardized test scores as the dependent variable produce the same story as for grades.

66. I think that "concrete" is a gross misnomer for these attitudes, and that it has confused the interpretation of Mickelson's work. They are just as abstract as the others: "fairness" is not concrete. They actually measure ambivalence or doubt about the "abstract" attitudes.

67. Coates (1972); Rubovits and Maehr (1973); Feldman and Orchowsky (1979); Taylor (1979). See also Babad (1980, 1985) for related research from Israel, where teachers in the experiment grade assignments on which the names are randomly either European or Moroccan.

68. Taylor (1979) designed her experiment in response to the possibility that confederate students' behaviors had confounded the findings of racial bias in Rubovits and Maehr (1973). By placing the phantom student behind a one-way glass, where they could allegedly see the teacher and respond to the teacher's questions and instruction, she removed any effects of targets' actual behaviors. Sessions were videotaped and the teachers' behaviors were coded. The participants were 105 white female undergraduates at the University of Massachusetts, Amherst. They were told that the purpose of the experiment was "to examine certain aspects of teaching behavior in a situation where feedback from pupil to teacher was limited." Discussions after the experiment show that they believed this premise.

69. There are many sources from which to draw this standard finding. Irvine (1990, table 3.3) tabulates studies conducted in naturalistic classroom settings. Of seventeen findings from sixteen studies, whites are favored in nine, there is no difference in four, the opposite race to the teacher is favored in two, the same race as the teacher is favored in one, and blacks are favored in one. One of these studies is from 1969 and the rest are from the 1970s and early 1980s. For discussion of earlier studies, see Brophy and Good (1974).

70. See Puma and others (1993).

71. See, for example, Solorzano (1992); Miller (1995).

72. On the types of student that teachers like to teach, see Brophy and Good (1974) and the literature that they discuss. Also, see below in the present chapter.

73. Teachers' expectations might be less flexible for black students than for whites. Inflexible perceptions, in turn, might lead to teacher behaviors that reinforce problem behaviors in

low-performing students and promote good behaviors in high-performing students. This is a ripe topic for future research.

74. Willis and Brophy (1974, p. 132). Extract is from Brophy and Good (1974, pp. 186–93).

75. Simply matching the race of the student and the teacher is too simple a prescription: social class and professional competence also appear to be important. In chapter 3, I discuss how a teacher's race and social class might affect student performance.

76. Cabello and Burstein (1995, pp. 289–90).

77. Jones (1997, p. 9).

78. See, for example, Katz (1973), cited in both Brophy and Good (1974) and Irvine (1990).

79. In particular, it is important that teachers make clear that academic ability is not immutable—that sustained effort mobilizes and develops ability. Dweck (1991) and Dweck and Leggett (1988) find statistically significant evidence among white children that those who believe that ability is fixed tend to adopt performance goals, whereas those who believe otherwise tend to adopt mastery goals. Among those who believe ability is fixed and that their own endowment is low, the performance goal serves to hide their ignorance. But both high and low achievers among those who believe that ability can be developed tend toward mastery goals. The same is probably true for blacks, but I do not know of any research that addresses this issue.

80. In a summary of the literature on wait time, Rowe (1986, p. 45) reports that teachers' "expectations change gradually, often signaled by remarks such as 'He never contributed like that before. Maybe he has a special "thing" for this topic.' . . . *This effect was particularly pronounced where minority students were concerned* [emphasis added]. They did more task relevant talking and took a more active part in discussions than they had before." Rowe also makes other references to the studies that develop these findings. Wait time is shorter for low-performing students (see chapter 8).

81. Guskey (1982).

82. For the ratings on probable achievement in the course and achievement potential, teachers assigned each student to one of five groups of equal size.

83. Studies find mixed results regarding techniques to improve corrective feedback. See, for example, Slavin's (1987) review of the literature on mastery learning.

84. Brattesani, Weinstein, and Marshall (1984). Their point in this paper is that teacher expectations become self-fulfilling prophecies only when communicated through differential treatment. They find that teacher expectations are stronger predictors in classrooms with higher levels of differential treatment. However, since they collected teachers' expectations in April of the school year, I would regard these as reports from the end of the school year rather than as self-fulfilling predictions. For interesting related work, see Weinstein and others (1987), who show that even first-graders can accurately report teachers' differential treatment of their peers, but that it is not until third grade that students begin to give accurate reports regarding their own differential treatment.

85. See Brattesani, Weinstein, and Marshall (1984, table 4). They find strong evidence that standardized test scores are predicted less well by past performance in classrooms where there is more differential treatment. The sample sizes are small, so that the difference in percentages of low achievers who make large gains does not reach statistical significance. Nevertheless, the magnitudes of the gains are large.

86. This summary draws from Ferguson (1993), which tells the story of the birth and early development of the initiative.

87. She maintained that most of the time the resistance could be reduced by a combination of two responses. First, she would assure the teacher that he or she could slip into the Great Expectations program gradually, implementing some elements first and others later. Second, she would model the specific practices to which the teacher was resistant. She would do so at that teacher's school, preferably in the teacher's classroom, and always with the

greatest respect and tact. When a teacher witnessed a mentor successfully demonstrating a method with the teacher's own students, he or she usually became (or claimed to become) more open to giving it a try.

88. One worst-case example involved a first grade teacher who had failed with a different new method during the previous year. Although several other teachers at her school were using the Great Expectations method and doing well, she was sure that it could not work for her, and she received no pressure to change from the passive principal.

89. In this and the following subsection, names of teachers and schools have been changed, but facts and quotations are real.

90. Chapter 3 discusses the Success for All program, which serves a large number of mostly black and Hispanic children across several states. It shows positive effects for all students, but larger effects for the bottom 25 percent of the class.

91. Robert Schuller is a popular television minister and proponent of positive thinking.

92. Guskey (1982).

93. Jussim, Eccles, and Madon (1996).

94. Casteel (1997).

95. In addition to strong leadership and professional development for teachers, better-conceived performance incentives, no matter what their expectations of their students, should be a part of this process. The search for ways to design and implement such incentives and standards of accountability is currently quite active; see, for example, Hanushek (1994); Hanushek and Jorgenson (1996); Ladd (1996).

References

Babad, E. Y. (1980). Expectancy bias in scoring as a function of ability and ethnic labels. *Psychological Reports, 46,* 625–626.

Babad, E. Y. (1985). Some correlates of teachers' expectancy bias. *American Educational Research Journal, 22,* 175–183.

Baker, S. H. (1973). *Teacher effectiveness and social class as factors in teacher expectancy effects on pupils' scholastic achievement.* Unpublished doctoral dissertation, Clark University, Worcester, MA.

Baron, R., Tom, D. Y. H., & Cooper, H. M. (1985). Social class, race and teacher expectations. In J. B. Dusek (Ed.), *Teacher expectancies.* Hillsdale, NJ: Erlbaum.

Brattesani, K. A., Weinstein, R. S., & Marshall, H. (1984). Student perceptions of differential teacher treatment as moderators of teacher expectation effects. *Journal of Educational Psychology, 76,* 236–247.

Brophy, J. (1985). Teacher-student interaction. In J. B. Dusek (Ed.), *Teacher expectancies.* Hillsdale, NJ: Erlbaum.

Brophy, J. E., Thomas, L., & Good, T. L. (1974). *Teacher-student relationships: Causes and consequences.* New York: Holt, Rinehart, and Winston.

Cabello, B., & Burstein, N. D. (1995). Examining teachers' beliefs about teaching in culturally diverse classrooms. *Journal of Teacher Education, 46,* 285–294.

Casteel, C. (1997). Attitudes of African American and Caucasian eighth grade students about praises, rewards, and punishments. *Elementary School Guidance and Counseling, 31,* 262–272.

Coates, B. (1972). White adult behavior toward black and white children. *Child Development, 43,* 143–154.

Committee on Policy for Racial Justice. (1989). *Visions of a better way.* Washington, DC: Joint Center for Political Studies.

Cook, P., & Ludwig, J. (1997). Weighing the burden of "acting white": Are there race differences in attitudes toward education? *Journal of Policy Analysis and Management, 16,* 656–678.

DeMeis, D. K., & Turner, R. R. (1978). Effects of students' race, physical attractiveness, and dialect on teachers' evaluations. *Contemporary Educational Psychology, 3*, 77–86.

Dweck, C. (1991). Self-theories and goals: Their role in motivation, personality and development. In R. A. Dienstbier (Ed.), *Nebraska symposium on motivation, 1990*. Lincoln: University of Nebraska Press.

Dweck, C., & Leggett, E. L. (1988). A social cognitive approach to motivation and personality. *Psychological Review, 95*, 256–273.

Eccles, J., & Wigfield, A. (1985). Teacher expectations and student motivation. In J. B. Dusek (Ed.), *Teacher expectancies*. Hillsdale, NJ: Erlbaum.

Egan, O., &Archer, P. (1985). The accuracy of teachers' ratings of ability: A regression model. *American Educational Research Journal, 22*, 25–34.

Entwisle, D. R., & Alexander, K. L. (1988). Factors affecting achievement test scores and marks of black and white first graders. *Elementary School Journal, 88*, 449–471.

Evertson, C. M., Brophy, J., & Good, T. L. (1972). Communication of teacher expectations: First grade (Report 91). Austin: University of Texas at Austin, Research and Development Center for Teacher Education.

Feldman, R. S., & Orchowsky, S. (1979). Race and performance of student as determinants of teacher nonverbal behavior. *Contemporary Educational Psychology, 4*, 324–333.

Ferguson, R. F. (1993). Spreading the paradigm of a master teacher: The Great Expectations Initiative in Oklahoma (Working Paper). Cambridge, MA: Harvard University, John F. Kennedy School of Government, Taubman Center for State and Local Government.

Ford, D. Y. (1996). *Reversing the underachievement among gifted black students*. New York: Teachers College Press.

Fordham, S., & Ogbu, J. (1986). Black students' school success: Coping with the burden of "acting white." *Urban Review, 18*, 176–206.

Gaines, M. L. (1990). Accuracy of teacher prediction of elementary student achievement. Paper prepared for the annual meeting of the American Educational Research Association.

Good, T L. (1987). Two decades of research on teacher expectations: Findings and future directions. *Journal of Teacher Education, 38*, 32–47.

Gross, S. (1993). Early mathematics performance and achievement: Results of a study within a large suburban school system. *Journal of Negro Education, 62*, 269–287.

Guskey, T. R. (1982). The effects of change in instructional effectiveness on the relationship of teacher expectations and student achievement. *Journal of Educational Research, 75*, 345–348.

Haller, E. J. (1985). Pupil race and elementary school ability grouping: Are teachers biased against black children? *American Educational Research Journal, 22*, 465–483.

Hanushek, E.A. (1994). *Making schools work: Improving performance and controlling costs*. Washington, DC: Brookings Institution Press.

Hanushek, E. A., & Jorgenson, D. W. (Eds.). (1996). *Improving America's schools: The role of incentives*. Washington, DC: National Academy Press.

Herrnstein, R. J., & Murray, C. (1994). *The bell curve: Intelligence and class structure in American life*. New York: Free Press.

Hoge, R., & Butcher, R. (1984). Analysis of teacher judgments of pupil achievement level. *Journal of Educational Psychology, 76*, 777–781.

Irvine, J. J. (1985). The accuracy and stability of teachers' achievement expectations as related to students' race and sex. Paper prepared for the annual meeting of the American Educational Research Association.

Irvine, J. J. (1990). *Black students and school failure: Policies, practices, and prescriptions*. New York: Greenwood Press.

Jones, J. (1997). The Message Project, Fort Wayne Urban League, phase I. Fort Wayne, IN: Urban League of Fort Wayne and Taylor University.

Jussim, L. (1989). Teacher expectations: Self-fulfilling prophecies, perceptual biases, and accuracy. *Journal of Personality and Social Psychology, 57,* 469–480.

Jussim, L., & Eccles, J. (1992). Teacher expectations II: Construction and reflection of student achievement. *Journal of Personality and Social Psychology, 63,* 947–961.

Jussim, L., Eccles, J., & Madon, S. (1996). Social perception, social stereotypes, and teacher expectations: Accuracy and the quest for the powerful self-fulfilling prophecy. *Advances in Experimental Social Psychology, 28,* 281–387.

Katz, M. (1973). *Attitudinal modernity, classroom power and status characteristics: An investigation.* Paper prepared for the annual meeting of the American Educational Research Association.

Kleinfeld, J. (1972). The relative importance of teachers and parents in the formation of negro and white students' academic self-concepts. *Journal of Educational Research, 65,* 211–212.

Kluegel, J. R. (1990). Trends in whites' explanations of the black-white gap in socioeconomic status, 1977–1989. *American Sociological Review, 55,* 512–525.

Krupczak, W. P. (1972). Relationships among student self-concept of academic ability, teacher perception of student academic ability and student achievement. Unpublished doctoral dissertation, University of Miami.

Ladd, H. F. (Ed.). (1996). *Holding schools accountable: Performance-based reform in education.* Washington, DC: Brookings.

Leacock, E. (1969). *Teaching and learning in city schools.* New York: Basic Books.

Lightfoot, S. L. (1978). *Worlds apart: Relationships between families and schools.* New York: Basic Books.

Merton, R. (1948). The self-fulfilling prophecy. *Antioch Review,* 8, 193–210.

Mickelson, R. A. (1990). The attitude-achievement paradox among black adolescents. *Sociology of Education, 63,* 44–61.

Miller, L. S. (1995). *An American imperative: Accelerating minority educational advancement.* New Haven, CT: Yale University Press.

Mitman, A. L. (1985). Teachers' differential behavior toward higher and lower achieving students and its relation to selected teacher characteristics. *Journal of Educational Psychology, 77,* 149–161.

Monk, M. J. (1983). Teacher expectations? Pupil responses to teacher mediated classroom climate. *British Educational Research Journal, 9,* 153–166.

Ogbu, J. (1978). *Minority education and caste: The American system in cross-cultural comparison.* New York: Academic Press.

Ogbu, J. (1983). Minority status and schooling in plural societies. *Comparative Education Review, 27,* 168–203.

Ogbu, J. (1987). Opportunity structure, cultural boundaries, and literacy. In J. Langer (Ed.), *Language, literacy, and culture: Issues of society and schooling.* Norwood, NJ: Ablex Press.

Pedulla, J. J., Airasian, P. W., & Madaus, G. F. (1980). Do teacher ratings and standardized test results of students yield the same information? *American Educational Research Journal, 17,* 303–307.

Puma, M., & others. (1993). *Prospects: The congressionally mandated study of educational growth and opportunity* (Interim Report). Washington, DC: U.S. Department of Education, Planning and Evaluation Service.

Raudenbush, S.W. (1984). Magnitude of teacher expectancy effects on pupil IQ as a function of the credibility of expectancy induction: A synthesis of findings from 18 experiments. *Journal of Educational Psychology, 76,* 85–97.

Rosenthal, R. (1994). Interpersonal expectancy effects: A 30-year perspective. *Current Directions in Psychological Science, 3*(6), 176–179.

Rosenthal, R., & Jacobson, L. (1968). *Pygmalion in the classroom.* New York: Holt, Rinehart and Winston.

Rowe, M. B. (1986). Wait time: Slowing down may be a way of speeding up! *Journal of Teacher Education, 37,* 43–50.

Rubovits, P. C., & Maehr, M. L. (1973). Pygmalion black and white. *Journal of Personality and Social Psychology, 25,* 210–218.

Shavelson, R. J., Cadwell, J., & Izu, T. (1977). Teachers' sensitivity to the reliability of information in making pedagogical decisions. *American Educational Research Journal, 14,* 83–97.

Slavin, R. E. (1987). Mastery learning reconsidered. *Review of Educational Research, 57,* 175–213.

Smith, M. L. (1980). Teachers' expectations. *Evaluation in Education, 4,* 53–56.

Smith, T. W. (1990). *Ethnic images* (GSS Topical Report 19). Chicago: University of Chicago, National Opinion Research Center.

Snyderman, M., & Rothman, S. (1986). Science, politics, and the IQ controversy. *Public Interest, 83,* 85.

Snyderman, M., & Rothman, S. (1987). Survey of expert opinion on intelligence and aptitude testing. *American Psychologist, 42,* 138–139.

Solorzano, D. G. (1992). An exploratory analysis of the effects of race, class, and gender on student and parent mobility aspirations. *Journal of Negro Education, 61,* 30–44.

Taylor, M. C. (1979). Race, sex, and the expression of self-fulfilling prophecies in a laboratory teaching situation. *Personality and Social Psychology, 6,* 897–912.

Weinstein, R. S. (1985). Student mediation of classroom expectancy effects. In J. B. Dusek (Ed.), *Teacher expectancies.* Hillsdate, NJ: Erlbaum.

Weinstein, R. S., & others. (1987). Pygmalion and the student: Age and classroom differences in children's awareness of teacher expectations. *Child Development, 58,* 1079–1092.

Wigfield, A., & others. (1991). Transitions at early adolescence: Changes in children's domain-specific self-perceptions and general self-esteem across the transition to junior high school. *Developmental Psychology, 27,* 552–565.

Willis, S. (1972). *Formation of teachers' expectations of students' academic performance.* Unpublished doctoral dissertation, University of Texas at Austin.

Willis, S., & Brophy, J. (1974). The origins of teachers' attitudes towards young children. *Journal of Educational Psychology, 66,* 520–529.

Yee, A. H. (1968). Interpersonal attitudes of teacher and disadvantaged pupils. *Journal of Human Resources, 3,* 327–345.

CHAPTER 5   A Diagnostic Analysis of Black-White GPA Disparities in Shaker Heights, Ohio

Notes

1. Students had the option to indicate any one of A, A–, B+, and so on, ranging down through F. For the 4-point scale, A = 4 points, A– = 3.67 points, B+ = 3.33 points, and so on ranging down through F = 0 points.

2. In effect, the question regarding each explanatory variable is: "How significant is it as a predictor of GPA [grade point average], considering both the magnitude and statistical uncertainty of the estimated relationship between that explanatory variable and GPA, holding constant the other explanatory variables?"

3. The homework completion question is: "When your teacher assigns homework, how much of the homework do you usually do?" It was asked separately for math, English, social studies, and science, with six forced-choice answers from which students could choose.

4. Perhaps if teachers knew more about the time and effort that students devoted to home-work and also kept in mind that even tough students want to learn (and usually respond to respect and caring), they might relate differently to students and engage them more effectively.

5. The most reasonable interpretation of why students who enroll in honors and Advanced Placement (AP) courses achieve at higher levels is that causation runs in both directions: High-achieving students tend to enroll in high-level courses, and high-level courses promote high levels of achievement.

6. Standardized test scores might be a more appropriate basis for this judgment, but the scores are not part of the data.

7. No evidence turned up that peer culture among black students is any more oppositional than among whites regarding hard work, and no important racial differences exist in reports of peer support for (or against) getting high grades. However, among males who take most of their courses at the honors and AP levels, 60 percent of whites, but only 37 percent of blacks, respond that their friends think it important to "be placed in the high achieving class."

8. Signithia Fordham, *Blacked Out: Dilemmas of Race, Identity, and Success at Capital High* (University of Chicago Press, 1996). The role of the "Other" is a theme of the book.

9. John Ogbu, *Minority Education and Caste: The American System in Cross-Cultural Comparison* (New York: Academic Press, 1978), p. 357. See also John Ogbu, "Minority Status and Schooling in Plural Societies," *Comparative Education Review*, vol. 27, no. 2 (1983), pp. 168–203; John Ogbu, "Opportunity Structure, Cultural Boundaries, and Literacy," in Judith Langer, ed., *Language, Literacy, and Culture: Issues of Society and Schooling* (Norwood, N.J.: Ablex Press, 1987); and Signithia Fordham and John Ogbu, "Black Students' School Success: Coping with the 'Burden of "Acting White,"'" *Urban Review*, vol. 18, no. 3 (1986), pp. 176–206.

10. Philip J. Cook and Jens Ludwig, "Weighing the Burden of Acting White: Are There Race Differences in Attitudes toward Education?" *Journal of Policy Analysis and Management*, vol. 16, no. 2 (1997), pp. 656–78; and Philip J. Cook and Jens Ludwig, "The Burden of 'Acting White': Do Black Adolescents Disparage Academic Achievement?" in Christopher Jencks and Meredith Phillips, eds., *The Black-White Test Score Gap* (Brookings, 1998), pp. 375–400. The data that they analyzed were from the National Education Longitudinal Study sponsored by the U.S. Department of Education. Cook and Ludwig use data from the 1990 follow-up when most students were in the tenth grade.

11. James W. Ainsworth-Darnell and Douglas B. Downey, "Assessing the Oppositional Culture Explanation for Racial/Ethnic Differences in School Performance," *American Sociological Review*, 63 (August 1998), pp. 536–53.

12. Examples are provided in Fordham, *Blacked Out*. Fordham also quotes Stephan L. Carter regarding a "burning drive to prove the racists wrong." Quote from Stephan L. Carter, "The Black Table, the Empty Seat, and the Tie," in Gerald Early, ed., *Lure and Loathing: Essays on Race, Identity, and the Ambivalence of Assimilation* (New York: Allen Lane, Penguin, 1993), p. 76.

13. See Claude Steele and Joshua Aronson, "Stereotype Threat and the Test Performance of Academically Successful African Americans," in Christopher Jencks and Meredith Phillips, eds., *The Black-White Test Score Gap* (Brookings, 1998). Steele and Aronson point out that their work builds on efforts by Irwin Katz and others during the 1960s, which studied how blacks' performance on IQ (intelligence quotient) tests depended on the conditions of test administration. See, for example, Irwin Katz, "Review of Evidence Relating to Effects of Desegregation on the Intellectual Performance of Negroes," *American Psychologist*, 19 (1964), pp. 381–99; Irwin Katz, E. G. Epps, and L. J. Axelson, "Effect upon Negro Digit Symbol Performance of Comparison with Whites and with Other Negroes," *Journal*

of Abnormal and Social Psychology, 69 (1964), pp. 963–70; and Irwin Katz, S. O. Roberts, and J. M. Robinson, "Effects of Task Difficulty, Race of Administrator, and Instructions on Digit Symbol Performance of Negroes," *Journal of Personality and Social Psychology,* 2 (1965), pp. 53–59. Katz's findings were analogous to what Steele and Aronson report. Building on his work with Steele, Aronson has collaborated on a recent work showing that black students' school performance could be improved by affecting their theories of intelligence. See Joshua Aronson and Carrie B. Fried, "Reducing the Effects of Stereotype Threat on African American College Students: The Role of Theories of Intelligence," unpublished manuscript, University of Texas, Austin.

14. See, for example, Christopher Peterson, Steven F. Maier, and Martin E. P. Seligman, *Learned Helplessness: A Theory for the Age of Personal Control* (New York: Oxford University Press, 1993).

15. John H. Bishop developed the survey as part of a project involving many schools across several states to study the effects of high school exit exams.

16. Data not used here include those for the 1 percent of respondents who are Latinos, 0.5 percent who are Native Americans, 3.5 percent who are Asians, 2 percent mixed black and Latino, 4.5 percent mixed black and white, and 5 percent who left the race variable blank. Preliminary analysis for groups other than blacks and whites was hampered by small sample sizes, and it also reached a level of complexity that was too much to attempt in the space of this paper.

17. This standardization included the whole sample, not just blacks and whites.

18. When a student left one of these variables blank, the average value for the racial group was substituted and a separate indicator variable was included in regression analyses to adjust for any systematic differences between students who left the variable blank and those who did not. Father's education was the variable most frequently missing, with 4 percent of white students and 18 percent of black students leaving it blank. Far fewer of the other variables in the analysis were blank. When they were blank, the missing values were predicted using the race and family background variables so that the observations would not have to be dropped from regression equations. When the missing value was for the dependent variable, that observation was dropped from the regression.

19. Versions of these four variables were first formed separately for mothers and for fathers as 0,1 indicator variables. Then, for each level of schooling, the indicators for mothers and fathers were added and divided by 2. Hence, for example, the "twelve years or fewer" variable that is used in the text equals 0 if both parents had more schooling than twelve years; it equals 0.50 if one parent had twelve years or fewer; and it equals 1 if both parents had twelve years or fewer. Analogous statements apply for the other three variables. In practice, these function the same as 0,1 indicator variables, even though each can take on three values. One parental education variable (for example, parents with graduate degrees) has to be omitted from each regression as the base category relative to which the coefficients for the other three are calibrated and can be interpreted. Hence, for example, the coefficient estimated for "parents have sixteen years of schooling" represents the difference in the value of the dependent variable for parents who have sixteen years of schooling versus parents in the base category. Here, parents with graduate degrees are always used as the base category.

20. The scale reliability coefficients are 0.45 for "simply decided not to bother," 0.40 for "carelessness and poor planning," and 0.34 for "the work was too difficult." These reliabilities would be too low for making judgments that have important consequences for individuals, and they are low even for exploratory work with fairly large samples as in this paper. Future work may develop (or locate) more refined measures of these constructs.

21. The question in the survey asked about hours watching television or playing video games, but the text refers only to watching television. This is to save on wording and because,

based on conversations with youth in Shaker Heights, television watching is the main activity that this variable is measuring.

22. The scale reliability coefficient is 0.50.

23. The scale reliability coefficient is 0.54.

24. Studies of peer effects in other contexts identify two main mechanisms. First is modeling and imitation. Sometimes on purpose and sometimes less consciously, youth copy or adapt some of the behaviors that they observe and use them in forming their own personal styles. They tend to imitate models that they admire and with whom they identify on race, gender, age, and other bases. There are limits, given that, for modeling to succeed, the behavior has to seem feasible for the person inclined to imitate it. The second mechanism is social reinforcement. See any textbook on adolescent development. For example, Rolf E. Muuss, *Theories of Adolescence* (McGraw-Hill, 1988).

25. About 60 percent of black students in grades seven through eleven report at least one person of a different race among their six closest friends at school. The same is true for about three quarters of whites. Thus, fewer than 25 percent of white students report that none of their six closest friends is of a different group, but about 40 percent of black students do. A larger segment of the black student body has, for whatever reasons, remained more insular.

26. Ordinary least squares (OLS) are used for the variables that have more than two values and probit for the variables that have 0,1 values. Ordered probit results for the variables that have several values did not differ from the OLS results.

27. "Thirteen to fifteen years" and "sixteen years" of parental education were also included in the estimated equations but are not reported here because of space considerations.

28. The ratio of coefficients to standard errors is 0.71 for parents with twelve years of schooling and 0.39 for living with only one parent. Students with more siblings are slightly more likely to hold back, and the ratio of the coefficient to standard error is 2.74.

29. The same multiple regressions include the desire to please adults as an additional explanatory variable. Students who hold back are more likely to say that pleasing adults is among the reasons that they work hard in school. Black students report this more than white students, which helps in predicting the black-white difference in holding back.

30. The estimate is that, other things being equal, black students' homework completion rate is about 0.15 to 0.20 standard deviations lower than for same-gender white students.

31. The coefficient on time watching television and video games was between 3.5 and 4.0 times its standard error, depending on what else was in the regression equation.

32. It does not significantly affect the homework completion rate, and it has a small positive and statistically significant predicted effect on grade point average, other things being equal. "Other things being equal" means that this result comes from an equation in which many other things were controlled. The result could mean that, among students whose homework is not done, those who keep trying to finish until the last possible minute do slightly better.

33. Whether a student has more black friends is determined from the question about the racial makeup among the student's six closest friends at school. Because 83 percent of all students are either black or white, the assumption is that when a white student says a friend is from a different racial group, that friend is probably black. There is no way of knowing for sure from these data.

34. This racial difference in television watching among teens is not unique to Shaker Heights. It is mirrored in national data and has been true for some time.

35. The data for Shaker Heights are not the kind of longitudinal or experimental data that would allow tracking of how changes in attitudes and behaviors lead to changes in school performance. Perhaps such data can be developed. In the meantime, causation in the models estimated presumably operates only in one direction—from the explanatory to

the outcome measures. The greater the extent to which this assumption is wrong, the more the estimates will be biased measures of the chosen relationships.

36. The only variables not included are some of the characteristics that students identified as those of the most popular crowd. The three perceived characteristics of the most popular crowd that are included in the regressions are "tough," "outgoing," and "self-confident."

37. Attitude and behavior effects might operate through the family background variables, but there is no way to calibrate how much. Black-white differences also could exist in the implicit standards relative to which blacks and whites are calibrating their answers. But that, too, is impossible to know and probably should not be assumed.

38. Consistent with these ideas, many things might affect school engagement and thereby the pace of progress toward raising school achievement—for example, personal standards (and, hence, goals) for what constitute acceptable behaviors, grades, and levels of achievement; long-term aspirations and the degree to which children believe that academic success is necessary or sufficient for getting what they want in life; (mis)understanding of effective strategies for securing supportive responses from helpers; initial skills and knowledge as they arrive at their particular grade levels and that affect their ability to keep up and assimilate new material during the year; self-concept of academic ability and beliefs about the nature of intelligence and personal capacity for intellectual growth; feelings of social fit with the school environment and beliefs about whether people at school have the obligation, will, and capacity to respond effectively in helping the child to learn; habits of mind and behavior related, for example, to attentiveness and communication in the classroom and also to effective time management routines for school-related tasks; psychological vulnerability and responsiveness to given social pressures, pro and con, related to achievement; extracurricular opportunities and experiences after school and during summers, and the degrees to which these experiences reinforce or compete with school; intellectual and social norms among the particular parents, peers, teachers, and others from whom the child receives supports and incentives; beliefs and feelings about the appropriateness of particular behaviors and achievements and the propensity to imagine, accept, and aspire to particular current and future selves and associated social worlds.

39. Muuss, *Theories of Adolescence,* p. 315.

40. Laurence Steinberg, Sanford M. Dornbusch, and B. Bradford Brown, "Ethnic Differences in Adolescent Achievement: An Ecological Perspective," *American Psychologist,* vol. 47, no. 6 (1992), pp. 723–29, quote on p. 727.

41. See Christopher Jencks and Meredith Phillips, eds., *The Black-White Test Score Gap* (Brookings, 1998), for a variety of explanations for the black-white test score gap. See also important new work by William T. Dickens and James R. Flynn, "The Interaction of Environment and Measured Intelligence," draft paper (Brookings, 2000), on the masking of environmental effects as genetic effects, and vice versa.

42. For an excellent piece of writing on racial stigmas, see Glenn C. Loury, "The Economics and Ethics of Racial Classification," paper prepared for the W. E. B. Du Bois Lectures at Harvard University, April 25–27, 2000.

43. See Jeff Howard and Raymond Hammond, "Rumors of Inferiority," *New Republic* (September 1985), pp. 17–21.

44. Among junior high and high school students, many strange interpretations are made of others' styles and behaviors, and even the most racially conscious acts can be misinterpreted as disloyalty. For example, black girls in suburban high schools are accused of acting white sometimes when they wear short afro haircuts and other low-maintenance hairdos. One reason is that they appear to be seeking the same freedom from hair problems that white girls experience after compulsory swimming during the gym period. I have

encountered this story in conversations in Shaker Heights and also with regard to a high school in Wisconsin.

45. The segment aired on June 7, 1999.

46. See, for example, Beverly Daniel Tatum, *Why Are All the Black Kids Sitting Together in the Cafeteria?* (Basic Books, 1997).

47. Fordham, *Blacked Out,* p. 291. The PSAT is a practice exam that eleventh graders often take in preparation for the Scholastic Assessment Test (SAT) college entrance exam that they take as twelfth graders.

48. Note that the foreign language department at Brookline High does not use a special term to refer to its nonaccelerated or lowest level of classes. These classes are referred to merely as Spanish 1 or Spanish 2. The two accelerated levels are called honors and Advanced Placement. To avoid confusion in the interview, Sara Stoutland asked this teacher to refer to the nonaccelerated as "standard" classes.

49. The probability value is 0.14 for the null hypothesis that black and white males at the mostly honors and AP level have the same opinion about whether studying a lot makes you less popular.

50. Fordham, *Blacked Out,* p. 306.

51. I have mentioned the importance of learning techniques both here and in the opening overview of the paper. However, developing this point is beyond the scope of the paper. For an introduction, see National Research Council, *Improving Student Learning: A Strategic Plan for Education Research and Its Utilization* (Washington: National Academy Press, 1999).

52. The survey finding is that blacks regard being tough as more important to popularity than whites do. School officials confirm that black students are much more likely to be involved in fights.

53. Blacks take fewer honors and AP courses, where homework assignments are longest, so on average they spend somewhat less time each day on homework than whites. The comparison in the text regarding homework time is between students who take the same classes. Most comparisons show that blacks self-report more time on homework than white classmates.

54. These differences of 4 percent among males and 3 percent among females are not statistically distinguishable from zero.

55. Because this study lacks a question about whether the student personally acts tough, it is not possible to estimate the relationship of tough behavior to measures of academic interest or achievement.

56. It would not be difficult to test whether standardized test scores overpredict or underpredict honors and AP enrollments for blacks versus whites in Shaker, but no such analysis has been done to date.

57. There are conflicting opinions in the district about whether the student advising system leads more or fewer blacks to take honors and AP courses than a race-blind advising system would produce.

58. Black students' SAT scores in Shaker are 100 points above the national average for all black students, but whites' scores are 150 points above the national average for whites.

CHAPTER 6   What *Doesn't* Meet the Eye: Understanding and Addressing Racial Disparities in High-Achieving Suburban Schools

Notes

1. For a discussion of racial achievement disparities and trends in disparity, see Ferguson (2001). Also see various publications of the National Center for Education Statistics at http://nces.ed.gov/. For other recent collections and overviews concerning racial achievement disparities and potential actions to reduce them, see Jencks and Phillips (1998),

National Task Force on Minority High Achievement (1999), and Walker-James, Jurich, and Estes (2001).

2. For a recent report on cities that are making progress, see Snipes, Doolittle, and Herlihy (2002).

3. Source: Calculated by the author from data available at http://factfinder.census.gov, Census 2000 Summary File 1: Detailed Tables, Tables P12A, B, D, and H. The numbers pertain to children ages 19 and under and exclude children for whom more than one race/ethnic category was indicated.

4. Since at least the time of *Brown v. Board of Education* (1954), the belief among many has been that nonwhite children would excel in school if only they could have access to the same high-quality classrooms that white children attended. Indeed, Kain and Persky (1969), and others over the years, have sometimes argued against "ghetto development" because, they assumed, educational and other opportunities for blacks and others were greater in the suburbs. Definitive evidence on whether black children in fact do better in the suburbs has been slow to accumulate because of data and methodological problems. See my discussion of this in Ferguson (2002) and references included there. An interesting recent paper on the effects of racial integration is Hanushek, Kain, and Rivkin (2001). They find that increasing the percentage of blacks in a school has the most adverse effects on high-achieving blacks.

5. Professor John Bishop of Cornell University developed the survey instrument.

6. A few schools surveyed sixth and 12th graders, but since only a small minority of the districts did so, sixth and 12th graders are not discussed in the present paper. In most instances, schools administered the questionnaire to all students in each surveyed grade who were present when the survey was given. Some districts surveyed only selected grades, such as seventh, ninth, and 11th.

7. "Mixed race" means that the student listed more than one race or ethnicity. There were many mixtures, about 40 percent of which were white mixed-race with one other group. Only 17 percent were black mixed-race with white. Some students indicated more than two groups. Hispanics and Asians reported more mixing with other groups than blacks or whites did.

8. Observations with missing data for any given variable are not included in tabulations of that variable. Generally, the number of missing observations for any given variable is small.

9. By class "level," I mean to distinguish whether students are taking honors or AP courses from whether they are *not* taking any. Whites and Asians enroll in honors and AP classes more often than blacks and Hispanics. Honors and AP classes typically require more homework, and students who take such courses spend more time on homework than students who do not—no matter what their race/ethnic group. Racial differences in rates of enrollment in honors and AP courses are not perfectly understood but seem due mostly to differences in academic proficiency. Most schools are working to increase black and Hispanic enrollments in honors and AP courses. However, there also are efforts underway to improve the quality of regular courses, so as to stem the flight of primarily white students away from them and to provide a higher-quality education to students who take them.

10. Because student surveys did not include official identification numbers, the author is not able to merge the data with standardized test scores or data from official transcripts.

11. The survey asked about specific letter grades and made no mention of whether grades for honors and AP courses might receive differential weighting in computing grade-point averages. There is no way of knowing whether honors and AP students might have inflated the letter grades they reported to account for differential weighting.

12. This was an extra question only for MSAN schools and was not on the printed Ed-Excel survey. Responses were entered in an extra response space at the end of the survey form.

13. Here, "about half or less" represents a composite of three options on the survey: "about half," "some," and "very little or none."
14. The data also include the fathers' years of schooling, but there are fewer missing values for the mothers'. The parents' education variables used in multiple-regression estimates combine mothers' and fathers' education data, and replace missing values using standard methods.
15. See, for example, various chapters in Jencks and Phillips (1998) and references included therein.
16. This finding comes from a multiple-regression analysis with fixed effects to control for school and grade level. Explanatory variables were the family background measures listed in Table 6–2, except that the parental education variable in regressions included the father's education as well. Missing values of explanatory variables were replaced with missing-value dummy variables.
17. Using the standard deviation for the whole data set, across all schools, grades, and racial groups.
18. Since they would correlate strongly with the variables we do have, it is uncertain how much more (or less) achievement disparity we could predict if such variables were included. Similarly, there is no way to know how much the findings might change if student responses were free of any errors or biases.
19. To form the SES categories, I began by using all of the SES measures in the data, but not race, to predict GPA. This multiple regression produced regression coefficients to use as weights in composite SES measures. The equation used a dummy variable for each value of each SES variable, in order to allow for nonlinearity in estimated effects. The equation also included school-grade-level fixed effects and gender. Missing values for explanatory variables were handled using dummy variables. The adjusted R-square for the equation was 0.23. Using the results, some students' SES characteristics (ignoring race/ethnicity) put them in the bottom 10 percent of predicted GPAs. I labeled this group the "lowest SES" group. Others' characteristics predict that they would be in the 40 percent of the distribution from the 10th to the 50th percentile (labeled "lower-middle SES") or in the 40 percent of the distribution from the 50th to the 90th percentile (labeled "upper-middle SES"). Finally, some would be in the top 10 percent, and this group is labeled "highest SES."
20. Multiple regressions for each achievement measure were estimated separately for each race/ethnic group, and the coefficients from these regressions were used to predict race/ethnic-specific achievement levels for each SES profile.
21. See, for example, McWhorter (2000).
22. For each subject, the Ed-Excel survey question asked, "When teachers assign homework or after-school work, how much of it do you usually do?" Students could indicate "homework is never assigned," "none of it," "some of it," "most of it," "all of it," and "more than required." For each subject, I created an index with three values. If the student's answer was "homework is never assigned," "none of it," or "some of it," the index had a value of 3. If the answer was "most of it," the value was 4, and if the answer was "all of it" or "more than required," the value was 5. Combining these across the four subjects creates an index with values ranging from 12 to 20. For Table 6–5, values of 15 or lower are labeled "some, or not much of it," values of 16 to 19 are labeled "most of it," and values of 20 are labeled "all of it."
23. Analysis of whether time on homework and homework-completion rates correlate with the GPA that students report for the end of the previous term shows that both homework measures help in predicting it. However, recall that there are few race/ethnic differences in time on homework among classmates. Therefore, homework-completion rates, but not

time on homework, help in predicting race/ethnic GPA gaps among students who take the same courses. Controlling for nothing but school and grade-level fixed effects, homework-completion rates predict about one-sixth of the GPA gap between whites and blacks, about one-fifth of the gap between whites and mixed-race students, and one-fourth of the gap between whites and Hispanic students, for those not enrolled in honors or AP classes. The analogous fractions are lower among students enrolled in honors or AP classes. About two-thirds to three-quarters of race/ethnic differences in homework completion are predicted by the MSAN Ed-Excel SES variables discussed above.

24. Another item in the table that shows race/ethnic differences is, "I don't want to embarrass my family." Here, the response ranges from 15 percent for whites to 33 percent for Asians, with blacks and Hispanics more like Asians than whites.

25. For other evidence of racial differences in motivational processes see Boykin and Bailey (2000); Steele and Aronson (1998); and Jussim, Eccles, and Madon (1996).

26. Indeed, the racial differences in some districts are large enough to deserve special attention, but to elaborate on this point is beyond the scope of this paper.

27. Among MSAN districts, interesting research in this regard is being done at Oak Park–River Forest High School in Illinois, where a team of teachers and researchers is carefully studying the school experiences and academic records of that high school's students.

28. For example, Supovitz and Poglinco (2001) conducted case studies of principals identified by their peers as outstanding instructional leaders. Among other things that they had in common, these instructional leaders cultivated a community of instructional practice, creating safe and collaborative environments for teachers to engage with one another and also with a wide range of outside actors to deepen the work. Similarly, Spillane (2002) describes a "situated" approach to teacher learning that engages teachers in constructing knowledge, playing roles as leaders, being active learners, and participating in activities that stress the social aspects of learning. Topics are integrated around areas of potential reform, with both internal and external actors providing guidance, and activities utilizing a curriculum involving several types of devices, including teachers' own practice. The approach is social rather than individualistic and it promotes teachers' identities as learners in school and classroom contexts where relationships matter a great deal.

29. For Erikson's tasks and stages of identity development, see Erikson (1963). For Tuckman's model of group process, see Baron, Kerr, and Miller (1992, p. 14). On innovation diffusion, see Rogers (1983). For a conceptually structured case example of social work with gangs, see Fox (1985). For a discussion of developing customer relations in marketing, see chapter 19 of Kotler (1986). For examples where I have applied the same model in other contexts, see Ferguson and Snipes (1996, available from the author) and Ferguson (1999, pp. 589–604).

30. The one hour includes a 10-minute stage-specific video; 10 minutes for teachers to respond in writing to a short list of prompts; 15 minutes for a panel of five students to respond to some prompts and take questions from the audience; then 25 minutes for open discussion among the faculty, leading to smaller group activities afterward.

31. Selected schools from a majority of MSAN districts as well as schools from an equal number of other districts are participating in the professional development, the research component, or both.

References

Baron, R. S., Kerr, N., & Miller, N. (1992). *Group process, group decision, group action*. Philadelphia, PA: Open University Press.

Boykin, A. W., & Bailey, C. T. (2000). *The role of cultural factors in school relevant cognitive functioning: Synthesis of findings on cultural contexts, cultural orientations, and individual differ-*

ences (Report No. 42). Baltimore, MD: Center for Research on the Education of Students Placed at Risk. Retrieved November 22, 2002, from http://www.csos.jhu.edu/crespar/techreports/report42.pdf

Erikson, E. H. (1963). *Childhood and society.* New York: W. W. Norton.

Ferguson, R. F. (1999). Conclusion: Social science research, urban problems, and community development alliances. In R. F. Ferguson & W. T. Dickens (Eds.), *Urban problems and community development* (pp. 569–610). Washington, DC: Brookings Institution Press. Retrieved November 22, 2002, from http://brookings.nap.edu/books/0815718756/html/569.html

Ferguson, R. F. (2001). Test-score trends along racial lines, 1971 to 1996: Popular culture and community academic standards. In N. Smelser, W. J. Wilson, & F. Mitchell (Eds.), *America becoming: Racial trends and their consequences* (Vol. I, pp. 348–390). Washington, DC: National Academies Press. Retrieved November 22, 2002, from http://books.nap.edu/books/030906838X/html/348.html

Ferguson, R. F. (2002). *Ed-Excel assessment of secondary school student culture tabulations by school district and race/ethnicity: Responses from middle school, junior high, and high school students in districts of the Minority Student Achievement Network (MSAN).* Retrieved November 22, 2002, from http://www.msanetwork.org/pub/edexcel.pdf

Ferguson, R. F. (with J. Mehta). (2002). Why racial integration and other policies since *Brown v. Board of Education* have only partially succeeded at narrowing the achievement gap. In T. Ready, C. Edley, Jr., & C. T. Snow (Eds.), *Achieving high educational standards for all* (Conference Summary). Washington, DC: National Academies Press (pp. 183–217). Retrieved November 22, 2002, from http://books.nap.edu/books/0309083036/html/183.html

Ferguson, R. F., & Snipes, J. C. (1996). Developmental tasks and stages in the YouthBuild experience. In R. Ferguson & P. Clay, *YouthBuild in developmental perspective: A formative evaluation of the YouthBuild program.* Cambridge, MA: MIT Department of Urban Studies and Planning.

Fox, J. R. (1985, January–February). Mission impossible? Social work practice with black urban youth gangs. *Social Work, 30*(1), 25–31.

Hanushek, E. A., Kain, J. F., & Rivkin, S. G. (2001). *New evidence about* Brown v. Board of Education: *The complex effects of school racial composition on achievement* (Working Paper). Dallas, TX: Cecil and Ida Green Center for the Study of Science and Society, University of Texas. Retrieved November 22, 2002, from http://www.utdallas.edu/research/greenctr/Papers/pdfpapers/paper27.pdf

Jencks, C., & Phillips, M. (Eds.). (1998). *The black-white test score gap.* Washington, DC: Brookings Institution Press. Retrieved November 22, 2002, from http://brookings.nap.edu/books/0815746091/html/index.html

Jussim, L., Eccles, J., & Madon, S. (1996). Social perception, social stereotypes, and teacher expectations: Accuracy and the quest for the powerful self-fulfilling prophecy. *Advances in Experimental Social Psychology, 28,* 281–399.

Kain, J. F., & Persky, J. J. (1969, Winter). Alternatives to the gilded ghetto. *The Public Interest, 14.*

Kotler, P. (1986). *Principles of marketing* (3rd ed.) Englewood Cliffs, NJ: Prentice-Hall.

McWhorter, J. H. (2000). *Losing the race: Self-sabotage in black America.* New York: Free Press.

National Task Force on Minority High Achievement. (1999). *Reaching the top: A report of the National Task Force on Minority High Achievement.* New York: College Board. Retrieved November 22, 2002, from http://www.collegeboard.com/about/association/taskforce/ReachingTheTop.pdf

Rogers, E. M. (1983). *Diffusion of innovations.* New York: Free Press.

Snipes, J., Doolittle, F., & Herlihy, C. (2002). *Foundations for success: Case studies of how urban school systems improve student achievement.* Washington, DC: Manpower Demonstration Research Corporation for the Council of Great City Schools.

Spillane, J. P. (2000, February). *District leaders' perceptions of teacher learning* (CPRE Occasional Paper Series OP-05). Philadelphia, PA: Consortium for Policy Research in Education. Retrieved November 22, 2002, from http://www.cpre.org/Publications/op-05.pdf

Steele, C. M., & Aronson, J. (1998). Stereotype threat and the test performance of academically successful African Americans. In C. Jencks & M. Phillips (Eds.), *The black-white test score gap* (pp. 401–428). Washington, DC: Brookings Institution Press. Retrieved November 22, 2002, from http://brookings.nap.edu/books/0815746091/html/401.html

Supovitz, J. A., & Poglinco, S. M. (2001, December). *Instructional leadership in a standards-based reform* (Research Report). Philadelphia, PA: Consortium for Policy Research in Education. Retrieved November 22, 2002, from http://www.cpre.org/Publications/ac-02.pdf

Walker-James, D., Jurich, S., & Estes, S. (2001). *Raising minority achievement: A compendium of education programs and practices.* Washington, DC: American Youth Policy Forum. Retrieved November 22, 2002, from http://www.aypf.org/rmaa/pdfs/toc.pdf

CHAPTER 7   Five Challenges to Effective Teacher Professional Development

Notes

1. See, for example: Fred Carrigg, Margaret Honey, and Ron Thorpe. 2005. "Moving from Successful Local Practice to Effective State Policy: Lessons from Union City." In C. Dede, J. Honan, and L. Peters, eds., *Scaling Up Success: Lessons Learned from Technology-Based Educational Improvement.* New York: Jossey-Bass; M. S Casserly, J. Lewis, J. Jepson, and J. Ceperich. 2002. *Beating the Odds II: A City-by-City Analysis of Student Performance and Achievement Gaps on State Assessments.* Washington DC: Council of Great City Schools; M. Casserly and J. C. Snipes. 2005. "Foundations for Success in the Great City Schools." In C. Dede, J. Honan, and L. Peters, eds., *Scaling Up Success: Lessons Learned from Technology-Based Educational Improvement.* New York: Jossey-Bass.

2. Several years ago, a framework incorporating these ideas became the centerpiece of the Tripod Project for School Improvement, which focused initially on classroom-level challenges of engaging students in learning. In this paper, we suggest how the same basic ideas can help leaders organize their thinking, and ultimately their actions, concerning the challenges of engaging teachers successfully in professional development for instructional improvement.

3. For a very good discussion of the importance of implementation, see, for example, Ann C. Linn, *Reform in the Making: The Implementation of Social Policy in Prison* (Princeton University Press, 2000). The book also includes an extensive bibliography on implementation.

4. See, for example: Jane Bumpers and Kristine K. Hipp, eds. 2003. *Reculturing Schools as Professional Learning Communities* (Toronto: Scarecrow Education); Michael Fullan. 2001. *The Meaning of Educational Change,* 3rd Edition (New York: Teachers College Press); Richard DuFour and Robert Eaker. 1998. *Professional Learning Communities at Work* (Alexandria, VA: Association for Supervision and Curriculum Development); Jonathan Supovitz and Jolley B. Christman. 2005. "Small Learning Communities That Actually Learn." *Phi Delta Kappan,* Vol. 86(9):649–51 (May).

5. Robert S. Baron, Norbert Kerr, and Norman Miller. 1992. *Group Process, Group Decision, Group Action* (Philadelphia, PA: Open University Press); Erik H. Erikson. 1963. *Childhood and Society* (New York: W. W. Norton & Company); Jerry R. Fox. 1985. "Mission Impossible? Social Work Practice with Black Urban Youth Gangs." *Social Work,* January–February; Philip Kotler. 1986. *Principles of Marketing,* Third Edition (Englewood Cliffs, NJ: Prentice-Hall); Everett M. Rogers. 1983. *Diffusion of Innovations* (New York: Free Press). Several years ago, a framework incorporating these ideas became the centerpiece of the Tripod Project

for School Improvement, which focused initially on classroom-level challenges of engaging students in learning (www.TripodProject.org).

CHAPTER 8   Toward Excellence with Equity: The Role of Parenting and Transformative School Reform

Notes

1. U.S. Department of Education (2005).
2. See Ferguson (2005) for a discussion of possible reasons progress in narrowing the reading score gap stopped at the end of the 1980s. Also see Neal (2005). Dickens and Flynn (2005) found evidence that the black-white IQ gap had narrowed since 1972.
3. U.S. Department of Education, National Center for Education Statistics, Early Childhood Longitudinal Study, Birth Cohort (ECLS-B), Restricted-Use File (NCES 2004–093), previously unpublished tabulation (January 2005), viewed at agi.harvard.edu/Topics/coe_table_35_3.xls?tableID=303, February 19, 2007. Also see Fryer and Levitt (2006).
4. Bronfenbrenner's (1979) micro-ecologies.
5. Bronfenbrenner's (1979) meso-ecologies.
6. Bronfenbrenner's (1979) exo-ecologies.
7. Bronfenbrenner's (1979) macro-ecology.
8. Eccles and Gootman (2002).
9. In discussing the attributes of supportive relationships, the NRC report emphasized the importance of responsiveness and fit: "On the surface these appear to be objective qualities, but research suggests that these qualities reside less in the adult than in the adolescent's perception of the adult and in the adolescent's experience of interactions with the adult. . . . Inasmuch as there is an underlying essential element here, it consists of attentiveness and responsiveness to adolescents' subjective worlds" (Eccles and Gootman, 2002, pp. 94–95). The same can be said of interactions of adults in training to be better parents or teachers, wherein parent or teacher receptivity to trainers or supervisors depends importantly upon subjective experiences of feeling valued and respected. It depends as well on perceptions of whether or not the trainer or supervisor is well meaning, competent, and reliable.
10. Eccles and Gootman (2002, pp. 90–91). The chapter in which these appear elaborates on each condition, with examples.
11. Key concerns include racial discrimination in hiring, promotion, and lending, which affects the family incomes and wealth that provide resources for rearing children. Further, it seems unfair that some segments of society benefit from exclusive social networks that carry valuable information or protect control over decisionmaking in key institutions. There is much about society that may stand in the way of reaching full potential in the domains addressed in this book.
12. Phillips and others (1998).
13. Neal (2005).
14. Dickens (1999); Loury (2002).
15. See discussion and references in Duncan and Magnuson (2005).
16. See, for example, Hanushek, Kain, and Rivkin (2002); Orfield (2005).
17. Lareau and Horvat (1999).
18. Brooks-Gunn and Markman (2005); Conger, Conger, and Elder (1997); McLoyd (1998).
19. Standard assessments of the degree to which socioeconomic resources affect achievement may be underestimates if important resource variables such as social network resources are poorly measured or absent from the analysis. Conversely, estimates may be too high if genetic differences correlate positively with SES. Specifically, if genetics contribute to

parental income and education and also to offspring's achievement levels, then contributions to achievement that are typically attributed to parental income and achievement may be at least partly due to genetics. Researchers tend to agree that genetics account for some within-race achievement disparities, but the importance of genetics for between-race disparities remains a matter of considerable dispute. Some researchers have concluded that genetics account for much of the correlation between family resources and student achievement—even between racial groups. Most prominently, Rushton and Jenson (2005) concluded that fixed, immutable genetic differences, not resources, discrimination, or environmental forces, accounted for half or more of racial IQ and achievement gaps. Supporting environmental (as opposed to genetic) explanations, Dickens and Flynn (2005) found that the black-white IQ gap narrowed between one-fifth and one-third (three to six points) between 1972 and 2002. They attributed this narrowing to environmental forces, although their work to identify such forces was only beginning. Research leaves little doubt that environmental forces are critically important determinants of achievement levels as well as achievement disparities. And among environmental forces, parenting constitutes the most important cluster in children's lives (Shonkoff and Phillips [2000]).

20. Brooks-Gunn and Markman (2005).
21. Epstein (1995) characterized six types of parental involvement: parenting, communicating, volunteering, learning at home, decisionmaking, and collaborating with community. Of the six, she argued that learning at home was the most reliably associated with gains in achievement. Typologies by other researchers (Bamber, Berla, and Henderson [1993]; Eccles and Harold [1993]); Shartrand and others [1997]) fit well with Epstein's.
22. Brooks-Gunn and Markman (2005).
23. Brooks-Gunn and Markman (2005, p. 148).
24. McLoyd and Smith (2002) found that spanking had less deleterious effects in black than in white households. The differential meaning of "tough love" in black families may help to explain why.
25. "Playing games and doing puzzles" is a single category in the ECLS-K; puzzles are not distinguished from other forms of playing.
26. See Fryer and Levitt (2004, table 2).
27. For example, the number of books may matter because new books provide new opportunities for parent-child discussions requiring higher-order thinking.
28. Fryer and Levitt (2004).
29. Sirin (2005, p. 441).
30. MSAN formed around 1998 so that these districts could share ideas and activities aimed at narrowing their racial achievement gaps. See Ferguson (2002); www.msanetwork.org.
31. I simulated achievement for each of the four standardized SES profiles. To form the SES categories, I began by using all the SES measures in the data, but not race, to predict grade point average (GPA). This multiple regression produced regression coefficients to use as weights in composite SES measures. The equation used an indicator variable for each value of each SES variable, in order to allow for nonlinearity in estimated effects. The equation also included school-grade-level fixed effects and gender. Missing values for explanatory variables were handled using dummy variables. The adjusted R-square for the equation was 0.23. Using the results, some students' SES characteristics (ignoring race or ethnicity) put them in the bottom 10 percent of predicted GPA. I labeled this group the "lowest SES" group. Others' characteristics predicted that they would be in the 40 percent of the distribution from the 10th to the 50th percentiles (labeled "lower-middle SES") or the 50th to the 90th percentiles (labeled "upper-middle SES"). Finally, some would be in the top 10 percent, and this group was labeled "highest SES."

32. Shaker Heights, Ohio, is one of these districts. Ogbu (2003) was incorrect when he suggested that blacks and whites in Shaker Heights had essentially equal SES.
33. See U.S. Department of Education (1995). Here, there is greater racial disparity in NAEP reading scores among 17-year-olds who say their parents are college graduates than among those who say their parents are high school graduates or dropouts.
34. Future work may link the data in this table to achievement disparities. Currently, however, the data have not been combined with grades or test scores.
35. Brooks-Gunn and Markman (2005, p. 139).
36. National Research Council (2001, p. 149).
37. Carey, Lewis, and Farris (1998); Christenson, Rounds, and Franklin (1992); Epstein (1996); Fruchter, Galletta, and White (1993); Moles (1993).
38. Ballen and Moles (1994, p. 2).
39. Henderson and Berla (1994, p. 1).
40. Ascher (1988); Baker and Soden (1998); Christenson, Rounds, and Franklin (1992); Rutherford, Billig, and Kettering (1993).
41. Baker and Soden (1998, p. 1). Joyce Epstein, a leader in this field, writes, "Research about school, family, and community connections needs to improve in many ways. Early research was often based on limited samples, too global or too narrow measures of involvement, and limited data on student outcomes. As research proceeds with clearer questions and better data, measurement models should be more fully specified, analyses more elegant, and results more useful for policy and practice" (Epstein [1996, p. 218]).
42. See, for example, Cook and others (1998); Davies (1993); Haynes and Comer (1993); Madden, Slavin, and Karweit (1993); Wong (1995).
43. See Chavkin (1993); Christenson, Rounds, and Franklin (1992), Dauber and Epstein (1989); Eccles and Harold (1993); Garlington (1992); Leitch and Tangri (1988); Moles (1993); Reglin (1993); Shartrand and others (1997); Swap (1993); Swick (1991); Wolfendale (1983).
44. Jeynes (2004).
45. Jeynes (2004, p. 6).
46. Turner, Nye, and Schwartz (2004).
47. Tizard, Schofield, and Hewison (1982).
48. Fantuzzo, Davis, and Ginsberg (1995).
49. Balli, Demo, and Wedman (1998).
50. Rodick and Henggeler (1980).
51. McKinney (1976).
52. McKinney (1976); Rodick and Henggeler (1980); Tizard, Schofield, and Hewison (1982).
53. Balli, Demo, and Wedman (1998).
54. Epstein (1991).
55. Walberg, Bole, and Waxman (1980).
56. For example, see the compendium of evaluation findings issued by the American Youth Policy Forum (James, Jurich, and Estes [2002]). Also see reviews in Molnar (2002).
57. Responses were voluntary; 82 elementary teachers from 21 schools and 233 secondary teachers from 20 schools responded. None was a deeply troubled school, but all were schools in cities, towns, and suburbs that had racial and ethnic achievement gaps that school officials were addressing with various types of professional development.
58. This section is based on Casserly and Snipes (2005); Casserly and others (2002); and Snipes, Doolittle, and Herlihy (2002).
59. Casserly and Snipes (2005, pp. 162–63).
60. Casserly and Snipes (2005, pp. 164–65).
61. The study with Jacobson applies our framework from the Tripod Project for School Improvement (www.tripodproject.org) to classify the ways leaders in higher and lower performing schools introduce ideas to teachers; balance administrative control with

teacher autonomy; get teachers to define and adopt school and personal goals; manage resistance, especially following setbacks; and celebrate success.

62. Especially in large districts, the right answer may be to grant exceptions on the basis of high levels of student performance. But equity concerns would remain even with this idea if schools work with different student populations, some more difficult than others.

References

Ascher, C. (1988). Improving the school-home connection for poor and minority urban students. *Urban Review, 20,* 109–123.

Baker, A., & Soden, L. M. (1998). *The challenges of parent involvement research* (ERIC/CUE Digest 134, ED 419030). New York: ERIC Clearinghouse on Urban Education.

Ballen, J., & Moles, O. (1994). *Strong families, strong schools: Building community partnerships for learning.* Retrieved from Department of Education, eric-web.tc.columbia.edu/families/strong/key_research.html

Balli, S. J., Demo, D. H., & Wedman, J. F. (1998). Family involvement with children's homework: An intervention in the middle grades. *Family Relations, 47,* 149–157.

Bamber, C., Berla, N., & Henderson, A. T. (1996). *Learning from others: Good programs and successful campaigns.* Washington, DC: Center for Law and Education.

Bronfenbrenner, U. (1979). *The ecology of human development.* Cambridge, MA: Harvard University Press.

Brooks-Gunn, J., & Markman, L. (2005). The contribution of parenting to racial and ethnic gaps in school readiness. *Future of Children, 15,* 139–168.

Carey, N., Lewis, L., & Farris, E. (1998). *Parent involvement in children's education: Efforts by public elementary schools* (Statistical Analysis Report, ED 416027). Washington, DC: National Center for Education Statistics.

Casserly, M., & Snipes, J. C. (2005). Foundations for success in the great city schools. In C. Dede, J. Honan, & L. Peters (Eds.), *Scaling up success: Lessons learned from technology-based educational improvement* (pp. 153–175). New York: Jossey-Bass.

Casserly, M., & others. (2002). *Beating the odds II: A city-by-city analysis of student performance and achievement gaps on state assessments.* Washington, DC: Council of Great City Schools.

Chavkin, N. F. (Ed.). (1993). *Families and schools in a pluralistic society.* Albany: State University of New York Press.

Christenson, S., Rounds, T., & Franklin, M. J. (1992). Home-school collaboration: Effects, issues, and opportunities. In S. Christenson & J. C. Conoley (Eds.), *Home-school collaboration: Enhancing children's academic and social competence* (ED 353492). Silver Spring, MD: National Association of School Psychologists.

Conger, R., Conger, K., & Elder, G. (1997). Family economic hardships and adolescent adjustment: Mediating and moderating processes. In G. Duncan & J. Brooks-Gunn (Eds.), *Consequences of growing up poor.* New York: Russell Sage Foundation.

Cook, T. D., & others. (1998). *Comer's school development program: A theory-based evaluation* (Evaluation Report). Chicago: Northwestern University.

Dauber, S. L., & Epstein, J. L. (1989). *Parent attitudes and practices of involvement in inner-city elementary and middle schools.* Paper presented at the annual meeting of the American Educational Research Association, San Francisco.

Davies, D. (1993). The league of schools reaching out. *School Community Journal, 3,* 37–46.

Dickens, W. T. (1999). Rebuilding urban labor markets: What community development can accomplish. In R. Ferguson & W. Dickens (Eds.), *Urban problems and community development.* Washington, DC: Brookings Institution Press.

Dickens, W. T., & Flynn, J. R. (2005). *Black Americans reduce the racial IQ gap: Evidence from standardization samples.* Washington, DC: Brookings Institution.

Duncan, G. J., & Magnuson, K. A. (2005). Can family socioeconomic resources account for racial and ethnic test score gaps? *Future of Children, 15,* 35–54.

Eccles, J., & Gootman, J. A. (Eds.). (2002). *Community programs to promote youth development.* Washington, DC: National Academies Press.

Eccles, J. S., & Harold, R. D. (1993). Parent-school involvement during the early adolescent years. *Teachers College Record, 94,* 568–587.

Epstein, J. L. (1991). Effects on student achievement of teachers' practices of parent involvement. In S. Silvern (Ed.), *Advances in reading/language research: Vol. 5. Literacy through family, community, and school interaction* (pp. 261–276). Greenwich, CT: JAI Press.

Epstein, J. L. (1995). School/family/community partnerships: Caring for the children we share. *Phi Delta Kappan, 76,* 701–713.

Epstein, J. L. (1996). Perspectives and previews on research and policy for school, family, and community partnerships. In A. Booth & J. F. Dunn (Eds.), *Family-school links: How do they affect educational outcomes?* (pp. 209–246). Mahwah, NJ: Lawrence Erlbaum.

Fantuzzo, J. W., Davis, G. Y. , & Ginsberg, M. D. (1995). Effects of parent involvement in isolation or in combination with peer tutoring on student self-concept and mathematics achievement. *Journal of Educational Psychology, 87,* 272–281.

Ferguson, R. (1998a). Teachers' perceptions and expectations and the black-white test score gap. In C. Jencks & M. Phillips (Eds.), *The black-white test score gap* (pp. 273–317. Washington, DC: Brookings Institution Press.

Ferguson, R. (1998b). Can schools narrow the black-white test score gap?" In C. Jencks & M. Phillips (Eds.), *The black-white test score gap* (pp. 318–374). Washington, DC: Brookings Institution Press.

Ferguson, R. (2002). *What doesn't meet the eye: Understanding and addressing racial disparities in high-achieving suburban schools.* Oak Brook, IL: North Central Regional Educational Laboratory.

Ferguson, R. (2005). Why America's black-white school achievement gap persists." In G. Loury, T. Modood, & S. Teles (Eds.), *Ethnicity, social mobility and public policy: Comparing the U.S. and Great Britain* (pp. 309–341). Cambridge, England: Cambridge University Press.

Fruchter, N., Galletta, A., & White, J. L. (1993). New directions in parent involvement. *Equity and Choice, 9*(3), 33–43.

Fryer, R., & Levitt, S. (2004). Understanding the black-white test score gap in the first two years of school. *Review of Economics and Statistics, 86,* 447–464.

Fryer, R., & Levitt, S. (2006). *Testing for racial differences in the mental ability of young children.* Cambridge, MA: National Bureau of Economic Research.

Garlington, J. A. (1992). *Helping dreams survive: The story of a project involving African-American families in the education of their children.* Washington, DC: National Committee for Citizens in Education.

Hanushek, E. A., Kain, J. F., & Rivkin, S. G. (2002). *New evidence about Brown v. Board of Education: The complex effects of school racial composition on achievement* (Working Paper 8741). Cambridge, MA: National Bureau of Economic Research.

Haynes, N. M., & Comer, J. P. (1993). The Yale School Development Program: Process, outcomes, and policy implications. *Urban Education, 28,* 166–199.

Henderson, A. T., & Berla, N. (Eds.). (1994). *A new generation of evidence: The family is critical to student achievement.* Washington, DC: National Committee for Citizens in Education.

James, D. W., Jurch, S., & Estes, S. (2002). *Raising minority academic achievement: A compendium of education programs and practices.* Washington, DC: American Youth Policy Forum.

Jeynes, W. H. (2004). Parental involvement and secondary school student educational outcomes: A meta-analysis. *Harvard Family Research Project: The Evaluation Exchange, 10*(4).

Lareau, A., & Horvat, E. M. (1999). Moments of social exclusion and inclusion: Race, class, and cultural capital in family-school relationships. *Sociology of Education, 72,* 37–53.

Leitch, L. M., & Tangri, S. S. (1988). Barriers to home-school collaboration. *Educational Horizons, 66,* 70–74.

Loury, G. C. (2002). *The anatomy of racial inequality (The W. E. B. Du Bois Lectures).* Cambridge, MA: Harvard University Press.

Madden, N. A., Slavin, R. E., & Karweit, N. L. (1993). Success for all: Longitudinal effects of a restructuring program for inner-city elementary schools. *American Educational Research Journal, 30,* 123–148.

McKinney, J. A. (1976). The development and implementation of a tutorial program for parents to improve the reading and mathematics achievement of their children. (ERIC Document Reproduction Service, ED 113703)

McLoyd, V. (1998). Socioeconomic disadvantage and child development. *American Psychologist, 53*(2).

McLoyd, V., & Smith, J. (2002). Physical discipline and behavior problems in African-American, European American, and Hispanic children: Emotional support as a moderator. *Journal of Marriage and Family, 64*(1).

Moles, O. C. (1993). Collaboration between schools and disadvantaged parents: Obstacles and openings. In N. F. Chavkin (Ed.), *Families and schools in a pluralistic society* (pp. 21–52). Albany: State University of New York Press.

Molnar, A. (Ed.). (2002). *School reform proposal: The research evidence.* Greenwich, CT: Information Age.

National Research Council. (2001). *Eager to learn: Educating our preschoolers.* Washington, DC: National Academy of Sciences.

Neal, D. (2005). *Why has black-white skill convergence stopped?* (Working Paper 11090). Cambridge, MA: National Bureau of Economic Research.

Ogbu, J. (2003). *Black American students in an affluent suburb: A study in academic disengagement.* Mahwah, NJ: Lawrence Erlbaum.

Orfield, G. (2005). Why segregation is inherently unequal: The abandonment of *Brown* and the continuing failure of *Plessy. New York Law School Law Review, 49,* 1041–1052.

Phillips, M., & others. (1998). Family background, parenting practices, and the black-white test score gap. In C. Jencks & M. Phillips, *The black-white test score gap.* Washington, DC: Brookings Institution Press.

Reglin, G. L. (1993). *At-risk "parent and family" school involvement: Strategies for low-income families and African-American families of unmotivated and underachieving students.* Springfield, IL: Charles C. Thomas.

Rodick, J. D., & Henggeler, S. W. (1980). The short-term and long-term amelioration of academic and motivational deficiencies among low-achieving inner-city adolescents. *Child Development, 51,* 1126–1132.

Rushton, J. P., & Jenson, A. R. (2005). Thirty years of research on race differences in cognitive ability. *Psychology, Public Policy, and Law, 11,* 235–294.

Rutherford, B., Billig, S., & Kettering, J. F. (1993). *Parent and community involvement in the middle grades: Evaluating education reform.* Denver: RMC Research.

Shartrand, A. M., & others. (1997). *New skills for new schools: Preparing teachers in family involvement.* Cambridge, MA: Harvard Graduate School of Education, Harvard Family Research Project.

Shonkoff, J. P., & Phillips, D. A. (Eds.). (2000). *From neurons to neighborhoods: The science of early childhood development.* Washington, DC: National Academies Press.

Sirin, S. R. (2005). Socioeconomic status and academic achievement: A meta-analytic review of research. *Review of Educational Research, 75,* 417–453.

Snipes, J., Doolittle, F., & Herlihy, C. (2002). *Foundations for success: Case studies of how urban school systems improve student achievement.* Washington, DC: Council of Great City Schools.

Swap, S. M. (1993). *Developing home-school partnerships: From concepts to practice*. New York: Teachers College Press.

Swick, K. J. (1991. *Teacher-parent partnerships to enhance school success in early childhood education*. Washington, DC: National Education Association of the United States.

Tizard, J., Schofield, W. N., & Hewison, J. (1982). Collaboration between teachers and parents in assisting children's reading. *British Journal of Educational Psychology, 52*, 1–15.

Turner, H., Nye, C., & Schwartz, J. (2004). Assessing the effects of parent involvement interventions on elementary school student achievement. *Harvard Family Research Project: The Evaluation Exchange (10)*4.

U.S. Department of Education. (1995). *Nation's report card: Reading 1994 for the nation*. Available from National Assessment of Educational Progress, nces.ed.gov/nationsreportcard/

U.S. Department of Education. (2005). *The nation's report card: NAEP 2004 trends in academic progress. Three decades of student performance in reading and mathematics*. Retrieved from nces.ed.gov/nationsreportcard

Walberg, H. J., Bole, R. E., & Waxman, H. C. (1980). School-based family socialization and reading achievement in the inner city. *Psychology in the Schools, 17*, 509–514.

Wolfendale, S. (1983). *Parental participation in children's development and education*. New York: Gordon and Breach.

Wong, P. L. (1995). *Accomplishments of accelerated schools*. Stanford, CA: Stanford University, Accelerated Schools Project.

CONCLUSION   Urgency and Possibility: A Call for a National Movement

Notes

1. Blacks and Latinos together are projected to be roughly 40 percent of the population by 2050, with whites making up less than 50 percent. American Indians, Asians, and other nonwhites will make up the rest.

2. Office of the Federal Register (1963–64, pp. 704–707).

3. Debates about the net impact of Great Society programs on social conditions, such as family formation norms, continue and may never be resolved. However, on balance, there is much to admire and defend.

4. On discrimination, see Davah Pager and Bruce Western (2005), "Race at Work: Realities of Race and Criminal Record in the NYC Job Market." The report was released as part of the NYC Commission on Human Rights conference, Race at Work: Realities of Race and Criminal Record in the NYC Job Market, held December 9, 2005, at the Schomburg Center for Research in Black Culture. Also see Pager and Quillan (2005, p. 3). On implicit, subconscious bias, see Gregg, Seibt, and Banaji (2006, pp. 1–20).

5. The best approach in many cases will be to test new ideas in ways that allow the collective to learn about their impacts, and to take the results into account in deciding how to proceed.

6. The Tripod Project for School Improvement is the source of the data for this summary. It operates in both inner-city and suburban schools across many states and provides survey-based data to inform strategic school-level interventions.

7. For example, on the Ed-Excel survey that the suburban Minority Student Achievement Network conducted in November of 2000, characteristics associated with academic engagement—both pro-achievement and anti-achievement—rated at the bottom of the list defining popularity. Among a dozen characteristics that might determine popularity, the top four (averaged across all racial groups) were "cool clothes," "attractive," "funny," and "good in sports," in that order (cool clothes ranked first). The *bottom* four were "not attentive in class," "attentive in class," "smart," and "make fun of those who study." The ranking varied only slightly between Asians, blacks, Hispanics, and whites.

8. Even for white and Asian females, fully a third fail to respond "mostly true" or "totally true" to the statement, *"If I didn't understand something, my classmates would be happy to help me."* The lowest percentage, at 45 percent, is for black males, though black males tend to report as much peer support as white males, when they share the same classrooms and have the same grade-point averages. Students with lower grade-point averages in any given classroom report roughly as much teacher support, but less peer support than students with higher grade-point averages. Black and Hispanic males tend to be in somewhat less supportive peer environments (classrooms) and to have lower grade-point averages than white males. The same is true when comparing black, Hispanic, and white females.

9. John McWhorter (2006) makes this point about not confusing entertainment with reality.

10. For a good assessment of the PYD movement during the 1990s, see Pittman, Irby, and Ferber (2000).

11. For contemporary versions see Gordon (2005), and see Harvard Family Research Project (2004) and materials on complementary education on the Harvard Family Research Project website at www.hfrp.org.

12. Durlak and Weissberg (2007) examined evaluations of 73 afterschool programs that targeted personal and social skills for youngsters in the 5- to 18-year-old age range and that had either control groups or high-quality comparison group designs. Of the 73 studies they identified, 39 met both the content and the process criteria, while 27 programs did not. All 39 showed statistically significant effects on key developmental dimensions, while none of the 27 did. Other more qualitative studies looking across programs have come to similar conclusions concerning the relationship of program quality to program effectiveness.

13. Retrieved September, 2007, from http://www.uschamber.com/icw/reportcard/default

14. Retrieved October, 2007, from http://www.philasafesound.org/about/

15. Retrieved September, 2007, from http://www.prichardcommittee.org/facts.html

16. Retrieved October, 2007, from http://www.publiceducation.org/aboutus.asp

17. Teams assembled by local engines would visit schools, afterschool programs, social service agencies, and other institutions to learn about practices and also provide feedback to the people in those places about ways of improving.

18. Accountability would operate to a large degree through formal authority structures, but perhaps even more through incentives created by the existence of public information on activities and performance.

19. See U.S. Department of Education, National Center for Education Statistics (2005) and Fryer and Levitt (2007).

20. See chapter 2 and the Afterword to that chapter.

References

Bronfenbrenner, U. (1979). *The ecology of human development.* Cambridge, MA: Harvard University Press.

Cohen, C. J. (2007). The *attitudes and behavior of young black Americans: Research summary.* Chicago: University of Chicago, Black Youth Project.

Durlak, J. A., & Weissberg, R. P. (2007). *The impact of after-school programs that promote personal and social skills.* Chicago: University of Illinois, Collaborative for Academic, Social, and Emotional Learning.

Eccles, J., & Gootman, J. (Eds.). (2002). *Community programs to promote youth development.* Washington, DC: National Academies Press.

Fryer, R., & Levitt, S. (2007). *Testing for racial differences in the mental ability of young children.* Retrieved June, 2007, from http://post.economics.harvard.edu/faculty/fryer/papers/fryer_levittbabiesrevision.pdf

Gordon, E. W. (2005). The idea of supplementary education. In E. W. Gordon, B. L. Bridglall, & A. S. Meroe (Eds.), *Supplementary education: The hidden curriculum of high academic achievement*. New York: Roman & Littlefield.

Gregg, A. P., Seibt, B., & Banaji, M. (2006). Easier done than undone: Asymmetry in the malleability of implicit preferences. *Journal of Personality and Social Psychology, 90*(1), 1–20.

Harvard Family Research Project. (2004). *Harvard Family Research Project: Evaluation Exchange, 10*(4), 6.

Lee, C. D. (2007). *Culture, literacy, and learning: Taking bloom in the midst of the whirlwind.* New York: Teachers College Press.

McWhorter, J. (2006). *Winning the race: Beyond the crisis in black America.* New York: Gotham.

Office of the Federal Register. (1963–64). *Public papers of the presidents of the United States: Lyndon B. Johnson, Book I.* Washington, DC: U.S. Government Printing Office.

Pager, D., & Quillan, L. (2005). Walking the talk? What employers say versus what they do. *American Sociological Review, 70,* 3.

Pager, D., & Western, B. (2005, December 9). *Race at work: Realities of race and criminal record in the NYC job market.* Report presented at the New York City Commission on Human Rights conference, New York.

Patterson, O. (2002). Unpublished paper. Retrieved October, 2007, from http://ksg.harvard.edu/inequality/Seminar/Papers/Patterson.pdf

Pittman, K., Irby, M., & Ferber, T. (2000). Unfinished business: Further reflections on a decade of promoting youth development. In Public Private Ventures (Ed.), *Youth development: Issues, challenges and directions* (pp. 18–64). Philadelphia: Public Private Ventures.

U.S. Department of Education, National Center for Education Statistics. (2005). *Early childhood longitudinal study, birth cohort (ECLS-B), restricted-use file (NCES 2004-093), previously unpublished tabulation.* Retrieved October, 2007, from http://nces.ed.gov/programs/coe/2005/section4/table.asp?tableID=303

Acknowledgments

My research and writing on the topics in this book began with two projects that Obie Clayton and later Christopher (Sandy) Jencks and Meredith Phillips commissioned me to do during the 1990s. Jencks and Phillips, in particular, called my attention to issues that will occupy me for the rest of my career. I am also grateful to John Bishop of Cornell University for inviting me to help fine-tune and road-test the Ed-Excel Survey of Secondary School Student Culture, which became an important part of my initial work with the Minority Student Achievement Network (MSAN). Data in chapters 5 and 6 come from Ed-Excel surveys of MSAN schools. Data in chapter 7 come from a different set of surveys that are part of the Tripod Project for school improvement. I founded the Tripod Project in 2001, and it continues to expand under the leadership of my colleague, Robert Ramsdell. I thank all of these colleagues for helping to inspire and shape the work that this book reports.

Among the many school administrators, teachers, and friends who deserve my thanks are Mark Freeman, Jim Paces, Bernice Stokes, Yvonne Allan, Jean Reinhold, Tom Kelly, and Rueben Harris of Shaker Heights, Ohio, the first school district that welcomed my work. In MSAN, Allan Alson, Laura Cooper, Carolyn Ash, Rossi Ray Taylor, and John Diamond (now teaching at Harvard) represent a much longer list of MSAN folks whose enthusiasm and cooperation have been much appreciated. The additional list of people in several dozen school districts whose cooperation has kept me involved in this work is much too long to present here, but I owe all of them—students, teachers, administrators, and others—a debt of gratitude.

Research assistants and staff associates who deserve my thanks include Lisa Carlos, Marian Valliant, Jason Snipes, Ann Ballantine, Carlos Santos, Sara Stoutland, Sarah McCann, Jordana Brown, Erin Hardy, and many others to whom I apologize for not listing their names. Sara Stoutland, in particular, worked with me for a full decade, participating in most of my work over that period, and I am deeply appreciative. Also, without listing them all by name, I thank the many colleagues who read and commented on various chapters or who provided data or advice, including Christopher Jencks, Meredith Phillips, William Dickens, Roland Fryer, Jens Ludwig, Jal Mehta, John Ballantine, Wilbur Rich, Karl Alexander, Henry Levin, James Flynn, John Kain, John Bishop, David Jacobson, and others. Sandy Jencks, in particular, has provided helpful and much appreciated feedback on most chapters of this volume.

Funders who have supported the work include the Rockefeller Foundation, the Russell Sage Foundation, the Martha Holden Jennings Foundation, the Gund Foundation, the Cleveland Foundation, and Marilyn T. Keane. Time Warner, Inc., has also been helpful as the core funder of the Achievement Gap Initiative (AGI) at Harvard. I thank my faculty colleagues in the AGI, including my cochairs Charles Ogletree and Richard Murnane, for their collegiality and continuing commitment to the work. I am also grateful to Dean David Ellwood of the Kennedy School of Government, Dean Katherine McCartney of the Harvard Graduate School of Education, and Julie Wilson, director of the Wiener Center for Social Policy, for their encouragement and support over the years.

Caroline Chauncey and her colleagues Dody Riggs and Jeff Perkins at the Harvard Education Press deserve special thanks. They guided my assistant Anaide Nahikian and me seamlessly through the various tasks necessary to get the book to press. Also, Caroline Chauncey and my research assistant Erin Hardy provided rapid and insightful feed back on initial drafts of the conclusion.

I thank my family for their steadfast love and support. My mother, Gloria Ferguson, has provided steadfast and continuing support from the day I was born. My wife, Helen Mont-Ferguson, sons Daniel and Darren, and nephew Marcus make my home a warm and joyous place. I thank them for their love, and for putting up with my busy schedule over the years that the work in this volume has progressed.

Finally, I thank the many colleagues who are fellow travelers in this work. I have been influenced by many of you and I look forward to the progress that is to come as we move forward together.

Ronald F. Ferguson
Cambridge, MA
November 28, 2007

About the Author

Ronald F. Ferguson is a lecturer in public policy and senior research associate at the Wiener Center for Social Policy at Harvard University's John F. Kennedy School of Government, where he has taught since 1983. In addition, he has recently joined the faculty at the Harvard Graduate School of Education. His research publications cover issues in education policy, youth development programming, community development, economic consequences of skill disparities, and state and local economic development. Much of his research since the mid-1990s has focused on racial achievement gaps, appearing in publications of the National Research Council, the Brookings Institution, the U.S. Department of Education, and the Educational Research Service, and in various other books and journals. Ferguson participates in a variety of local, state, and national consulting and policy advisory activities, including with state and local school districts, on closing achievement gaps. He is the founder of the Tripod Project for school improvement and the faculty cochair and director of the Achievement Gap Initiative (AGI) at Harvard. The AGI is a university-wide initiative to help close the nation's achievement gaps by supporting new research and connecting research to policy and practice. Ferguson attended public schools in Cleveland, Ohio, later earning an undergraduate degree from Cornell University and a PhD from MIT, both in economics. He lives with his sons, Daniel and Darren, a nephew, Marcus, and his wife, Helen Mont-Ferguson, to whom he has been happily married for twenty-nine years.

Index

Note: Figures and tables are indicated by *f* or *t*, respectively, following page numbers.

Homework
  and black-white GPA gap, 151, 158–159
  completion of, 5, 151, 158–159, 198–199*t*,
    213*t*, 214–215, 214*t*
  gender differences in, 171*f*
  racial differences in, 60–62, 61–62*t*, 171*f*,
    213–215, 213*t*, 214*t*
  Shaker Heights study results, 196–199*t*
  television watching and, 169–171
  time spent on, 60, 61–62*t*, 151, 198–199*t*,
    213–214, 213*t*
Honors courses. *See* Higher-level courses
Household composition, 158, 165–166,
    209–210
Houston, Texas, 274–277
Humans, motivations of, 239

Identity
  African American, 58–59, 64, 155, 181–182
  aspects of, 64–65
  formation of, 64
  hip hop and, 63–64
  rap and, 65
Immigration, 21, 23
Implementation, significance of, 239, 245
Incarceration
  employment (weeks worked) and, 31–33
  predictors of, 32
Institutional capacity, for educational reform,
    299–302
Instructional interventions
  for at-risk children, 96
  Success for All program, 97–98
  See also Teaching
Instructional tripod
  defined, 5, 225
  implementation of, 227–230
  necessity of, 225, 226
  teachers and, 292–293
Involuntary minorities, 155
Iowa Test of Basic Skills, 82, 121, 140
IQ effects, 80, 84, 255, 316n4
Irvine, Jacqueline, 121, 128

Jacobson, David, 277
Jacobson, Lenore, 124
Jencks, Christopher, 3, 62
Jenson, A. R., 353n19
Jeynes, William, 270
Job Corps, 273
Johns Hopkins University, 97

Johnson, J., 65–66
Johnson, Lyndon B., 25, 283–284
Jones, J., 321n54
Jussim, Lee, 125–129, 132, 134, 147

Kane, T., 316n4
Kennedy, John F., 284
Kentucky, 300–301
Kleinfeld, Judith, 128
Knowledge, and black-white GPA gap, 152
Krueger, Alan, 14–17, 21, 45, 110, 309n33
Kulik, Chen-Lin, 86
Kulik, James, 84, 86, 95

Laine, Richard, 109
Lazar, I., 316n4
Leadership
  civic, 298–302
  of professional development initiatives,
    237–253
  of school reform, 274
Learned helplessness, 156
Learning
  input goals for, 289–298
  redundancy in, 289
  resources for, 225
Learning behaviors, and black-white GPA
    gap, 152
Lee, Carol, 287–288
Leisure reading, 59–60, 60*t*, 62–63, 63*f*
Leonard, Jonathan, 25
Level of schooling
  earnings by, 18*f*, 22
  employment-to-population by, 20*f*
  gains in, 17, 307n18
  of parents, 158, 165, 209, 261–262, 263–
    265*t*, 267*t*, 268, 279
Levin, Henry, 96
Levitt, S., 262
Lifestyles, 278–279
Lightfoot, Sara Lawrence, 118
Ludwig, Jens, 137, 155, 180–181, 313n3

Madon, Stephanie, 125–129, 132, 134, 147
Markman, L., 260–261, 268–269
Marshall, Hermine, 138
Mastery goals, 337n79
McLoyd, V., 353n24
MDRC, 274–275
Medicaid, 284
Medicare, 284

and black-white GPA gap, 151–152, 159–
162, 166, 168–171, 173–174, 177–184
and GPA prediction, 174, 178*t*, 179*t*
race and, 129–131, 155–156
about school, 70–74, 72*t*
about teachers, 71–73, 74*t*, 136, 222–223,
222*t*, 223*t*
about tracking, 94–96
Student behavior
attitudes about, 151
and black-white GPA gap, 151–152, 159–
162, 166, 168–171, 173–174, 177–184
and GPA prediction, 174, 178*t*, 179*t*
popularity and, 160–162, 186*t*, 218, 220*t*
Student effort
holding back, 153–154, 167*t*, 168–169,
177, 179, 182–184, 234, 296
on homework, 151
household composition and, 165
learning strategies and, 152
motivations for, 216–218, 217*t*
peer culture and, 153
race and, 206, 221*t*
stereotype anxiety and, 156
teacher demands versus teacher
encouragement and, 205–206, 216–218,
219*t*, 226
See also Disengagement, student;
Engagement, student
Students
ambitiousness of, 228–229
autonomy of, 228
classifications of, 180
community support for, 297
enjoyment of studies by, 221–222, 222*t*
help seeking by, 224*t*, 229
interracial friendships among, 344n25
motivations of, 72, 73*t*, 160, 224
participation of, in tracking decisions,
317n19
response of, to teachers, 127–131, 160,
205–206, 216–218, 219*t*
and teacher-student relations, 225, 227–
230
See also African American students; Asian
students; Hispanic students
Suburban schools, racial disparities in, 203–
235
in achievement, 205, 206, 207*t*, 209
in family background, 205, 209–213
in homework, 206, 213–215

recommendations concerning, 224–225,
228–230
in skills, 205
in socioeconomic status, 205, 208*t*, 210–
213
in student effort, 205–206, 216–218
study of, 204, 347n4
Success for All, 96–98, 99*t*, 114, 273, 321n62
Supovitz, J. A., 349n28

Talent Development, 273
Taylor, Marylee, 132–133
Taylor, Ollie, 94
Teacher behavior
race of students and, 132–136
racial bias and, 118–124
Teacher expectations
accuracy of, 120–121
flexibility of, 121, 126, 332n17, 336n73
Great Expectations program, 139–146
impact of, 69, 125
race of students and, 69–70, 285–286
racial bias and, 118–124
racial factors in, 125–127
and self-fulfilling prophecies, 124–127
tracking and, 95
Teacher perceptions
accuracy of, 120–121, 137–138
of African American students, 69, 134–135
flexibility of, 121, 126, 336n73
racial bias and, 118–124
and self-fulfilling prophecies, 124–127
of student effort, 133*f*
Teacher professional learning committees,
239
Teacher quality
goal of, 292–294
race of students and, 104
Teachers
ambitiousness of, 240
autonomy of, 240
certification testing of, 55, 107–108
and control, 228
demands by, 205–206, 216–218, 219*t*
effective, 293
encouragement offered by, 205–206, 216–
218, 219*t*, 224–225, 226
race-matching of, 100–103, 101*t*, 102*t*,
135–136
racial bias of, 117–124
resistance of, 140, 337n87

Permissions

"Shifting Challenges: Fifty Years of Economic Change toward Black-White Earnings Equality." This chapter originally appeared in *Daedalus, Journal of the American Academy of Arts and Sciences*, Winter 1995, Vol. 24, No. 1. Reprinted with permission.

"Test-Score Trends along Racial Lines, 1971 to 1996: Popular Culture and Community Academic Standards." Reprinted with permission from the National Academies Press, copyright © 2001, National Academy of Sciences. This chapter originally appeared in *America Becoming: Racial Trends and Their Consequences*, edited by Neil J. Smelser, William Julius Wilson, and Faith Mitchell. Washington, DC: The National Academies Press, 2001.

"Can Schools Narrow the Black-White Test Score Gap?" and "Teachers' Perceptions and Expectations and the Black-White Test Score Gap" originally appeared in *The Black-White Test Score Gap*, edited by Christopher Jencks and Meredith Phillips. Washington, DC: Brookings Institution Press, 1998. Reprinted with permission.

"A Diagnostic Analysis of Black-White GPA Disparities in Shaker Heights, Ohio" originally appeared in *Brookings Papers on Education Policy: 2001*, edited by Diane Ravitch. Washington, DC: Brookings Institution Press, 2001. Reprinted with permission.

A shorter version of "Five Challenges to Effective Teacher Professional Development" appeared in the *Journal of Staff Development*, Fall 2006, Vol. 27, No. 4.

"Toward Excellence with Equity: The Role of Parenting and Transformative School Reform" also appears in *The Price We Pay: Economic and Social Consequences of Inadequate Education*, edited by Clive R. Belfield and Henry M. Levin. Washington, DC: Brookings Institution Press, 2007.

Prof. Ferguson's class

1. The white & esp black pop's are not homogeneous and monolithic. Need to unpack these racial labels.

\# 2. Is the research done there for a national movement. This Q is relevant if one wants to initiate reform. But what if the objective is to motivate interest in the achievement gap & the political will to do sth about it.

3. p. 259 parenting - build on this within the black community. Take advantage of the heterogeneity in the black community.

4. p. 283 - sense of urgency. Cf 2003 Sup Ct. Sandra Day O'Connor - 25 yr sunset.

\# 5. p. 285 the Goal of group proportional equality. Can we proceed in 2 steps?
    ① no B-W difference within income groups
    ② same income dist'n b/t B & W.

\# 6. p. 289 proximate determinants. Which is most important? And within that, where are the most effective points of intervention? Do we know the answers to these Q's? If not, is it a failure of later research. what? Maybe this lays the groundwork for discussing the new Manhattan Project. Where is the rate of return the highest? It's the problem of the NPL draft. where do draft 1st 2nd 3rd etc.